The Digital Continent

The Digital Continent

Placing Africa in Planetary Networks of Work

Mohammad Amir Anwar
Mark Graham

OXFORD
UNIVERSITY PRESS

OXFORD
UNIVERSITY PRESS

Great Clarendon Street, Oxford, OX2 6DP,
United Kingdom

Oxford University Press is a department of the University of Oxford.
It furthers the University's objective of excellence in research, scholarship,
and education by publishing worldwide. Oxford is a registered trade mark of
Oxford University Press in the UK and in certain other countries

First Edition published 2022
Impression: 1

Published in the United States of America by Oxford University Press
198 Madison Avenue, New York, NY 10016, United States of America

British Library Cataloguing in Publication Data
Data available

Library of Congress Control Number: 2021941851

ISBN 978-0-19-884080-0

DOI: 10.1093/oso/9780198840800.001.0001
Printed and bound in
Great Britain by Clays Ltd, Elcograf S.p.A.

Acknowledgments

First and foremost, our wholehearted thanks go to African workers, without them the book would not have been made possible. They generously offered their precious time to share with us stories of their lives, for us to make sense of the future of work and what it means for workers. Their hospitality, honesty and openness are central to the finished book. We sincerely hope that we have adequately represented your voices and concerns. We would also like to extend our thanks to employers, business leaders, social enterprises, policy makers, civil servants, activists, and industry experts, who found time in their busy schedule to share their insights on digital work and its relevance to Africa.

We travelled to five countries in Africa for fieldwork: Ghana, Kenya, Nigeria, South Africa, and Uganda. Here, we met old colleagues and made some new friends. We relied on them to provide expert advice on navigating the treacherous terrain of protracted fieldwork. Their connections provided a useful entry point for us to understand the networks of work in which the lives of African workers are entangled. We would like to especially thank: Diane Abrahams, Chris Rogerson, Jayne Rogerson, Rob Urquhart, Luvendra Naidu, Lynnette Morris, Tebogo Molapisane, Traci Freeman, Evan Jones, Rod Jones, Gareth Pritchard, Alicia Fortuin, Alison Gillwald and Julia Taylor in South Africa; Bitange Ndemo, Kaburo Kobia, Mercy Mugure, Patrick Karanja, Bundi Teresios, and Elly Otieno in Kenya; Patrick Kagenda and Clive Moses in Uganda; Amal Hassan, Rechard Timm, and Anil and Tushar Hathiramani in Nigeria; Pius Siakwah, Eric Delali, and Emmanuel Fiagbenu in Ghana. Our team of transcribers: Elly Otieno (Kenya), Eric Delali (Ghana), and Belinda and Hope (South Africa) diligently transcribed thousands of minutes of audio-recorded interviews and we thank them for their hard work and patience.

The findings in the book were presented at various avenues including conferences, workshops, and seminars: 4th Uni-Africa Regional Conference, Dakar 2017; DIODE Group Workshop, Oxford 2017; Reshaping Work Conference, Amsterdam 2017; Digitalization of Labour Workshop, Lausanne 2017; International Labour Process Conference, Buenos

Aires 2018; Global Conference on Economic Geography, Cologne 2018; Workshop on Work and Employment in the Era of Platform Capitalism, Paris 2018; Workshop on Social Life of Work, Oxford 2018; Knowledge Exchange Workshop, Johannesburg 2019; Regulating Decent Work Conference, Geneva 2019; and with audiences at University of Johannesburg, Harambee Youth Employment Accelerator Johannesburg, Wissenschaftszentrum Berlin für Sozialforschung Berlin, Confederazione Generale Italiana del Lavoro Rome, University of Milan, University of Oxford, Turing Institute, and University of Edinburgh. We thank all participants for their insightful feedback.

This book emerged from a five-year European Research Council (ERC) funded project called Geonet. The project (ERC-2013-StG335716-GeoNet) gave us the opportunity to fund the salaries of Amir as full-time Researcher on the project and Mark as the Principal Investigator. It also allowed us the opportunity to engage in the extensive fieldwork that was required to undertake a research project of this size. Needless to say, our research in this area—and by extension, this book—would not have existed without the support of the ERC. The Geonet project incorporated three core research areas, of which the work in the book represents one. Each area of the project has been shaped by the innovative research and hard work of our colleagues in the rest of the team. Therefore, we would like to thank our Geonet collaborators: Fabian Braesemann, Chris Foster Nicolas Friederici, Sanna Ojanperä, Stefano De Sabbata, Ralph Straumann, and Michel Wahome.

The book is also shaped by countless discussions with colleagues and friends at the Oxford Internet Institute, and their feedback on our work tremendously enriched the research behind this book. At the Oxford Internet Institute, our appreciation goes to: Greetje Corporaal, Alex Wood, Jamie Woodcock, Villi Lehdonvirta, Otto Kässi, Bernie Hogan, Joe Shaw, Margie Cheesman, Heather Ford, Marie-Therese Png, Srujana Katta, Kelle Howson, Funda Ustek-Spilda, Alessio Bertolini, Pablo Aguera, Daniel Arbuayi, Nancy Salem, Robbie Warin, Fabian Ferrari, and Martin Dittus. Countless discussions held with them and their feedback on our work enriched the research behind this book tremendously. Beyond Oxford, our thanks are due to: Richard Heeks, Pádraig Carmody, Uma Rani, Niels van Doorn, Elvis Melia, Julian Posada, Mira Wallis, Jelena Sapic, Slobodan Golušin, Susann Schäfer, Hannah Dawson, Lauren Graham, Julia Giddy, Matt Zook, and Esther Kroll. Their friendship, encouragement, and erudite commentary on our writing are greatly valued.

We have also deeply benefited from the conversations, debates, and political engagements that the authors have carried out as part of the Fairwork project based at the Oxford Internet Institute and Berlin Social Science Centre. Thank you very much to Fabian Brasemann, Stefano De Sabbata, Chris Foster, Sanna Ojanperä, Fabian Stephany, Ralph Straumann, Daniel Abs, Iftikhar Ahmad, María Belén Albornoz, Moritz Altenried, Paula Alves, Oğuz Alyanak, Branka Andjelkovic, Thomas Anning-Dorson, Arturo Arriagada, Daniel Arubayi, Tat Chor Au-Yeung, Alessio Bertolini, Louise Bezuidenhout, Gautam Bhatia, Richard Boateng, Manuela Bojadzijev, Macarena Bonhomme, Maren Borkert, Joseph Budu, Rodrigo Carelli, Henry Chavez, Sonata Cepik, Aradhana Cherupara Vadekkethil, Chris King Chi Chan, Matthew Cole, Paska Darmawan, Markieta Domecka, Darcy du Toit, Veena Dubal, Trevilliana Eka Putri, Fabian Ferrari, Patrick Feuerstein, Roseli Figaro, Milena Franke, Sandra Fredman, Pia Garavaglia, Farah Ghazal, Anita Ghazi Rahman, Shikoh Gitau, Slobodan Golusin, Markus Griesser, Rafael Grohman, Martin Gruber-Risak, Sayema Haque Bidisha, Khadiga Hassan, Richard Heeks, Mabel Rocío Hernández Díaz, Luis Jorge Hernández Flores, Benjamin Herr, Salma Hindy, Kelle Howson, Francisco Ibáñez, Sehrish Irfan, Tanja Jakobi, Athar Jameel, Hannah Johnston, Srujana Katta, Maja Kovac, Martin Krzywdzinski, Larry Kwan, Sebastian Lew, Jorge Leyton, Melissa Malala, Oscar Javier Maldonado, Shabana Malik, Laura Clemencia Mantilla León, Claudia Marà, Évilin Matos, Sabrina Mustabin Jaigirdar, Tasnim Mustaque, Baraka Mwaura, Mounika Neerukonda, Sidra Nizamuddin, Thando Nkohla-Ramunenyiwa, Caroline Omware, Adel Osama, Balaji Parthasarathy, Leonhard Plank, Valeria Pulignano, Jack Qui, Ananya Raihan, Pablo Aguera Reneses, Nabiyla Risfa Izzati, Nagla Rizk, Cheryll Ruth Soriano, Nancy Salem, Julice Salvagni, Derly Yohanna Sánchez Vargas, Kanikka Sersia, Murali Shanmugavelan, Shanza Sohail, Janaki Srinivasan, Shelly Steward, Zuly Bibiana Suárez Morales, Sophie Sun, David Sutcliffe, Pradyumna Taduri, Kristin Thompson, Pitso Tsibolane, Anna Tsui, Funda Ustek-Spilda, Jean-Paul Van Belle, Laura Vogel, Zoya Waheed, Jing Wang, Robbie Warin, Nadine Weheba, and Yihan Zhu.

The Oxford Internet Institute was the perfect home for this project. Duncan Passey, Tim Davies, Emily Shipway, Adham Tamer, and Arthur Bullard provided extensive administrative support over the life of the project. David Sutcliffe, thanks a million for your invaluable editorial support on our early drafts.

At OUP, the editorial team consisting of Katie Bishop, Samantha Downes, Christina Fleischer, and Henry Clarke, were exceptionally patient while we finished the manuscript. They provided valuable feedback and advocacy for the book. The copy-editor, Patricia Baxter, was diligent and the epitome of patience. Thank you to Geoff Bailey for compiling the index.

We would like to also extend our thanks to the United Nations Conference on Trade and Development (UNCTAD) for permission to reproduce Figure 2.1: In worldwide dependence on commodity exports (UNCTAD, 2019a); the International Telecommunications Union for permission to reproduce Figure 2.3: on Individuals using the internet 2005–19 (ITU, 2019); and the World Bank for permission to reproduce Figure 2.2: Distribution of income in Africa by quintile, published under CC BY 4.0 licence.

We are also grateful to the publishers of the following materials for allowing us to draw on substantially for this book. These include:

- Anwar, M.A. and Graham, M. 2019. Does economic upgrading lead to social upgrading in contact centers? Evidence from South Africa. African Geographical Review 38, 209–226. https://doi.org/10.1080/19376812.2019.1589730
- Anwar, M.A. and Graham, M. 2020a. Between a rock and a hard place: freedom, flexibility, precarity and vulnerability in the gig economy in Africa. Competition and Change. https://doi.org/10.1177/1024529420914473
- Anwar, M.A. and Graham, M. 2020b. Digital labour at economic margins: African workers and the global information economy. Review of African Political Economy 47, 95–105. https://doi.org/10.1080/03056244.2020.1728243
- Anwar, M.A. and Graham, M. 2020c. Hidden transcripts of the gig economy: labour agency and the new art of resistance among African gig workers. Environment and Planning A 52(7), 1269–1291. https://doi:10.1177/0308518X19894584
- Graham, M. and Anwar, M.A. 2018a. Two models for a fairer sharing economy, in Davidson, N., Finck, M., and Infranca, J. (Eds), Cambridge Handbook on Law and Regulation of the Sharing Economy. Cambridge University Press, Cambridge, pp. 328–340. https://doi.org/10.1017/9781108255882.025
- Graham, M. and Anwar, M.A. 2018b. Labour, in Ash, J., Kitchin, R. and Leszczynski, A. (Eds), Digital Geographies. SAGE Publications, London, pp. 177–187.

- Graham, M. and Anwar, M.A. 2019. The global gig economy: towards a planetary labour market? First Monday 24. https://doi.org/10.5210/fm.v24i4.9913

Finally, researching for this book meant we spent days and in some cases months away from home. Hence, we would like to express indebtedness to our families for their sacrifice, encouragement, and mental support during the course of our work for this book.

Contents

List of Figures

List of Tables

List of Boxes

Prologue

Making Visible the Invisible

In discussions about the locations that make up the key productive nodes of the digital economy, Africa rarely gets a mention. Autonomous vehicles, artificial intelligence and machine learning systems, next-generation search engines, recommendations systems, and online content: how many of these technologies do you think are 'made in Africa'? The answer is actually 'all of them'. More importantly, few of these digital work types are typically thought to be associated with human labour—let alone with African workers participating as a central cog in them. In fact, there are thousands and thousands of African workers helping create some of the most sophisticated technologies available today, from some fairly unlikely locations.

In 2017, we visited a machine learning training centre in a rural African town. Despite being a ten-hour drive from the nearest international airport, we found workers who are helping to build some of the world's most advanced technological goods and services. The foreign-owned centre began in 2012 in old shipping containers with communication towers and satellites for the internet connection (Figure 0.1). It was in these shipping containers that workers started to train machine-learning systems that had been designed in other continents.

Today the company operates out of a large open-plan office—albeit still constructed from shipping containers. In it, three 8-hour shifts a day enable 300 workers to sit over their computer screens to train machine-learning systems. These tasks might involve workers matching names to photographs of celebrities they had never heard of, or correcting information about hotels on travel booking sites, tagging images, and identifying objects in photographs—usually of suburban America. What these myriad tasks have in common is that computers are unable to do these jobs as effectively as humans—that is, to structure unstructured information.

The work is secured by the parent company's (US-based) sales team, which liaises with large technology firms which are building products

Fig. 0.1 Shipping containers acting as a makeshift training centre
Source: Anwar and Graham, 2020b. Reproduced with permission.

and services that involve machine-learning approaches—for example, autonomous vehicles. This typically requires extremely large annotated image and video data sets to train the system. In order for autonomous vehicles to share roads safely and react appropriately to every possible context in which they might find themselves, their cameras must be able to identify objects, road markings, people, trees, and traffic lights with complete accuracy. Therefore, millions of images and videos of cities need to be manually tagged so that computers can learn the difference between a pavement, a road, a tree, and a person. The level of detail needed from the workers who build the training data set is astonishing. Workers annotate not just large features on the road, but also wires, leaves, the outlines of door numbers, and—in one case that we saw—a bird sitting atop a pole (Figure 0.2). Each image takes a worker anywhere from one to five hours to identify and tag all its content, with workers having a target of seven images per shift. A supervisor then checks the quality of the annotation before they are sent back to the clients, primarily in the US.

What is most noteworthy about the centre and the work that it does is that the workers are never told what is the purpose of their work. One worker, when asked to describe their job, said 'I am tagging images'. We then pressed for more detail: 'But, why? What is somebody doing with these tagged images?' The response was: 'They don't tell me; they just want lots of tagged images.' Workers know that they need to tell the computer in front of them what the difference is between a house and a road sign, but they are told nothing about the end client, or what products are being built with

(a)   (b)

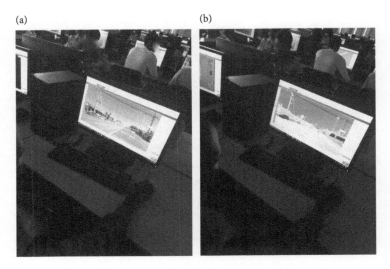

Fig. 0.2 Image annotation for a machine learning system
Source: Anwar and Graham, 2020b. Reproduced with permission.

all this information. Labour could not be more alienated: workers selling their labour power to far-off unknown firms, building products that they are unlikely to ever see or use.

One of the key objectives of this book is to resist this—to make visible the invisible and put the human back in the machine. Doing so allows us to explore the ways in which Africa is embedded into contemporary digital economy activities, and to shine a light on the role African workers are playing in digital capitalism. In the book we will describe African workers doing various types of work, most requiring them to manipulate digital data or provide digital services, often over the internet. These workers come primarily from poor socio-economic contexts, which influence their experience of the work. Consider the words of some of the workers we interviewed. For example Kenyangi,[1] a transcriber and content writer we interviewed in Kampala in 2017:

I come from a large family of ten siblings. My father is a carpenter and my mother is a housewife. Professionally, I am supposed to be a social worker; at least that is what I studied. I worked at a consulting firm as a junior editor and later became assistant editor. I had health problems. My boss was not very supportive and

---

[1] We have pseudonymised all the worker interviews in this book.

could not give me three months off. So, I decided to leave and ventured into online work through Upwork.

My first job was writing subtitles for movies. The client was based in the US. I did that for about three months and eventually stopped. I earned around US$95 for three movies. It was paid per movie. You were given a specific timeframe to complete the task. You do not get paid if you do not finish on time. One movie I did not complete and I lost about 10 hours' worth of my labour and there is nothing I could do. My clients on Upwork are from all over the world. My top client is a news agency based in Washington DC and a big data firm. I do transcription for them and also content writing for business websites. Sometimes I do not work for a week, because everything is contract based. Sometimes you have three contracts and they all end at the same time and you haven't got a new contract yet.

I work from home, on my laptop. I have a desk and a chair in my bedroom. I work eight to ten hours a day. I do most of my work at night between 9 pm and 5 am. I usually keep my weekends free. I feel there is more freedom with this home working than local work, but it is not absolute. I think it gives me the freedom to dictate my own work you know, hours and speed. Although that is not exclusively true because you know clients give you jobs and they dictate hours. But I do not have to go to the office every day. The traffic is awful and you can sit for two hours every morning and two hours in the evening to go to work. Even if I get something $10 per hour locally, I will not do it.

But online clients look at South-East Asia and Africa for cheaper labour. I started at US$10 an hour on Upwork but now I am at US$15 an hour. I will not get a job in Uganda that pays that much and then you have to pay taxes. I probably will not be making half of this working locally. I make on an average US$500 a week now, which is my main source of income and is the single most important contribution of this work to my life. I have private health insurance. I have invested in some side projects such as farming back in my village, where there was land available, something to earn a bit of income for my family.

In Kenyangi's case, her work through the internet is well-paid even if that means she does not have control over her working hours. She also understands that jobs are hard to come by in Uganda, and clients on the internet are leveraging it to access cheaper labour from Africa, which she is willing to do. This point was confirmed to us by most workers we spoke to, despite little work-life balance in these jobs. Dabiku, a video editor we interviewed in Nairobi in 2016, who is trained to be a veterinary surgeon, but after graduating in 2011 struggled to get a job locally. He told us:

> I tried private practice but only rich people can afford it. In villages, if you are vaccinating a dog, people would think twice, should I eat or vaccinate the animal. One time I was given a bottle of milk and bananas for helping a cow deliver her calf. I quit afterwards.

> I started doing online jobs in 2012. A friend helped me set up my profile on Upwork (then Odesk). I remember the first job I got was to flip a video from upside down. The client paid $10 and I did it in less than 30 minutes. I realised this is a field that I could venture into and do it without a lot of hustle. The next contract I got was to convert videos from one format to another. The client sent me 20 videos for $20. He kept on sending videos and considering I was a newbie back then, I did not even ask for money. I did about 80 videos for the client and he paid me US$150. The clients in America think why hire a graphic designer for US$35 per hour to sit in an office and that is the only kind of work he can do. They can use US$35 to hire seven guys in Asia or in Africa with an array of skills that can do graphic design, video editing and transcription.

> I do not have a work schedule now. I work when I want, when I feel like it. But when I have a deadline, I work long hours. I used to sleep from 3 am till 9 am. I still work for more than 60 hours a week. I don't take holidays. I have a lot of work now. I subcontract fixed priced jobs on Upwork, while I do the hourly work. I also re-outsource through Facebook groups.

> It is actually not for everybody and not many people can sacrifice the way I did. Most people do not realise that online work is actually work. People do not understand what you are doing. You know it's a new thing here. While my friends would go and watch football in the evening, I would bid on Upwork. When you are doing this kind of work, you tend to shut off people. I cannot say the last time I actually communicated with guys I went to school with. Only on WhatsApp groups.

The above two cases of workers describe jobs that can be done over the internet and mostly from the confines of workers' home, though these jobs do involve long and irregular working hours, and have health implications. Now *compare* the case of another worker who does customer service work at a call centre in Nairobi. Kenneth has a diploma in international relations from the University of Nairobi. We interviewed him in 2016 and he explained how a lack of work that matches his skills set results in African workers like him being driven towards new forms of digital work which can be underpaid and defined by strict workplace control. He told us:

I applied for a few jobs but only got called for an interview for this call centre job. It is not that people want to work in a call centre but basically, they need a job. They need money and that is how they get into it. But there is a lot of pressure, deliverables are difficult, long working hours and low compensation.

My company operates on the basis of shift work. They call it split-shift where you work from 8:00 am to 1:00 pm then you break and then back at 6:00 pm for work till 11:00 pm. You get one-hour break and break is not paid. That one hour is not continuous. You get a 15 minutes coffee break, then you get a half an hour lunch and then another 15 minutes break. I was working 10 hours a day or 50 hours a week. They were also calling me for overtime when they would get busy periods.

As an agent, we would deal with customer queries. Normally, we would be receiving anywhere between 150 and 180 calls per day during our shifts. Deliverables or targets now come in when you're doing an outbound campaign, which is primarily sales. You know, it is like I have been given this cup and I have been told do not come home with it. Come with money. So, I have to find a way to sell this cup. Outbound is chaotic and hell.

I am supposed to receive 100 calls, but after 20 calls basically, I will go home tired, with migraines. Basically, when you work in a call centre, you leave that office, you do not want to speak to anybody. You just want to go home, eat and sleep.

There were issues with workers not getting paid on time or their transport money. But they rarely speak because they fear so much about victimization at the workplace. There are lots of malpractices happening but guys fear losing their jobs.

We also do not get compensated properly. At my firm, as an agent I was getting KSH22,000 (approx. US$200) a month before taxes. As a team leader, now I am paid KSH35,000 (approx. US$318). I have known people who work for in-house call centres in Nairobi to earn KSH35-40,000 a month. But we are an outsourced centre. For me to survive it has never been sufficient. I have to pay school fees for my baby brother. Currently, I am dealing with my baby sister who is completing high school. I think the government needs to regulate the sector and that people get compensated equally.

Besides, there are few jobs locally and our jobs in contact centres are insecure. There is no job security, I would say. When you sign a contract, it says I am a permanent employee. But the next day you can get a call from your superior and your job is gone. They can fire you at any time. No benefits. The legal process would incur an expense. Who is willing to pay for this. Nobody. We do not have that money to get a lawyer. So, you move on. Go and get another job. Hence, I wake up and go to work to get that little money so that I can survive.

Unions are weak as well. I tried joining a union and recruiting workers. But my boss told me either you have your job or you want a union. So, I thought, if I am fired, he will not feed me. So, let me just get oppressed here. I think from the moment we understand that people who are united can achieve something [and] that we will not be fired as a group. Workers do not understand this thing and the value of unions or collective power. I tried recruiting and convincing 150 people in my firm. Then, all of sudden 70 people were fired. So, I have to start again.

I would not work in a call centre. Just need my life outside it. Basically, if I get a job in my line of education, yes, I would work there.

The experiences of the three workers described highlight that these jobs are an important economic lifeline to Africans who struggle to find paid-work locally. As a result, big hopes about African development are pinned on the digital economy activities, ranging from employment generation to reduction of poverty and inequality. In the context of widespread job-lessness on the continent, young African workers—who are often highly-educated—are turning to the new job opportunities presented by an emerging information-based economy not necessarily out of choice but necessity. This book is about these new digital jobs in Africa and the workers who perform them.

The stories from the young African workers quoted above underline both the potential and the constraints represented by contemporary digital cap-italism for workers in Africa. Each of these stories involves an African worker doing work that can be quickly transmitted digitally to another cor-ner of the planet. The work described by Kenyangi and Dabiku offers them some flexibility to work wherever and whenever they want, and economic possibilities and freedom to earn a living. This is also true of the work described by Kenneth who provides the type of back-office customer services work that keeps the motor of the digital economy running. In fact, many of these digital jobs are touted as an important stepping stone in the professional careers of African workers. But these jobs are also characterized by short-term contracts, job insecurity, long and irregular working hours, and lack of social welfare and freedom of association. These impacts also have gender, racial, ethnic and migrant dimensions (e.g. women and migrants experiencing precarious conditions at work). Most importantly, workers are subjected to a harsh regime of algorithmic surveillance of workplace and labour processes exerted through the application of advanced digital technologies. As a result, promises of the new digital economy have also brought about a degree of uncertainty for African workers and their livelihoods.

In this book we therefore want to shed light on the digital jobs that are currently taking place in Africa, and use what we know about where those jobs go, what types of work people do, and how those jobs are experienced, to reflect on the increasingly planetary-scale labour market through which futures of digital work will be played out.

1

Hopes and Realities of the Digital

Introduction

In 2000, there were almost ten times as many internet users in Belgium than in all of East Africa (Roser et al., 2015). The latest estimates from 2020 suggest that there are 590 million internet users in Africa (Internet World Stats, 2020), representing a penetration rate of around 47 per cent—the lowest in the world. Furthermore, while in 2005 there were only 87 million mobile phone subscriptions in the whole of Africa (ITU 2019), today, the continent has some of the highest mobile phone penetration rates in the world, with rates well above 100 per cent in some countries, as many people own multiple sim cards to offset peak call charges, through which a majority access the internet. The International Telecommunications Union (ITU) has estimated over 800 million mobile phone subscriptions in Africa in 2019 (ITU 2019).

Such tremendous diffusion of information and communication technologies (ICTs), including mobile phones, computers, and the internet, has led observers to examine the myriad ways in which technology-driven political, economic, social, and cultural transformations are happening on the continent (e.g. Adera et al., 2014; Africa Partnership Forum, 2008; Britz et al., 2006; Buskens and Webb, 2009; Butare et al., 2013; Chowdhury, 2006; Diga and May, 2012). Many see digital technologies and their adoption on the continent as a stimulus for Africa to connect more closely with the world digital economy. Indeed, digital technologies are acknowledged as a powerful driver of socio-economic transformation on the continent, as described by Dr Hamadoun Touré, former Secretary General of the ITU:

ICTs are truly transformational. With the power of technology, we can educate every African citizen, right across the continent. With the power of technology, we can open new opportunities and create new well-paid jobs for our people. With the power of technology, we can deliver healthcare services to every African citizen, even in the remotest villages. And with the power of technology

The Digital Continent. Mohammad Amir Anwar and Mark Graham, Oxford University Press.
© Mohammad Amir Anwar and Mark Graham (2022). DOI: 10.1093/oso/9780198840800.003.0001

we can empower African women and leverage the fantastic energy and passion of young Africans. This is not just a pipe-dream: this is real.

Touré, 2013

The potential of digital technologies to transform the political and economic landscape in Africa is deeply entrenched in the thinking of such organizations as the World Bank, which sees digital technologies as allowing people to access goods and services, and therefore as crucial in strengthening the continent's economies (Yonazi et al., 2012). A recent issue of *Africa's Pulse*, the World Bank's biannual publication on the outlook of the African economy, states that 'the digital transformation of Africa would foster economic growth and reduce poverty. It has the potential to create more jobs, encourage entrepreneurship among the youth, increase farmers' productivity, bring more women into the labour force, and create markets' (Calderon et al., 2019: 3). Such is the confidence around the emergence of the digital economy that some commentators argue that Africa's place in the world economy will be redefined, as it transitions into the so-called 'Fourth Industrial Revolution' (Nsengimana, 2018). The African Union (AU) Commissioner for Infrastructure and Energy, Dr Amani Abou-Zeid, has recently commented that 'All the stars are aligned for Africa to take advantage of Revolution 4.0 and digitalisation' (World Bank, 2019a).

This does not suggest that a digital economy has become either pervasive or prevalent across the continent. As we will later show, there exists a highly uneven pattern of engagement with the digital economy. For example, the cost of accessing the internet on the continent remains high in comparison to the rest of the world. According to the Alliance for Affordable Internet (2019), there is a wide disparity in the cost of 1 gigabyte of mobile broadband data on the continent, with the cost in Egypt just under 1 per cent of the average monthly income, while in the Democratic Republic of Congo the cost is about a third of average monthly income. In two of the continent's largest economies, Nigeria and South Africa, it costs 1.58 per cent and 2.3 per cent of average monthly income, respectively. In the continent as a whole, it averages around 8 per cent, while the world average is 5.76 per cent. There also exists a divide in terms of internet access between rural and urban areas in Africa, with rural populations 58 per cent less likely to have access (GSMA, 2019a). These divides can also be seen in the various forms of digital economy activity that are emerging on the continent. In 2019, an estimated 618 technology hubs—(i.e. organizations offering infrastructure support for technology start-up companies and digital entrepreneurs—were active on the continent, with almost half of those hubs present in just four countries, namely Nigeria, South Africa, Kenya, and Egypt (GSMA, 2019b). The rise of digital labour platforms has also been heralded as revolutionary for the continent's unemployment problem, as these platforms connect workers to economic opportunities around the world (Kuek et al., 2015). However, according to our own calculations, in 2019, almost all (92 per cent) of the African workers registered on the biggest digital work platform came from just seven countries, namely Morocco, Algeria, Tunisia, Egypt, Kenya, South Africa, and Nigeria.

In fact, the very uneven development of Africa's digital economy has led us to engage critically in this book with the wider debate around digital technologies and economic development—commonly referred to as the 'information and communication technology for development' (ICT4D) discourse (Unwin, 2009, 2017). While critical research has already pointed out the potential and limitations of ICTs in the African context (see, for example, Adera et al., 2014; Aker and Mbiti, 2010; Asongu, 2013; Attwood et al., 2013; Bornman, 2016; Carmody, 2013a; Diga and May, 2012; Donner, 2006; Etzo and Collander, 2010; Mamba and Isabirye, 2015; Molla and Heeks, 2007; Muto and Yamano, 2009; Okpaku, 2006; Oyelaran-Oyeyinka and Lal, 2006; Taylor, 2016), much of the focus so far has been on the impact of ICTs on the traditional sectors of the economy, such as manufacturing, tourism, and agriculture (Anwar et al., 2014; Foster et al., 2018; Murphy and Carmody, 2015). The newly emerging activities of the digital economy in Africa—and its associated digital labour—have received less attention. The book addresses this issue.

Scope of the Book

By digital economy, we mean 'that part of the economic output derived solely or primarily from the application of digital technologies with a business model based on digital goods or services' (Bukht and Heeks, 2017: 12). Most of these activities involve human labour. 'Digital labour', by contrast, has attracted a more varied set of conceptualizations. Heeks (2017) presents a useful schema of the ways in which the term is understood and used. There are multiple definitions to the term, for example, 'waged and unwaged work undertaken on digital media' (Scholz 2012); 'the organisation of human experiences with the help of the human brain, digital media and speech in such a way that new products are created' (Fuchs and Sevignani 2013); 'digitally-mediated service work' (van Doorn 2017); 'work done in an online labour market where (1) labour is exchanged for money, (2) the product of that labour is delivered "over a wire" and (3) the allocation of labour and money is determined by a collection of buyers and sellers operating within a price system' (Horton 2010); and 'work done in online labour markets that bring together buyers and sellers of intangible knowledge and service work' (Lehdonvirta et al., 2014).[1]

While these definitions are helpful and certainly illustrate the fact that work is changing and becoming more digital in nature, 'digital labour cannot be regarded as a discrete form of labour, separated hermetically from the rest of the economy' (Huws, 2014: 157). There are two points to consider here. First, there has been an explosion of all sorts of work required to keep the machinery of the digital economy going—for example, production of tangible goods such as computers, cables, batteries, etc., much of which still requires human labour (see Fuchs, 2014). Second, the contemporary digital economy is increasingly reliant on 'hidden value-generating digital practices' (Gregory, 2017), which some have described as 'ghost work' (Gray and Suri, 2019). This behind-the-scenes work can be found in telemediated services (Benner, 2006; Gareis et al., 2006) and various other forms of new digital tasks including machine learning, software development, transcription, proofreading, and search engine optimization (Anwar and Graham, 2020b; Tubaro et al., 2020). Many of these activities can in theory be outsourced to locations around the world to be performed by humans.

For Huws (2014), an appropriate way to understand digital labour is to recognize the growing division of labour in the contemporary digital economy—in part driven by the easy fragmentation of digital production into smaller tasks—and for digital labour to be geographically relocated to different parts of the world. The work during the early twentieth-century assembly line production (e.g. car assembly) would typically be done under one factory roof. However, some work has become digital in nature,

---

[1] Note that the very concept of 'work' has been hotly contested in the social sciences, primarily between the capitalist notion of waged employment and non-waged work (e.g. care work) which is often hidden from official figures and is otherwise considered informal and precarious. Hidden and informal work now accounts for 60% of global employment and has been a norm in low—and middle-income—countries for decades. An urgent need here is to understand 'work' from the perspective of these groups of people who have sometimes been labelled as 'precariat' and 'dangerous' (see Standing, 2014). They continue to play an increasingly important role in the contemporary world economy, through work activities such as artisanal mining, domestic work, farm labour, and most recently digital labour.

meaning that digital tasks can be performed by workers around the world with minimum requirements—essentially, basic computing skills, computers, and an internet connection. Common examples of such work include transcription, and the image annotation/tagging work described in the Prologue. In other words, the emerging digital production landscape has become ever more complex, often opaque, and has the potential to expand into new locations. Some of these new locations are now in Africa. We therefore use the term 'digital labour' in this book to describe *types of work activities involving the paid manipulation of digital data by humans through ICTs such as mobile phones, computers, laptops, etc.*; in so doing we emphasize the centrality of human labour in the makings of digital capitalism. We also emphasize the role of geography in the ways in which digital work is organized and managed across a range of newer locations which have not previously been considered central to the global digital economy.[2] Our focus in the book is on two key forms of digital economy activities in Africa: business process outsourcing (BPO), and the remote gig economy.

Business process outsourcing is understood as the practice of a firm contracting out some of its non-core services or functions to a different specialized firm or firms. It involves both the domestic and foreign relocation of these services, commonly referred to as onshore or offshore outsourcing, respectively (see Bryson, 2007; Troaca and Bodislav, 2012). While this process of sourcing of services has been going on for decades, advances in digital technologies since the 1990s have radically altered the spatial organization of production—and hence the geographic and sectoral reach of global services sourcing as new actors join global networks (Beerepoot et al., 2017; Peck, 2017). The BPO industry that emerged in India and the Philippines in the 1990s has had a great impact on local economic development in these two countries (Bardhan et al., 2013; Dossani and Kenny, 2009; Kleibert, 2015). More recently, some of this offshoring work has moved into various countries in Africa. In particular, the growth of mobile phone subscriptions has led to the emergence of a domestic market serving BPO operations, particularly customer services centres across a number of countries on the continent (Anwar and Graham, 2019; Graham and Mann, 2013). However, apart from a few reports produced by management consultancies (e.g. Deloitte, 2015, 2016; Everest Group, 2012; Frost

---

[2] Africa already occupies a central location in global digital production networks through the raw materials that go into the production of computers, mobile phones, cables, and other machinery. These materials include coltan, cobalt, gold, silver, platinum, bauxite, and copper (Carmody, 2016). More on this in Chapter 2.

and Sullivan, 2018) and a handful of scholarly works on BPO operations in Africa (for example, Anwar and Graham, 2019 Benner, 2006; Kleibert and Mann, 2020; Mann and Graham, 2016), not much has been written about the African labour involved in this industry.[3] This book contributes to the emerging literature by focusing in part on entry-level activities such as call and contact centre work which includes diverse range of activities e.g. inbound and outbound customer service, technical support, back office admin functions, digitization, etc. in Africa.

The second focus of the book is the remote gig economy. The gig economy can be understood as a system of economic exchange whereby organizations and individuals come together to get a variety of work done via digital transaction platforms acting as intermediaries (see Lehdonvirta et al., 2019; Woodcock and Graham, 2019). Digital platforms enable transactions between buyers and sellers of a particular service or tasks digitally through their proprietary platforms or websites. An estimated 4.8 million workers have already performed various types of gig economy tasks in just seven countries on the African continent (Insight2impact, 2019). We use the term 'gig economy' to refer to the work tasks that are digitally mediated or transacted through a multitude of digital platforms and that can be delivered either remotely or performed locally. The term 'gig' refers to the short-term nature of the work, with tasks lasting from a few minutes to several months. Conceptually, we acknowledge a range of competing understandings of the gig economy, such as microwork, online outsourcing, crowdwork, etc. (see Heeks, 2017), but we stress explicitly the geographical and digital focus of the term and distinguish between two types of gig work: 'remote work' that is geographically untethered (e.g. transcription and graphic design work secured via platforms such as Upwork) and 'geographically tethered' work which is geographically sticky and performed locally by workers (for example, ride-hailing apps like Uber) (Graham and Anwar, 2018a, 2018b, 2019). Our focus in the book is on remote work. That is, where workers apply for and carry out a variety of remote jobs for clients who themselves can be located anywhere in the world. Some of these tasks include article writing, virtual assistance, transcription, and machine-learning and search engine optimization, which can be perfomed by workers either via platforms or through firms (e.g. BPO firms). With increasing diffusion of digital technologies, and rising internet penetration

---

[3] The literature on working conditions in the global BPO industry is huge, and we engage with it in later parts of the book. Key works include Hastings and Mackinnon, 2017; Woodcock, 2016; Hunter and Hachimi, 2012; Noronha and D'Cruz, 2009; Glucksmann, 2004; Belt, 2002; Callaghan and Thompson, 2002; Taylor and Bain, 1999, 2005.

in low- and middle-income regions of Africa, there is a potential for more of this labour to be performed across the continent.

The core question we attempt to answer in this book is as follows. How are these new digital economy activities influencing African workers' lives and livelihoods? To address this question, we undertake a geographical and political economic analysis of the consequences of digital labour for African workers. Empirically, we draw on in-depth qualitative evidence gathered from African call and contact centre operations and the remote gig economy to analyse paid digital work and its flows, networks, geographies, and development implications in five African countries, namely: Ghana, Kenya, Nigeria, South Africa, and Uganda.

Case Study Contexts

The selection of our five case study countries was strategic, and they represent a diversity of experiences and contemporary development challenges, such as growth in joblessness, unemployment, income inequality, and high levels of informal employment. We also wanted to cover places where both types of digital work activities, i.e. business process outsourcing and remote work, are happening in Africa. We conducted fieldwork in Ghana, Kenya, Nigeria, South Africa, and Uganda between July 2016 and November 2017 (see Appendix for more details).[4]

Concerning the state of digital work in these countries, Ghana and Kenya are noted for their potential for digital outsourcing activities in various management consultancy indexes, and South Africa remains a top destination for international BPO work in Africa. Other countries, like Nigeria and Uganda, face serious challenges, and in several cases, we found some BPO operations closing down. Our five case countries account for 40 per cent of the labour supply from the African continent on the biggest digital work platform in the world, Upwork. Kenya, Nigeria, and South Africa have some of the highest concentrations of platform workers in Africa (only Egypt had a higher number of registered workers on Upwork from Africa, at the time of data collection), but by contrast, Uganda and Ghana are still catching up.

---

[4] We acknowledge that our focus here is largely on Anglophone Africa, though given the digital economy is largely driven by the US (and therefore English-speaking), this made sense to us when setting up the study. Our study countries are also relatively prosperous compared to some of their neighbours, though again: we wanted to select countries with a significant digital economy.

Our case study countries also have some of the fast-growing information technology sectors on the continent, with Kenya, for example, heralded as a 'Silicon Savannah' in the popular press (Financial Times, 2016). Kenya's tech-hub ecosystem is big, with forty-eight hubs (GSMA, 2019b), over 200 start-ups, and a valuation of US$1 billion (Mallonee, 2018). Our five case study countries account for 40 per cent of all the technology hubs currently in Africa. South Africa has a highly developed information technology infrastructure and ranks fairly highly on the ICT Development Index in comparison to other African countries—only outranked by Mauritius and the Seychelles.

All five countries are also quite varied in terms of development indicators. Nigeria and South Africa are the two biggest economies on the continent, and are classed as middle-income countries; however, both have high income inequality. In South Africa, the Gini index (a measure of income inequality) has remained persistently above 60 per cent, and in a recent study, Chatterjee et al. (2020) found that the wealthiest 10 per cent of the South African population owns 86 per cent of the aggregate wealth. Furthermore, they find that half the adult population survives on near-zero savings. While South Africa fares better on the human development index, Nigeria fares very low, largely due to the unstable political situation marred by violence and terrorism in the northern parts of the country. Ghana is also a middle-income country, is fairly stable politically and economically, and ranks highly in various socio-economic indicators in comparison to its West African neighbours. Uganda is a low-income country and is classified as very low on the human development index (162nd of the 189 countries for which data are available), with poverty rates standing at 41 per cent in 2016 (World Bank, n.d.). Table 1.1 summarizes the key development indicators of our case study countries.

Contribution and Argument

Theoretically, this book bridges research in the fields of economic geography and development studies—what Vira and James (2011) have referred to as 'interdisciplinary trading zones' (also see Barnes and Shepard, 2010)—to engage with the intersections between these disciplines. Economic geographers are typically concerned with geographical enquiry into the production, distribution, and consumption of goods and services (Clark et al., 2018). They have long used concepts like space, place, and positionality to make sense of contemporary economic globalization and the uneven

Table 1.1 Key development indicators in our case study countries

	Ghana	Nigeria	Uganda	Kenya	South Africa
Unemployment % (Youth (Unemployment)	4.4 (9.1)	9.0 (18.3)	10.0 (15.6)	9.3 (12.8)	32.6* (59.4)
Informal Employment (%)	90.1	92.9	93.7	83.6	34
Human Development Index (Rank)	0.611 (138)	0.539 (161)	0.544 (159)	0.601 (143)	0.709 (114)
Multidimensional Poverty Index (MPI)	0.138	0.254	0.269	0.178	0.025
Income Inequality (Gini Index)	43.5	43	42.8	40.8	63
Mobile Phone subscriptions per 100 people	137.5	88.2	57.3	96.3	153.2
ICT Affordability: 1 Gigabyte Data in US$ (% of average income)	2.27 (1.36)	2.70 (1.71)	3.75 (5.95)	3.69 (2.62)	5.68 (1.41)
ICT Development Index Value (Rank)	4.05 (116)	2.60 (143)	2.19 (152)	2.91 (138)	4.96 (92)

* This figure is the official unemployment rate in South Africa in the first quarter of 2021 as per Statistics South Africa (2021). Unemployment statistics have been a political matter in South Africa since the country moved away from a broad unemployment indicator towards a narrow ILO definition (see Alenda-Demoutiez and Mugge, 2020). The expanded unemployment rate is well over 43%.
Notes: A high MPI value indicates a high incidence of poverty.
Sources: Statistics South Africa, 2021; ILOSTAT Data Bank; United Nations Development Programme (UNDP), 2019, 2020; ITU, 2017b; Kenya National Bureau of Statistics, 2019; Alliance for Affordable Internet, 2020.

distribution of production activities around the world (Barnes, 1989; Coe and Yeung, 2015; Dicken, 2011; Harvey, 1982, 1989a; Massey, 1995; Scott, 1988; Sheppard, 2002; Storper and Christopherson, 1987). However, the emergence of information technology and its increasingly important role in the production process has led some observers to describe an altering of the geographical landscape of production—perhaps most famously in Thomas Friedman's assertion that the world has become 'flat'. In other words, this heralds the so-called 'death of geography' (Ohmae, 1990) as globalization and digitalization render obsolete various key factors for structuring of production processes, such as physical proximity to the market. In this view, a *relational* understanding of space is much more helpful, i.e. space is seen as emerging from social relations (Massey, 2005), rather than being a mere physical quantity. It draws attention to the actor networks formed through the subtle blending of digital technologies and human actors, which are then implicated in the 'active construction of space and place, rather than making it somehow redundant' (Graham, 1998: 174). The underlying point is that even in the highly technologically mediated production systems and markets of the digital economy, geography still matters. In this book, we highlight uneven geographies in digital economy networks. We then draw on conceptual frameworks within the sociological research and development studies literature (e.g. job quality) to examine digital economy's developmental impacts on workers on the African continent.

There are two main advantages to the bringing together of many disciplines into discussion of Africa's digital economies. First, by bringing the lens of economic geography into the study of Africa's digital economy, we can examine the continent's place in the contemporary world of digital work. We will show that there exists an emerging market for a variety of digital work activities, which presents economic opportunities for African workers that are unequally distributed. It also enables us to broaden the scope of analysis of digital capitalism into low- and middle-income regions. Second, having a multidisciplinary focus improves its utility for public policy. This is hugely important, given the high rates of poverty and unemployment across the continent, which forces governments to uncritically adopt narratives around digital technologies as a panacea for economic development without appropriate empirical evidence. We hope this book will enrich the debates around the role of digital technologies in effecting a broader structural transformation of the African labour force—an aspect that is often neglected in the ICT4D literature.

Core Arguments

Practically, this book has two central arguments. One is that *digital capitalism is bringing some jobs to Africa but is also generating uneven economic geographies*. Historically, the outsourcing of economic production (primarily industrial manufacturing) was done from a handful of geographical locations around the world. Because of the tangible nature of industrial activities involving movements of raw materials and finished goods over long distances, a number of factors—socio-political, cultural, and technological—have generated uneven economic geographies of production. Digital technologies are expected to have an equally profound impact on the way economic production is spatially organized. The digitization of production processes generates new digital forms of value, such as IT-enabled services. Much of this value remains geographically untethered and can therefore move around the world much more easily than, say, industrial goods. As a result, new places have been brought into these digital networks—most notably, places like India and the Philippines (Beerepoot et al., 2017; Kleibert and Mann, 2020), but also a number of countries across Africa. By examining the economic geographies of business process outsourcing and the remote gig economy in these countries, we are able to unveil processes of integration and marginalization (e.g. political, economic, social, and technological infrastructures) to highlight uneven developments on the continent as it is brought more closely into the circuits of digital capitalism.

The second central argument we present is that while digital capitalism is bringing much needed jobs to Africa, *the use of digital technologies is also enabling so-called 'digital Taylorism' in contemporary workplaces and digital work platforms, where management and control techniques are being applied with increasing efficiency.* This is simply the latest manifestation of the scientific principles introduced by Frederick W. Taylor in the early twentieth century to organize work on the factory floor. This revolution in organizational efficiency was laid out in Taylor's book 'The Principles of Scientific Management' (1911), and is still referred to today as Taylorism or Taylor's Principles. By breaking complex jobs into simpler ones, managerial control of workers could be increased, as could quantification of worker performance, and thus linking of wages to performance. These techniques were widely adopted both in the assembly line production of the early twentieth century (Frobel et al., 1981; Lipietz, 1987) and the BPO industry of the late twentiethth century. Indeed, since the 1990s, call and contact centres have become synonymous with Taylorist control systems, with research done on BPOs around the world showing high levels of monitoring, commodification of work, and a lack of work autonomy (Taylor and Bain, 2005; Woodcock, 2016). Some have equated work organization at call and contact centres with an 'assembly line in the head' (Taylor and Bain, 1999), or even to an 'electronic sweatshop' (Garson, 1988).

Much recent research is documenting how the use of digital technologies is altering work, labour processes, workplaces, and employment relations (Aroles et al., 2019; Bonekamp and Sure, 2015; Gandini, 2019; Kellog et al., 2020; Prassl, 2018). The Economist (2015a) has noted that Amazon's use of Taylorist techniques to measure its workers in order to achieve maximum efficiency embodies a new trend of 'Digital Taylorism'. This form of digital control is also very much evident in the global gig economy, where managerial control of workers through the use of technologies and algorithms is quite common (Gerber and Krzydwinski, 2019; Kellog et al., 2020; Anwar and Graham, 2020a, 2020c). In essence, Digital Taylorism is seeping into various forms of low-paid informal work (Krishna, 2019; Wonolo, 2019), which has great development implications in many low and middle-income countries, where informal work is the dominant form of employment opportunity (International Labour Organisation (ILO), 2018). While digital technologies have been leveraged in a variety of workplaces since the 1990s in order to achieve efficiency, the latest drive also affects working conditions (Anwar and Graham, 2019; Taylor et al., 2013). This fundamental tension between efficiency and working conditions raises questions about the limits of digital technologies in bringing about a positive socio-economic transformation of labour on the continent.

One of the underlying arguments we want to make in our analysis of BPO work and the gig economy in Africa is that these work types are only made possible because of the commodification of work. We would also argue that the digital Taylorism that sustains these digital economy activities is more powerful and more dehumanizing than earlier versions, mainly because technological innovations have given management the ability to control labour processes remotely, allowing Taylorist principles to be exerted from far beyond the place of production (Frischmann and Selinger, 2017). In more practical terms, we will pinpoint and discuss a number of bottlenecks or challenges to a sustainable and equitable transformation of the lives of African digital workers.

Among many policy institutions, development organizations, and management consultancies, there is an implicit assumption that many of the changes we see in contemporary work organization are technologically driven, and hence inevitable (for example, see European Commission, 2019; Mckinsey & Company, 2016; Manyika, 2015; World Bank, 2016). However, we will argue that these changes in the world of work are also (even largely) political and economic. In organizational studies, there has been a shift away from technologically deterministic explanations of technology use in organizations (e.g. Lawrence and Lorsch 1967; Perrow, 1967; Thompson 1967; Woodward, 1958) towards socio-material, institutional, and practice-driven views of technology-induced organizational change (eg. Barley, 1990; Leonardi, 2013). Some scholars have, for instance highlighted the inseparability of the technical and social aspects of work and organizations (see Orlikowski and Scott, 2008). Leonardi and Barley (2010), in their review of the application of technology in organizations and further suggest that scholars should pay closer attention to the geographical variability of social dynamics, to the dynamics of power, and the role of institutions in shaping technological trajectories. Such geographically sensitive and socially constructed explanations of digital technologies, we posit, can help advance understanding of the nature of digital work, especially regarding the uneven geographies of contemporary digital economy. More importantly, it will hopefully build social consciousness and help shape political and regulatory responses to the normalization of Taylorist techniques in the digital economy.

Chapter Overview

Following this introductory chapter, in Chapter 2 we discuss Africa's digital connectivities to understand the nature of digital production networks on the continent. The objective of this chapter is to examine continuity and change in the extractive nature of contemporary capitalism in Africa. The overall argument is that the internet is bringing globalization to Africa, and the resulting digitalization and fragmentation of production processes have enabled an African information economy to emerge and integrate into global production networks. However, there is a danger of African economies getting locked structurally into a system of value extraction, which will ultimately impact workers' livelihoods.

To explore this, we first carry out a brief overview of the colonial and post-colonial linkages of the African continent with the world capitalist economy. A number of studies have shown that Africa's underdevelopment is a result of poor articulation in the global political economy (Bond, 2006; Carmody, 2010; Rodney, 2012) rather than due to its physical distance from core economies or lack of market access. Indeed, many hope that through the rapid adoption and diffusion of digital technologies, Africa's adverse articulation can be reversed, and the continent put on track for economic development. This is best symbolized in the ICT4D (European Commission, 2017; Unwin, 2009) and 'data for development' (D4D) discourses (Mann, 2018). One uncritical assumption among some of the studies is that digital technologies are transforming Africa's place in the global economy, and are also having a progressive impact on its workers (e.g. World Bank, 2012, 2013b, 2016). While it is true that technological revolutions have transformed the production landscapes of the twenty-first century by bringing various places into the ambit of capitalist production, we argue that it is the nature and type of integration that is key to understanding the development implications of increasing digitalization.

In Chapter 3 we present a vivid account of the economic geographies of the emerging digital economy in Africa through an examination of the production, distribution, and consumption of digital goods and services in Africa. The underlying objective of this chapter is to provide a visual and descriptive outline of call and contact centre work and remote gig work in Africa, revealing a highly uneven landscape of informational capitalism. We argue that geography matters for the networks and flows of the global information economy, and the way that labour is allocated within it. In doing so, we ask what type of remote/digital work gets done in Africa, and what that means for value creation and capture across the region.

Drawing on our empirical work on BPO firms in our five case study countries, we first examine and analyse the geographies of the outsourcing industry, the nature and types of activities taking place, and the level of integration with global outsourcing production networks. We point to the uneven development of the African outsourced services industry. For example, South Africa's outsourcing industry is more outward looking and has a deeper connection with international buyers than Kenya, Nigeria, Ghana, and Uganda. In some cases, such as in Kenya and Ghana, international BPO operations have shut down, due to companies moving abroad in search of cheaper locations. While there has been a certain lifting of technological barriers (such as internet connectivity), other political and socio-economic bottlenecks, which are preventing the region from moving into high-value added functions (e.g. upgrading), still remain. That is, the uptake of digital technologies does not necessarily transform the power relations and political–economic structures of global production networks in such a way as to allow African firms to participate equally in the global information economy.

The final part of the chapter deals with the rise of the African gig economy. By sourcing data from, Upwork, which boasts over two million registered workers worldwide, we provide an empirical and visual account of the geography of remote work in Africa through mapping of remote work activities. Upwork is the go-to platform for African workers to source gig work, although most workers set up profiles on multiple platforms, including Freelancer.com, Fiverr, and PeoplePerHour. We find there to be a highly uneven distribution of remote work across the continent, with only a handful of countries accounting for the majority of the African workers registered on Upwork. This uneven geography is also represented globally, with the United States, India, Pakistan, and the Philippines accounting for more than half of the global labour supply on Upwork. Our argument here is that while in the world of digital work there exists the possibility of a planetary-scale labour market, it is very far from being a level playing field (Graham and Anwar, 2019). Digital labour markets are characterized by multi-scalar and asymmetrical technological, political, social, cultural, and institutional factors, which can lead to an uneven geography of labour both in Africa and beyond.

With CEOs in the Global North proclaiming that 'location is a thing of the past' (Upwork, 2018) and governments and civil society in Africa promising to create millions of digital jobs on the continent, we need to understand that geographies *still matter* to the flows of digital work and to the lives of the African workers who undertake these activities. More importantly, the emergence of digital jobs has wider development implications.

Chapter 4 conceptualizes the developmental impact of new digital work activities by drawing from the literature on the quality of work (e.g. ILO, 1999, 2014; Green, 2006; Kalleberg, 2013). While this framework has its theoretical origins in high-income countries, there are certain commonalities to be found in low- and middle-income regions. We therefore conceptualiseize the impacts of two digital economy activities (namely call and contact centre work, and remote gig work) on African labour in terms of income, autonomy at work, worker power, freedom of association, economic inclusion, skills upgrading, and labour agency.

Chapter 5 examines the developmental impacts of digital jobs on labour in Africa. It frames several key questions: Who does this type of work? What factors determine who does it? And how do these jobs impact workers' lives and livelihoods? We provide a detailed description of the labour processes involved in both platform-based remote work, and call and contact centre work. This we believe is key to understanding how workers perform different types of digital jobs, and how this affects their well-being. We draw on interviews with workers to explore the lived experiences of African digital labour. One of the key arguments we make is that while digital work can certainly bring a degree of freedom and flexibility to African workers' lives, it can also contribute to precarity and vulnerability.

We discuss various forms of social divisions such as class, gender, and race, and how these shape the way workers get access to digital work. We also stress that there is no straightforward narrative about positive or negative outcomes, but rather a great variety of lived worker experience— shaped by workers' socio-economic, political, and cultural backgrounds, education levels, and types of work activities. That said, there is an element of agency involved, and workers have the ability to create 'fixes' for their own production and reproduction and to influence their working conditions.

Chapter 6 examines the agency of African gig workers to shape their own labour geographies. By incorporating various strands of research on labour geography, this chapter asserts that labour agency, as understood in the existing literature, needs further conceptual and theoretical development that speaks for emerging digital work activities and the labour that goes into them. We theorize agency not just in the form of collective and organized action, but also in the way in which workers are able to exert individual and unorganized agency in digital workplaces. These can be understood as the everyday actions and practices of workers, described as 'hidden transcripts' by Scott (1990) in his portrayal of subaltern resistance in the face of power. We also place specific focus on agency practices that extend beyond the realm of production into the realm of reproduction, i.e. worker homes and the new digital communication spaces that provide workers with an outlet for their voices to be heard and for mobilizing collective action. In doing so, we highlight a number of 'fixes' created by workers beyond their workplaces in response to capital's tendency to undermine their labour. However, we show how these agency practices are shaped and restricted by a number of factors, including the socio-economic background of workers and the types of work activities they undertake.

Chapter 7 brings together several key threads and arguments made in the book to discuss what the future of work means for the African continent and how to create a fairer world for labour. Here we note that the future of work in Africa is still emerging and emergent vis-à-vis the processes of digital transformation. If that future is to contain decent jobs and fair outcomes for African workers, we need to ensure that we appropriately understand the transnational networks in which those jobs are embedded. Here we propose the idea of a planetary labour market in digital work. Planetary labour markets transcend the spatial boundaries that constrain the convergence of employers and workers, but that is characterized by multi-scalar and asymmetrical technological, political, social, cultural, and institutional factors. This allows us to think about labour futures in such scenarios.

We end the chapter by asking the following. Does a planetary market for digital work mean that African workers can transcend some of the constraints of the local labour markets in which they are embedded, or will they continue to suffer from those constraints? There is no simple yes or no answer. However, the opportunities and constraints placed on labour power must be better understood if we are to create a better future for African workers. Finally, we draw attention to the key role that political actors (e.g. the state) and civil society (third sector organizations and advocacy groups) can play in ensuring that digital work contributes positively to workers' lives. We also call for greater involvement of labour unions in expanding the way they organize workers, especially in thinking about cross-national ways of fostering solidarities and worker voice. In summary, we need to understand that economic production is embedded in socio-political and cultural contexts, and that state institutions are required to govern and regulate it. It is those institutions, together with trade unions and civil society organizations, that must rise to the challenge of not just thinking at a planetary scale, but also *acting* at a planetary scale if we want labour markets to represent anything other than a global race to the bottom.

2

Africa's New Digital Connectivity and Economic Change

Introduction

Historically, Africa was seen as a key supplier of natural resources, such as minerals and oil, in the world economy. This was the main driver for European colonialism in Africa (Rodney, 2012), and many of its economies still depend predominantly on the export of low-value added commodities. However, many new actors have emerged in the contemporary scramble for Africa (Carmody, 2016; Southall and Melber, 2009). The rapid adoption and diffusion of digital technologies on the continent in the last decade has led many governments and observers to talk about Africa's 'Fourth Industrial Revolution' (The Brookings Institution, 2020; Du Preez, 2019; Morsy, 2020). The underlying assertion here is that digital technologies will help African economies move away from the primary sector towards tertiary economic activities, and therefore put them on track for economic development. However, there are genuine concerns about the extent to which digital technologies will alter the existing modes and structures of production that currently harm the African continent (see Anwar, 2019; Gillwald, 2019; Murphy and Carmody, 2015). In this chapter, we argue that Africa continues to be locked into a value-extractive position in the global economy. Digital production, predominantly characterized by low value-added economic activities that do not necessarily translate into socio-economic improvements for the African working classes, represents a new arena for these dynamics to play out.

Africa's Linkages with the World Economy

As one of the most resource-rich regions of the world, Africa is estimated to contain about 42 per cent of the world's bauxite, 38 per cent of its uranium, 40 per cent of its gold, 73 per cent of its platinum, 88 per cent of its

The Digital Continent. Mohammad Amir Anwar and Mark Graham, Oxford University Press.
© Mohammad Amir Anwar and Mark Graham (2022). DOI: 10.1093/oso/9780198840800.003.0002

diamonds, and 10 per cent of its oil. However, over 40 per cent of Africans live on less than what US$1.90 a day would buy you in the US (cited from Carmody, 2016: 1–2). Further, the unemployment rates on the continent are some of the highest in the world, with youth unemployment in North Africa standing at around 28 per cent—more than twice the global average (ILO, 2017a).[1] South Africa has youth unemployment in excess of 64 per cent. Furthermore, the ILO estimates over 85 per cent of African employment to be informal, representing the highest rate in the world (ILO, 2018, 2020b).[2] While we can find numerous explanations for these rather dismal development indicators, there is no denying that much of this is the result of Africa's poor articulation with the world economy—which itself has been influenced by its long colonial legacy. Walter Rodney in his classic *How Europe underdeveloped Africa* (2012: xvi) has noted that 'the operation of the imperialist system bears major responsibility for African economic retardation by draining African wealth and by making it impossible to develop more rapidly the resources of the continent'.

Put in very broad terms, the colonial powers—including Britain, France, Belgium, the Netherlands, Portugal, Spain, Italy, and Germany—instituted and structured the rules of the game in such a way as to support regimes of accumulation in which the benefits accrued to the European territories.[3] These strategies set up the economic system in Africa in which natural resources became central to the 'scramble for Africa'—and which continue to this day even after the independence movements that swept the continent from the 1950s onwards (Carmody, 2016).[4] Politically, independence for many African states brought hopes of a structural transformation of their political economy; however, in failing to resolve the structure of their relationship with global powers, their economic dependence on their ex-colonial masters was preserved, leading to a situation of neocolonialism. As Kwame Nkrumah (1965) has described, the essence of neocolonialism is that the state which is subject to it is, in theory, independent and has all

---

[1] In the region, among those aged 15–29, those not in education, employment or training (NEETs) account for 32% in Tunisia and 40% in Egypt (ILO, 2016).

[2] Informality is often understood to be economic activities and employment outside the purview of legal and regulatory frameworks of the state. From the workers' point of view, informal employment is often low-paid and lacks social protection. The ILO advocates for the transition from informal to formal employment as a route to development. However, this does not mean the formal sector jobs always offer better pay and social protection, as has been the case with the call-centre work we describe in this book.

[3] African colonization was made possible not just by sheer violence but also by several rules enforced by European colonial powers, such as terra nullius and trusteeship (see Boisen, 2013).

[4] Egypt achieved its independence from Britain in 1922, long before successive waves of independence in the rest of the continent began in the 1950s.

the outward trappings of international sovereignty. However, in reality, its economic system and thus its political policy is directed from outside.[5]

An example of this in the post-colonial era in Africa is the series of structural adjustment programmes (SAPs) forced on it by the International Monetary Fund (IMF) and the World Bank. These programmes have had a lasting impact on African political economy, leading in some cases to deindustrialization, corruption, and inequalities (see Carmody, 1998; Gibbon and Mkandawire, 1995; Nyang'oro and Shaw, 1992). The local political elites within many African societies also became agents in 'the process of political centralization and economic accumulation' (Bayart, 2000: 219).[6] At the same time, support by the US and Europe of a number of dictators (e.g. President Mobutu in Zaire, present-day Democratic Republic of the Congo (DRC)), financial aid, and free markets and free trade advocated by the IMF and the World Bank served the purpose of drawing African wealth away from the continent (Bond, 2006; Gibbon, 1993; Moyo, 2009).[7] A 2017 report by a coalition of NGOs suggests that the continent is a net creditor to the rest of the world, i.e. more wealth leaves Africa every year, through debt payments and profit repatriation by foreign corporations, than it receives (see Honest Accounts, 2017).[8]

Africa's structural place in the global economy is such that mining and agriculture still dominate the political–economic landscape of the region, which has dragged several African countries into long-term conflicts, civil wars, and insurgency (on oil, see Ovadia, 2016; on gold, see Engels, 2017; on diamonds and coltan, see Mantz, 2008; Nest, 2013).[9] The global financial crisis of 2008, coupled with a rise in food grain prices, led to a surge in large-scale land deals (i.e. acquisition of land by both domestic and foreign investors) which served the purpose of supplying food and energy security to investor countries (Cotula et al., 2009; Matondi et al., 2011; Oya, 2013)

---

[5] France's involvement in Francophone Africa is a classic example of a power continuing to exert control over its former colonies, both militarily and monetarily, in order to protect its interests (see Aggad-Clerx, 2013; Charbonneau, 2016; Kamel, 2018; Kane, 2017).

[6] That said, Bayart's thesis of extraversion has been criticized for downplaying the influence of colonialism, and homogenizing African political experience (see Young, 1999).

[7] The US, by some accounts, has provided military assistance to 36 of the 49 dictatorships around the world as of 2015, that is, to around three-quarters of them (Whitney, 2017).

[8] In 2019, remittances flows to Africa stood at about US$82 billion (World Bank, 2020), higher than the foreign direct investment (FDI) in flows (US$45 billion) (UNCTAD, 2020) and the total overseas development assistance (ODA) or government aid (about $30 billion in 2019) (Organisation for Economic Co-operation and Development (OECD) Stats, n.d.). Put simply, not only do foreign actors extract more wealth from Africa, they give back less than Africans abroad.

[9] Botswana and South Africa may be outliers here, with relatively stable political–economic environments and an economic output largely built around mining. That said, they are still highly unequal societies, with South Africa's GINI coefficient of 0.61 still the highest in the world.

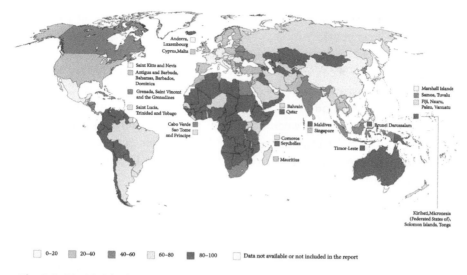

Fig. 2.1 Worldwide dependence on commodity exports, 2013–17 (percentage)
Source: UNCTAD, 2019a. Reproduced with permission.

and entrenching control over politics and resources by the host African states, along with international investors (Carmody and Taylor, 2016; Lavers and Boamah, 2016). In 2011, an estimated 70 per cent of the land acquired globally by both the private sector and governments was sourced from the African continent (Cheru and Modi, 2013). Recently, new powers, including Brazil, Russia, India, and China, are reconfiguring Africa's economic geography and development but are also reinforcing old patterns of economy and politics (Bond and Garcia, 2015; Carmody, 2013b). Indeed, a majority of Africa's economies still depend on natural resources and agricultural goods (see Figure 2.1), which have a critical role in deepening the processes of contemporary globalization on the continent (Carmody, 2016).

Africa's mineral exports to the rest of the world accounted for around half of its total exports in 2018 (UNCTAD, 2019b). The major export from the continent's biggest economy, Nigeria, is crude petroleum (74 per cent by value), while the second biggest economy, South Africa, depends largely on the exporting of minerals such as gold, platinum, diamonds, coal, and iron ore, amounting to 42.8 per cent. The smaller economies are even more dependent on natural resources export, including Equatorial Guinea (petroleum 87 per cent); DRC (metal ores 53 per cent, copper 13 per cent); Ghana (gold 49 per cent, crude oil 17 per cent, cocoa 10 per cent); Ethiopia (coffee 32 per cent, oilseeds 16 per cent, gold 11 per cent, cut flowers 9 per cent); Zambia (copper 74 per cent); and Uganda (coffee 20 per cent, gold 15 per cent). The North African economies are slightly more diversified—Morocco's major exports are textiles and machines, while in Egypt, minerals are followed by chemical and vegetable exports.[10] This dependence on commodities makes them susceptible to commodity price shocks. For example, between 2008 and 2017 the external debt to gross domestic product of Uganda increased from 16 per cent to 43 per cent; in Ghana the figure increased from 19 per cent to 47 per cent, while in Mozambique it is now close to 97 per cent (UNCTAD, 2019c). In the Republic of the Congo and Zambia, external debt payments account for more than 40 per cent and 50 per cent, respectively, of government revenue in 2019, with Republic of the Congo cutting public spending by almost 50 per cent between 2015 and 2018 (Jubilee Debt Campaign, 2020).

Despite African economies growing by 4.1 per cent between 2000 and 2019, which is higher than figures for South American countries, the region has performed poorly on various socio-economic indicators.[11] Income inequality remains a major problem, with ten of the nineteen most unequal countries in the world being found on the African continent (UNDP, 2017). Even within different African countries, the distribution of income remains highly unequal, with the richest quintile having a disproportionately high income (see Figure 2.2). The rates of extreme poverty (i.e. US$1.90 per day per capita as poverty threshold) have declined from 54.3 per cent in 1990 to about 41 per cent in 2015, but absolute numbers have gone up from 280 million to 412 million during the same period (Roser and Ortiz-Ospina, 2019). These numbers are expected to increase further as a result of the COVID-19 pandemic, with the United Nations Economic Commission for Africa estimating that an additional 23 million Africans will be pushed into extreme poverty (United Nations Economic Commission for Africa (UNECA), 2020). The World Bank estimates that the pandemic will push around 50 million people into extreme poverty on the continent. Other indicators also reveal the grim reality for the African population. The average life expectancy at birth in Nigeria, the continent's biggest economy, is fifty-four years, whereas the world average

---

[10] These data come from the Observatory for Economic Complexity. Available at https://oec.world/en/resources/about/, accessed 8 July 2021.

[11] Data extracted from the Data Bank World Development Indicators. Available at https://data.worldbank.org/indicator/NY.GDP.MKTP.KD.ZG, accessed 8 July 2021.

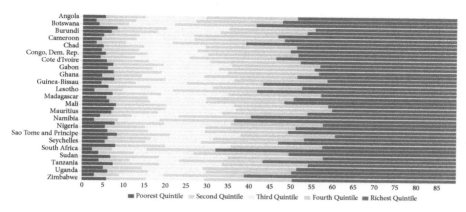

Fig. 2.2 Distribution of income in Africa by quintile

Source: Reproduced with permission from the World Bank (n.d.) under CC BY 4.0 Licence.

is seventy-one years.[12] While average adult literacy rates have historically increased worldwide, at least twelve African countries still have literacy rates of less than 50 per cent (Roser and Ortiz-Ospina, 2016). According to WHO data, only 30.1 per cent of the population on the continent have access to safely managed water, which is fewer than the number of mobile phone subscribers.[13] Furthermore, on the 2019 Human Development Index, eighteen of the bottom twenty countries are on the African continent (UNDP, 2019). While these statistics make sombre reading, they do not necessarily indicate that change on the continent will be hard to come by.

The processes of contemporary globalization are changing (see Hirst and Thompson, 2019), and in particular, processes of digitization and automation driven by advancements in digital technologies have transformed the global production landscape, with new business models and new sectors of the economy opening up (Elding and Morris, 2018; OECD, 2017, 2020; WEF, 2018). The world economy has become more information technology and services intensive since the 1970s (Amin, 1994; Harvey, 1989a; Sassen, 2001), with IT-enabled services often regarded as a potential new pathway to economic development opportunities (Dossani and Kenny, 2007; UNCTAD, 2004). Not surprisingly, the emergence of a digital

---

[12] Data from the Data Bank, World Development Indicators. Available at https://data.worldbank.org/indicator/SP.DYN.LE00.IN?locations=ZG-1W, accessed 8 July 2021.
[13] Available at https://washdata.org/data/household#!/, accessed 8 July 2021.

economy has ushered in renewed optimism among observers and commentators that the African economies will embark on a process of political and socio-economic transformation.

Digital Economy

The 'digital economy' has been variously defined since Tapscott (1996) first coined the term (also see Brynjolfsson and Kahin, 2000; Malecki and Moriset, 2007). Bukht and Heeks's (2017: 12) definition of the digital economy is flexible enough to incorporate a wide range of digital goods and services. However, they acknowledge the challenge of measuring or quantifying them due to the interwoven nature of the physical and digital economies (e.g. through digitalization of production processes), problems of data quality, and the invisibility of activities (e.g. intermediate services and cross-border data flows) (Elms and Low, 2013).[14] That said, there are some metrics that allow us to put the growth and value of the global digital economy in perspective (also Bukht and Heeks, 2017).

In 2019, roughly 87,500 tweets and 188 million emails were sent per minute (Desjardins, 2019a). It is also estimated that by 2025, 463 exabytes of data will be created each day globally, equivalent to 212,765,957 DVDs per day (Desjardins, 2019b).[15] While it is hard to quantify the value of all this digital data, one estimate suggests the global digital economy to be worth US$11.3 trillion (World Bank, 2019b).[16] Furthermore, statistics from UNCTAD (2017: 15) suggest that the global production of ICT goods and services contributes about 6.5 per cent to the global economic output, with Taiwan, Ireland, and Malaysia's ICT sectors contributing the most to their own national gross domestic products (UNCTAD, 2019a). Some observers

---

[14] This is also part of the bigger problem with the services sector in general, which is increasingly dependent on digital technologies. The services sector, unlike manufactured goods like garments, can be heterogeneous, generally not seen, and hence can remain invisible in statistical and analytical expressions (Low, 2013).

[15] The market intelligence company International Data Corporation (IDC) estimates that by 2025 annual data creation will reach 175 zettabytes, which if one was to store on DVDs, would be long enough to circle the earth 222 times (IDC, 2018).

[16] An important aspect of the growth of the global digital economy which is often sidelined is the externalities that it creates. For example, in 2016, 44.7 metric tonnes of e-waste, i.e. discarded electronic waste including mobile phones, laptops, tablets, desktop monitors, etc. was generated, equivalent to 4,500 Eiffel Towers (ITU, 2017c). A significant proportion of European e-waste is shipped to West Africa. This has not only environmental and health implications but also economic ones. The e-waste often contains rich deposits of recoverable minerals gold, silver, copper, platinum, palladium, etc., whose total value is estimated at $55 billion (UN News, 2017). It by no means suggests that this value can be easily recovered as the minerals are hard to extract from the electronic goods; instead, these goods become environmental hazards.

have noted that much of this points to the digital revolution taking place across the world (Brynjolfsson and McAfee, 2014). However, one of the genuine concerns about the growth of the global digital economy is about the unevenness of developments around the world.

The UNCTAD's report (2019a: 3) on the digital economy finds a deep digital divide between countries. Just two countries, China and the US, account for 40 per cent of the total value added in the ICT sector. They also account for 75 per cent of the patents relating to blockchain technologies, 50 per cent of global spending on the Internet of Things (IoT), and more than 75 per cent of the world market for public cloud computing. The report also finds that both countries account for 90 per cent of the market capitalization value of the world's seventy largest digital firms. Europe's share is 4 per cent and Africa and Latin America's share together accounts for only 1 per cent. In other words, there is a concentration of economic power taking place in the global information economy.

That said, the proliferation of digital technologies among the general population in Africa is growing rapidly, and various types of digital economy activities are emerging. The growth of Mpesa, a mobile money transfer scheme launched in 2007 by Safaricom Kenya, has been dubbed a huge success, and other telecom services providers are now providing mobile money transfer services in other parts of the continent (Jack and Suri, 2011, 2014; Jalakasi, 2019; Suri and Jack, 2016).[17] Africa accounts for roughly 45.6 per cent of the mobile money market, with US$26.8 billion in transactions in 2018 (GSMA, 2018). Mobile money has also had an impact on the wider IT industry and digital entrepreneurship across the continent, with an increasing number of digital technology start-ups being launched (Andjelkovic and Imaizumi, 2012; Deloitte, 2017; Friederici et al., 2020). There are already 618 tech-hubs established across Africa, which aim to support local tech start-ups, and software and app developers (GSMA, 2019b). Two of the most widely talked about African tech start-ups are Andela (a talent accelerator that trains software developers) and Jumia (a digital marketplace), both of which were launched from Nigeria.[18]

Furthermore, a nascent BPO industry has emerged in various parts of the continent, offering customer services, customer retention, sales, data management, consultancy, etc. (Anwar and Graham, 2019; Beerepoot and

---

[17] A critique of Jack and Suri's assessment of M-Pesa is given in Bateman et al. (2019).

[18] Andela is now headquartered in New York, receiving funding from the Chan Zuckerberg Initiative. Jumia's founders are French, the company's headquarters are in Berlin and its technology and product team is based in Portugal.

Keijser, 2015; Benner, 2006; Mann and Graham, 2016). South Africa and Egypt have emerged as two such preferred offshore destinations on the continent, with Amazon, Microsoft, and Vodafone—among many others—operating their service centres in these countries (Anwar and Graham, 2019). In Kearney's 2019 Global Services Location Index (Kearney, 2019), both Kenya and Ghana were ranked higher than Ireland as preferred locations for offshore services work. The demand for various types of business services is growing globally, as firms are increasingly looking to outsource some of their operations in order to remain cost competitive, and to focus on their core services (Deloitte, 2018a; Sassen, 2001). Many of these services operations can now be mediated digitally through platforms or websites which connect clients to a global workforce (Lehdonvirta et al., 2019).[19] These digital transaction platforms have grown globally to provide services to buyer clients, with an estimated 365 digital work platforms operating in just eight countries on the continent, of which 301 are African (Insight2impact, 2019). Thousands of African workers are turning to these platforms to perform a variety of digital services and tasks for clients both abroad and within their own countries (see Anwar and Graham, 2020b; Graham and Anwar, 2019).

Outsourcing and Production Spaces

One way to think about contemporary configurations of digital economy landscapes and networks in which Africa is being incorporated is to look at the construction of capitalism across geographies, and how new networked spaces of production are being built. For Marx (1954), capitalism is inherently crisis ridden. In order to overcome its crises and survive, capital creates a physical landscape (Harvey, 1978) or produces space in its own image (Lefebvre, 1991; Smith, 1983). David Harvey (2003) referred to such processes as 'spatio-temporal fixes'.[20] 'Fix' has two meanings here: first, there is a literal fixing of capital in place in physical forms (e.g. in factories or transportation infrastructure); second, a more metaphorical fixing of crises in capitalism through spatial reorganization of capital, and

---

[19] With the COVID-19 pandemic forcing many companies to adopt a digital transition and encourage working from home, it is likely that many more services will be outsourced to remotely located workers.

[20] Spatio-temporal fixes refers to 'a metaphor for a particular kind of solution to capitalist crises through temporal deferral and geographical expansion' and involves many different 'ways to absorb existing capital and labour surpluses' (e.g. production of space) (Harvey, 2003: 115–116).

specific strategies to address these crises. In other words, fixes represent capitalism's ability to create a landscape (only to have it destroyed at a subsequent point in time) so that profits are made, albeit temporarily. Fixes lead to newer contradictions, and therefore new rounds of fixes are introduced (Harvey, 2014). Fixes can therefore be understood as a never-ending search for both internal and external transformation of capitalism through 'geographical expansion and geographical restructuring' (Harvey, 2001).

In this section we outline three key waves of restructuring in capitalist production since the end of the World War II: (1) the relocation of industrial production; (2) services outsourcing; and (3) platform-based outsourcing. Our argument is that each of these waves represents a distinct spatio-temporal fix—namely geographical expansion, technological innovation, and organizational change—in contemporary capitalism (Harvey, 1982: 373–412; Hoogvelt, 2001; Jessop, 2006; Peet, 1983)[21] that aims to restore the accumulation process and class power—a key feature of neoliberalism (Harvey, 2005; Peck and Tickell, 2002). Each of these waves is the result of long and regular cycles of boom and bust in capitalism, which generate particular production landscapes. In its constant search for profits, new markets, commodities, and cheap labour, capitalism must always create new spaces of production, and some of these are now located in Africa.

Industrial and Services Outsourcing

In practice, the contemporary outsourcing of production can be traced back to the 1960s with the relocation of industrial manufacturing (Fröbel et al., 1981). The attempt by American (as well as European) transnational corporations (Dicken, 2011) to relocate labour-intensive production to low-wage locations in South America and East Asian countries led to a new international division of labour (Fröbel et al., 1981). On the one hand, this division of labour allows production to be subdivided and relocated to multiple locations, and on the other hand it has made it easier for many low-wage locations to be potentially integrated into industrial production networks. For example, the emergence of China as a major

---

[21] The famous maxim that every crisis is an opportunity applies as capitalism emerges from crises and attempts to restart the cycle of accumulation by cutting costs or capturing cheaper assets and new markets, and forcing out competitors (Harvey, 2011, 2014).

manufacturing hub has largely been driven by transnational firms relocating their industrial units to its many special economic zones (SEZs) (Zhang, 2006). This relocation was driven not just by a desire for market capture, but also to restore corporate profits by seeking cheap labour, tax breaks, and capable suppliers offshore.[22] As Fröbel et al. (1981) observe, division of labour is an ongoing process, with transformative implications for social relations as they are increasingly stretched over larger distances (Massey, 1995; also see Manwaring, 1984). Massey (1995: 3) emphasized that 'whole new sets of relations between activities in different places, new spatial patterns of social organisation, new dimensions of inequality and new relations of dominance and dependence' have emerged as production has become increasingly international and complex.[23]

The globalization of production processes has ultimately resulted in the dismantling of existing social contracts and destroyed hard-fought collective bargaining in many high-cost locations (Gereffi, 2014; Lipietz, 1982)—in effect setting off a global race to the bottom (see Mehmet, 2006; Rodrik, 1997; Davies and Vadlamannati, 2013). Low-income countries with a large supply of low-wage labour set up policies and plans to attract incoming investment. This is achieved by various means, for example by adopting free market and free trade policies and deregulation, incentivizing production, and flexibilizing labour supply. Many countries established industrial zones—India and China set up SEZs (Anwar, 2014; Levien, 2018), Mexico has its 'Maquiladoras' (MacLachlan and Aguilar, 1998), and in Egypt and Jordan, they are referred to as qualifying industrial zones (Azmeh, 2014). More recently, there is a trend of SEZs being set up in Africa, for example in South Africa, Nigeria, and Ethiopia (Adunbi, 2019; Bräutigram and Xiaoyang, 2011; Dannenberg et al., 2013; Farole and Moberg, 2017; Giannecchini and Taylor, 2018). But an important point to note here is that these zones are not limited to industrial production alone. The Philippines

---

[22] SEZs are later rendition of export processing zones (Anwar, 2014). The first EPZ is said to have been built in the Republic of Ireland. The 1960s saw India's first EPZ built in 1965, Mexico's in 1966, and Taiwan's in 1967. An estimated 5,000 exist around the world today (UNCTAD, 2019d).

[23] The French regulationist scholars have been quite influential in explaining the transformation of the capitalist production landscape and accompanying economic and socio-political relations (Aglietta, 1979; Boyer and Saillard, 2002; Lipietz, 1987, 1997; on its adoption among Marxian political economy scholars see Jessop, 2001). The regulationist approach uses two concepts: 'regime of accumulation' (the way production, distribution, circulation, and consumption is organized to create a stable economic system) and 'mode of regulation' (set of laws, norms, forms of state and policy that create a supporting environment for regimes of accumulation). The transition from Fordism (industrial mass production) towards post-Fordism (flexible specialization) represents a shift in the way production is spatially organized (see Storper and Christopherson, 1987) and also the socio-cultural changes associated with it (Harvey, 1989a).

and India both have zones especially dedicated to outsourced services that cater to the needs of both foreign and domestic markets (Anwar, 2014; Anwar and Carmody, 2016; Kleibert, 2014).

The term 'outsourcing' emerged in the 1970s in the US as a corporate managerial strategy of firms to relocate production and jobs to multiple low-cost locations such as East Asia and Latin America (Barnett and Muller, 1974). This outsourcing soon came to be seen as a threat to domestic labour markets, particularly in the US. Business Week's cover story titled 'Is your job next?' (Engardio et al., 2003) noted that:

> [I]t is globalisation's next wave—and one of the biggest trends reshaping the global economy. The first wave started two decades ago with the exodus of jobs making shoes, cheap electronics, and toys to developing countries. After that, simple service work, like processing credit card receipts, and mind-numbing digital toil, like writing software code, began fleeing high-cost countries . . . Now all kinds of knowledge work can be done anywhere . . . The rise of globally integrated knowledge economy is a blessing for developing nations. What it means for the US skilled labour force is less clear. At the least, many white-collar workers may be headed for a tough readjustment.

By the late 1990s, outsourcing had achieved a commonplace status in the political and economic sphere, being understood as practices involving lengthening of supply chains, modularization, standardization, lean managerial practices, fragmentation of production, and flexible specialization (see Peck, 2017: 26–27). With more firms actively looking to divest non-core functions such as administrative processing and information technology, the foundation for the outsourcing of back office functions was laid through the establishment of customer service centres across India and the Philippines. As Peck (2017) has noted recently, these outsourcing production networks have become increasingly sophisticated, widening their sectoral reach to include not just labour-intensive production, for example garments, leather goods, toys, consumer electronics, and automobiles, but also standardized service work (e.g. back office processing and customer support), as well as more knowledge-intensive and high value-added operations such as research and development, finance, and consulting. Outsourcing is a dynamic process, with firms constantly searching for new ways to generate value through strategies of nearshoring, onshoring, and multishoring (Abbott and Jones, 2012; Crane et al., 2007;

The Economist, 2005; Finnemore et al., 2010; Jacques, 2006).[24] In other words, the emergence of a suite of outsourced services activities, ranging from low value-added to high value-added functions, and the offshoring, onshoring, and nearshoring of production has set the foundation of today's far-reaching and complex global production networks, resulting in a significant reorganization of the world economy (see Coe and Yeung, 2015).

This vision of a new globalized world of production and work seemingly overcoming the constraints of the physical geography is epitomized in Thomas Friedman's *The World is Flat*. This contemporary round of globalization, he argued (Friedman, 2005: 176), is enabling 'the sharing of knowledge and work in real time, without regard to geography, distance, or, in the near future, even language'. Friedman's persuasive account shed light on the global networks that are bringing many different places into the realm of the world economy. However, he ignored the socio-political factors that affect the ways people and places participate in these networks. While it is true that many new places were integrated into global production networks, the inherent power relations in these networks meant that not all places found themselves on a level playing field. India and the Philippines today occupy more than half of the global services market, while new regions like Africa have struggled to capture the market, with countries like Kenya—seen a decade ago as a potential location for outsourced services work—struggling to tap into it (Kleibert and Mann, 2020). In the case of South Africa, the BPO industry has grown over the last decade, but functional upgrading (i.e. moving into high value-added services) among local firms is constrained (Anwar and Graham, 2019).

Furthermore, while it is true that many low-income countries have been able to connect to the world economy in wholly new ways, new sets of structures and power relations in the world economy have emerged (see Gereffi et al., 2005). The geographical relocation and dispersal of economic production—the quintessential hallmark of globalization—has simultaneously been linked with the integration of many more corporate activities. New forms of high-end complex services have emerged that require highly specialized skills to support and manage the operations of large firms. Some

---

[24] Nearshoring is a strategy of outsourcing of business processes to suppliers or service providers to a country closer to the buyer's home country. Onshoring refers to moving these services to rural areas or other small cities within the home country of the buyer firm.

of these services tend to cluster around only a handful of localities, to take advantage of agglomeration economies (see Sassen, 2001).[25]

Through all of this linking and delinking of economic activities, corporate organizational structures and patterns of trade have also changed. As firms have become less involved in production they have increasingly bought goods and services from specialized suppliers, often with strict quality control and based on the lead firm's original design (Gereffi et al., 2005). The best-known example of this is Apple. The company's flagship iPhone range of mobile phones is designed at the company's headquarters in California but its individual component parts (such as batteries, processors, and networking chips) are produced by a large number of contract manufacturers or original design manufacturers (ODMs) located globally. These component parts are then assembled by Hon Hai Precision Industry Co. Ltd (aka Foxconn) and Pegatron, both Taiwanese firms, primarily in assembly plants in China and also in other parts of the world (see Costello, 2020; Duhigg and Bradsher, 2012; Moorhead, 2019).[26] In fact, this practice of firms buying goods and services directly from a specialized seller or supplier is the hallmark of the contemporary global outsourced services industry, with around 80 per cent of the Fortune 500 companies outsourcing mostly to overseas suppliers, of which India captures the majority share (Poster and Yolmo, 2016: 585, cited from Peck, 2017: 2).

There is no doubt that outsourcing is a spatio-temporal fix that allows firms to extend their production networks on a global scale, often by leveraging advanced digital technologies (Oshri et al., 2015)—which is what Friedman understood as the revolution that is 'flattening' the world. However, the patterns of trade and investments that are emerging point to an uneven landscape (see Dicken, 2015) of regionalizing tendencies, clusters, and agglomerations (see Dunning, 2002; Storper, 1997). Indeed, some have dismissed Friedman's account 'as a series of exaggerated visions' about globalization (see Ghemawat, 2009). Nonetheless, underneath the corporate rhetoric lie insights into the complex

---

[25] The financial services industry developed around London and New York, the motion picture industry in Hollywood (Storper and Christopherson, 1987), information technology cluster developed around Silicon Valley in California, with Bangalore emerging as the Silicon Valley of India (the location of Friedman's eureka moment) primarily as outsourcing destinations for American firms (Parthasarathy, 2004). Similarly, many more specialized global cities or regions can be seen around the world. Milan and Paris became centres of the fashion industry (though the bulk of garment production takes place in China), Gurgaon and Manilla emerged as call centre hubs of the world (but customers are based in the US and EU countries).

[26] According to Dedrick et al. (2018) the US captures the bulk of the value of the iPhone 7 (US$237.45 per handset) while China only gets 3.6% of the value of its factory cost. While it is true that China has been able to capture a slightly higher share of the value from Apple's latest iPhone X than from the iPhone 3G, the total value capture is still only 10.4% (Xing, 2019; also see Applebaum et al., 2018).

technological, organizational, and social transformations that have enabled the emergence of a new global-spanning but uneven digital production landscape.

New Digital Spaces of Production

Complex long-distance trading networks have existed for centuries. For instance, two thousand years ago, the Silk Road allowed Roman glassware to be sold in China and Chinese silk to be sold in the Roman Empire.[27] Similarly, Chinese goods such as porcelain have been found in Great Zimbabwe, an ancient city in Southern Zimbabwe. The trans-Saharan trade in gold, textiles, and slaves which connected West Africa to North Africa and the Roman Empire and beyond (Mattingly et al., 2017) flourished long before the later European colonial powers entered Africa. Centuries later, the advent of contemporary technologies has changed the temporality of such relationships: a Kenyan rose grower who picks and packages her flowers on a Monday on the shores of Lake Naivasha could have her products bought and displayed in a home in Rome or London by the end of the week. However, even with the advancements made in transportation technologies, perishable goods tend to be produced closer to home (e.g. dairy production), with non-perishable goods (e.g. shoes or cars) being produced at great distances from sites of consumption. Many other factors undoubtedly also come into play (e.g. regulatory environments, regional specializations, commodifiability of goods), but the point remains that there has traditionally been an important relationship between what is produced, and where it is produced and consumed. It is also noteworthy that while many sites of production (and associated labour) can be spread out across the planet, some types of work remain geographically bound to the places in which it is used or consumed. While a Chinese silk weaver or Kenyan rose grower can perform their work thousands of miles from the place of consumption, a shopkeeper or a delivery person is still needed to bring those goods to consumers. Put differently, some jobs carry with them an inherent geographic stickiness.

That said, digital technologies are fast changing the geographies of production, distribution, consumption, and organization of work, and the relationship between workers and place is becoming more complicated as a result. Cheap computers and connectivity have drastically lowered the cost

---

[27] Part of this section is reproduced with permission from Graham and Anwar, 2018a.

of some production processes. If workers can do information-based work that can be quickly transmitted around the world, then that work can, in theory, be done from anywhere and by anyone who has access to the right machines and connectivity. When you file a complaint because your train was late or call an airline to request a refund for your flight, the workers who handle your requests could be either down the road from you or on the other side of the planet. Put simply, unlike a farmer or a factory worker, today's digital workers have far less need to be physically proximate to the object of their labour.

For many types of digital service work, geography has thus become less sticky, with a whole host of services activities being endlessly divided, repackaged, rebundled, and allocated to various suppliers around the world (Peck, 2017). The modularization, commodification, and standardization of work tasks (Scott, 2001), and advances in automation and robotization all present ways to digitally connect service work with different places. In other words, an increasingly digitally connected world has enabled complex virtual production networks to emerge (Tuma, 1998).

At the centre of these production networks are digital platforms. Such has been the tremendous growth of these new corporate entities that some scholars have termed this the emergence of 'platform capitalism' (Srnicek, 2016). In his lucid account of how capitalism evolves between cycles of growth and downturn with technology playing a key role, Srnicek argues that the capitalism that emerged after the 2008 global financial crisis is built around the application of digital technologies in production, and the monopolizing, extracting, manipulating, and analysing of large quantities of a key raw material: digital data (also see Couldry and Meijas, 2019).[28] Because digital data is codified and can be moved relatively easily across borders, firms' business models have changed as platforms have become the new organizational structures of digital capitalism, bringing users together to interact and undertake business transactions (Lehdonvirta et al., 2019). This has led some to call such platforms the 'dominant forms of rentier in contemporary capitalism' (Sadowski, 2020: 575).[29] Srnicek describes

---

[28] The 2008 global financial crisis became a watershed moment in the history of capitalism as the focus shifted towards the rise of new technologies (the Internet of Things, artificial intelligence, machine learning, automation) and new models of accumulation (the fourth industrial revolution, platform economy, sharing economy, on-demand economy) (see Schwab, 2016; Sundarajan, 2016).

[29] Despite often positioning themselves as intermediaries or platforms, big technology companies have set in motion a new regime of accumulation by setting the rules of the marketplaces and products. The politics of some of the biggest technology corporations, their monopolistic tendencies, and the effects they have on the market and consumer is covered in great detail elsewhere. Rana Foroohar's

various types of emerging platforms, e.g. product platforms, industrial platforms, and advertising platforms. While this is a useful classification, our primary concern in this book is with digital platforms that connect buyers and sellers of services (Lehdonvirta et al., 2019). Some of the biggest and most notable of these digital work platforms are Upwork, Freelancer.com, and Amazon Mechanical Turk, representing a workforce of many millions around the world.[30]

Unlike the outsourcing of the 1990s that took place between different firms and organizations (Manning et al., 2017 cited from Lehdonvirta et al., 2019), digital work platforms can now match big firms, small businesses, and individual clients directly with individual workers and small enterprises anywhere. In theorizing the new 'global platform economy', Lehdonvirta et al. (2019) argue that platforms have emerged as new technology-enabled offshoring institutions that enable gains for organizations and individuals by mediating and managing cross-border services. Vallas and Schor (2020: 1) refer to these digital platforms as 'a distinct type of governance mechanism different from markets, hierarchies, or networks'. Similarly, Langley and Leyshon (2017) argue that platforms play the role of 'socio-technical intermediary' and facilitate 'business arrangement' between buyers and suppliers of certain digital services. Firms no longer have to take advantage of low-cost locations to set up their offices or customer service centres. A small business in London, for instance, can now directly hire a worker in Kenya to make a website for them and also hire a Nigerian virtual assistant to do customer support and up-selling via web chat. Already Kenyan workers are doing article writing for clients based in the US, the UK, and the EU for a variety of purposes, for example magazines and web content.[31] Some Fortune 500 firms are already using platform-based workers globally to undertake complex knowledge-intensive work such as graphic design, software development, and data management work (Corporaal and Lehdonvirta, 2017). In other words, the global platform economy leverages the changing nature of internet connectivity and digital technologies to provide firms with access to skilled

---

(2019) excellent exposé *Don't Be Evil: The Case against Big Tech* and Soshanna Zuboff's (2019) *The Age of Surveillance Capitalism* are good starting points.

[30] Other platforms enabling local work such as taxi services, domestic help, care work, and online deliveries are not the subject of this book. The most notable local work platforms are Uber, Deliveroo, Task Rabbit, Care.com, Bolt, Helpling, and Airtasker.

[31] Some of the writing done by Kenyan workers fills relatively niche areas. In one case, we spoke to a worker who specialized in writing paid online reviews for doctor surgeries in the US (even though he had never been to the US).

and cheap labour power in areas (such as Africa) not necessarily associated with outsourcing networks, while enabling workers to seek alternative employment outside their local labour markets. Our argument is that labour arbitrage still remains at the centre of global sourcing activities—these platforms are simply the latest digital spaces of outsourced production in the contemporary digital economy, where workers are bought and sold as a commodity on a planetary scale (Graham and Anwar, 2019). However, as we have already noted, these labour markets are very much concentrated in only a few geographical locations (see Graham and Anwar, 2018b, 2019). As such, the new division of labour we are witnessing with the emergence of a global platform economy has the potential to exacerbate geographical inequality, by entrenching the social and economic relations that are embedded within it.

Previously, outsourcing firms got access to cheap and skilled labour by buying services directly from a provider or a vendor located in a select few low-cost locations. But while earlier modes of outsourcing and offshoring were constrained by technological infrastructure, regulatory factors, and other socio-political and cultural factors to cluster around a handful of locations (Gereffi and Lee, 2016; Manning et al., 2017), digital work platforms have eliminated some of these constraints, enabling the platform economy to theoretically operate globally and have access to cheap labour. Whereas the earlier modes of outsourcing did not bring economic production or jobs to Africa on a scale comparable with China and India, digital outsourcing has the potential to bring some forms of digital production and jobs to the African continent. The information economy is characterized by digital forms of value, which are intangible in nature. The raw material is primarily digital data which can be extracted and moved across locations with relative ease, compared with, say, gold or oil. With improved digital connectivity, digital data can flow to locations such as Africa and thus bring new forms of economic activities. The potential of the digital economy and its associated jobs to support development in Africa is now deeply entrenched in the thinking of international development organizations, policymakers, and businesses. Terms like the Fourth Industrial Revolution and Industry 4.0 are rapidly gaining ground among various observers in the African context, and digital jobs are being touted to solve the long-standing unemployment problem. But to understand the potential of new digital production networks emerging in Africa, we should first take stock of the ways in which digital technologies and internet connectivity are understood to impact development.

ICTs and Digital Connectivity in Africa: Development Contradictions

Digital technologies have undoubtedly driven transformative changes in the global economy, with newly emerging digital economy activities now widely regarded as critical drivers for economic development, with profound social, political, economic, and cultural implications for individuals, businesses, and the state (Brynjolfsson and Kahin, 2000; Lane, 1999; World Bank, 2016). The importance of the digital economy for economic development in low- and middle-income countries is also underscored by UNCTAD's Secretary-General, Mr Mukhisa Kituyi, in its 2019 Digital Economy Report. He states:

> The rapid spread of digital technologies is transforming many economic and social activities. However, widening digital divides threaten to leave developing countries, and especially least developed countries, even further behind. A smart embrace of new technologies, enhanced partnerships and greater intellectual leadership are needed to redefine digital development strategies and the future contours of globalisation.
>
> **UNCTAD, 2019a: v**

Today more than half of humanity is connected to the internet—that is, well over 4.1 billion people—with more people from the low- and middle-income regions of the world expected to join in the future (Figure 2.3). By some estimates, the African continent has witnessed one of the fastest growth rates in internet penetration over the last decade, though it still lags behind the world average in terms of the percentage of population that is connected to the internet (ITU, 2019). The cost of mobile broadband remains the highest in the world (ITU, 2019) which prevents further penetration of these technologies.

Nonetheless, policymakers, development organizations, and the private sector have invested huge sums of money into various highly ambitious (and perhaps overly optimistic) programmes to bring the world's digitally unconnected people into the networks of digital technologies. These include Facebook's Free Basics, Google's balloon-powered internet provision for all through Project Loon, the One Laptop per Child initiative, the Connect Africa initiative of the African Development Bank (AfDB), and programmes run by several African governments to connect their citizens with free internet services through public WiFi hotspots such

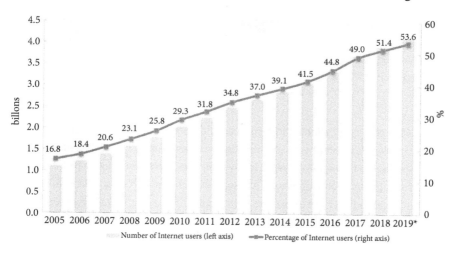

Fig. 2.3 Individuals using the internet 2005–19

Source: ITU, 2019: 1. Reproduced with permission from the International Telecommunication Union (ITU).

as Project Isizwe (South Africa) and MYUG (Uganda).[32] The logic is that digital technologies can help bring progressive change, particularly in the case of low- and middle-income regions (e.g. Radelet, 2010, 2015; Sachs, 2005). The World Bank in its 2016 report titled 'Digital Dividends' noted that:

Digital technologies have dramatically expanded the information base, lowered information costs, and created information goods. This has facilitated searching, matching, and sharing of information and contributed to greater organization and collaboration among economic agents—influencing how firms operate, people seek opportunities, and citizens interact with their governments. The changes are not limited to economic transactions—they also influence the participation of women in the labour force, the ease of communication for people with disabilities, and the way people spend their leisure. By overcoming information barriers, augmenting factors, and transforming products, digital technologies can make development more inclusive, efficient, and innovative.

World Bank, 2016: 8–9

---

[32] Google has also partnered with local cable network providers to set up free WiFi spots in Nigeria (Akinyelure, 2018). Facebook Free Basics is now accessible in 32 countries on the continent (Nothias, 2020). In January 2021, Google's parent firm Alphabet decided to shut down its Loon project.

Debates around the impact of digital technologies have gained considerable traction in recent years, particularly around the idea that ICTs could be a means to deliver 'development' (see Heeks, 2006). Heeks (2009: 1) has argued that

> ICT4D – the application of information and communication technologies for international development – is moving to a new phase. This will require new technologies, new approaches to innovation and implementation, new intellectual perspectives and, above all, a new view of the world's poor. All these must be understood if we are to harness digital technologies in the service of some of our world's most pressing problems.

(On the growing body of ICT4D research, see Aker and Mbiti, 2010; Akpan-Obong, 2009; Avgerou, 2010; De' et al., 2018; Donner, 2015; Heeks and Krishna, 2016; Juma and Agwara, 2006; Kleine and Unwin, 2009; Mamba and Isabirye, 2015; Poveda and Roberts, 2018; Qureshi, 2015; Roztocki et al., 2019; Unwin, 2009, 2017; Walsham, 2017); for critical reflections, see Anwar, 2018; Chaudhuri, 2012; Díaz and Urquhart, 2012; Friederici et al., 2017; Murphy and Carmody, 2015: chs 1–2). The upshot of this growing body of research is that digital tools have wide-ranging social, political, and economic impact—including on economic growth (Qiang and Rossotto, 2009; Waverman et al., 2005); bridging the digital divide (Norris, 2001); social inclusion (Warschauer, 2003); services delivery such as education and health (Blaya et al., 2010; Khan and Ghadially, 2010); better governance, political well-being, and reduction of corruption (Asongu and Nwachukwu, 2019; Bailard, 2009; Bratton, 2013); economic and industrial development (Oyelaran-Oyeyinka and Lal, 2006); financial development (Asongu, 2013); increased market integration (Muto and Yamano, 2009); reduced transaction costs (Molony, 2006); the reduction of information asymmetries (Aker, 2010); and enabling of enterprise development to allow firms to tap into global markets and generate new kinds of IT-based employment opportunities (Asamoah et al., 2020; Benner, 2006; Graham and Mann, 2013; Okpaku, 2006). Such has been the unwavering support for these technologies that ICT tools like mobile phones have been called 'the single most transformative technology for development' (Jeffery Sachs quoted from Cable News Network (CNN), 2011).

Africa Rising

Such powerful imaginaries concerning, digital tools such as mobile phones, and 'internet for African development' efforts, are perhaps best symbolized by the 'Africa Rising' narrative (The Economist, 2011; Perry, 2012). This was driven in large part by the arrival of the fibre-optic undersea cable in 2009 to the eastern coast of Africa, hailed by SeaCom, the company backing these cables, as a 'revolution' (SeaCom Live, 2009). Of course, Africa was already connected to the world economy, albeit based on commodities export on terms that favoured rich countries. Nonetheless, in recent years, major international organizations and institutions such as the World Bank (2009, 2012, 2015, 2016), African Development Bank (AfDB, 2013), Rockefeller Foundation (2014), and the World Economic Forum (Schwab, 2016) have fuelled further speculation about the potential of digital technologies for development on the continent. Talks of a Fourth Industrial Revolution, automation, the 'machine age', robotization, machine learning, and artificial intelligence have seeped into the linguistic repertoire of politicians, businesses, development organizations, aid agencies, lobbying groups, and the mainstream media.[33] The World Economic Forum has established a hub called the Centre for the Fourth Industrial Revolution, and two affiliate centres have already been set up in Rwanda and South Africa.[34]

Nevertheless, these predictions of an African Rising have been strongly criticized. One of the main criticisms stems from the privileging of economic growth as an indicator for development, despite this telling us little about broad-based development (Taylor, 2016; also Meagher, 2016). Lopes and Kararach (2020) point to the fragility of economic growth on the continent, and a worrying tendency of the continent's economies to grow rapidly but for structural transformation to remain slow, making them vulnerable to crises (also see Cheru, 2017). Rwanda, Botswana, and Ethiopia are often portrayed as countries that have turned their fortunes around through state-directed development strategies, with high economic growth in the last ten years. However, much of that wealth has accrued to

---

[33] See, for example: World Economic Forum (WEF): *Here's how Africa Can Take Advantage of the Fourth Industrial Revolution;* Forbes: *How Africa Wins the 4th Industrial Revolution;* African Development Bank: *Unlocking the Potential of the Fourth Industrial Revolution in Africa.* The COVID-19 pandemic has further fuelled debates and anxiety about automation and artificial intelligence in the post-pandemic era in Africa (see Africa Renewal, 2020; Daramola, 2020; Turnbull, 2020).

[34] In a way, the future of African development is now hyped around digital innovation (see Liu, 2019) rather than industrialization, which was the case a few decades ago.

elite interest groups (see Goodfellow, 2014; Mann and Berry, 2016; Matfess, 2015).[35] Similarly, Phillips et al.'s (2016) study of the growth of the Ghanain oil sector points to the problem of elite accumulation with benefits rarely reaching the poor. In other words, while the Africa Rising narrative is built around—and depends on—high economic growth and good governance (see World Bank, 2000), economic growth by itself will not transform African economies and their structural position in the world economy (Gray and Khan, 2010; Noman et al., 2012). As Taylor (2016: 8) has noted, 'a rise based on an intensification of resource extraction whilst dependency deepens, inequality increases and de-industrialisation continues apace, cannot be taken seriously'.

Mkandawire (2014) argues that much of the discussion within these Africa Rising accounts often ignore the issue of socio-economic inequality emerging from recent economic growth. Not to say inequality is a uniquely African problem—UNDP figures suggest that income inequality is on the rise globally, with the richest 10 per cent receiving up to 40 per cent of global income, and the poorest 10 per cent earning only between 2 per cent and 7 per cent.[36] Oxfam's latest report, 'Time to Care' (Oxfam, 2020), finds that the combined wealth of the world's 2,153 billionaires is greater than that of 4.6 billion people—or 60 per cent of the world's population—and also that the twenty-two richest men in the world have more wealth than all the women in Africa. Another criticism of Africa Rising narratives comes from the lack of clear evidence on the role of digital technologies and internet connectivity in economic development in general, and for low- and middle-income regions in particular (see Friederici et al., 2017). Thompson (2004) cautions that the way ICT4D discourse is legitimized and replicated in practice, for example in the speeches of the President of the World Bank, can blur the problematic link between ICTs and development for many low- and middle-income countries.

Digital: A Fix for Africa's Problems?

Ambitious visions of the power of digital technologies to effect economic development are recreated repeatedly, acting to encourage greater economic integration of Africa with the world economy. Advocates such

[35] Kagame was a de facto leader between 1994 and 2000 and has been the President of Rwanda since 2000. Ethiopia is effectively a single party democracy which has recently faced serious internal conflicts.
[36] Available at https://www.africa.undp.org/content/rba/en/home/sustainable-development-goals/goal-10-reduced-inequalities.html, accessed 8 July 2021

as the World Bank often argue that ICTs have great potential to bring about socio-economic and political transformations around the world. First and foremost, digital technologies are seen to overcome physical geography and increase the flows of information, enhance communications, and allow greater market integration (World Bank, 2009; but see Harvey, 2009 for a critique). Second, ICTs are assumed to reduce poverty and inequality, increase productivity and economic growth, and improve accountability and governance (World Bank, 2012). ICTs and improved connectivity are therefore regarded by some observers as a 'technological fix' to Africa's myriad political, economic, and social development problems (Royal Geographical Society, n.d.). The World Bank argues that:

> [T]he challenge for the next decade is to build on the mobile success story and complete the transformation. This will require reducing the cost of access for mobile broadband, supporting government private-sector collaboration, improving the e-commerce environment, enhancing ICT labour market skills, encouraging innovative business models that drive employment, such as micro-work and business process outsourcing, and creating spaces that support ICT entrepreneurship, such as ICT incubators, and local ICT development clusters.
>
> **World Bank, 2012: 17**

This kind of ideology gives preference to ICT-driven connectivities, open markets, free trade, economic growth, and property rights as critical drivers of development. Development for Africa is therefore reduced to a process of spatial diffusion of capitalism from the (high-income) centre, with digital technology playing a key role in this. The World Bank (2009;2016) for example, argues that African countries should improve their connectivity-enhancing infrastructure (including digital technologies) in order to make development more inclusive, efficient, and innovative. However, there is a danger here that these digital connectivities could act to amplify existing economic, political, and social inequalities (Fuchs and Horak, 2008) rather than necessarily create a level playing field. As we shall see in the following chapters, much as we might think of digital outsourcing as a frictionless (Parker et al., 2016) and free-market product of capitalism, it is also generating uneven economic geographies.

In a similar vein, UNCTAD in their 2019 Digital Economy Report (UNCTAD, 2019a) have warned that while digital advances have generated enormous wealth in the world in a record amount of time, that wealth has been concentrated around a small number of individuals, companies, and countries. Indeed, there is evidence that ICTs and connectivity have a variegated impacts across different geographical contexts (e.g. low income vs high income countries), and that more evidence is available from high-income countries than low- and middle-income countries (Friederici et al., 2017: 4). In other words, digital connectivities can reinforce the production of spatially uneven development.

In fact, the emerging critical research on ICT4D in relation to African development presents a contradictory and complex picture, with some of this work suggesting that there is a greater amount of hype than reality vis-à-vis technological connectivity and its role in economic development (e.g. Anwar, 2019; Friederici et al., 2017; Graham and Mann, 2013; Murphy and Carmody, 2015; Murphy et al., 2014). In their review, Murphy and Carmody (2015: xv) maintain that the ICT4D literature in relation to Africa often lacks 'geographic contextualization, theoretical grounding, and/or inter-study comparability or transferability'. Friederici et al. (2017) in their extensive review of the literature on the impact of digital connectivity found that the evidence of the transformative potential of ICTs for African development is inconclusive at best. More specific empirical studies also support this depressing reality. Murphy and Carmody (2015) in examining the use of digital technologies in the wooden furniture and tourism industry in South Africa and Tanzania, for example, found that the use of ICT tools has limited positive transformative impact on furniture producers and hotel owners as they seek to extract more value. Similarly, Friederici et al. (2020: 209) in their multi-city study on the emerging phenomenon of digital entrepreneurship find that in Africa 'digital enterprises are creatively and productively applying and adapting digital technologies to their local economic, social, and political contexts'; but they also find that digital entrepreneurship is highly unevenly distributed, recreates post-colonial dependencies, and 'positive local impacts have so far happened at neither the rate nor the scale that widespread narratives about African digital entrepreneurship had suggested' (Friederici et al., 2020). Furthermore, the role of financial technologies (fin-tech) on African development is also highly celebrated. For example, M-Pesa in Kenya is now widely acknowledged as a success story (see Jack and Suri, 2011, 2014; Suri and Jack, 2016), finds support even among international institutions, and is now seen as critical for achieving sustainable development goals (SDGs). However, Suri and Jack's research on M-Pesa in Kenya is criticized by Bateman et al. (2019) who highlight a number of problems in their work, including omission of key impact factors and the use of false logic and faulty methodology.

They argue that these have 'helped to catalyse into existence a largely *false narrative* surrounding the power of the fin-tech industry to advance the cause of poverty reduction and sustainable development in Africa and elsewhere'. They conclude that while 'the fin-tech has the potential to liberate enormous value . . . the bulk of this value does not go to the poor. Rather, fin-tech is very clearly designed to hoover up value and deposit it into the hands of a narrow global digital-financial elite' (Bateman et al., 2019: 490).

There is no doubt that ICT penetration has increased over the last five years across Africa, and the region has witnessed some growth of ICT-based economic activities. But there is a danger of replicating old-style adverse economic integration of African economies into global digital production networks. Local firms might be generating new forms of digital value on the continent but because of the digital nature of the goods, the value might flow out of the regions—indeed, more easily than commodities such as oil, coffee, gold, wood, etc. This might be the case, for example, in those sectors of the economy that depend on digital technologies, but also those where the products are intangible and not digital in nature, like the tourism sector. There are indications from some parts of the continent that value is being captured by foreign lead firms while local actors simply become dependent on these foreign entities for their survival (for South Africa, see Anwar et al., 2014; for Zanzibar, see Murphy, 2019). Similarly, in digitally intensive sectors such as the outsourced services sector in South Africa, local firms can get locked into low value-added activities, and opportunities for upgrading into high-value complex activities are relatively few (Anwar and Graham, 2019).

As the world economy becomes increasingly digital, the flows of digital data (which is considered by some a resource in itself) will play a crucial role in development and act as a source of power (see Couldry and Meijas, 2019). Digital data is the source of economic value, and firms do everything to exercise control over its ownership and flows—for accumulation (Sadowski, 2019, 2020). In their latest book, Couldry and Mejias (2019) argue that at the heart of the contemporary capitalist mode of production is extraction and exploitation of digital data (also see Sadowski, 2019).[37] Information technology firms, along with international organizations (e.g. United Nations (UN) and World Bank) and private sector lobby groups

---

[37] The dangers of surveillance using digital data and services are all too real too (see Donovan and Martin, 2014).

(e.g. World Economic Forum) have pushed for the valorization of digital data, hence the emerging narrative around data for development (including open data and big data) (Hilbert, 2016; UN Global Pulse, 2012;).[38] For example, International Business Machines Corporation's (IBM) Project Lucy—a US$100 million cognitive computing project—is expected to learn and discover insights from big data and develop commercially viable solutions to Africa's grand challenges in health care, education, water and sanitation, human mobility, and agriculture (IBM, n.d).

This data for development (D4D) discourse fits into broader ICT4D discourses, whereby digital data has become a justification for new and old kinds of ICT4D engagement (Mann, 2018 also see European Commission, 2017). Many African countries have also bought into these narratives to create governance and regulatory environments that facilitate flows of data outside the continent, and ultimately (economic) developmental opportunities to be missed. (Mann, 2018).

While digital capitalism holds the promise of bringing new forms of economic production to the continent, to be able to say something meaningful about its implications for development we need to examine its economic geographies. We do this in the next chapter by focusing more closely on BPOs and the remote gig economy. We shall see that uneven distribution of these activities across the continent forces us to ask whether and how the digital is implicated in generating new forms of uneven development at multiple scales.

[38] See Big Data for Development (BD4D). Available at http://bd4d.net/about.html, accessed 8 July 2021.

3

Economic Geographies of Digital Work in Africa

with Fabian Braesemann

Introduction

Workers perform a diverse range of activities both in BPOs and on platforms, and one of our objectives in this book is therefore to understand the digital economy as a continuum with a great deal of heterogeneity. In this chapter we will provide a snapshot of how and where these diverse work activities get done in Africa, showing that African workers remain very much a part of contemporary digital capitalism. They perform a wide range of digital work activities from diverse locations—from an office block in the centre of a lively metropolis, to a makeshift room in a town recovering from civil war, as well as a multitude of bedrooms, cafes, and libraries across the continent. In summary, this chapter will provide a visual and descriptive outline of the various types of digital activities being performed in newer spaces that are connecting to the global information economy. In doing so, we ask what types of work get done in Africa, and what that means for value creation and capture.

Uneven Geographies of Outsourcing in Africa

As part of our study, we examined the outsourced services landscape in five case study countries by collecting information on the presence of BPO firms (both foreign and domestic), their country of origin, locations of their customers and clients, source of work, presence of intermediaries, kinds of operations such as captive or outsourced, types of activities in the value chains (e.g. low value-added or high value-added), and the distribution of firms in each country. We focused specifically on

The Digital Continent. Mohammad Amir Anwar and Mark Graham, Oxford University Press.
© Mohammad Amir Anwar, Mark Graham, and Fabian Braesemann (2022). DOI: 10.1093/oso/9780198840800.003.0003

BPOs—that is, on entry-level activities in the outsourcing sector's value chains (Fernandez-Stark et al., 2011), including both voice-based (telephone calls) and non-voice services (e.g. emails and webchat) involving customer support, data-capture, outbound sales, document conversion, transcription, and digitization.

The rapid diffusion and penetration of ICTs in Africa has led to a nascent BPO industry in recent years (Anwar and Graham, 2019; Benner 2006; Benner and Rossi, 2016; Kleibert and Mann, 2020). These BPO operations, such as call and contact centres, provide African economies with an important entry point into digital outsourcing production networks. With the uptake in digital production generating a 'tradability revolution' in services—now considered a key component for economic development (UNCTAD, 2004)—BPOs have become a key policy initiative in a number of African countries, including Kenya, South Africa, Nigeria, Uganda, Ghana, and Egypt (see Ndemo, n.d.). However, the outsourcing industry is buyer driven (Fernandez-Stark et al., 2011), characterized by asymmetrical power relations, and highly cost sensitive which often benefit lead firms (Peck, 2017) to the detriment of smaller firms and local assets. It therefore places some limits on regions and their institutions' attempts to plug into these networks and gain from these dynamics (Gereffi and Lee, 2016). Indeed, we found a varied landscape of outsourcing in our case study countries (Table 3.1).

Coupling and Decoupling in BPOs in Africa

The literature on value chains and production networks has been useful in making sense of the various production nodes in the global economy (Coe and Yeung, 2015; Gereffi, 1999, 2005; Henderson et al. 2002). One of the important concepts in the GPN literature has been that of 'strategic coupling', defined as 'a mutually dependent and constitutive process involving particular ties, shared interests, and cooperation between two or more groups of economic actors who otherwise might not act in tandem to achieve a common strategic objective' (Yeung, 2016: 54). But coupling is also 'time–space contingent' and geographically and institutionally dependent (Yeung, 2016: 57). It can change over time, and in different geographical contexts can even lead to decoupling of an entire region, defined by disinvestment, the exit of foreign firms, and loss of access to foreign markets (see Horner, 2014; MacKinnon, 2012, 2013).

Table 3.1 Summary characteristics of the outsourcing industry in our case studies

Outsourced services landscape	South Africa	Kenya	Nigeria	Ghana	Uganda
Outlook	International	Domestic; regional leader (East Africa)	Domestic; regional leader (West Africa)	Domestic	Domestic; regional connections to Kenya and Tanzania
Market focus	Local and global	Local and regional; subcontracted work from India and intermediaries connecting the US market	Local; subcontracted work from India; some offshore work for the US market	Local; the US market in the past	Local and regional; intermediaries connecting the US market
Types of firms	Domestic and international firms; UK firms dominate	Domestic firms; international intermediaries and Indian-origin firms	Domestic firms; established presence of Indian-origin firms	Domestic firms; established presence of Indian-origin firms	Domestic firms; international intermediaries and Indian-origin firms
Value-added activities	Diversified activities with a mix of high to low value-added work	Low value-added (prevalence of subcontracted work e.g. transcription, digitization, image tagging); failed attempts at high-value work	Low value-added (inbound and outbound customer service; outbound sales; digitization)	Low value-added (inbound and outbound customer service; document conversion; transcription)	Low value-added work (customer service; subcontracted work e.g. digitization, image tagging)
Urbanized geography	Three cities (Johannesburg, Cape Town, and Durban)	Concentrated around Nairobi	Concentrated around Lagos and Abuja	Concentrated in Accra	Concentrated in Kampala

Broadly speaking, strategic coupling is evident in South Africa, with the South African government actively promoting the industry through a variety of incentives. Foreign lead firms have established captive operations (i.e. run and managed by the parent firm) as well as outsourced their services to local vendors in South Africa. Some of the key lead firms are Teleperformance, WNS, Webhelp, and Aegis, all of whom have set up off-shore delivery centres in the country. Webhelp has a workforce of 4,000 workers across six different offices in South Africa. A host of regional shared service operations of global corporations like Amazon, Microsoft, British Petroleum, Shell, and Lufthansa have also emerged.[1] Despite the increasing presence of international lead firms in South Africa, a majority of the BPO operations are still serving the domestic market. This is not surprising given that most call centres globally (86 per cent) serve the local rather than international market (Holman et al., 2007). However, the BPO industry in Kenya, Nigeria, Ghana, and Uganda can be characterized by structural coupling, defined by unequal power relations in networks with lead firms attracted to a region for their labour surpluses, and often associated by branch plant syndrome (Mackinnon, 2013).[2] These destinations are primarily seen by lead firms as low-cost destinations for low value-added work, and the countries' dependence on third-party vendors or intermediaries make them prone to decoupling.[3] BPO operations tend to be footloose, meaning that production can relocate with relative ease. In fact, we found examples of contraction in the outsourcing industry in some locations in Kenya, Ghana, and Nigeria, with BPO operations closing down.

The existing literature has already identified the potential and limits of technological connectivities in influencing BPO operations in Africa (Graham et al., 2015; Mann and Graham, 2016). One of the central arguments in this literature is that while digital infrastructure overcomes some constraints for African enterprises (namely technical skills), there are various other forms of control and imbalanced power relationships embedded in these global production networks which need to be overcome (Foster et al., 2018). In the following we discuss African countries' attempts to integrate into digital outsourcing production networks and the uneven landscape that results.

---

[1] For a detailed account of the South African BPO industry, see Anwar and Graham (2019).

[2] Branch plant refers to the fully owned subsidiaries of a larger transnational corporation characterized by low-value added activities, external ownership, remotely controlled by the firm's headquarters, and offering limited economic development opportunities (Kleibert, 2016; Sonn and Lee, 2012).

[3] Decoupling is a very likely outcome in structural coupling formations (see Coe et al., 2004; Horner, 2014; Mackinnon, 2012).

Incentivizing Outsourcing

Opportunities to develop BPO operations have improved for only a handful of African countries, including South Africa, Egypt, and Mauritius. This is surprising, since in our interviews with executives of BPO firms, government officials, and private sector associations, almost everyone pointed to similar value propositions of their respective countries, including a skilled workforce with English language skills, low labour costs, favourable time zones, and good internet connectivity. Ironically, Ghana and Kenya have both ranked higher than South Africa for the last two years in the offshore locations rankings of various management consultancy firms. Yet, their offshore segment has not grown, while South Africa is slowly becoming a destination of choice for offshore work; albeit still not as popular as India and the Philippines (Anwar and Graham, 2019). Various economic, socio-political, and reputational factors were noted by several industry experts as key for the BPO industry to develop further in South Africa.

As the second biggest economy on the continent, a member of the BRICS bloc, and the only African member of the G20, South Africa acts as a gateway to regional African markets. It is also relatively politically stable, and its infrastructure and education levels are considered by industry members to be optimal for offshore work to take place. While cost remains the main factor in locating BPO operations—in particular labour cost, which accounts for 60 per cent of operational expenditure (Interview, pers. comm., BPO Executive Johannesburg, 2016)[4]—there are combinations of other factors that can shape the offshoring landscape. According to an industry expert from the US, the buyer community in the US is looking to minimize their business risk and reduce their dependence on India and the Philippines, and South Africa offers to them low cost and a skilled workforce (Interview, pers. comm., Johannesburg, 2016). For BPO firms in South Africa the declining value of the South African Rand in the post-2008 period means the country has become reasonably competitive compared to locations such as the Philippines and India for entry-level work. According to one business executive from an international firm operating a call centre in South Africa:

We bill a large portion in [GB] Pounds, and so the worse the Rand is, more feasible and stronger our financial performances are because we have revenue in

---

[4] Managers of the BPO firms in our sample agreed that labour accounts for the highest proportion of their operational cost.

Pounds and we have a cost base (e.g. wages and workspace) in Rand, which is a
dream.

Interview, pers. comm., Johannesburg, 2016

South Africa also has a stable base of graduate entrants to the labour market. An estimated 150,000 people graduate every year from South African universities into the labour market, and most of them are considered to be suited for entry-level BPO work (BPESA, 2015a). One of the officials of the industry body, Business Process Enabling South Africa (BPESA), told us that the availability and scalability of a skilled workforce at competitive prices remains key to South Africa's success (Interview, pers. comm., Johannesburg, 2016). The fact that South Africa has one of the highest youth unemployment rates in the world means that the government's industrial policy action plan is geared to supporting sectors which can contribute to employment generation, hence its prioritization of the 'business process services' (BPS) sector; a point confirmed to us by a Department of Trade and Industry (DTI) official (Interview, pers. comm., Johannesburg, 2016).[5]

The South African government's policy initiatives, such as generous cash incentives especially for outsourced services (in place since 2014) provide a further impetus to attracting foreign lead firms in the hopes of creating jobs for South Africans. According to the DTI official we interviewed, these incentives are provided with a view to narrowing the cost gap between South Africa and other destinations to secure contracts for offshore markets (Interview, pers. comm., Johannesburg, 2016). The incentive programme was further revised in 2018, to include cash grants for firms creating at least fifty 'offshore jobs' within the first three years. For entry-level work (e.g. inbound customer services), a firm gets paid US$9,375 per job created over five years. There is also a 20 per cent one-off 'bonus incentive' for creating more than 500 jobs and maintaining these for five years.[6] By comparison, Egypt provides subsidies for vocational training, telecommunications costs, and rents (Reuters, 2010b), and has an export-based cash rebate programme for IT firms (ITIDA, 2018). No similar incentives were found in any of the other four case study countries, although alternative initiatives exist.

Spatial zoning policies seem to be the key planning instrument used by governments in Kenya and Ghana to kick-start the nascent IT and BPO

---

[5] The government of South Africa uses the term BPS instead of BPO in their strategy.
[6] The lowest wage we found among contact centre workers in South Africa was ZAR 5,000 per month (US$860 at purchasing power parity (PPP) levels) paid by an international firm running an offshore operation for a UK client.

sector—however, with relatively little success in attracting investments and creating jobs. Examples include dedicated free trade zones or parks such as Konza City (Kenya), Tema ICT Park (Ghana), and the BPO Incubation Centre (Uganda). Such zoning policies have precedents outside Africa, for example in India where the government has allowed 100 per cent foreign direct investment into the IT-sector driven special economic zones and tax exemptions on export and import (Anwar, 2014). The Kenyan state has experimented with exemption from corporate income tax and stamp duty, employment-based grants, and duty-free import of materials in Konza City. The Kenyan government also subsidized bandwidth costs for BPO companies in 2007–08 by redirecting funds from an e-government project of the World Bank (cited from Mann and Graham, 2016). The Ghanaian government, meanwhile, has set up the Accra Digital Centre on the site of an old public works warehouse in Accra, which, according to its managing director, provides cheap office space and ancillary services to attract BPO companies to the site (Interview, pers. comm., Accra, May 2017).[7] Unfortunately, the Tema ICT Park in Ghana, which is expected to host IT and BPO firms, had only one tenant (a local private sector firm doing customer services work) when we visited their offices in 2017 (Figure 3.1).[8] Similarly, the BPO Incubation Centre (Uganda) had only one big regional firm, which was doing sales and customer retention campaigns for a cable television company and their customers in East Africa.

Marketing Abroad

Markets do not exist in a vaccum, they need the protective covering of state institutions (Polanyi, 2001). Despite the push for privatization and deregulation on the continent (under the stuctural adjustment programmes) by the World Bank and IMF, the need for markets to be supported and developed in close collaboration with state was clearly evident in our work on the outsourcing sector. Several BPO executives and private sector associations conceded that the state needs to play an active role for the local BPO industry to develop and flourish. For them state can help with the brand marketing abroad, especially in buyer locations such as the US and United

---

[7] When we visited the centre in 2017, it was empty. At the time of writing this chapter in mid-2020, the centre houses Ghana Tech Lab and Ghana Innovation Lab, two incubators for start-ups and also for hosting various industry events.

[8] The Government of Mauritius entered into a US$260 million agreement with the Government of Ghana to develop the park.

Fig. 3.1 ICT Park in Tema, Ghana, with its only local BPO firm in the background
Source: Authors, May 2017.

Kingdom (UK). This helps create awareness and also improve the image of the country in order to attract offshore work. However, The level of institutional capacity of the state and its relevant institutions varied across our case-study countries.

The South African government, through the DTI, led the country's marketing effort as far back as 2002–03 in partnership with the private sector and management consultancies to formulate a sector development strategy for the BPO industry, which has made it easier to sell the country's location abroad, attract investment, and create jobs (Interview, pers. comm., BPESA official, 2016). The South African Government has a close relationship with BPESA and is actively involved in supporting the sector through marketing. As one of the DTI officials explained to us:

Another part of our strategy [for development of the outsourcing sector] is investor promotion, what we call broad based marketing. So, creating awareness in an offshore market is about the fact that South Africa is the place to go to do BPO. We have a South African value proposition that gets offered to a prospective investor that wants to come in. We also provide all the investor facil-itation and logistic services, work permits, etc. It makes it easier to get into South Africa. And then obviously there is the talent development path which is where the skills development strategy falls into. And then another part of the govern-ment's role is to mobilise industry. The way we do that is by working through with the industry body [BPESA]. Although we do not fund the industry body, we have a working relationship with the industry body in order to support them in terms of marketing abroad.

Interview, pers. comm., Johannesburg, September 2016

An important aspect of the South African state's role in the outsourcing sector is the increasing number of business trips and participation in buyer forums, which have created awareness among international buyers. In col-laboration with BPESA, the South African government has been leading the way in this regard. In 2019 alone, BPESA delegates along with DTI of-ficials went on several marketing and investment promotion trips to the UK, Australia, and the US—three major offshore markets for South Africa (Anwar and Graham, 2019). The DTI's new Global Business Services (GBS) incentives were launched in London in 2018.[9] At the launch, the BPESA's CEO was quoted as saying '[The] government's continued support for this sector is applauded and hopefully sends a clear message to investors in the UK and elsewhere that South Africa is very serious about your business and will continue to put great effort and resources into attracting and retaining your investment in South Africa' (DTI, 2018).

The South African BPO industry is now the biggest in our sample in terms of number of firms and jobs created, with only Egypt as its closest rival (see Table 3.2). Of course, South Africa is an economic heavyweight on the continent with its well-developed infrastructure and better educa-tion levels, which many smaller economies such as Uganda simply cannot match. Even though both Kenya and Rwanda are considered to have po-tential for offshore services, their IT and BPO industry lags behind South Africa's.

International bodies such as the Netherlands Trust Fund (NTF) have funded projects in Kenya and Uganda with the aim of enhancing the export competitiveness of the IT and IT-enabled service sector (ITC, 2015). The NTF in partnership with the International Trade Centre has selected a few small and medium enterprises to increase their capacity and create and

---

[9] The previous scheme was also launched in London, in 2014.

validate an export plan, thus improving the capacity of trade support institutions and expanding business linkages and partnerships in target export markets. The CEO of a local Ugandan firm told us that 'the NTF project provided Ugandan companies skills development training, evaluated their marketing materials online and offline, and offered advice on rebranding their websites and business cards' (Interview, pers. comm., Kampala, 2017). The NTF project helped bring together a group of companies to form a private sector association, the Alliance for Trade and Information Technology and Services (ATIS), to undertake advocacy work and marketing of Uganda as a destination for offshore work (Interview, pers. comm., ATIS Official Kampala, 2017). However, it has failed to bring in more offshore work. They also noted lead firms' prejudices about Africa as a location for BPO work. The CEO of the local Ugandan firm also told us that international clients often ask, 'Uganda is known for tourism, it is not known for software work, so give us a reason why we should actually come to you.'

Many BPO executives told us a number of governance challenges associated with their participation in global production networks (Gereffit et al., 2005), which brand marketing alone cannot overcome. For example, lead firms exercise strict control in the networks for quality (e.g. through business standards certification from the likes of International Organization for Standardization (ISO)) which can prevent new local firms from winning international contracts. These are mostly voluntary, and often costly. Buyers also have specific requirements for certain types of accreditations, including for data security, project management, and quality control (Anwar and Graham, 2019). Lynnette Morris, Chair of the South African Technical Review Committee for South African Business Standards, revealed that some US firms like IBM and Microsoft are already using their own business standards. Some of them cost at least one million ZAR (almost US$75,000) for South African firms to accredit themselves, in order to gain the reputation and trust required for securing international contracts. This point was also made to us by the CEO of the Kenyan Information Technology and Outsourcing Services (KITOS), a trade association for outsourcing and IT firms in Kenya (Interview, pers. comm., November 2016). As a result, some smaller domestic firms struggle to operate profitably in the face of competition from international firms, expensive certification costs for business standards, and their lack of capacity and market reputation to secure contracts. The CEO of one Ugandan firm told us that one of their potential clients in the US once asked them if they have Microsoft-certified developers and software engineers. He went on to explain the kind of conditions clients place on African firms before awarding any contract:

> [T]here are so many conditions you have to meet before you can get work from international buyers. Clients ask do you have professional certifications and do you have Microsoft certified developers or engineers. I believe if we overcome this, then we should be able to compete internationally. But at times there are many conditions for us. One of them is your certifications. You must be having the industrial certifications. Then the way you deliver your work. Do you have your project management system, like quality control? Then what is your delivery approach? Do you have servers where you do your development? How are your security controls? The clients would say Why should I come to Africa? The US itself has firms and organisations and also, we know where to outsource, we will go to India.
>
> **Interview, pers. comm., Kampala, November 2017**

Nigeria faces these reputational challenges more evidently. As the most populous country in Africa, Nigeria has the potential for a BPO market due to its growing population which can act both as a consumer market and also as the supplier of the labour force for the BPO industry. But its image among the business community abroad is a major hinderance to attracting offshore work. Nigeria is known for online scamming and there are also security and terrorism concerns in the northern parts of the country. The CEO of a local BPO firm told us:

> In Nigeria offshore work is a gold mine for us in the outsourcing space but that has not taken off. There are snippets of it occurring but not fully . . . There are lots of reasons why. Obviously, the political landscape. In the early days, it used to be technology and connectivity but we have since moved on from that—you know that the technology is available, connectivity is available now. For example, a conference bridge service (through IP PBX)[10] that allows international calls to be routed directly to us from the US and the UK. But I think the biggest challenge is the confidence in the country. Well think of Nigeria as an address. As a service provider or product provider in the UK or in Europe you are thinking of offshoring to a destination somewhere across the world where when you turn on the news you are seeing Boko Haram. And you are thinking, am I making the right decision here. If you just listen to the news people are wary of coming to Nigeria, let alone

---

[10] An IP PBX (Internet Protocol private branch exchange) is a system that provides internal communication for business in the form of audio, video, and instant messaging over the internet.

outsourcing their business to Nigeria. So that for me I think is a big challenge, there is an image challenge.

Interview, pers. comm., Lagos, March 2017

Similarly, one of executives of the Association of Outsourcing Professionals in Nigeria (AOPN) told us that the image and perception of Nigeria among international buyers is of a corruption-ridden country, which 'is working seriously against us and the government is not helping the matters' (Interview, pers. comm., Lagos, March 2017). The National Information Technology Development Agency (NITDA), the Nigerian government agency tasked with developing the local IT industry, struggles with its leadership and a lack of a clear policy framework to create a political–economic space in which the outsourcing industry can germinate.

The NITDA officials we interviewed maintained that the government is actively trying to improve the image of the country and letting the business community know that 'we are not corrupt people. We are not lazy people. We are very disciplined people and we are hardworking people' (Interview, pers. comm., Abuja, 2017).

According to one of the NITDA's officials, there are three main challenges that Nigeria's BPO industry faces: lack of a clear policy framework, poor infrastructure (electricity, transport, internet), and the country's image. When we conducted our fieldwork in early 2017 the government was holding discussions about a new outsourcing bill that would include several incentives, including tax breaks. The NITDA officials told us that in order to enhance the perception of Nigeria the state needs to set up a dedicated office for outsourcing, step up its marketing campaigns abroad among the business and buyer communities, and demonstrate the suitability of the business environment in the foreign media (Interview, pers. comm., Abuja, 2017). It took the COVID-19 pandemic in 2020 for the NITDA to unveil a new National Outsourcing Strategy for Nigeria 2020–25, which contains some fairly bold claims—such as one million direct and indirect jobs and 500 new outsourcing entrepreneurs employing an average of fifty staff to be created within three years of implementing the strategy (NITDA, 2020). Nigeria already had a National Outsourcing Policy, dating from 2007, which contained less ambitious targets of 10,000 jobs and '500 new outsourcing entrepreneurs employing an average of twenty staff within the next three years of implementing the outsourcing programme' (NITDA, 2007). While the targets are bigger in the new policy, the mechanisms to achieve these aims have remained virtually the same. For example, the 'special Outsourcing Development Fund', which was to be established under the 2007 policy, features again in the 2020 policy, suggesting it has not been set up yet during the last thirteen years. We observed similar issues in Kenya.

The Kenyan case is somewhat paradoxical in the sense that it has a slightly better image than Nigeria among international buyers, is noted for its growing IT and tech-hub scene, and has been dubbed the 'Silicon Savannah' in the press (Financial Times, 2016). However, its BPO industry did not take off in the way that industry experts, policymakers and development organizations predicted almost a decade ago. Kleibert and Mann (2020) have noted that the Kenyan government did not put in place a proper strategy to develop the BPO sector, and in fact, preferential treatment for certain firms has meant that many inexperienced domestic firms struggled to compete and were crowded out of the market. The CEO of KITOS told us that:

> there was a lot of push with the studies by McKinsey that highlighted Kenya's potential for international BPO work and I think that was what was sold . . . Unfortunately, IT and BPO has not been in the forefront of the government's priority. Maybe tourism or other things have been very forefront for Kenya. The branding from the government I do not think is very clear on the BPOs and the sector I think is getting smaller. Interview, pers. comm., Nairobi 2016[11]

Recently, the ICT Authority Kenya, the government body responsible for Kenya's wider ICT sector, has been very active in promoting various digital economy activities. It has drafted a Strategic Plan 2019–23 'to take advantage of the "Fourth Industrial Revolution"' (Kenya ICT Authority, 2019: 3), although the plan has little to say about the outsourcing industry and its growth. The BPO industry in Kenya (and also Uganda) is now reliant on a handful of firms and new intermediaries (who are foreign entities) for the bulk of its offshoring work, which affects local value creation and capture within the country. The increasing reliance on foreign firms for offshore work and a focus on low value-added activities (e.g. customer support services and data entry) make decoupling very likely.

---

[11] The study referred to here was the study commissioned by the Kenyan ICT Board in 2009 to develop Kenya's BPO Value Proposition. The study was conducted by McKinsey and made 13 recommendations. One of those recommendations was to improve the international perception of Kenya abroad, specifically through the Brand Kenya Initiative (see Kariuki, 2010).

By the time we did our fieldwork in 2016–17, many foreign firms had already left Kenya, Ghana, and Nigeria. According to one of the managers of a local firm in Kenya, the government's marketing campaign in 2006 (before the fibre-optic undersea cables landed in Mombasa in 2009), did help bring some work to Kenya, but the government failed to develop the necessary infrastructure (e.g. adequate office spaces, electricity supply) and a skilled labour force (Interview, pers. comm., Nairobi, 2016). As a result, companies which came to Kenya for offshore work left because they could get the work done with a skilled workforce more cheaply elsewhere, for example in the Philippines. We met the owner of a newly established local firm doing entry-level digitization work for the domestic banking and financial sector in Ghana. He told us that previously he used to work for a US firm called Affiliated Computer Services (ACS), which began operations in 2000 in Ghana and left in 2013. Similarly, another US-based firm, Teletec, left Ghana in 2014. Because outsourcing value chains are cost driven, buyers often shift the risks to vendors (i.e. the company providing or selling the service), including infrastructure and sunk costs, making it easier for the buyer firms to relocate to other places if the cost goes up or service quality declines, leaving local suppliers struggling to stay in the market.

The local firms in most of our case study countries lacked managerial experience, technological know-how, personal connections, and some were facing financial and operational difficulties after the 2008 financial crisis, despite a recent reduction in telecommunications costs and improvements in internet connectivity. For example, Kencall, the winner of the Best Non-European Call Centre at the Call Centre Focus Conference in 2008, was facing liquidation due to unpaid debts. We visited their call centre just off the Mombasa Road on the southern outskirts of Nairobi only to find it closed.[12] The CEO of a small IT services firm which also runs call centre operations in Nairobi told us that finance has been their main challenge to expanding their operations, to undertake complex high value-added work, and attract offshore work (Interview, pers. comm., Nairobi, 2016). At the time we did our interviews the company was primarily doing transcription work subcontracted by other bigger local and regional buyers. In South Africa, there were also indications of domestic firms shutting down operations due to foreign competition and governance challenges (e.g. maintaining business standards and data security in the value chain, see

---

[12] The co-founder of Kencall, Nicholas Nesbitt, was working for IBM at the time of the fieldwork in 2016.

Anwar and Graham, 2019). The development implications of this uneven landscape of outsourcing are briefly explored next.

Economic Development Trajectories

Data on the BPO industry on the continent remains sketchy at best. Most countries in Africa do not have good-quality official data, and estimates derived from reports by development organizations and management consultancies remain scattered and outdated, which makes comparable analysis even more difficult. We therefore attempted to collect estimates on the size of the wider IT or IT-enabled services (ITES) industry in our case study countries, since some official figures on the ITES industry also include the BPO segment (Table 3.2). The data come from a range of sources, including interviews with private-sector associations and secondary sources (reports and publications), and physical trips to firms' offices. In 2014, the IT sector made up around 2.7 per cent of the gross domestic product of South Africa, slightly higher than the agriculture sector but less than the tourism sector (Statistics South Africa, 2017). Figures for Nigeria and Uganda remain unavailable. We further collected information on the number of firms doing BPO work in our case studies, along with Egypt and Mauritius, to understand the size of the market on a larger regional scale. In Kenya, we were told by an official at KITOS that they had a total of sixty members, of whom ten were doing entry-level BPO work, primarily data entry, transcription, inbound customer support, and sales, while they had no record in their database of any firm doing high-value work such as knowledge process outsourcing. In Uganda, a newly formed private-sector association, ATIS, has twenty-four registered firms (Interview, pers. comm., ATIS official, 2017). Comparable figures for Ghana and Nigeria are more difficult to ascertain. During our fieldwork, we found only twelve companies doing entry-level BPO work in Accra.[13] In Nigeria, we interviewed officials from the Association of Outsourcing Professionals Nigeria (AOPN) and the Nigeria Association of Information Technology Enabled Outsourcing Companies (NAITEOC). While they connected us to a few local industry players, neither organization had estimates of the BPO industry. We triangulated web-based research and field visits to the known firms' offices in Lagos and Abuja in 2017 to build a database of just fourteen BPO firms.[14]

---

[13] In an earlier study, Beerepoot and Keijser (2015) found 34 companies doing IT work in Accra.

[14] We visited the offices of a firm in Lagos in 2017. They had vacated the offices and the site was occupied by another local IT firm.

Table 3.2 Summary of the size of the outsourced services industry in key African countries

Countries	Share of GDP	Jobs	No. of Firms	Government Body	Industry Bodies
Egypt	4%[1]	169,000	n/a	ITIDA	n/a
South Africa	2.7%	236,000	91	DTI	BPESA
Kenya	0.9%[2]	2,500[3]	10[4]	ICT Authority Kenya	KITOS
Uganda	n/a	4,000	24	National Information Technology Agency Uganda (NITA-U)	ATIS; Information Communication Technology Association of Uganda (ICTAU).
Nigeria	n/a	n/a	14	NITDA	Association of Outsourcing Professionals Nigeria (AOPN); NAITEOC
Ghana	3.3%	3,500[5]	12	National Information Technology Agency Ghana (NITA-G)	Ghana Association of Software and IT Services Companies (GASSCOM)
Mauritius	5.6%	25,000	216[6]	Ministry of Technology, Communication and Innovation (MTCI)	Outsourcing and Telecommunications Association of Mauritius (OTAM); Mauritius IT Industry Association (MITIA)

[1] 2018 figures (Manek, 2018).
[2] Frost and Sullivan (2018) estimated the Kenyan ICT sector to be worth US$5.16 billion.
[3] Reported in the media (Kamau, 2016).
[4] Data from Frost and Sullivan (2018) suggest it had 16 firms in 2018.
[5] Figures from 2012 in Kennedy et al. (2013).
[6] Database from the Ministry of Technology, Communication and Innovation, Mauritius.

The Domestic Market and Low Value-Added Services

There is no denying the fact that the improvement in internet connectivity in Africa since 2009 has increasingly made some of its economies competitive in wider global outsourcing value chains (Anwar and Graham, 2019; Kleibert and Mann, 2020; Mann and Graham, 2016). Other elements have also contributed to the development of the BPO industry in several parts of Africa. One in particular has been the trend in the Indian BPO industry of moving away from entry-level work (generally classified as low value-added) into high-value and skilled professional services including complex IT-enabled services. India has some of the world's best-known and most valuable IT and software development companies in the world.[15] Many Indian IT companies owe their success to outsourced business process functions for clients or corporations in high-income countries like the US and UK (Peck, 2017; also Parthasarathy, 2004; Parthasarathy and Aoyama, 2006). More recently, the national industry body, the National Association of Software and Services Companies (NASSCOM), has started using the term Business Process Management (BPM) in its reports and various other outputs as they reorient their value proposition from low-cost locations to domain expertise and high value-added offerings such as data science and artificial intelligence capabilities (see NASSCOM, 2018).[16]

This shift has opened up the space for some of the low-value work to be relocated and re-outsourced to other locations which are cost effective. This point was emphasized by a Ugandan CEO, who told us that 'the Indian BPO industry is looking to sell themselves for higher-end professional services such as the web support services and cloud computing. The cost of doing bottom of the value chain work such as inbound customer service, transcription and digitization is increasing in India which means many African countries can fill the gap as our costs are fairly low' (Interview, pers. comm., Kampala, November 2017). That said, without accurate data it is hard to ascertain how much BPO work is being redirected from India to Africa. It is clear, however, that low value-added activities such as inbound customer services, digitization, transcription, and content generation have emerged in our sample—the bulk of these services being primarily targeted at domestic markets. That said, in South Africa, some firms were doing various forms of high value-added work (see Anwar and Graham, 2019: 213–214).

The growth of domestic market-oriented BPOs we see in our sample is also reflective of services demand coming from mobile operators such as MTN, Vodacom, Safaricom, and Airtel, who have a growing subscriber

---

[15] Tata Consultancy Services (TCS) is the first Indian IT company to be valued at US$100 billion. TCS and Infosys are the only two Indian companies on the Forbes Top 100 Digital Companies in the world (Forbes, 2019).

[16] The main objective towards transitioning from the term 'BPO' to 'BPM' is to change the public image of the BPO industry and attract foreign clients to outsource their higher-end services or functions (The Times of India, 2013).

base. For example, in South Africa, telecom operators are the biggest segment buying entry-level services, both from foreign firms and domestic firms, such as customer and technical support (BPESA, 2018). Spurred on by improvements in digital infrastructure technologies, most notably broadband fibre-optic cables, the potential for low value-added BPO work to be done on the continent remains. However, digital economy activities can also lead to new forms of intermediation with implications for economic development (through value capture) (Murphy et al., 2014).

Third-Party Intermediaries

The contraction of the local BPO industry in Kenya and Uganda has created an economic space for re-intermediation by new types of players, which we term 'third party coupling', through US-based intermediaries. These intermediaries are not lead firms as in direct buyers of services. Instead, they source work from Silicon Valley corporations and then subcontract that work to local firms in Africa. In essence, they are becoming the 'bridge' between Silicon Valley and the 'Silicon Savannah'.

From the Kenyan perspective, Mann and Graham (2016) noted that trust was a major issue facing local firms in sourcing offshore work directly, as well as the power of incumbents. Indeed, many local industry players became reliant on new foreign intermediaries. One of these US-based intermediaries started with a 70-seater centre doing entry-level data annotation and image tagging work (also referred as machine learning and artificial intelligence work) for Silicon Valley corporations. Their initial business model was based on subcontracting services delivery to local firms in Kenya. They now have offices in both Kenya and Uganda. In 2016, when we visited their offices, they had expanded their inhouse delivery centres, and do limited subcontracting to local firms. At the time of our fieldwork, this intermediary had capacity for 600 employees in a 200-seater office space in Nairobi, with three eight-hour shifts a day (Interview, pers. comm., business manager, Nairobi, 2016).

Since these intermediaries have the significant advantage of a base in the US, they control a sizeable portion of the entry-level work coming into the East African region. Overall, these intermediaries provide much-needed work for local firms to stay afloat in the market. One of the managers of a local Kenyan firm told us that the industry has not grown and the demand for work has slowed down, however, they have survived because of their dependence on this international intermediary, which provides them with a majority of their business contracts (generally short-term) doing transcription work (Interview, pers. comm., Nairobi, 2016). That said, some local firms had taken a direct approach to bringing offshore work into their respective countries, given that intermediaries can significantly affect the value capture and upgrading opportunities for regional economies.

The director of the BPO segment of one of the big regional IT firms, with an extensive presence in East Africa, told us that international intermediaries were important for them to break entry barriers into these value chains, though this intermediation affected the value that they were able to capture. In 2014, they set up offices in California and approached clients directly, bypassing the intermediary, and now have long-term contracts with two of the biggest Fortune 500 companies, doing data capture and data processing.[17] The director also told us these intermediaries were effectively charging a huge mark-up to take a large cut of the profit, so when they approached Silicon Valley clients directly with their pricing for similar work, the clients were surprised and decided to buy those services directly from them (Interview, pers. comm., Nairobi, 2016). Similarly, in Nigeria, two local firms told us that they had succeeded in securing small contracts from US-based clients. According to the chief operations officer of one of these firms, the buyer was unhappy with the insurance sales service they were getting from a company in India, so they outsourced a portion of that work to Nigeria, despite slightly higher cost per agent in the country (Interview, pers. comm., Abuja, 2017). In essence, while enhancing digital footprints (e.g. through online marketing and improving websites) can integrate firms into global networks, physical presence in buyer locations is still a significant factor for firms to be able to win contracts for offshore work.

Regional Networks

There are strong indications of regionally oriented value chains emerging in outsourcing in Africa (Kleibert and Mann, 2020). In the BPO sector, where foreign-owned firms have shown less enthusiasm for engaging in the local or regional markets in our sample, Indian-diasporic businesses are filling the gap. The Indian diaspora has long been present in Africa

---

[17] The company began operations in Tanzania in the 1990s, and now has corporate headquarters in Dubai.

and is received with a mixture of friendliness and hostility in local socio-political circles. Some observers have called Indian entrepreneurs in East Africa 'settled strangers' (Oonk, 2013), while in West Africa, the colloquial term used is 'briefcase businessmen' (according to an Indian immigrant we interviewed in Nigeria). Some of the well-known BPO firms run by Indian diasporic businesses in Africa are ISON, Technobrain, Acreaty, and Simbatech.[18] Another big IT firm, Tech Mahindra, which is a subsidiary of the Indian conglomerate Mahindra Group, has offices in thirteen African countries and serves primarily local markets. According to the regional head at Tech Mahindra, their company deals mostly in call centre operations for telecom services providers such as MTN and Airtel (two of the major networks in Africa) (Interview, pers. comm., Lagos, March 2017). Similarly, a high-ranking ISON executive told us that if telecom operators in sub-Saharan Africa outsourced customer services, 90 per cent went to ISON (Interview, pers. comm., Lagos, March 2017).[19]

These regionally oriented players and networks have the potential for wider industry-level upgrading into complex value chain activities, for example data management and legal process outsourcing. The shifting of local firms' priorities towards domestic and regional value chains is also reflective of a trend towards regionally oriented value chains as a pathway to economic development (Morris et al., 2016). The expansion of regional value chains can generate South–South trade, which is considered more important for high-value capture among African firms than North–South value chains and networks (see Franssen, 2019). However, it should be pointed out here that in the value chain literature, there is a recognition that the risk in value chains shifts towards lower-end suppliers (see Selwyn, 2018), as has been the case for supermarket value chains in Southern Africa, where supermarkets' demand for private standards and requirements affects upgrading among the lower-end suppliers (Nair et al., 2018). While the potential for local firms to upgrade into complex value chains and high value-added activities remains to be seen in Africa, the employment generation potential through digital outsourcing is evident.

---

[18] We were told by a high-ranking executive of Simbatech in Nairobi that the company was acquired by a South African firm in 2016.

[19] We cannot verify this claim.

Employment Generation

In the context of high levels of working poverty across the continent, employment within the newly emerging outsourcing industry is seen as a critical economic development on the continent. Grand claims are often made by governments about job creation through the digital economy, with BPO work predicted to be a provider of formal-sector jobs to the African population (Ndemo, n.d.). Similarly, the World Bank's 2016 World Development Report noted the potential of digital technologies in creating jobs in low- and middle-income countries, both through internet-enabled offshoring (e.g. call centre work) and online work (World Bank, 2016). The Rockefeller Foundation's Digital Jobs Africa initiative, a US$100 million project, was designed 'to create new jobs' and employment opportunities in the IT sector, including BPO and online outsourcing jobs.

There is some evidence that jobs are emerging on the continent. South Africa's BPO industry, for example, supports around 236,000 jobs, yet this represents only 0.6 per cent of South Africa's total labour force. However, data on employment in the outsourcing industry is sketchy for our other case countries. In Kenya, a country which was once regarded as best placed to tap into outsourcing value chains, data on job creation are often inconsistent and speculative. The Kenyan government expected Konza City (a US$14 billion project conceived in 2008) to create 200,000 high value IT-enabled services and entry-level BPO jobs in the zone (Ncube and Ondiege, 2013). Yet, expectations from projects like Konza City to kick-start digital outsourcing services in Kenya remains far-fetched (see Saraswati, 2014). In fact, at the time of writing in 2021, Konza City is still under construction.

Uneven Development in the Remote Gig Economy

Remote work has gone mainstream and the genie is not going back into the bottle.

CEO of Upwork, quoted in Consumer News and Business Channel (CNBC, 2020)

We have already considered the emergence of the gig economy in Chapter 2. Such has been the uptake of gig economy platforms around the world that various terms such as 'gigification' (Veen et al., 2019) and 'platformization' (Casilli and Posada, 2019) are now commonly used to underscore their importance for the world economy. There is no doubting the potential of gig economy platforms to provide new services (Srnicek, 2016). Platforms are implicated in moving jobs from one part of the world to another (Graham and Anwar, 2019; Kässi and Lehdonvirta, 2018), commodifying work (Anwar and Graham, 2020a; Rani and Furrer, 2020; Wood et al., 2019), and expanding contingent employment relations around the world (Morgan and Nelligan, 2018; Panteli et al., 2020; Todolí-Signes, 2017). Put simply, gig economy platforms have unleashed tremendous change in work and employment relations around the world (Anwar and Graham, 2020a; Berg et al., 2018; Prassl, 2018). With the onset of the COVID-19 pandemic, remote work has gained even more traction, as the quote from the CEO of Upwork above illustrates (CNBC, 2020). Latest estimates by Kässi et al., (2021) suggest that there are 165 million registered worker profiles globally on 162 digital labour platforms for remote work.

In the context of Africa, Insight2impact in their database[20] list ninety-one freelancing platforms that connect buyers and sellers of remote work in Africa. African workers use a variety of major platforms, including Upwork, Fiverr, Freelancer.com, PeopleperHour, and Figure Eight (previously CrowdFlower). Other platforms are less well-known but nevertheless still widely used by African workers for niche work such as writing, including Uvocorp, iWriter, and Gotranscript. Indeed, workers usually register profiles on multiple platforms. To examine the geographies of remote work, we studied Upwork, the world's largest platform in terms of registered workers, and the most commonly used by African workers.

To understand the economic geographies of remote gig work in Africa, we used Upwork's filter menu (Figure 3.2).[21] This allows users to select freelancers based on their locations, hourly rate, skills set, number of hours worked, and income earned. While the filter menu provides enough quantitative information to get some sense of the size of remote work and the relative market shares of countries, the filter mechanism is nevertheless a 'black box'; that is, Upwork doesn't publish details on how its back-end data feeds into the information returned by the search interface. On their website, Upwork claims to have 12 million workers with 2,900 skills.[22] However, on 22 May 2019, when the screenshot was taken (Figure 3.2),

---

[20] Available at http://access.i2ifacility.org/Digital_platforms/, accessed 10 July 2021.

[21] At the time of writing in May 2020, Upwork's filter feature has changed. While one can still use the filters Upwork does not allow users to see the number of workers against each category.

[22] Available at https://www.upwork.com/hiring/for-clients/3-tips-finding-best-talent-upwork/, accessed 10 July 2021. Because there is no detailed information available on the way data is updated in the filter menu, we don't know if the numbers reflect all users who have ever registered.

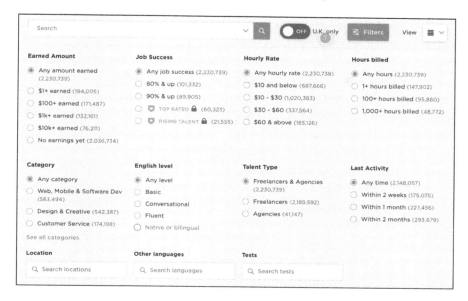

Fig. 3.2 Upwork's filter menu
Source: Screenshot from 22 May 2019.

(a)   (b)

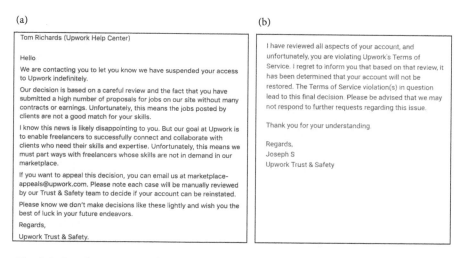

Fig. 3.3 Emails sent to workers notifying them of suspension and cancellation of their accounts

Upwork had 2.3 million searchable worker profiles. Upwork also cancels certain workers' accounts and deletes their profiles, which essentially means workers can easily be excluded from these platforms (Figure 3.3).

Another difficulty when trying to estimate the number of workers on Upwork is that interactions between different filters considerably affect the aggregated numbers reported through the search form, requiring cautious interpretation. For example, workers who have worked at least one hour will almost certainly have earned at least one dollar, but there are also workers listed who have earned at least one dollar, but worked zero hours. Those workers might have been hired on piece-meal contracts. Additionally, the numbers are aggregated into large groups. For instance, it is only possible to select freelancers who have earned at least one dollar, 100 dollars, 1,000 dollars, or 10,000 dollars. However, despite these caveats, the filter menu provides a means to assess the size and composition of the labour supply on Upwork in Africa, and worldwide.

To assess the relevance of different online labour platforms in African countries we also collected data on aggregate monthly clicks from SimilarWeb.com, a web-traffic monitoring website, between May 2018 and November 2018. The tool provides web analytics, including insights into the number of visitors to a web page, and the country from where these visits took place (using visitor IP addresses). The SimilarWeb-API allowed us to automate the collection of aggregated visitor statistics for our five case study countries.

Upwork is one of the leaders in the remote gig economy, with roughly one third of the overall market share in Africa, as measured by the monthly visits to the website. Figure 3.4 shows the relative market shares of the five most important digital work platforms as measured by the aggregated monthly clicks in the six months between May 2018 and November 2018 (data source: SimilarWeb). The African online labour market is dominated by the global market leaders Upwork and Fiverr, with Upwork being the largest or second largest platform in all African countries. Overall, the market share of Upwork is 36 per cent (similar to Fiverr's market share), but it is even higher in a number of countries such as Egypt and Kenya, two of the largest online labour suppliers from Africa. Freelancer.com also has a substantial market share in some countries, while Peopleperhour and Guru have only a tiny share of the African market.

Relative Supply and Demand of Remote Work

To get a comprehensive perspective on the overall supply and demand trends of remote work worldwide, we collected data from Upwork.com by setting up a web-scraping tool based in Python to access Upwork's main

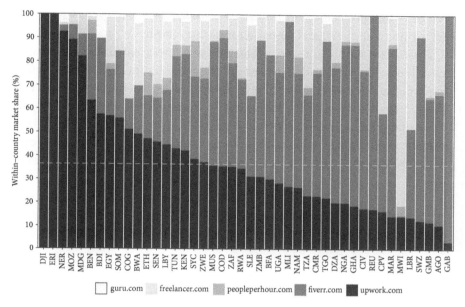

Fig. 3.4 Market share of different platforms in Africa (May–November 2018)
Source: Authors' calculations based on data from SimilarWeb.com.

search interface. To do so, we used the 'Selenium' package, a web-based automation tool that simulates a human user opening a web browser and clicking through web pages. This scraping tool allowed us to automatically apply different filters to Upwork's search interface, such as 'country', minimum number of 'hours billed', and 'amount earned'. Each filter results in different numbers of freelancers being returned. We therefore performed several hundred search requests to obtain detailed figures on supply, demand, and hourly rates for all the African countries we were interested in. Given the need for relatively long sleeping intervals in the scraping tool between requests (in order to avoid CAPTCHA controls), we needed several weeks to complete the data collection. During that time, overall numbers of supply and demand on the platform appeared largely constant. We noted slight fluctuations on a daily basis, but these did not seem to be systematic in any direction. To estimate the demand for online labour from our five case study countries we counted the number of open projects listed on Upwork. Both the global supply of workers on Upwork and the demand for their labour are highly concentrated (Figure 3.5). Much of the labour demand comes from high-income countries, primarily the US, UK, Germany, Canada, and Australia. With 33,000 projects listed on Upwork, out of 70,000 projects listed at the time of data collection, the US accounts for around half the global demand for online labour.

The labour supply is also concentrated in a few countries, and low- and middle-income countries are some of the largest suppliers of this digital labour. The three largest labour suppliers—namely, the US, India, and the Philippines—were home to more than 1.13 million registered workers, or close to half of the total registered workers on Upwork, at the time of data collection (Table 3.3). Indeed, these three countries represent the forefront of global outsourcing value chains: the US is the leader in terms of demand

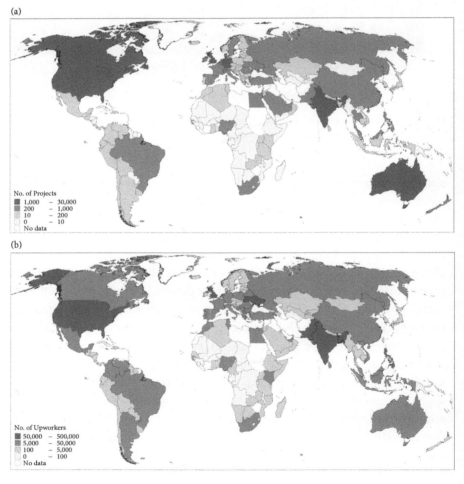

Fig. 3.5 The global distribution of online labour supply and demand (Upwork)
Source: Authors' calculations based on data from Upwork from November 2018.

for outsourced services, and India and the Philippines together account for well over half of the global market share in terms of global services delivery (Beerepoot et al., 2017; Peck, 2017). These three countries therefore enjoy a network effect and reputational advantage in online labour markets. With just over 120,000 registered freelancers on Upwork, the African continent as a whole has a global market share of just 5.2 per cent, which is less than the Philippines (Table 3.3).

Regionally, there is some unevenness in the labour supply on Upwork. While countries on the Asian continent and most Latin American countries are major labour suppliers, almost all African countries have a

Table 3.3 Labour supply in selected countries on Upwork on 21 June 2019.

Country	Potential Workforce	Min. $1 earned	No earnings	Over supply (%)
Global	**2,302,902**	**196,538**	**2,106,364**	91.4
United States	758,845	40,214	718,631	94.7
India	271,460	32,692	238,768	87.9
Philippines	179,689	24,339	155,350	86.4
Eastern Europe	N/A	N/A	N/A	N/A
Ukraine	69,076	12,531	56,545	81.8
Serbia	31,109	4,169	26,940	86.5
Romania	20,842	2,087	18,755	89.9
South and Central America	N/A	N/A	N/A	N/A
Brazil	27,169	1,490	25,679	94.5
Argentina	14,337	1,475	12,862	89.7
Mexico	14,709	1,140	13,569	92.2
Colombia	10,317	824	9,493	92
Africa	**120,345**	**7,024**	**113,320**	**94.1**
Egypt	44,270	2,091	42,179	95.2
Kenya	21,412	1,616	19,796	92.4
South Africa	15,474	957	14,517	94.1
Nigeria	9,499	827	8,672	91.2
Morocco	9,041	376	8,665	95.8
Tunisia	6,424	270	6,151	95.7
Algeria	4,383	165	4,218	96.2
Ghana	1,799	94	1,705	94.7
Uganda	1,311	54	1,257	95.8

Source: Authors calculations based on data scraped from Upwork.com.

relatively low labour supply, with most being in the lowest quartile of global distribution in terms of labour supply on Upwork. Two of the key factors influencing labour supply from the continent are the relatively low penetration of ICT tools, and costly broadband services. In fact, ITU (2019) has noted that internet penetration in Africa, despite a recent surge in mobile phone adoption, is still the lowest in the world, with affordability and lack of digital skills among the population representing key barriers to uptake. Although there are some significant labour suppliers on Upwork such as Egypt, Kenya, South Africa, Nigeria, and Morocco, the other African countries either have small workforces far below the global median, or are absent altogether (Figure 3.6).

Within-Africa Remote Work Market Distribution

Despite these large differences in labour supply, most African countries show a similar composition of remote labour in terms of job categories.

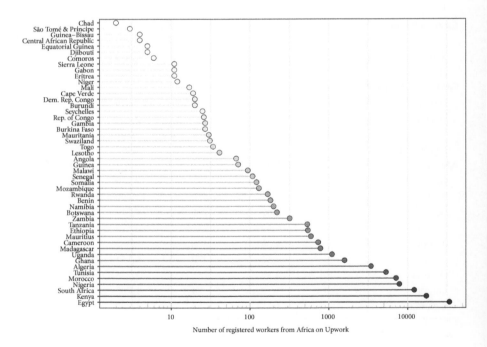

Fig. 3.6 Remote labour supply in Africa

Source: Authors' calculations via web-scraping on Upwork in November 2018.

Figure 3.7 shows the composition of online jobs within each African region and for the market leaders (i.e. the US, India, and the UK) on Upwork. In contrast to India, most African countries provide fewer workers in 'IT' than in 'Admin support'. In the largest labour-supplying countries, most jobs are conducted in the 'writing and creative' category. Such jobs include translation and blog writing. The second largest category is 'Admin support', including data entry, virtual assistance, and transcription. The other main categories are 'IT' including software development or analytics, and 'Legal and consulting' including tasks like accounting, paralegal jobs, and business plan writing.

If we expand our analysis and include more platforms, the regional and global outlook stays roughly the same. For example, the Online Labour Index (OLI) (Kässi and Lehdonvirta, 2018) measures the supply and demand of online labour across countries and occupations by tracking the number of projects and tasks across a number of platforms in real time. Though limited to only English language platforms, it tracks 70 per cent of the market by traffic. In June 2020, the US was the leader in terms of the employer market share on the major platforms around the world, followed by India and the UK (Figure 3.8). Worker distribution is also concentrated,

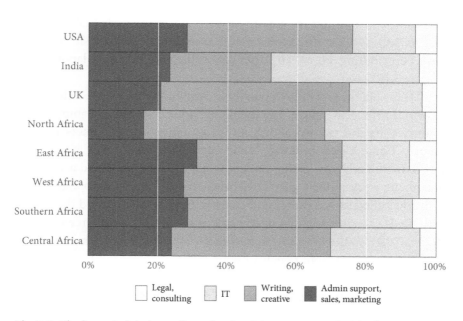

Fig. 3.7 The largest global suppliers of online labour compared with African regions
Source: Authors' calculations via web-scraping on Upwork in November 2018.

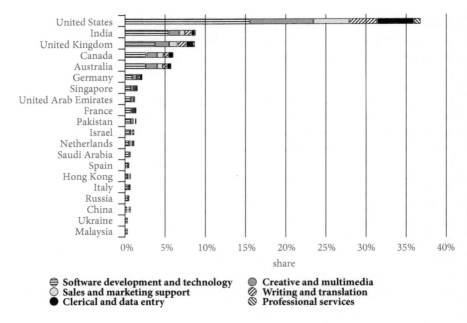

Fig. 3.8 Market share of countries with vacancies posted on major online labour platforms in June 2020

with Asia contributing more than 65 per cent of the global labour force (Figure 3.9), and just three countries, namely India, Bangladesh, and Pakistan, contributing more than 50 per cent of the world's remote labour force (Figure 3.10).

All this said, the COVID-19 pandemic will undoubtedly affect the world of work in the near future. The pandemic and the lockdown imposed by countries around the world has forced employers and workers to shift towards home-based working,[23] and a few large enterprises around the world are already advocating remote working to be the standard way of organizing work in the future (UN News, 2020).[24] Furthermore, the pandemic has affected businesses and threatened job losses around the world, with the ILO estimating that nearly half of the world's workforce is at risk (ILO, 2020a). In the US alone, an estimated 42.6 million workers had applied for unemployment benefits by June 2020 (Lambert, 2020). Many of these workers could look for online work to earn a living. This could mean changes to some of these geographies of remote work.

---

[23] Available at https://www.youtube.com/watch?v=DCaxXiHKOhY, accessed 10 July 2021.
[24] Twitter has already announced that its employees can work from home going forward (Paul, 2020).

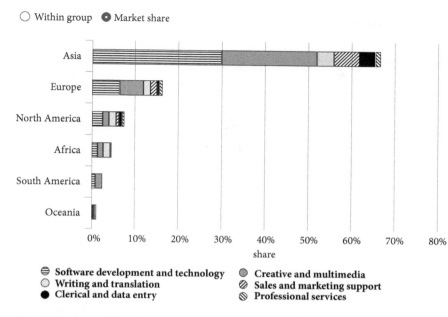

○ Within group   ● Market share

Fig. 3.9 Regional distribution of labour supply on work platforms

⊜ **Software development and technology**   ◉ **Creative and multimedia**
○ **Writing and translation**   ◎ **Sales and marketing support**
● **Clerical and data entry**   ⊘ **Professional services**

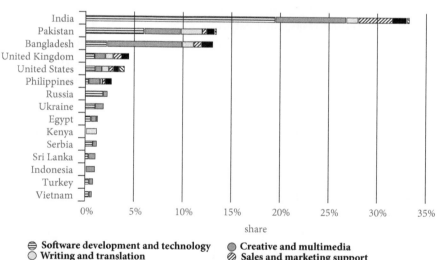

⊜ **Software development and technology**   ◉ **Creative and multimedia**
○ **Writing and translation**   ◎ **Sales and marketing support**
● **Clerical and data entry**   ⊘ **Professional services**

Fig. 3.10 Top 15 countries and their market share for labour supply on work platforms

Source: for 3.8, 3.9, 3.10: Online Labour Index at Kässi & Lehdonvirta, 2018.

Global Income and Wage Distribution

The imbalances in the supply of remote digital labour we have discussed above translate into an even more skewed global distribution of income and wages. Figure 3.11 compares the market shares of the different world regions in two groups: (a) amount earned, and (b) hourly rate. Africa, Latin America, and the Middle-East together account for less than 15 per cent of the overall market share; and account for even less in the high-income bracket (a) and high hourly rate groups (b). Africa's market share is low overall, and it is basically absent in the high income groups (a) and high hourly rates (b).

From the above observations, we can safely say that there is excess supply of online labour globally (Graham and Anwar, 2019). This can significantly affect the bargaining power of workers on platforms (Anwar and Graham, 2020a; Graham et al., 2017b). Second, most workers who earned more than US$1,000 have come from India, Pakistan, the Philippines, the Ukraine, and Russia. In particular, India and the Philippines have the largest market shares in the high-income bracket (that is, US$1,000+ and US$10,000+) (Figure 3.11a). That said, while workers from these countries perform the majority of online tasks, they earn low wages per hour. The high hourly rate groups (US$30+ and US$60+ per hour) are dominated by workers from high-income countries, such as the US (Figure 3.11b). The issue of bias among employers towards workers of the same nationality is also well known in the gig economy (Ghani et al., 2014 and World Bank, 2016). Additionally, people from low- and middle-income regions—in particular Africa—are even more marginalized in the remote gig economy. Low overall market shares are coupled with low incomes and low wages.

Gender and Racial Dimensions

The gig economy is also structured along gender lines, with a varied distribution of men and women globally. The Online Labour Observatory estimates that female workers make up about 39% of the labour force in the remote gig economy (Stephany et al., 2021). A 2018 study by the ILO covering 3,500 gig workers in seventy-five countries found that a third of those were women (Berg et al., 2018). More men are also likely to participate in the gig economy than women in the US (Farrell et al., 2018) and Australia (Churchill and Craig, 2019). In Europe more men take part in the gig economy than women, with the sole exception of Italy (Huws et al.,

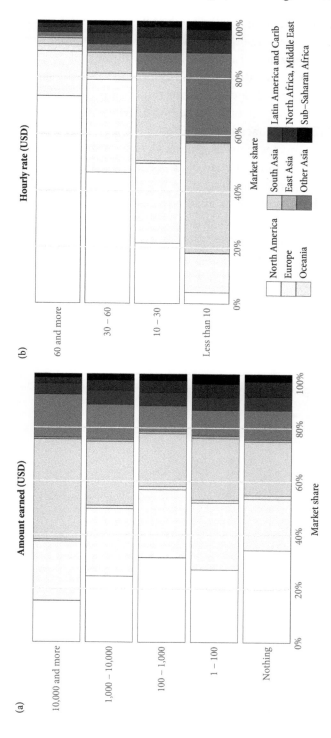

Fig. 3.11 Total amount and hourly rates earned on Upwork by world region
Source: Authors' calculations via web-scraping on Upwork in November 2018.

2017). However, a study done by Research ICT Africa across seven countries found that more women than men participated in remote work from Ghana, Kenya, Nigeria, and Tanzania, despite a significant gender divide in terms of internet access (Research ICT Africa, 2017).

We also scraped data of South African remote workers [3500 profiles or 25% workers] by total income earned on Upwork in November 2018 (Figure 3.12). We applied facial-recognition software on the workers' profile images to get estimates of users' gender. Details on the face-recognition algorithm can be found in Dehghan et al. (2017). The authors report high accuracy of their algorithm through having trained it on more than four million images from more than 40,000 individuals. The algorithm also reports confidence scores which help the user to assess the accuracy of the estimate. If the image is, for instance, of low resolution, the confidence score might be lower. The results do come with some uncertainty. To assess the uncertainty involved, the software reports probabilistic estimates of gender of the individuals on the profile images. In our case, the algorithm identifies the users' gender with high average confidence: the algorithm identified users as 'male' with a mean confidence of 94.8%, 'female' users with a confidence of 94%; for users identified as 'White' the

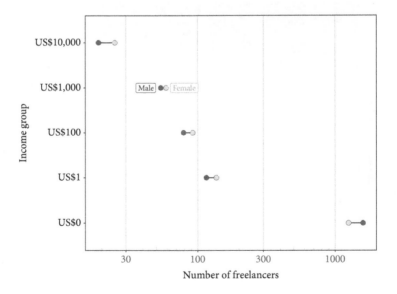

Fig. 3.12 Gender distribution in the South African remote gig economy

Source: Authors' calculations based on data from Upwork from November 2018.

mean confidence is 98.4%, for 'Black' users it is 91.1%, and it is 83.9% for 'Asian' users. Overall, the software provides outstanding results in image recognition. While this is not the ultimate method to identify someone's gender, it gives us some indication of gig economy's socio-economic distribution. Overall, we found slightly more male users (54 per cent) than female ones. But there are more women in the subset of users who successfully conducted projects on the platform: 54 per cent within the US$1+ and US$100+ groups, 52 per cent in the US$1,000+ group, and 56 per cent in the US$10,000+ group.

To gain insights into the racial composition of the gig economy workforce in Africa, we analysed South African workers' profiles in the high-income bracket on Upwork manually to understand who succeeded in earning a higher income. At the time of analysis in June 2019, ninety-one of the ninety-nine workers from South Africa, who had earned more than US$10,000 and worked over 1,000 hours, were white South Africans (person with lighter skin tone). Access to technology is lowest among the low-income groups or poor (Research ICT Africa, 2018), who often happen to be Black South Africans (persons with darker skin tones) (Statistics South Africa, 2014). Hence, they hardly succeed in earning high-income on platforms.

Contrastingly, White South Africans have better access to education and better material conditions (resulting from the institutional and political manipulations of the colonial and the apartheid regimes) than Black South Africans, who So, our categorization of remote workers in South Africa based on their racial categories is to highlight how race as an idea or a social construct and its political–economic application has inter-generational impacts in society and on inequality (also see Box 3.1). The point here is that the current socio-economic imbalances in South Africa are amplified in the new gig economy as well.

Box 3.1   Race and the gig economy

'Race' as a term is problematic and a highly contested category which evolved historically from theological justifications to scientific rationale and biological groupings (Meer 2014). In fact, the biological divide (between the whites and the Blacks) provided the intellectual [sic] justification for colonialism around the world and the scramble for Africa as well. Though there is no biological basis for race as a distinct category to categorize humans (Meer, 2014), yet, race as 'both

continued

Box 3.1 *continued*

a historical idea and a social category' continues to shape the power, politics, economies and societies around the world (Omi, 2001). As Howard Winant (2001: 1) observed that 'it [race] continues to signify and structure social life not only experientially and locally, but nationally and globally. Race is present everywhere: it is evident in the distribution of resources and power, and in the desires and fears of individuals from Alberta to Zimbabwe. Race has shaped the modern economy and the nation-state.'

As a matter of fact, the understanding of race as a social construct has been hotly debated for decades (Smaje, 1997; also see Coates, 2013; Hartigan Jr, 2008). Some have even highlighted that the issue of race has been sidelined in various sociological inquiries and other terms are used such as ethnicity (see Bhattcharya and Murji, 2013; Song, 2018). Song (2018: 1135), in fact, argues that the 'reluctance to use the term 'race', and the preference for 'ethnicity', as others too have argued, translates into an equivocation about race'.

Actually, the very nature of race as socially constructed that we use the term to understand the divisions that it continues to create in societies whether the term race is used in public discourse or not. The continuous brutality of law enforcement on Blacks in the US and the recent murder of George Floyd on 26 May 2020 have brought attention to the racial injustices in the country and beyond. Therefore, it is still very much appropriate to talk about race and race relations, especially in regions where a history of racial divisions has been at the heart of its politics, economy, culture, and society. This is the case of South Africa.

The fact that 'race' was used as a tool to create divisions in South Africa historically, does not mean that racial labels such as 'whites' or 'Blacks' are less important. Instead, we should make sure to highlight the implications of such social fractures in contemporary societies. This is nowhere better exemplified than South Africa, where European powers used race as a political tool to further their economic interests at expense of locals. In South Africa, the European colonization (Dutch and English) and the apartheid rule (also an extension of Europe) were built on racial divisions (inspired by the colour of the skins of certain groups of people): whites with lighter skin tone are superiors and people of colour with darker skin tones are savages. These divisions or segregation were enshrined in the constitution of pre-1994 South Africa. These two white-dominated racist, minority, and exploitative regimes left Blacks dispossessed of their land and other assets, maimed, traumatized, and politically, socially and economically marginalized. The effects of these two regimes can still be seen in the domestic political economy of post-apartheid South Africa with high-levels of poverty and unemployment among Blacks in comparison to other social groups such as Whites, Indians and Coloured (Statistics South Africa, 2014). Despite the establishment of democracy in 1994, which theoretically created more equal political opportunities, the material conditions of most Blacks have not improved substantially. A more balanced society is still in pursuit (a useful analysis is given in Bond, 2014). A recent study by Chatterjee et al (2020: 25) finds a lop-sided income and wealth distribution in the country and concluded 'there is no evidence that wealth concentration has decreased since apartheid'. (also see Bassier and Woolard, 2018, who argue that richest 1 per cent have seen an increasing income share). Another study by Bhorat and Khan (2018) found that wage inequality has increased since the end of apartheid with wages growing at about twice the rate for the highest percentile of the wage distribution in comparison to lower end group, which is primarily Black. Bhorat and Khan (2018) also concluded that race is a significant determinant of employment outcomes in South Africa and that Blacks are less likely to be employed than whites, a figure which has increased since 1995, though there has been a declining trend recently. Similarly, Gradín (2019) notes that labour markets remain segmented and segregated with Blacks disproportionately holding low-paying jobs (compared to whites).

Put differently, Blacks are discriminated in the labour markets both in terms of income and the occupation types. In fact, what we see in the context of the gig economy in South Africa is the trend towards further entrenchment of socio-economic inequalities. Those with material and social capital (mainly whites) continue to prosper and succeed on Upwork, while Blacks, the poorest segment in South Africa struggle.

This can also be explored further in other country contexts where racial divisions are historically present along the socio-economic or material opportunities (e.g. the UK and the US). In the UK, The Mcgregor-Smith Review found racial discrimination to be present in the labour market with Blacks and minorities only accounting for 10 per cent of the workforce and just 6 per cent of the top management position (McGregor-Smith, 2017). The review noted that 'in the UK today, there is a structural, historical bias that favours certain individuals'. Similarly, analysis done by the Trade Union Congress (TUC) found the Black and minority population continue to experience high-levels of unemployment and that between 2011 and 2016 Black workers in temporary contracts increased by 58% (TUC, 2017).

There is already some literature on the racial discrimination in the gig economy. Hannák et al. (2017) examined TaskRabbit and Fiverr to find that race (along with gender) is significantly correlated with worker evaluations, which could harm

continued

Box 3.1 *continued*

---

the employment opportunities afforded to the workers on these labour markets. They found that on Fiverr, Black and Asian workers received lower ratings than whites, while on TaskRabbit Black workers received lower ratings than white ones. Similar example of racial discrimination and bias was found on the Airbnb, where researchers found that distinctively African American names are 16 per cent less likely to be accepted relative to identical guests with distinctively white names (Edelman et al., 2017).

This brings us to an important question. How do these digital work activities affect African workers' lives and livelihoods? In Chapter 4, we will discuss job quality issues in the remote work and call centre work that we have discussed above.

Acknowledgements

This study was part of the bigger GeoNet project funded by the European Research Council 2013, ERC-2013-StG335716—GeoNet (see Graham et al., 2017a).

4

Digital Work, Human Labour, and Development

> Access to paid work is no guarantee of decent work.
>
> **(ILO, 2020c: 12)**

Work and Development

Employment is considered a central piece of the development puzzle. In recent times, numerous reports have come out from some of the leading international organizations on the theme of work and its importance for human development. These include the UNDP's 2015 Human Development Report on Work for Human Development and the World Bank's 2019c World Development Report on The Changing Nature of Work. From the African continent's point of view, the African Development Bank's 2012 African Economic Outlook had a special theme on 'Youth Employment in Africa'. For their 2018b and 2019 Outlooks, jobs featured as a separate chapter, and the latest 2020 Outlook is titled Developing Africa's Workforce for the Future. Highlighting the significance of jobs for development,[1] the World Bank's 2013 Report Jobs (2013a: 2) states:

> Jobs are the cornerstone of economic and social development. Indeed, development happens through jobs. People work their way out of poverty and hardship through better livelihoods. Economies grow as people get better at what they do, as they move from farms to firms, and as more productive jobs are created and less productive ones disappear. Societies flourish as jobs bring together

---

[1] The very notion of 'jobs' has been argued as overly restrictive and is often used in capitalistic terms of 'waged employment' (see Komlosy, 2018). But this fails to capture the many kinds of work experience that are more flexible and open-ended, and possibly unpaid (e.g. care, voluntary, and creative work) (UNDP, 2015). Hence, our use of the term 'jobs' and 'employment' includes paid, unpaid, formal, informal, waged, and non-waged forms of work. As we note in this book, digital jobs in many cases are informal and can be unpaid.

The Digital Continent. Mohammad Amir Anwar and Mark Graham, Oxford University Press.
© Mohammad Amir Anwar and Mark Graham (2022). DOI: 10.1093/oso/9780198840800.003.0004

people from different ethnic and social backgrounds and nurture a sense of opportunity. Jobs are thus transformational—they can transform what we earn, what we do, and even who we are.

Taking a broader view on work and human development, the UNDP's 2015 report further argues that:

> Work enables people to earn a livelihood and be economically secure. It is critical for equitable economic growth, poverty reduction and gender equality. It also allows people to fully participate in society while affording them a sense of dignity and worth. Work can contribute to the public good, and work that involves caring for others builds cohesion and bonds within families and communities.

> Work also strengthens societies. Human beings working together not only increase material well-being, they also accumulate a wide body of knowledge that is the basis for cultures and civilisations. And when all this work is environmentally friendly, the benefits extend across generations. Ultimately, work unleashes human potential, human creativity and the human spirit.

UNDP, 2015: 1

Despite growing international recognition of the role of work and development, numerous studies have pointed out deteriorating working conditions and labour standards in a variety of industries across the globe (e.g. Barker and Christensen, 1998; Bernards, 2018; Kalleberg, 2000, 2003, 2013; Lambert, 2008; Pai, 2012; Webster et al., 2009, 2016).[2] In 2019 the global working age population (i.e. aged 15 and above) stood at 5.7 billion, out of which 3.3 billion were employed (ILO, 2020c). However, the ILO's 2020c World Employment and Social Outlook argues that there are significant deficiencies in work quality around the world, and warns that the global labour income share has declined from 54 per cent in 2004 to 51 per cent in 2017. Thus, while more workers may be accessing jobs in the labour market, their work may be eroding their earning power.

Furthermore, there are over 2 billion workers employed in the informal sector, accounting for 61 per cent of the global workforce: a section of the population who are less likely to enjoy full rights and entitlements at

---

[2] The education sector is a key exemplar of the neoliberalization of universities and schools, primarily in the UK and the US, where employment contracts are often offered on a fixed-term or temporary basis (Archer, 2008; Berg et al., 2016; Olssen, 2016).

work or benefit from social protection measures (ILO, 2018). Some 635 million workers globally, i.e. a fifth of all workers, live in poverty.[3] The poor working conditions endured by a majority of the global workforce reflect the prevalence of non-standard employment relations in a diversity of workplaces (ILO, 2016, 2018, 2020c). Employers are increasingly offering workers fixed-term or temporary contracts, zero-hour contracts, casual work, using temporary staffing agencies and subcontractors to hire workers, and often misclassifying employees as self-employed (Kalleberg, 2000; Theodore, 2016; Vallas and Prenner, 2012; also see De Stefano, 2016 on misclassification in the ride-hailing sector).[4] In the European Union, the share of temporary employment stood at only 9 per cent in 1987 (ILO, 2016), rising to 14.1 per cent in 2018 (Eurostat, 2020). As a result, decent working conditions have become one of the main challenges faced by workers today.

In Africa, the economic growth promised by the 'Africa Rising' narrative (discussed in Chapter 2) has not been matched by job creation. While economic growth remained high on the continent between 2000 and 2014, much of this growth has been jobless (AU/OECD, 2018; Barrett et al., 2017). For the period 2000–08, employment only grew at an annual rate of about 2.8 per cent, and for 2009–14 it grew at 3.1 per cent; roughly half the rate of economic growth in the region (AfDB, 2018b). The African Development Bank's (AfDB) 2019 African Economic Outlook estimated that Africa's potential labour force will grow to one billion by 2030, and that to prevent unemployment from rising, the continent needs to create about 12 million new jobs every year during this period. The same report also highlighted that between 1.3 and 3 million jobs are lost every year (AfDB, 2019).

Regarding the nature of African labour markets, non-standard employment relations have been the norm for decades, despite some form of standard employment relations emerging towards the end of the last century (Meagher, 2016; Scully, 2016; Webster et al., 2009).[5] Estimates from

---

[3] Working poor refers to people who earn less than US$1.90 per day at purchasing power parity (i.e. the standard international poverty line).

[4] The definition of casual employment varies. Generally speaking, casual work is stipulated for a short period of time (hours or days) and in some countries like the UK takes the form of zero-hour contracts.

[5] The term 'standard employment' is used to describe work that is full time, indefinite, and may also include a set workplace that is outside the home. Hence, work that falls outside the purview of the standard employment relationship can be understood as non-standard (see ILO, 2016). The ILO (2016: 7) considers four types of employment relationships as non-standard: temporary employment, part-time work, temporary agency work, other forms of employment involving multiple parties, disguised

the ILO suggest that while the labour force participation rate has increased on the continent (albeit only marginally between 2000 and 2017), many workers have been absorbed by the informal sectors of the economy—that is, those which are characterized by low-pay, insecure contracts, and poor working conditions (ILO, 2017b, 2018; see Box 4.1). One in four Kenyan employees is casual, and temporary employment represents over half of the Ethiopian workforce. The use of fixed-term contracts has also grown in South Africa and Morocco (ILO, 2016). Unsurprisingly, the continent has the highest proportion of the working population classified as 'working poor' (ILO, 2020c). An estimated 53.9 per cent of workers live in poverty on the continent, compared to 18.8 per cent in the Asia-Pacific region (ILO, 2020c). This roughly equates to 245 million African workers living in poverty, or 38 per cent of the world's working poor (ILO, 2020c). The AfDB has also reported that the continent has the highest share of people employed in low-skilled jobs and the lowest shares employed in medium- and high-skilled jobs globally (AfDB, 2020). Responding to these grim figures, national policymakers and international organizations have made a priority of creative solutions for job creation and improvement of working conditions for the continent's quickly growing workforce. It is at this moment that many look to the digital economy as a panacea for the region's chronic unemployment and informality.

Box 4.1   Ambiguity in defining the informal sector and informal employment

Much ink has been spilled over the years on the issue of conceptualizing, defining, and measuring the informal economy (Hart, 1973, 1985; ILO, 1993a, 2013, 2016; Sengenberger, 2011; also Hoskyns and Rai, 2007; Rakowski, 1994); on the politics of statistics: Desrosières, 2002; Dorling and Simpson, 1998; Linsi and Mügge, 2019). While the term 'informal economy' first appeared in the 1972 ILO report, also known as the Kenya Report (ILO, 1972), Keith Hart, an anthropologist, is credited with coining the term (Hart, 1973). Hart described the low-income economic activities among migrants in Accra who could not find waged employment elsewhere. The ILO's Kenya Report (1972) argues that much of these activities exist

---

employment relationships, and dependent self-employment (also see Barker and Christensen, 1998; Barley and Kunda, 2006 on contingent employment). These employment relationships are commonly found in the gig economy (see De Stefano, 2016).

'largely outside of the system of government benefits and regulations' and hence could be categorized as 'illegal'. But the term attracted mixed reviews in scholarly circles. The neat mapping and distinction between informal and formal sectors is a problem. Workers in the formal economy supplement their incomes by engaging in informal work (see Meagher 2016). As a result, the boundaries between formal and informal intersect in various settings and remain blurred. Hart himself has been critical of the way the concept was taken up and argues that now 'the term informal says what these activities are not, but not what they are' (Hart, 2009: 6; also Hart, 2006). Nonetheless, various definitions and criteria are used to define terms like the 'informal sector' and 'informal employment'. For example, the ILO has adopted different definitions over the years to standardize these concepts, from the early usage of the terms like 'traditional sector' (as opposed to the 'modern sector'), 'disguised employment', and 'employment in the informal sector' (Bangasser, 2000; Benanav, 2019).

There are three key concepts used by the ILO. First is the informal sector, which primarily concerns the characteristics of production units (firm or enterprise-based concept). Hence, the informal economy refers to all economic activities by workers and economic units that are in law or in practice not covered or insufficiently covered by formal arrangements (ILO, 2015: 4). The definition excludes illicit activities. Second is informal employment, which focuses on characteristics of jobs, and the third is employment in the informal economy, that is, the total employment in the informal sector and informal employment which is outside the informal sector. The ILO refers to informal employment as work arrangements that are de facto or de jure not subject to national labour legislation, income taxation, or entitlement to social protection or certain other employment benefits, such as advance notice of dismissal, severance pay, paid annual or sick leave (see ILO, 2018). The common criteria used to define informal jobs are: lack of coverage by the social security system; lack of entitlement to paid, annual, or sick leave; and lack of a written employment contract. Informal employment is also included as a statistical indicator in the UN Sustainable Development Goals (8.3.1) (available at https://unstats.un.org/sdgs/metadata/files/Metadata-08-03-01.pdf, accessed 2.8.21).

Many countries have attempted to align their definitions and operationalization of these terms based on their own criteria (see OECD/ILO, 2019) and some have aligned these to the standards of the ILO (e.g. South Africa), even though local contexts may not fit well (Posel et al., 2014; on challenges of measuring informality, see Stuart et al., 2018). In India, the National Commission for Enterprises in the Unorganised Sector (NCEUS) defines the informal sector as 'all

continued

Box 4.1 *continued*

---

unincorporated private enterprises owned by individuals or households engaged in the sale and production of goods and services operated on a proprietary or partnership basis and with less than ten total workers' (NCEUS, 2008: 2). The NCEUS defines informal employment thus: 'Informal workers consist of those working in the informal sector or households, excluding regular workers with social security benefits provided by the employers, and the workers in the formal sector without any employment or social security benefits provided by the employers' (NCEUS, 2008: 2). Then there are different organizations within India that have their own definitions such as the National Sample Survey Organisation (NSSO), which makes estimation on the size and scope of informality in India extremely difficult. However, some have estimated that about 90 per cent of workers in India are informally employed (ILO, 2018).

The South African case is quite peculiar, considering its history of racial segregation and the unequal access to paid work for different racial groups. In the immediate post-apartheid period, its key labour market indicators (e.g. the unemployment indicator) were broad and captured a better picture of the scale and characteristics of unemployment in the country. But the ruling African National Congress (ANC), sees the expanded definition as counterproductive to its political ambition. The expanded definition points to the dire labour market positions of the Black South Africans and ANC's failure to address inequalities in the country since 1994. An estimated 34 per cent of the country's workforce are in informal employment and Black South Africans have the highest unemployment rates among all racial groups. During the 2000s, the ANC began to align itself with the narrower definitions of the ILO, which does not capture the full extent of the unemployment contexts in South Africa. Statistics South Africa, the office for national statistics, which has faced backlash in the past over its use of the narrow definition, has more recently begun to include expanded definitions in its publications (see Alenda-Demoutiez and Mügge, 2020).

Digital Jobs and Development

The emergence of information economy activities on the African continent has been perceived by policymakers and development practitioners as a silver bullet for solving the continent's many socio-economic problems, including joblessness and poverty (Kuek et al., 2015; UNDP, 2015, 2016; World Bank, 2016). Following this view, digital jobs are considered as an alternative to traditional forms of employment, and various tasks, including essay/article writing, proofreading, graphic design, video editing, ride-hailing services, deliveries, and customer service work all receive an overly positive assessment in terms of the socio-economic prospects for African workers (Kuek et al., 2015; UNDP, 2016; World Bank, 2016). Yet, many of these new digital jobs have also emerged in other parts of the world (Kässi and Lehdonvirta, 2018), where they are characterized by low-pay and insecurity in high-income contexts and countries where standard employment relations are common, for example in the European Union (see Berg, 2016; De Stefano, 2016; Huws et al., 2017). While a large body of work examining the developmental impacts of various forms of digital labour has emerged from high-income countries' perspectives—highlighting its potential and constraints for workers (Cant, 2019; Gray and Suri, 2019; Holland and Brewster, 2020; Ravenelle, 2019; Scholz, 2016; Shibata, 2019; Tassinari and Maccarrone, 2019, van Doorn, 2017; Woodcock, 2020a)—there is a lack of critical scholarly work engaging with African digital labour.

An important aspect of this neglect is the fact that Africa as a region, as well as its workers, is not necessarily considered to be central to the global information economy. Our previous research has shown this is not the case, and that African workers are increasingly playing a key role in digital capitalism (Anwar and Graham, 2020b). For example, the training of artificial intelligence, machine learning, offshore customer services, search engine optimization, business consulting, data management, and graphic design are some of the services that African workers are already providing to the world economy. More importantly, as more and more segments of the African population get access to mobile phone technologies and the internet, there will be many more people joining the world of digital work.

However, the digital nature of work in the global information economy means it can be relocated with relative ease, making regulation difficult, and hence digital jobs might represent the geographical expansion of informality at multiple scales. As the African labour force is increasingly drawn into digital economy production networks, there may be genuine benefits for African workers (e.g. wages) but there are also concerns about the kind of employment relations and working conditions these digital jobs will bring. Undeniably, job creation is critical for development in Africa (AfDB, 2018b; ILO, 2018; Kawar, 2011; World Bank, 2013, 2019c). But in the context of dysfunctional labour markets and rampant poverty in Africa, there is also a need to move beyond the reliance on job growth and an overly optimistic narrative of digital jobs to properly understand the implications of digital labour on African workers. Examining job quality can give us a better picture of the development implications of the new world of digital work.

Job Quality in Digital Work

In recent decades a large body of work has developed on the quality of work (European Commission, 2001; Fernández-Macías and Hurley, 2017; Gallie, 2009; Green, 2006; ILO, 1999; Rubery and Grimshaw, 2001; Visser, 2019). The ILO in particular argues that in the context of low-income countries, where workers may struggle to find work and have few choices available, employment figures that look encouragingly high might mask a deterioration of working conditions (ILO, 2014)—hence, a better route to a country's development is to generate high quality jobs. Job quality was further adopted by the ILO under its 'Decent Work' programme and later included in 2015 as one of the UNDP's Sustainable Development Goals.[6]

Job quality is understood to be multidimensional, and various factors can influence what constitute a good or a bad job (de Bustillo et al., 2011; Findlay et al., 2013 Kalleberg, 2013). For example, some workers report higher levels of job satisfaction despite being on zero-hour contracts (see CIPD, 2015; Financial Times, 2015), and unionized workers report being less satisfied with their jobs than non-unionized workforce (Bessa et al., 2020). Put simply, the issue around job quality is between subjective and objective aspects of good or bad work (Brown et al., 2012; Dolan et al., 2008; Findlay et al., 2013; Kalleberg, 2013).

Scholars have long emphasized both the economic and non-economic characteristics of work (Green, 2006; Kalleberg, 2013). The ILO's (2019) definition of decent work includes adequate earnings, sociable working time, job security, work/family time, workplace safety, and social protection. Similarly, issues around compensation, skills levels, autonomy, work

[6] The ILO's Decent Work Agenda is a rights-based approach with a set of standardized indicators. The Decent Work Agenda has four important strategic objectives: rights at work, employment, social protection, and social dialogue (Ghai, 2003; ILO, 1999). Criticisms of this approach include its co-option by elite institutions, lack of clarity on why non-decent working conditions exist, and its inability to fully consider the role of the systemic exploitation that is characteristic of capitalist social relations (see Selwyn, 2013: 81–82). Relatedly, there are concerns about its utility for the informal sector. For example, 'social dialogue' among informal workers and representation takes place through informal networks and associations, rather than the trades unions of the formal sectors (Lindell, 2013).

intensity, the extent of control over one's work, stress, and employment terms and conditions are also noted to impact job quality (Osterman, 2013). For Kalleberg (2013), job quality depends on economic compensation (earnings and fringe benefits), and non-economic rewards such as the degree of job security and opportunities for advancement to better jobs, the degree of control over work and non-work activities, and the experience of a meaningful job. Kalleberg argues that the (non-)provision of these economic compensations and non-economic benefits can influence job quality.

Although there continues to be a debate on their applicability in low- and middle-income countries (Burchell et al., 2014), certain key aspects of job quality are considered transferable and are generally understood to differentiate between good and bad jobs (Green, 2006; Kalleberg, 2013). As Rubery and Grimshaw (2001) have noted, job quality is not only a concern for skilled jobs in high-income countries but also for low-skill jobs and low-income countries. The challenge for researchers is in conceptualizing, characterizing, and measuring job quality (Kalleberg, 2013), especially when dealing with different socio-political and economic contexts.

Considering that many low-income countries have seen an increase in non-standard employment and rising informalization in labour markets (ILO, 2018, 2020c), examining job quality is critical. Some studies have investigated job quality in low- and middle-income countries (Burchell et al., 2014; Monteith and Giesbert, 2017). Monteith and Giesbert (2017) found that income, health, and autonomy and social contact are valued by informal workers in Uganda, Sri Lanka, and Burkina Faso, factors which are also crucial for job quality in richer parts of the world. Their research shows that job quality in low- and middle-income countries is influenced by socio-environmental conversion factors such as the cost and availability of education and health care, the division of domestic labour, economic competition, market [de]regulation, and gender and class relations.

Here, we are also mindful that investigating the quality of work requires close attention to the types of work tasks undertaken, their geographical and temporal contexts, and personal positionalities (Brown et al., 2012; Holman, 2013). For example, during the time of the 2008 global financial crisis, a sales worker in Southern California (who had been made redundant) was quoted as saying that 'there are no bad jobs now. Any job is a good job' (quoted in Kalleberg, 2013: 9). Similarly, in the video games industry, workers earn high incomes but have little separation between work and leisure (Bulut, 2015). Put differently, a worker may experience various outcomes of a good job but can achieve low levels of wellbeing (Monteith and Giesbert, 2017).

In the context of the digital labour that we described in Chapter 3, another important factor influencing job quality outcomes is the use of digital technologies in the organization of production and labour processes (Rubery and Grimshaw, 2001). There are many accounts of technologies being used to control and organize work, and which outline high levels of workplace monitoring and surveillance (Crowley et al., 2010; Giordano, 2016; Holland and Brewster, 2020; Melachrinoudis and Olafsson, 1995; Moore, et al., 2017; Taylor and Bain, 2005). This highlights a Taylorist control of work that subjects workers to detailed performance measurement and puts them under the intense pressure of an 'electronic panopticon' (Fernie and Metcalf, 1998; for a critique see Bain and Taylor, 2000) or 'electronic sweatshop' (Garson, 1988). Even in call and contact centre operations, where some home-based agents handle customer calls and queries, companies use software and electronic tools to control and monitor workers (see Shellenbarger, 2008). Though a large proportion of these accounts originate in the BPO industry, they have applicability in modern workplaces as well. For example, Amazon warehouses have been at the centre of controversy on intense monitoring of workers through tracking wristbands (Solon, 2018; Spicer, 2018).[7] Similar accounts can be found in more recent studies on gig economy activities where working remotely or from home is common. Wood et al. (2019), for example, find that gig work platforms exert digital control through algorithmic management of the labour process, which in turn affects the autonomy of workers. Rani and Furrer (2020) in their study of 675 workers in twenty-seven low- and middle-income countries found that algorithmic management of labour processes on digital work platforms shaped their working conditions, primarily concerning remuneration and working hours (also Anwar and Graham, 2020a, 2020c). Algorithmic management of labour processes is becoming integral to contemporary digital production networks and many other forms of economic activity, controlling all aspects of work and labour process (Möhlmann and Zalmanson, 2017; Moore et al., 2017), inspiring some observers to talk of a new 'digital Taylorism' (The Economist, 2015a). Our argument in this chapter is that the (non-)provision of both economic and non-economic

---

[7] More recently, during the COVID-19 pandemic, Amazon has been censoring employees by monitoring their activities on social media for evidence of activism (Sainato, 2020).

rewards (Kalleberg, 2013), technological control of labour processes (Gandini, 2019), and the various political–economic and socio-cultural contexts in which the work gets done all determine job quality outcomes. We focus here on seven key job quality indicators, namely income, autonomy at work, worker power, freedom of association, socio-economic inclusion, skills and mobility, and labour agency.

Income, or job earnings, is considered to be a fairly reliable indicator of job quality (Clark, 2005; European Commission, 2001; Ginzberg, 1979; Green, 2006; ILO, 1999; Nadler and Lawler, 1983; Rosenthal, 1989; Tilly, 1997). Kalleberg (2013), in distinguishing between good and bad jobs, highlighted that good jobs usually involve high earnings, offer opportunities for salary increment over time, and provide fringe benefits. One of the measures of the United Nations Human Development Index is income per capita, given this provides workers with the freedom to achieve well-being and positive development outcomes such as access to food, clothing, and housing (Sen, 2001). In a number of recent studies on digital labour around the world, income has been considered a key element of job quality (e.g. Anwar and Graham, 2020a; Berg et al., 2018; Kessler, 2018; Rani and Furrer, 2020).

Autonomy at work can be understood as discretion and control over tasks and working hours, which is considered critical for work quality (Lin et al., 2013; Reinardy, 2014). In digital jobs, worker autonomy is influenced both by the forms of work organization (e.g. subcontracting and commodification) and by the use of technologies in the organization of that work (Gandini, 2019). BPO work has long been characterized as 'an assembly line in the head' because of the standardized and repetitive nature of the work and the expectation that workers will adhere to strictly set work schedules or risk the cancellation of contracts and non-payment of wages (Taylor and Bain, 1999). Gig work rests on similar principles (Graham and Anwar, 2019) and thus worker autonomy can be compromised. In fact, while there is some evidence that workers actually gain some autonomy in the gig economy, they are in practice rarely able to exercise their power over employers, such as by Uber drivers and workers on Amazon Mechanical Turk (Lehdonvirta, 2016; Möhlmann and Zalmanson, 2017).

Worker power is affected by modern-day technologies in various ways (Silver, 2003). Worker power, here, refers to the ability of workers to gain an advantageous position in the system vis-à-vis employers (Kalleberg, 2013: 31; also see Schmalz et al., 2018). Two key forms of power are structural power and associational power (Silver, 2003; Wright, 2000). Structural power can be further divided into marketplace bargaining power (i.e. power derived by workers due to tight labour markets and shortage of skills) and workplace bargaining power (i.e. power derived through the position of workers in the production process) (Silver, 2003). Both these types of structural power can lead to some positive outcomes such as class compromise with employers (Pahle, 2014), though these powers can be compromised for workers in digital jobs. In the gig economy, platforms provide employers with access to a potentially global pool of workers, and can also eliminate geographical barriers to labour process management and managerial control. This can adversely affect workers' marketplace bargaining power because there is global competition for work; that is surplus labour creates a global race to the bottom. Algorithmic control via platforms also influences workplace bargaining power. For workers in the BPO industry, this power is affected by the nature and type of the operations (inbound vs outbound and captive vs hybrid) and the structures of the local labour markets, which are themselves shaped by what Peck (1996) refers to as the production–reproduction dialectic and the regulatory dialectic.[8] For example, BPO workers in India are able to move within the industry, and beyond it (Vira and James, 2012). By contrast, South African BPO workers find their opportunities constrained due to the small size of the industry, a non-unionized workforce, and dysfunctional labour markets which make it hard for workers to find jobs (Anwar and Graham, 2019).

Freedom of association is the individual and collective right for workers to join a group and leave it. It is enshrined in the ILO's Declaration on Fundamental Principles and Rights at Work. Associational power by workers is achieved by being part of organizations; typically trades unions that can serve as a front for collective action, which can take place at multiple scales (Schmalz et al., 2018). Trades unions in Africa have long been central in the struggle against colonialism, apartheid, and structural adjustment programmes (Beckman et al., 2010; Cooper, 1996; Mboya, 1956; Orr, 1966; Pfeffermann, 1967; Rizzo, 2013; Southall, 1988; Webster, 2015), and have also recently mobilized against dictatorships in North Africa (Beinin, 2015; Bishara, 2018; Feltrin, 2019; Hartshorn, 2019). However, union membership is in decline not just across the continent (Steyn, 2014;

---

[8] The production–reproduction dialectic can be understood as an interaction between the structures and processes of labour supply (reproduction) and demand (production). The regulatory dialectic means institutional forms and functions that influence the structures of labour markets, which are geographically unique (see Peck, 1996).

Times Live, 2015) but also globally (Topping, 2017; Kopf, 2019).[9] In the US, union membership has declined from a peak of 20 million workers in 1979 to 14.5 million in 2013; and in Britain the corresponding figures are 12 million and 6.5 million (The Economist, 2015b). In response, von Holdt and Webster (2008) argue that the weakening of structural power of workers should be compensated with associational and symbolic power to develop new forms of labour movements.[10] Workers have long used symbolic power in combination with associational power as a powerful means to articulate moral issues in order to build wider public pressure and generate social movements (on symbolic power, see Chun, 2009).

In the remote gig economy, workers may use alternative spaces to express their associational and symbolic power, including social media networks (Anwar and Graham, 2020b), which have become a front for informal organization (Schradie, 2015, 2018). The use of Facebook groups has lately emerged as an important outlet for individuals to seek support from other workers or signal a need for assistance with a task (Beuhler et al., 2019; Otieno et al., 2020). There are already multiple Facebook communities of African digital workers with thousands of members, and these are critical for understanding workers' expanding spaces for mobilization, sense of belonging, and socio-economic inclusion in society (Anwar and Graham, 2020c).

Socio-economic inclusion is a commitment of the United Nations 2013 report on A New Global Partnership in development policy, together with a determination to 'leave no one behind' (United Nations, 2013). Similarly, in their 2016 World Development Report, the World Bank (2016) puts its weight behind digital jobs and their potential for economic inclusion particularly for the workers in the informal sector.[11] Considering the rise in joblessness in Africa, digital jobs can be a catalyst for the inclusion of workers from certain demographics (e.g. women and migrants, who make

---

[9] The highest trades union densities in Africa, defined as the share of employees who are union members, are found in Egypt at 43.2%, South Africa at 28.1%, and Ghana at 20.1%. By contrast, in some Scandinavian countries such as Denmark and Sweden, union density is well over 65% (data from ILOSTAT).

[10] But symbolic power can also be used differently as opposed to peaceful movements—for example the case of South African Post Office (SAPO) workers mobilization, which used violence and intimidation instead of articulating moral issues Dickinson (2017).

[11] Buoyed by the figures on population surge and digital jobs, international organizations such as the World Bank, African Development Bank, OECD, and UNDP have shared optimism over the development role of informal employment in Africa. For example, the World Bank's (2013a) World Development Report noted that informal jobs can be transformational and the African Development Bank's African Economic Outlook (AfDB et al., 2012), argued that that the informal sector can generate entrepreneurial spirit and job creation.

up a large share of the informal economy around the world) who may be excluded from their local labour markets. Certainly, many types of new digital jobs have enabled workers in Africa to participate in new labour markets (Graham et al., 2017) and importantly, enhance their skills and mobility (Anwar and Graham, 2020a).

Skills and mobility are closely related to each other (Wen and Maani, 2018) and influence job quality (European Commission, 2012, 2019).[12] As the world economy moves towards knowledge-intensive production, there is an increasing demand for workers with a particular set of skills and educational training. Simply put, the digital economy is dependent on a skilled workforce. There is therefore an incentive for policymakers in low- and middle-income regions like Africa to place an emphasis on transforming the national education system to offer skills development and enhance workforce mobility. Here, skills development refers to gaining tacit and explicit knowledge about work and technical skills that can enable workers' upward mobility in their professions (e.g. Campbell et al., 1991; Green et al., 2002; Vira and James, 2011). Labour mobility in the most basic sense refers to the movement of workers both geographically across the space (geographical mobility) and across a set of jobs (occupational mobility) (Long and Ferrie, 2003).

Participation in the digital economy may generate livelihoods but there can be hidden dangers. Workers can suffer from an 'opportunity trap', where they join the global knowledge economy in order to further their careers but find that the intense competition hinders their progression up the job ladder (Brown, 2003). Take for example, BPO jobs, considered to be ideal for the tech-savvy twenty-first-century youth. But BPOs are also flat organizations and prospects for entry-level workers to progress to managerial positions are few (Beerepoot and Hendriks, 2013; Benner, 2006). In the gig economy, learning and skills development can be highly self-regulated, which means opportunities for developing careers are few and far between (Margaryan, 2019a, 2019b). Importantly, platforms can reduce social mobility, as the short-term nature of jobs could become 'traps', rather than 'bridges' into permanent or more regular work (Lehdonvirta et al., 2019).

---

[12] Skills development is a key component in job quality research (Felstead et al., 2019; Green, 2006). The ILO has argued that 'learning new skills, upgrading existing ones and lifelong learning can all help workers to maintain their employability and enterprises to adapt and remain competitive' (ILO, 2010: 18). However, see Moore (2018) on how the quantification of tacit skills and attitudes of workers can lead to increased labour control.

Worker mobility has a geographical dimension too (Eliasson et al., 2003; Hackl, 2018; McGrath, 2013). South African job seekers, for example, face both economic and spatial barriers to work—and their restricted geographical mobility, including high cost of transportation costs, can act to deter work seekers (Graham et al., 2019). Recognizing the benefits of free movement of people, the African Union adopted a Free Movement Protocol in 2018 (African Union, 2018). Unfortunately, it has yet to achieve recognition by all members, and therefore faces further problems in realizing African Union passports.[13] For workers, both types of labour mobility (geographical and occupational) can enable material improvements, political participation, and collective organization (Smith, 2006), all of which provide them with some agency to influence their working conditions.

Labour agency as a concept has a long pedigree in labour geography, with much written about its effects on working conditions (Cumbers et al., 2008, 2010; Featherstone and Griffin, 2016; Herod, 1997, 2001; Katz, 2004; Oseland et al., 2012; Pratten, 1993). In this book we argue that worker actions are both constrained and enabled by the social, cultural, and political structures around them (Coe and Jordhus-Lier, 2011). From this theoretical standpoint, there is a need to consider not only workers' collective actions through unions but also their individual actions (Rogaly, 2009). These individual actions can take the form of everyday resistance practices (Scott, 1985; also, Abu-Lughod, 1990). However, Katz (2004) argues that not every autonomous act is an act of resistance, but rather that there exists a variety of oppositional practices.[14]

Resistance, according to Katz (2004: 251), requires 'a critical consciousness to confront and redress historically and geographically specific conditions of oppression and exploitation'. For Ackroyd and Thompson (1999), resistance can also include misbehaviour and counterproductive practices towards work itself, and the use of work material for non-work purposes. Thus, resistance can be seen as both the direct and indirect confrontation of workers to management, including challenging and subverting exploitative production regimes. Worker actions such as strikes and demonstrations are more direct forms of resistance, while indirect confrontations include wage negotiations. As employment relations become more contingent, and the

---

[13] Only a quarter of countries in the African Union allow visa-free travel for people from other African countries (Maru, 2019).

[14] There are other forms of workplace deviance or aggression such as theft (Greenberg, 1990; see also Lawrence and Robinson, 2007); and sabotage (Ambrose et al., 2002).

workforce becomes less organized, workers complement resistance with resilience and reworking strategies to maximize their chances of survival.

Resilience refers to small acts of 'getting by' or coping with everyday realities without necessarily changing existing social relations (Katz, 2004: 244).[15] These acts include autonomous initiatives like education, training, and taking care of community members, and may therefore be neither progressive nor transformative. Workers also complement these with 're-working efforts' in an attempt to redistribute resources and power by recalibrating oppressive and unequal power relations to improve their material conditions. Katz understood reworking as focused and pragmatic responses to problematic conditions faced by people. For example, workers might subcontract the work of one client to their friends while they finish a second job themselves (see Graham and Anwar, 2018b).

In the digital jobs that we describe in this book, these everyday practices of resistance, resilience, and reworking by workers will be critical for job quality. While worker actions in the workplace or the site of production are well known, in the gig economy work gets done remotely, and workers and employers are rarely in the same location (Graham and Anwar, 2018a, 2019). In the gig economy, collective organization and unionization are therefore largely absent (Lehdonvirta, 2016), except in some place-based work (see Aslam and Woodcock, 2020; Tassinari and Maccarrone, 2017; Woodcock, 2020a). However, gig workers have been devising new ways of resisting the constraints of their work and attempting to form communities on social media (see Anwar and Graham, 2019; Wood et al., 2018). Here, the use of digital tools in the forms of new communication channels, such as Facebook groups, can influence workers' agency practices. An important point to note here is that these practices vary and are shaped by workers' socio-economic backgrounds, positionality, and the types of work they do (Carswell and De Neve, 2013).

Development Dimensions in Digital Jobs: A Heuristic Framework

By studying these job quality aspects, we are able to examine how digital jobs contribute to African workers' lives and livelihoods. We analysed the

---

[15] For some, resilience can mean putting up with precarious livelihoods and inequality in society, and relocating the responsibility for well-being and change onto the individual (see Diprose, 2014).

developmental impacts of digital jobs through the twin lenses of freedom and flexibility, and precarity and vulnerability. We expand on these below.

Freedom and Flexibility

Digital jobs are seen to hold considerable potential for development in Africa (Rockefeller Foundation, 2013a, 2013b; UNDP, 2015, 2016, 2019; World Bank, 2016). The Rockefeller Foundation's Digital Jobs Africa Initiative identified both online work and 'impact sourcing'[16] as a way to solve unemployment on the continent. It argues:

> [T]he digital economy holds significant potential for creating formal jobs that are accessible to historically marginalized youth. These 'digital jobs' – defined as any short-term or permanent positions that use information technology to deliver a product or service – are in the formal sector and therefore provide higher wages and long-term job stability, which are two key mechanisms that enable people to work their way out of poverty.
>
> **Rockefeller Foundation, 2013a: 3**

In the expectation that digital jobs will act as 'a pathway out of poverty' for many of the continent's unemployed (Rockefeller Foundation, 2013a), the Digital Jobs Africa Initiative has invested nearly US$100 million in skills training in order to 'impact one million lives'. Several governments are also touting the development potential of gig work and have undertaken policy-level interventions of their own to promote it. The Nigerian government in partnership with the Rockefeller Foundation set up the Naija Cloud initiative to promote gig work. The Kenyan Government introduced the Ajira Digital Programme in late 2016. Recently, Egypt has launched its own programme to train youths for digital jobs (ITIDA, 2020).

In addition to tackling unemployment, the digital economy is often described as providing both freedom and flexibility to workers (Kuek et al., 2015; Rockefeller Foundation, 2013a; Solutions for Youth Employment (S4YE), 2018). Gary Swart, the former CEO of O-Desk (now Upwork, a digital labour market), has stated that:

---

[16] Impact sourcing is the socially responsible arm of traditional outsourcing, where businesses target historically disadvantaged youth for employment. How these individuals are identified as disadvantaged is not clear.

with the Internet increasingly enabling popular work approaches such as telecommuting, distributed teams, online work, and even entirely virtual companies, both businesses and workers are finding more freedom and flexibility to work whenever, however and with whomever they like.

Swart, 2013

In a survey conducted by O-Desk with online freelancers, it was found that 89 per cent of respondents valued the freedom and flexibility that comes with freelancing, and 72 per cent were willing to quit their regular jobs (Schawbel, 2013).[17] Furthermore, a World Bank-commissioned report (Kuek et al., 2015: 39) found that besides income generation and flexible working conditions, remote work enables workers to 'develop skills and progress professionally' (Kuek et al., 2015: 4). Similarly, the Rockefeller Foundation (2014) has portrayed gig work as a disruptive innovation for African youths, which:

offers significant income earning potential for those who can successfully navigate the platforms. For employees, particularly young people, online work provides a low-barrier-to-entry opportunity to earn an income, while building their skills and digital work experience.

Indeed, digital economy jobs have received much media hype and corporate backing recently, driven largely by the ICT revolution currently taking place in Africa.[18] However, there are a number of problems with such expectations around digital economy jobs, both globally and for African workers in particular. One such problem is assertions that digital work brings a welcome freedom and flexibility to a worker are loaded with the language of neoliberalism (Holborow, 2015; also Massey, 2013).[19]

Polanyi (2001) has argued that in a market-based society, meanings of freedom become complicated. On the one hand, a market-based society provides capital with the freedom to exploit labour, the freedom to accumulate inordinate amounts of wealth, and the freedom to prevent sharing

---

[17] O-Desk merged with Elance in 2013 to create the world's largest online work platform, Upwork.

[18] There are various ambitious initiatives in Africa for creating digital jobs. The Mastercard Foundation has a US$200 million programme for job creation (Mastercard Foundation, 2019) and IBM has a US$70 million programme for building digital skills (IBM, 2017). The African Development Bank has the Coding for Employment Programme, from which it expects to create 9 million jobs (AfDB, 2018a).

[19] Neoliberalism refers to the political economic framework that rest on the principles of free market and free trade, i.e. fewer government interventions in the operations of the market (see Harvey, 2005). A critique of neoliberalism as a term and a concept is given in Venugopal (2015).

of technological gains for public benefit, which Polanyi refers to as bad free-dom. On the other hand, a market economy also provides freedoms that are good, such as freedom of speech and the freedom to choose one's own job, for example.[20] However, the 'good freedom' offered by the market economy to society can also threaten to disrupt—for example through worker collec-tive action—capital's push towards a liberal utopianism, i.e. a market free from government intervention (Harvey, 2005). Hence, for advocates of a free market society (e.g. the World Bank) the individual freedom of work-ers is given more importance than freedom of association and collective action (Neff, 2012). As we shall see in the following chapters, digital jobs are becoming highly atomized, commoditized, and in many cases lack col-lective bargaining. As a result, the alleged freedom in digital work becomes problematic. Our argument here is that the new market-based principles and contingent employment relations found in the world of digital work are being used to great effect in restricting freedom of association of work-ers in the global digital economy, and are also shifting risk from capital to labour.

There is no doubt that digital jobs offer employment opportunities for workers (both in Africa and in other low- and middle-income regions) and provide them with much-needed livelihoods, and we recognize this as one of the most important contributions of digital jobs to African work-ers' lives (Anwar and Graham, 2020a, 2020b; Graham and Anwar, 2018a, 2019). In essence, these jobs offer workers considerable freedom to achieve personal goals and well-being (Sen, 2001). Alongside the provision of in-come, there are also benefits to digital workers in the form of flexible working. The World Bank's World Development Report on 'Digital Div-idends' also argues that flexible working hours are the main advantage of online outsourcing work for women, young people, and older people (World Bank, 2016: 108), despite the relatively poor wages and lack of future prospects. The 2015 United Nations Human Development Report (UNDP, 2015) made a similar point on flexibility at work associated with information economy activities. However, it also raises the concern that for digital workers who are already living in poverty, the distinction between work and personal life will be challenging since it is never clear to them when the next work opportunity will come their way.

---

[20] China is an interesting example here, with a market-based economy, but freedom of expression being curtailed by the government.

With non-standard work arrangements gaining in popularity among businesses, firms are increasingly offering temporary, part-time, and remote work arrangements (Barley and Kunda, 2006; Huws, 2013). Some see these flexible work arrangements as key to attaining multiple life choices, offering freedom from corporate hierarchies, and facilitating social innovation (Coenen and Kok, 2014; Howe, 2009). Policy and legislative reforms have been created (e.g. in the EU) to facilitate the use of temporary employment, which has further increased labour market flexibility (ILO, 2016). However, much of the mainstream literature has tended to understand and define the idea of flexibility from the perspective of firms and not workers. The European Commission's (2007) concept of 'flexicurity' is a good example. Building on the idea that flexibility in work arrangements and security in job transitions should not be seen as opposites but as complementary, flexicurity is seen as an integrated strategy to bring flexibility and security to the labour market. Though an ambitious idea, it has its limitations. What is regarded as flexible for firms may not be flexible from workers' perspectives. It also depoliticizes the relationship between capital and labour, individualizes social protection, and increases risk for workers (Keune and Serrano, 2014)—an important example of neoliberalism's drive to restore the power of capital over labour. In other words, flexible working arrangements can act to transfer the economic burden from businesses to workers (Arnold and Bongiovi, 2013; Kalleberg, 2003).

Flexibility from a worker's perspectives means the ability to define and control their working hours, place of work, and pace and scheduling of work—all important aspects of job quality (Green, 2006; Kalleberg, 2013). However, such flexibility remains a myth for most workers (Lehdonvirta, 2018). In BPO work, managers have developed a system of controlling labour in the production process through the application of technology to ensure that workers are often glued to their computers for the maximum amount of time (Brophy, 2017; Mosese and Mearns, 2016). The use of software technologies (e.g. customer relationship management and workforce management tools) is quite prevalent in order to optimize the number of workers and workforce productivity in what can be referred to as 'shift work' (Beers, 2000; McMenamin, 2007; also Bohle, 2016). Rather than working on a regular eight-hour set schedule, workers are allocated two daily shifts of shorter working hours to fit the needs of the business. This can seriously affect their autonomy at work.

Precarity and Vulnerability

The second way we analyse the developmental impacts of digital jobs is through the lens of precarity and vulnerability. Precarity and vulnerability have both been contextualized in the literature from a variety of perspectives (Lambert and Herod, 2016; Lewis et al., 2015; Waite et al., 2015). One of the most recent and influential analyses on precarity has come through the work of Guy Standing, who in his book *The Precariat* argues that in the contemporary neoliberal era we are witnessing the emergence of a new working class (the 'precariat'), that lacks various forms of labour securities, has insufficient social income, lacks community benefits, and lacks a work-related identity (Standing, 2014). The ILO (2016) has adopted the term and broadly defines precarious work as non-standard employment that is poorly paid, insecure, and unprotected—while cautioning that non-standard employment and precariousness are not necessarily synonymous. In other words, workers can experience precarity in both standard and non-standard employment. While very influential, Standing's theorization has been critiqued powerfully by some (Paret, 2016; Scully, 2016; Wright, 2016; see also Lawlor, 2013).

First, Wright (2016) questions whether 'precariat' are a distinct class from then 'core' working class when their 'material interest' and political objectives might be aligned (e.g. socialist alternative) (see Paret, 2016: 113). Relatedly, Scully (2016) cautions against viewing precarity as a recent universal phenomenon. He argues that while precarious work has been on the rise globally, Standing ignores the longer history of precarious work in low- and middle-income regions like Africa (see also Munck, 2013). In Africa, precarious work forms are the norm and workers often employ mixed-livelihood strategies that shape the way they experience wage work (Callebert, 2017).[21] But workers' increasing reliance on wage work also signals the increasing commodification of labour in the contemporary neoliberal era. At the same time, state-led attempts to offer social protection programmes in some of the countries in the Global South represent a Polanyian double movement, whereby the state creates conditions for markets to prosper without much government intervention and

[21] Another important aspect to remember here is that the category of 'wage work' is developed within the narrow economic sense of capitalism, and hence work that exists outside these norms is considered as 'informal', and working-class dependent on such 'informal' work is termed a 'dangerous class' by Standing because 'insecurities induce the bitterness, ill-health, and anger that can be the fodder of right-wing populism', but also aiming for progressive political movements (e.g. Occupy movement) (Standing, 2018: 1).

also creates social protection measures against that liberalization (Harris and Scully, 2015).[22] Thus, for Munck (2013: 757), 'a perspective from the low and middle-income countries would understand precarity as part of the broader process of dispossession and the generation of new surplus populations'.

Second, Alberti et al. (2018) have voiced concern over the incorporation of a wide variety of working classes by Standing, which leads to the conceptual overstretching of 'precarity' and diminishes its explanatory power. Alberti et al. (2018) suggest that there can be 'explicit' and 'implicit' forms of precarization with both the state and management playing an active role. These forms can differ in a range of labour market contexts. In digital labour contexts, managerial surveillance of workers through the use of technology, and temporary contracts, can influence workers' experiences of both implicit and explicit precariousness; implicit by introducing a climate of fear where workers feel replaceable, and explicit through use of zero-hour contracts, for example. In the gig economy and call centre jobs, workers are noted to have irregular working hours and a high work intensity (on the gig economy, see Berg et al., 2018; on call centre jobs, see Holman, 2013).

It is also important to remember that workers' experiences differ based on the socio-political landscape in which they are embedded, particularly those who have lived their lives in precarious situations. In many parts of the African continent, standard employment relations have remained largely absent (Wood and Brewster, 2007). Although some forms of standard employment relations have developed, this has mainly occurred in the formal sectors of the economy rather than the informal (i.e. more vulnerable) sectors, which host the majority of the workforce (Webster et al., 2009). Under the ILO's definition, vulnerable employment comprises own-account workers (or the self-employed) and family workers who lack the most basic of worker rights, social security, and voice at work.[23] Yet, the policy rhetoric for international organizations like the World Bank is to promote self-employment for people who work on gig economy platforms (often referring to these as 'entrepreneurs'; see Kuek et al., 2015), despite

---

[22] Karl Polanyi in his famous book, *The Great Transformation* (2001) argues that establishment of unregulated markets goes hand in hand with the efforts of social forces (e.g. the state) to protect society from the ravages of the free market (e.g. social protection measures).

[23] The ILO defines own account workers who hold a self- employed job, engaged in the production of goods exclusively for own final use by their household (e.g. subsistence farming or do-it-yourself construction of own dwellings) and have not engaged on a continuous basis any employees to work for them during the reference period (see ILO, 1993b).

evidence that such entrepreneurial tactics ignore the structural constraints faced by both African workers and entrepreneurs (Friederici et al., 2020). Also, the ILO's definition of vulnerable employment does not capture the experiences of other types of new non-standard employment, which include digital jobs. A more practical definition of vulnerable employment has been adopted by the Trades Union Congress Commission on Vulnerable Employment, which defines it as a form of employment in which workers, despite accessing work, remain at risk of continuing poverty and injustice resulting from an imbalance of power in the employer–worker relationship (TUC Commission on Vulnerable Employment, 2008: 3). Thus, whereas precarity can be an experiential outcome of the working class's embeddedness in the wider socio-economic and political landscape, vulnerability can be understood as 'a situation in which the person involved has no real and acceptable alternative but to submit to the abuse involved' (O'Neill, 2011: 10).

In the digital economy jobs that we cover in this book, precarity and vulnerability relate to the mechanisms used to track and rate worker performance. The reputational scoring and rating systems used by platforms put workers in an imbalanced power relationship vis-à-vis clients and platforms, where workers have to constantly appease the client in order to gain higher ratings and feedback. Workers not conforming to the platform's values are blocked immediately and can also be removed from

Table 4.1 Heuristic framework for developmental impacts of digital jobs

| | Developmental dimensions | | | |
	Freedom	*Flexibility*	*Precarity*	*Vulnerability*
Drivers	Algorithmic management of labour process.	Internet and computer-based work. Shift work.	Managerial surveillance. Temporary contracts. Labour oversupply.	Reputational scoring system (feedback, ranking, ratings). Key performance indicators. Non-unionized sectors.
Outcomes	Waged employment. Skills upgrading.	Autonomy at work. Socio-economic inclusion.	High work intensity. Labour insecurities.	Lack of bargaining power. Physical and psychological impacts.

Source: Adapted from Anwar and Graham, 2020a: tab. 2. Reproduced with permission.

the platform permanently (see Chapter 3). Because there are significant costs involved in joining the gig economy platforms, workers need to maintain high scores, which can influence their work intensity (e.g. involving unsociable working hours). Organizational management strategies to constantly monitor workers against strict key performance indicators (KPI) are a central feature in much of the outsourcing sector, especially in BPO jobs. KPIs can involve a number of variables, such as punctuality, time spent on calls, break times, number of calls answered, etc. Woodcock (2016: 65) has described the workings of a call centre as 'a regimented labour process driven by quantified targets', where technology is used to collect data on worker performance. Workers not performing well risk monetary penalties or even dismissal from the job (Anwar and Graham, 2019). These performance mechanisms can generate significant psychological and physical impacts. Therefore, it is not only critical to understand how digital jobs contribute towards the implicit and explicit precariousness in the lives of African gig workers but also how their vulnerability is abused and amplified within the employment relationship, leading to adverse mental and physical impacts. We therefore problematize the development discourse of freedom and flexibility in the mainstream literature through empirical accounts of digital workers' experiences of precarity and vulnerability. Table 4.1 presents a framework to understand the development implications of the digital jobs discussed in this chapter.

We would like to emphasize that our separate treatment of freedom, flexibility, precarity, and vulnerability in this chapter is not intended to compartmentalize them. Instead, we take these development dimensions to be dynamic and existing in a continuum for any particular job. We can understand these dimensions as 'moments' which may exist with other dimensions in any given job for a particular person or even a social group, but may be lacking in another job or for a different person. The advantage of thinking of these as moments is that workers will experience them differently during different times in their jobs. Workers may experience greater autonomy at certain times and feel more insecure at others. For example, the regular availability of work through platforms provides workers with a steady stream of income, which in turn helps them achieve some goals in their lives and personal well-being, while worker performance measurement in the form of ratings can affect their bargaining power in that same job.

5

Digital Taylorism

Freedom, Flexibility, Precarity, and Vulnerability

Introduction

Work has always been tethered to place. However, the increasing use of digital technologies in the production process is transforming the fundamental relationship between work and place. The penetration of ICT tools and internet connectivity have now made it possible for digital work to be distributed across large distances and carried out in parts of the world where it would have seemed improbable just a few years ago. In this chapter, we explore the lived experiences of African workers who participate in digital economy activities, including the gig economy and BPO activities.

Just to reiterate, there is no clear separation between the digital tasks undertaken on gig economy platforms and through outsourcing firms. Indeed, in many cases, work done on platforms can also be done through outsourcing firms, and vice versa. For example, image tagging work is done both through platforms like Upwork and Appen (etc.) and also through BPO firms. In fact, many Kenyan BPO firms are involved in this type of tagging work. Similarly, while customer service work is often associated with call centre firms, workers are also doing this work from their homes via platforms like Upwork.

At the heart of many worker experiences of digital work is the widespread nature of so-called digital Taylorism (The Economist, 2015a), i.e. the intense use of digital technologies by management in the workplace to monitor workers and control the labour process. Employment relations have always required a system of control (Granovetter, 2005), and there is an established body of work that has examined the use of technology by management to exert control over labour processes with a view to maximizing labour productivity (see Braverman, 1974; Burawoy, 1979; Edwards, 1979; Smith, 2006). More recently, the literature has begun to explore

The Digital Continent. Mohammad Amir Anwar and Mark Graham, Oxford University Press.
© Mohammad Amir Anwar and Mark Graham (2022). DOI: 10.1093/oso/9780198840800.003.0005

the connection between new technologies (e.g. algorithms), surveillance, and control in modern-day workplaces (Ball and Margulis, 2011; Gandini, 2019; Gorwa et al., 2020; Jamil, 2020; Kellog et al., 2020; Woodcock, 2020b). However, technology is socially embedded (MacKenzie and Wajcman, 1999) and modern-day technologies like algorithms are developed, designed, and implemented through human labour (Anwar and Graham, 2020b; Tubaro et al., 2020). Concerns have already been raised about opacity and algorithmic bias (see Burrell, 2016; Noble, 2018; Smith, 2019; Wachter-Boettcher, 2017). Therefore, we understand digital Taylorism as not just simply technology intensive, e.g. algorithm driven or automatic, but as *fused* with forms of structural control deployed by management, which Callaghan and Thompson (2001) have argued can be both intensive and unobtrusive as it blends various technological and bureaucratic elements.

Our underlying argument in this chapter is that the use of algorithms in digital work is giving managers power to exert new forms of control and discrimination in workplaces, which is in turn affecting worker experience. Of course, African digital workers' experiences are influenced not just by digital Taylorism, but also by their socio-economic, political, and cultural backgrounds, education levels, and types of work activities. For example, the way two virtual assistants on a platform experience their work will depend on their family background, education, gender, ethnicity, employment contracts, and marital status. Similarly, two contact centre workers who are employed by one firm can have different experiences of work depending on whether they are performing outbound sales or inbound customer services. Outbound sales are often considered to be one of the toughest jobs in the contact centre environment (Woodcock, 2016). Therefore we argue in this chapter that there is no straightforward narrative about positive or negative outcomes in digital work, but rather a great variety of lived worker experience.

In this chapter we will explore further the four development dimensions of digital work we introduced in Chapter 4, i.e. freedom, flexibility, precarity, and vulnerability. Practically, we investigate African workers' everyday struggles to find paid work and to make a living in a highly commoditized form of global economic production. Undoubtedly, emergence of the digital economy on the continent has generated new economic opportunities for workers. At the same time, we have also uncovered in our fieldwork various technological and social-economic barriers that influence workers' experience of digital work.

Freedom from the Constraints of Local Labour Markets

Digital work is commodified and fragmentated into minute tasks (Graham and Anwar, 2019). The digital nature of work means it is relatively foot-loose and can now be done from a great variety of locations. Several leading Silicon Valley technology companies are subcontracting these types of work to outsourcing firms who get it done from a variety of locations (Corporaal and Lehdonvirta, 2017). Take the examples of image tagging, transcription—two of the common tasks that are easily deliverable digitally from a range of locations. Image tagging work (the one we described in the Prologue) is at the core of many types of digital goods and services of today, for example driverless cars (Anwar and Graham, 2020b). For algorithms and computers to correctly identify images and their contents, they need to be trained with thousands upon thousands of such images. These images can be distributed to a global workforce through a variety of platforms such as Amazon Mechanical Turk, Appen, and Upwork (Anwar and Graham, 2020b; Gray and Suri, 2019; Kessler, 2018). Similarly, transcription work is extensively used in academic research, legal and judicial work, corporate houses, and media and communication services (Thompson, 2020). An hour-long audio recording can take anywhere between four and five hours for one person to transcribe. But the transcription can be done more quickly if the audio is subdivided into smaller files. These smaller files can be distributed by clients directly to workers through specialized transcription platforms (e.g. GoTranscripts, Rev.com), or clients can hire BPO companies. The manager of a Kenyan BPO company told us that they were fragmenting audio files into 10-minute segments to complete transcription for an Indian client, who was sourcing this work from the United States.

Another example of digital work is the web content creation; for example, Google's info box which is curated by many of the workers we spoke to in Africa.[1] Here is a worker at a Ugandan outsourcing firm telling us how Google gets some of this work done from Kenya and Uganda (possibly other locations as well) and the kind of work they do:

So, Google pays the BPO. The BPO hires youths. First, we come and we work on different domains that Google wants. For example, they might want us to update

---

[1] Info box is the panel that appears (on the right-hand side) when we search a term, person, or a place on Google's search engine. Google calls them 'knowledge panels' and says they are generated and updated 'automatically'. Available at https://support.google.com/knowledgepanel/answer/9163198?hl=en-GB, acessed 8 July 2021.

something about a film, or a music video, something about sports game, something about books. Anything you search on Google is what we edit. There is this software that we do work on. So, from that software you are able to search from different websites and pick what you are specifically working on. For example, I'm working on a book and maybe I am supposed to edit the authors, the editors, or adjust the date of publication. I go to the author's official website, I pick what is necessary and attach. I can check other local sources. For example, the author is from India and I can go through our company's team in India. I can even send an email to the Indian team, a local team in India who are doing the same project and I tell them I need some information, maybe the date of first publication . . . Maybe the source that I have on Google is in Hindi. Maybe I want them to translate for me. So, I send an email to them then they translate for me. Then here I will edit it. So, next time someone goes on Google and searches for that same book, it will appear what we edited. You see the system of editing comes with specific instructions on what to do. So, you have to search for different sources and there are guidelines and rules. It tells the author's official website has the highest priority when it comes to the date of publication. So, in case you do not get the official website there are some other websites we also use. Like for books we use Good Reads, World Cut and for films we believe in IMDB . . . The workflow system gives you different choices like there are topics about people, books, films so it is just up to you what you want to work on. Sometimes, there are priorities. It will show you this one is needed urgently. You have to work on it very fast. Or that one has a lower priority.

Examples can also be found in routing back office work which has a longer history across large distances (Peck, 2017). For example, in call centres customer queries are routinely allocated to workers through automated tools such as workforce management and customer relationship management software (Taylor and Bain, 1999; Taylor et al., 2002). If a customer in the UK has a problem with their airline tickets or any other goods they bought, chances are they will be speaking to customer services agents abroad, likely in India or the Philippines, or lately South Africa. Indeed, we found one of the customer services centres of Sport Direct (the UK's largest sports goods retailer) to be based in Johannesburg, South Africa, and run by an international BPO firm (headquartered in Paris, France). Put simply, the emerging networks of the digital economy are often complex and opaque, and importantly, becoming global in nature. As a result, some of this workforce is now based in Africa, alongside other places like India (Anwar and Graham, 2020b).

Indeed, the digital economy is bringing new jobs and offering new connectivities (both technological and socio-economic) for the African population. The affordances of digital technologies and the internet create a sense of connection and network to the wider world among the African population (Burrell, 2012). On the question of the importance of the internet on their work and lives, Adaobi, a Nigerian gig worker who does online English language teaching for primarily Chinese students, told us, 'it is now a global village, global world' (Interview, pers. comm., Lagos, February 2017). These imaginaries are tied to people's aspirations and agency (see Appadurai, 1996), but also to the uncomfortable realities of constrained opportunities for material improvement in African workers' immediate locality. In countries like Kenya, Ghana, and Uganda, over 80 per cent of the workforce is informally employed. In South Africa, the post-apartheid period can be characterized with jobless economic growth with young people struggling to find paid work (Bond, 2014).

Digital economy jobs are seen by many stakeholders (including workers, policymakers, and development organizations) to be a panacea for unemployment, and also an escape from the current realities of dysfunctional labour markets on the continent, which primarily offer underpaid and unpaid work (ILO, 2018). Narratives around digital work's development potential in Africa are further reinforced by leading development organizations such as the World Bank and the private sector (e.g. Kuek et al., 2015; Rockefeller Foundation, 2013a; Solutions for Youth Employment, S4YE, 2018; World Bank, 2016). The Rockefeller Foundation has underlined the importance of job creation in the new digital economy in Africa by arguing that:

> [T]he digital economy holds significant potential for creating formal jobs that are accessible to historically marginalized youth. These 'digital jobs'—defined as any short-term or permanent positions that use information technology to deliver a product or service—are in the formal sector and therefore provide higher wages and long-term job stability, which are two key mechanisms that enable people to work their way out of poverty.
>
> **Rockefeller Foundation, 2013a: 3**

A growing literature on digital work has documented the potential of these jobs for livelihood opportunities (D'Cruz and Noronha, 2016; Graham et al., 2017b), offering workers considerable freedom to achieve their personal goals and well-being (Sen, 2001). In fact, a majority of the African workers we interviewed for this study noted that digital jobs were their main source of income, providing them and their family with food, clothing, and medicines. In the African context, the importance of such new jobs is even more pronounced as opportunities for paid work are hard to come by, and the conditions of poverty make it harder for people to find work outside their locality (Graham and Lannoy, 2016). A majority of our workers had university degrees and yet struggled to find jobs in their local labour markets.

Formal-sector employment can provide a great deal of importance and meaning to the lives of workers in Africa who face a social welfare system that is under considerable strain due to government debts and neglect of welfare services such as education and health. For example, call centre jobs provide a good entry point into formal sector employment and are seen as a source of income, employment benefits, transport to and from work, and recreational facilities. This is particularly important for migrant and poor segments of society, who often occupy the lowest-paying jobs in the global economy. Migrants often move to urban areas for jobs and better material opportunities and end up working in low-wage service work such as care work, call centres, security services, and street trading (see, for example, Bauman, 2003; Gautié and Schmitt, 2010; Kincses and Tóth, 2020; Lewis et al., 2015; Ngai, 2007; Shah and Lerche, 2020).[2] Migrants have long played a central role in the call centre industry around the world, especially in low- and middle-income countries (see Alarcón-Medina, 2018; Cruz, 2018; Golash-Boza, 2016; McDuie-Ra, 2012). In Johannesburg, South Africa, a majority of the workers we spoke to in our sample came from impoverished areas, including Soweto, Alexandria, and Tembisa. These localities are largely populated by Black South Africans (often migrants from other parts of the country), that is, the poorest racial group with significantly higher rates of unemployment than any other group in the country (Statistics South Africa, 2014). Similarly, in Kenya, Nigeria, and Ghana, workers we spoke to were primarily domestic migrants who moved to urban areas in search of jobs or education, and call centres became one of their options for work.

For more than half of the call centre workers we interviewed, this job was their first formal sector employment opportunity. This by no means suggests that workers did not work or that other opportunities for paid work were not available. Some scholars have pointed out that in some

---

[2] Ride-hailing has also emerged as an important source of livelihood for migrants both in Africa and abroad (see Otieno et al., 2020).

cases, young workers refuse work they consider undesirable and that doing low-paid work can affect their ability to find better-paid jobs (e.g. Mains, 2007). In fact, there is ample evidence of resistance to waged work in Africa, and that African workers will combine multiple sources of income (Cooper, 1987; Freund, 1988; Kinyanjui, 2014, 2019; see also Hart, 1973). The workers in our sample were similarly involved in a diverse range of economic activities to supplement their incomes. These ranged from informal trading, running community-based food joints, seasonal work such as plumbing and welding, and various forms of online work activities such as transcription, translation, and essay writing.[3] Although online jobs on platforms can be characterized as primarily informal in nature—typically defined by non-standard employment relations such as short-term contracts and being unregulated—the workers we spoke with noted that they struggled to find jobs locally and had to resort to working online as a way to earn a living and provide support to their immediate family members. That is, online work emerged not as a matter of choice for workers in our sample, but a necessity. As an online transcriber in Kenya, Elias, who also worked for a local BPO company doing entry-level data annotation work, told us: 'When there is work, I can do like 30 minutes. I can transcribe like 30 minutes audio. It can go beyond that or even 40 minutes. It is now your ability. It is your effort. If you can do more, you can work like you want. I want to do more.' We asked him why, and he replied, 'the same reason. At least you earn some extra money' (Interview, pers. comm., Nairobi, 2016).

An important aspect of the contribution of digital jobs to workers' freedom from the constraints of local labour markets is that some of these jobs offer higher levels of income for workers than they would get from local jobs. Workers who had been previously employed in jobs such as retail and hospitality, and artisan and craftsman work (such as welding, painting, and plumbing), described their income from their new digital jobs as being better than their previous work. However, wages varied across job types.

On the call centre front, payment models differ between call centres, and salary structures varied across different countries. Some call centres have a commission- or incentives-based income model; others provide a fixed

---

[3] It is only recently becoming common knowledge that Kenyan workers are central to the academic writing for secondary school students, undergraduate, and post-graduate studies in the US and the UK (see Stockman and Mureithi, 2019).

monthly income, and some even pay hourly wages. We spoke to a call centre agent in South Africa working for Merchants.[4] He was on a sales and retention campaign for a South African telecom company who outsourced this work to Merchants. He was getting paid a rate of about ZAR20 per hour (US$7.84 at PPP levels) when he joined in January 2015.[5] His working hours were flexible and varied regularly depending on the demand at the centre and the needs of the client, which meant his wages fluctuated as well. On the other hand, we also spoke to workers like Mwenga, an agent at the in-house contact centre of the Standard Bank South Africa (the biggest bank in Africa in terms of assets).[6] He started as a temporary worker contracted through an employment agency in 2014. In 2015, he was given a full-time contract by the bank, which he told us brought a sense of security to his life. Full-time employees at his company also qualify for employment benefits like health insurance, unlike temporary or agency staff (Interview, pers. comm., October, 2016). His salary before taxes was ZAR18,799 per month (US$3,300 at PPP levels), highest among the South African workers we spoke to, while the minimum was ZAR5,000 (US$860 at PPP levels) for temporary workers on flexible contracts.

Call centre firms also recruit temporary workers (primarily through staffing agencies) on flexible contracts to work during high-volume call times or at different times of the year, for example the period leading up to Christmas (see Doellgast et al., 2009; Frade and Darmon, 2005; Hannif and Lamm, 2005; Shire et al., 2009). For South Africa, where we have the data, the use of temporary and flexible contracts in call and contact centres seems to have increased in recent years. A 2018 report by BPESA highlighted that since 2015 the use of contractual workforce (both full-time and part-time) has increased from 2.2 per cent of the total workforce in call centres in the country to 15.1 per cent in 2018. It has to be said that the proportion of full-time permanent workforce in call centres is still high in South Africa, though it had declined from 91.7 per cent in 2015 to around 75.9 per cent in 2017. The use of temporary staffing agencies has

---

[4] This South African-based BPO firm is a subsidiary of Dimension Data Holdings, owned by Nippon Telegraph and Telephone, a Tokyo-based telecommunication giant.

[5] The national minimum wage of ZAR20 per hour was introduced in May 2017 in South Africa (Mail and Guardian, 2017).

[6] S&P Global 2020 Data. Available at https://www.spglobal.com/marketintelligence/en/news-insights/latest-news-headlines/top-30-banks-by-assets-in-africa-and-middle-east-2020-58040885, accessed 18 July 2021.

Table 5.1 Call centre agents' salaries per month in our case study countries

Countries	Minimum (US$)	Maximum (US$)	National Minimum Wage
South Africa	ZAR5,000 ($300)	18,799 ($1,128)	ZAR20 per hour ($1.2)
Kenya	KSH20,000 ($186)	50,000 ($465)	KSH20,904 per month[a] ($192)
Uganda	UGX541,919 ($150)	N/A	N/A[b]
Nigeria	N40,000 ($103)	85,000 ($220)	N18,000 per month (2017)[c] ($47)
Ghana	GHC350 ($60)	650 ($112)	GHC8.8 per day (2017)[d] ($1.5)

[a] Kenya has a minimum wage policy for different occupations. This figure is for telephone operators.
[b] Uganda does not have a set minimum wage though parliament has passed the Minimum Wage Bill, 2015. The bill mandates the process for determining the minimum wage but does not clarify what the minimum wage should be.
[c] In 2019, the minimum wage was raised to N30,000 per month.
[d] In 2020, the minimum wage was increased to GHC11.82 per day.
Source: Data collected by authors from a variety of sources, including interviews with respondents and secondary data.

been widely recognized as a key driver in suppressing wages (see Barrientos, 2013; Coe et al., 2009, 2010; Elcioglu, 2010; Peck and Theodore, 2016; Theodore and Peck, 2002).

There are differences in wages between countries (Table 5.1) and within the industry as well as between industry segments.[7] In Kenya, respondents told us that salaries were higher at in-house call centres than in outsourced call centres. We observed similar trends in Nigeria and Ghana; because the industry is so small in these countries, call centre workers in one firm would often know workers (either friends or family members) from other firms and hence were aware of the salaries paid to workers. In South Africa, a report from BPESA shows that captive in-house contact centres (both domestic and international) have higher wages than outsourced third-party centres (BPESA, 2018). Captive operations have declined in South Africa since 2015, while outsourced operations have increased, further confirming the downward trend in wages on offer at call and contact centres in the country. Overall, the trend of lower wages among outsourced call and contact centre operations is also observed globally (see Holman, 2013; Holman et al., 2007).

There is a potential for higher salaries in remote gig work compared with local work alternatives in Africa (also see Beerepoot and Lambregts, 2015;

---

[7] In Kenya and Nigeria, minimum wages are defined based on sector and municipalities.

Wood et al., 2019). In our own sample of workers, Pat, in South Africa, told us that compared to the wages from local jobs, gig work pays better salaries (Interview, pers. comm., Johannesburg, August 2016). Likewise, Kufuo, a user-interface designer in Ghana, told us that he now earns double what he earned in his previous job as an app developer for a local start-up (Interview, pers. comm., Accra, May 2017). One respondent, Abaeze from Nigeria, who has a university degree in geography, told us that over a period of five months preceding our interview, he was able to earn more than US$2,500, or roughly US$500 a month (Interview, pers. comm., Abuja, March 2017). We found this to be comparable to or higher than entry-level graduate jobs in some of the private companies operating in Nigeria, including Proctor and Gamble (consumer goods), Zenith Bank (banking), Glo, MTN (telecom), PricewaterhouseCoopers (consultancy), and Shell (oil).[8] We also compared Abaeze's wages with entry-level call centre salaries in Lagos and Abuja. We found that agents at outsourced providers were earning a quarter of Abaeze's income from gig work. Agents working at in-house or captive centres were only marginally better off than those working for third-party providers. A virtual assistant, Dave in Nigeria, told us,

> I have a friend of mine who works for a local firm. He wakes up by 4:00 am every morning, by 6:00 am he is at work. He gets back home by between 9.00 pm and 10:00 pm everyday Monday to Friday and he is being paid just about 120,000 Naira. And here in Nigeria they see 120,000 Naira as big money. Some companies do not want to pay that much. I have this online job and it is paid more. It has afforded me the chance to actually be free, independent, work from home. I am actually internet savvy. I am that kind of person, and I love it. It is a passion for me.
>
> **Interview, pers. comm., Lagos, March 2017**

The income potential of remote work in Africa should be read with some caution. First, not everyone who joins remote gig economy platforms is able to earn an income. As a result, income generation through gig work is highly variable. Berg et al. (2018) in their study across six platforms found that wages per hour on platforms are generally low (also see Rani and Furrer, 2020). There are also geographical dimensions to this earning potential. Beerepoot and Lambregts (2015) found that experienced

---

[8] Since it is very difficult to find out about salaries in Nigeria due to the unavailability of official records and sources, we reviewed salaries for entry-level positions in these sectors through Glassdoor, a website that anonymously collects information about salaries and company reviews.

gig workers from low- and middle-income countries (e.g. India and the Philippines) can earn relatively high wages per hour, although workers in high-income countries earn higher absolute wages. Similarly, the ILO's survey of remote gig workers found that gig workers in North America and Europe typically earned higher incomes than workers in Africa and the Asia and Pacific region (Berg et al., 2018; also see Rani and Furrer's (2020) study across twenty-seven low- and middle-income countries). Even between low- and middle-income countries, there is variation. For example, African workers earn slightly less than workers in Asia and South America (Berg et al., 2018), and while workers from countries in Eastern Europe and Asia are fairly successful in earning an income from Upwork, African workers find this more difficult (see Table 3.3). There is also variation within Africa, as workers from Kenya are more successful in earning an income from Upwork than Ghanaian, Ugandan, Egyptian, or Moroccan workers. In addition, workers with adequate skills and technological affordances are more likely to break the barriers to entry on platforms and earn a higher income online than those without adequate skills and education (Anwar and Graham, 2020a, 2020c; Graham et al., 2017b). That said, securing the first job on a gigwork platform like Upwork can be extremely difficult, with many workers in our sample spending several weeks or months bidding for jobs on Upwork before winning their first contract (see Anwar and Graham, 2020a, 2020c). A majority of the workforce which join Upwork are not able to earn any income at all.

Second, it is noteworthy that economic compensation in the form of income may not necessarily transform into a person's ability to achieve all the outcomes they value. There are two key issues here. While access to the internet and communications technology has increased over the years in Africa, research has shown that people in some African countries might spend more money on phone credit than on family welfare and education (Carmody, 2012). Indeed, we found some gig workers in our sample were spending more money on broadband internet than on food, hoping that with a good internet connection they would be able to work and earn more. Kufuo, a user experience and product designer in Accra survived on Coca-Cola and bread on multiple occasions, with no other food in the house. He said he would 'rather pay for the internet and go hungry' to impress the client/employer by delivering good quality work on time. The fact that gig work is dependent on the internet and other technologies (computer and electricity, for example), and the added cost of these for workers to be able to perform this work, can alter workers' job experiences. Very rarely is it acknowledged that the high cost of mobile subscriptions in Africa (ITU, 2017a), through which most Africans access the internet, is a major hindrance to workers seeking jobs online.

Social Recognition

While wage earning was the thing our respondents claimed as digital work's main contribution to their lives, social recognition (Honneth, 1996) also emerged as a sought after element. Imageries of unemployed workforce on the continent as involving in crime, drugs, and passing time are quite common (Desta et al., 2017) to an extent even deprecated by political leaders as 'lazy' and this has historical precedence since the colonial times (Cooper, 2017). Paid jobs provide workers with a chance to move out of poverty and also gain acceptance and prestige in their immediate social circles. Our respondents commonly made reference to gaining confidence, developing a dress sense, an ability to communicate, and developing interpersonal skills. For workers, their work helped them gain social recognition and identity, a key aspect to autonomy and agency (Rossiter, 2014). This was indicated by Kenyangi in Uganda, who told us that a lot of people do not know about or understand freelancing and therefore, it is hard for her to explain to people what she does for a living. She said: 'I am sure my parents still do not quite get it, but they are okay with it. They know I have a job that I earn money from' (Interview, pers. comm., Kampala, November 2017).

However, the social perception of internet-based jobs or new information economy jobs in Africa is not positive everywhere. The recognition and respect workers gain by being able to earn a livelihood from digital jobs is also dependent upon workers' location, and their social and cultural backgrounds. Nigerian workers, in particular, face a stigma attached to online work, primarily due to the online scamming networks prevalent in the country, colloquially referred to as the 'Yahoo Boys' (Reuters, 2018). A Nigerian virtual assistant told us:

> Freelancing in Nigeria is not something we are actually used to—when you tell somebody you are a freelancer in Nigeria, they think you are a witch worker. They tend to look at you like a scammer. Anybody who makes money, who claims to work from home should be a scammer and I try to like no, it is not so. I work. I earn my money. I work hard to make money.

Another virtual assistant and translator, Onochie in Nigeria, told us that he was stopped by a policeman, who asked him about his work because he was carrying two laptops. When the policeman heard online work, he said: 'You are a scammer. You are doing all that work. You are scamming people. So, they took me to the police station. I sat with them and I opened my Upwork profile and Skype. And then they let me go' (Interview, pers. comm., Lagos, February 2017). Nonetheless, digital jobs are seen by African workers as prestigious and provide them with some sense of pride. Some of this has to do with the way IT-sector jobs are considered as skilled and come with a better workplace environment, particularly in the BPO industry.

Workplace Environment

Call centre work offers a safer and healthier work environment than most local work such as in retail and hospitality. Workers acknowledged the presence of recreational facilities, such as a gym and cafeteria, in call and contact centres to have a positive impact on their work, output, and stress management. There were examples of outsourcing firms providing meals to workers during their shifts, and also offering transport between the offices and homes of the workers. The cost of finding jobs, which includes transportation costs, is noted to be one of the reasons that discourage work seekers in South Africa to find work (Graham and Lannoy, 2016). By comparison, such facilities are rarely available in jobs such as the hospitality industry.

There were differences between countries and different types of firms (captive or outsourced). The BPO firms in South Africa were generally found to be offering healthier work spaces, in comparison to firms in Kenya, Nigeria, or Uganda, for example. The South African BPO industry is slightly more advanced than other countries in our sample and has a large presence of international outsourcing firms. BPESA and the Government of South Africa are actively involved in marketing the country as a location for offshore work, and firms are investing a great deal in maintaining and benchmarking business and workplace standards. As a result, firms are investing in improved infrastructure and ICT tools, which influence working conditions (including health and safety issues) inside the centres. These are considered essential for securing contracts with international buyers (see Anwar and Graham, 2019). Some of the firms we visited were air-conditioned workplaces, had expensive office furniture, canteens, and leisure areas (Figure 5.1). However, there are no set standards for the working environment, and the work spaces of local firms who are dependent upon subcontracted work (for example in Kenya, Ghana, and Nigeria) are generally less advanced than those with international contracts (e.g. in South Africa).

Flexibility: The Dilemma

As well as the material affordances offered by digital jobs, there are also benefits to workers in the form of flexible working, particularly in remote work. The World Bank's World Development Report on *Digital Dividends* argues that flexible working hours is the main attraction of online outsourcing for women, young people, and older people (World Bank, 2016: 108). In one of the World Bank's studies on the gig economy (Kuek et al., 2015), one Nigerian worker was quoted as saying that:

> [O]nline outsourcing gives me the freedom to choose who I work with, when I work, and how I work. I love that I can work without borders, on interesting jobs, and with clients spanning several countries and organizations.

Similarly, in a survey of over 1,000 workers on Amazon Mechanical Turk and Crowdworker, Berg (2016) found that workers place great value on

Fig. 5.1 Working environment of two contact centres in Johannesburg
Source: Reproduced with permission from Anwar and Graham, 2019: fig. 1.

flexibility. A 2017 survey of gig workers in the UK by the Chartered Institute of Personnel and Development also found that workers favoured flexible working and independence over job security (CIPD, 2017). Also, the advocacy work done by numerous platform executives has further reinforced the image of the wider gig economy as offering increased autonomy at work. The CEOs of a number of platforms have released statements supporting the flexible arrangements found in the gig economy. Stephane Kasriel, ex-CEO of Upwork, said that 'people are increasingly building flexible careers on their own terms' (Upwork, 2015); Uber's ex-CEO Travis Kalanick said that 'for the first time, I think in possibly history, work is flexible to life and not the other way around' (Squawk Box Today, 2016); and Oisin Hanrahan, the co-founder of Handy, has said that the platform 'provides income opportunities and flexible arrangements that may not have been available otherwise' (Hanrahan, 2015).

In our own sample, gig workers largely appreciated the ability to work from any place and at any time. For example, one customer support executive from Nigeria remarked that 'knowing you are the boss comes with some swag' (Interview, pers. comm., Lagos, April 2017). Indeed, most African workers in our sample highly valued the autonomy that comes with remote work, i.e. the ability to work at one's own pace, and discretion over the time and location of work. This idea of worker autonomy was echoed by several gig workers:

> I am the kind of a person that loves freedom and having the opportunity to set your own schedule and do your own thing.
>
> **Kenny, pers. comm., online writer, Abuja, 2017**

> It is a bit scary and at the same time it is easy. As long as my work is done I can do anything I want. I can be watching movies while I work. I have even gone partying with my laptop on. Basically, my work is done and if my clients need me it is on.
>
> **Ben, pers. comm., virtual assistant, Nairobi, 2016**

> Each time I work from home I am usually excited and happy because I think about people on the road, the traffic, how they suffer, they walk. They sit down from morning to night at the desk and they get paid peanuts. And I am in the house, I can do anything I want. I can take a nap, wake-up, eat, do anything I want. I am just free. I can fire my boss, get a new job.
>
> **Dave, pers. comm., online sales agent, Lagos, 2017**

I work 40 hours a week for an Australian client . . . Eight hours a day. But you just distribute the hours. So, like if you say, I want to work for four hours in the morning and rest until the end of the day, and then four hours later, you can do that. I think that is what I enjoy the most. I am almost like my own boss. I have a client but I run my own hours and time. So, I do not have to login at a certain time and you know actually log off at a certain time, I can just keep working, and if I do not want to work tomorrow, I put in my hours the next day.

Nicola, pers. comm., digital marketing specialist, Johannesburg, 2016

However, this autonomy associated with remote work is not as simple as it looks. First, not all workers experience autonomy or flexible working. In our sample, well-educated workers with graduate degrees, and who come from financially well-off socio-economic backgrounds, were able to overcome these barriers to earn themselves a meaningful livelihood. These are also workers who have been able to maintain high reputation scores and ratings on the platform and who were doing specialized digital work such as article writing, software development, and content generation. In contrast, new workers, the less well-educated, the already unemployed, and workers from poor family backgrounds do not have such opportunities and were doing low value-added entry-level work such as data annotation. Additionally, workers often work under deadlines and have time constraints put in place by clients and employers, which seriously affects their experiences of autonomy. This flexibility paradox is exemplified by Kenyangi, a transcriber in Uganda, who said, 'I think basically for me the best thing is the freedom to dictate my own working hours and speed. Although that is not exclusively true because you know clients give you jobs and they dictate hours' (Interview, pers. comm., Kampala, 2017).

In fact, some researchers have questioned the notion of 'flexibility' in the gig economy. Lehdonvirta's (2018: 25) study on three different types of online work platforms found the ability of gig workers to control their time was often curtailed by structural (for example, the availability of work and degree of worker dependence on the work) as well as cultural-cognitive constraints (such as procrastination). Kessler's (2018) account of American workers on some of the major platforms like Uber and Amazon Mechanical Turk uncovers workers in less flexible arrangements (e.g. doing high-intensity work and long working hours) in contrast to what the platforms portray. Similarly, Ravenelle's (2019) ethnographic study on workers on TaskRabbit, Helpling, Uber, and Airbnb, documents working conditions. Ravenelle found that despite some workers achieving a high income, they experience strict control over work. Rani and Furrer's (2020) study on remote workers in low- and middle-income countries also found that workers spend a considerable time on platforms as unpaid work. It is safe to say that while workers may enjoy considerable autonomy in scheduling their work, such flexibility remains elusive for most gig workers (see Wood et al., 2019; also Shibata, 2019). The gig workers in our sample often talked about long and irregular working hours, sometimes involving late night work. In other words, the flexibility offered to workers in the gig economy is a double-edged sword. It is actually the client and the platform that dictate how work is done. Nonetheless, in the gig economy workers still retain a slightly greater degree of autonomy than is typical of other forms of work such as call centre work.

In BPOs, the management deploys a mix of digital technologies—including customer relationship management (CRM) and workforce management (WFM) tools, automatic call distributors, predictive diallers, interactive voice response, and call recording systems—and communications channels such as social media, smartphone applications, and webchat to deliver services and control the labour process (Bain et al., 2002; Taylor and Bain, 2005). The adoption of WFM tools in call centres ensures workforce productivity and efficiency (Brophy, 2017; Mosese and Mearns, 2016). Management will also optimize their workforce by putting more workers at certain times of the day; a practice of workforce allocation commonly referred to as 'non-standard scheduling' or irregular scheduling in the industrial relations literature (Wood, 2020), and also referred to as 'shift work' where the scheduling of shifts is done to fit the needs of the business (Beers, 2000; Bohle, 2016; McMenamin, 2007). Wood (2020) in his ethnographic study of two contemporary firms (one in the US and one in the UK) highlighted a regime of control built around flexible scheduling implemented by management, which he terms 'flexible despotism'. This, Wood explains, involves managers disciplining workers by assigning them irregular hours and shifts, and at the same time workers trying to win 'schedule gifts' or favour from the management in the form of better hours.

In some of the call centres that we examined in Africa, flexible scheduling takes the form of 'split shifts' (see Chapela, 2015; Zaller, 2012). Rather than working on a regular eight-hour set schedule, workers are allocated two shifts of shorter working hours. We found this in outsourced call centres both in Nairobi and Accra, where BPO firms were doing customer services work for telecommunication companies. For example, in Nairobi, call centre workers at ISON (which was handling Airtel's customer services centre) had two shifts: one in the morning and one in the evening. Workers on split shifts would start working at 8 am and finish at 1 pm, and then they have to start again for the second shift at 6 pm until 11 pm. In Accra, Tech Mahindra was handling Airtel's customer services centres and was using split shifts to manage their workforce. One of their agents, Iffi, told us:

> I am on the split shift, and with the split shift we start at 7:30 am and close at 12 pm. And then I come back at 5 pm till 9:30 pm. So, we have a break of 5 hours . . . You know most of the time the calls come early morning and then in the evening. Normally, in the afternoon calls do not come in. So, it is like, we are there to pick or to assist the other agents when call volume is high. And we have agents who are doing the straight shift. Some start at 8 am and finish at 5 pm. We have those who also start at 6 am to 3 pm, 5 am to 2 pm and then we also have the night shift.

Workers' shifts would change every week. Agents who did day shifts one week would be transferred to night shifts the next week and vice versa. Agents also told us that there is a possibility of requesting a change of shift if someone has personal issues. But this request needs to be put in place in advance to the team leader, and there is no guarantee it will be approved. In other words, the scheduling of shifts in call centres can be very much subjective depending on a worker's relationship with their management (see D'Cruz and Noronha, 2013). Flexible scheduling is known to have an adverse impact on mental health, e.g. depression, particularly among women (Torquati et al., 2019; also Chapela, 2015; Lambert et al., 2012).

Another key aspect of digital Taylorism in call centres is managerial control over the labour process through the use of sophisticated CRM tools. These tools ensure that workers are glued to their computers for the maximum amount of time. CRM tools enable customer calls to be organized and allocated to agents automatically. Rushd, one of the customer services agents at a call centre in Nigeria, described the process:

> The calls are automatic. We are not the ones who dial. The software handles the call for you. You just see the customer's detail and speak to the customer. It does not even ring. You just hear hello. The customer is already saying hello, so, we have to talk to the customer.
>
> **Interview, pers. comm., Lagos, 2017**

A senior verification officer at a call centre in South Africa explained to us the way CRM tools handle the calls in BPOs.[9] He called it 'predictive dialling' and told us that 'it dials automatically. It has customer leads [contact details]. So, the moment you log in to the system, it starts dialling. It is a free-flow system which means the moment I end the first call, it automatically picks up another customer'. However, it is not just the routinization of calls that is controlled by the management. The management also controls what the agents have to say to customers, as part of the quality control of the firm. The management provides workers with scripts that they have to use while they talk to customers (see Woodcock, 2016). Rushd explains:

> When a customer calls, we say, hello and introduce ourselves. It is a script. It has to be very accurate. You say: 'my name is XYZ, I'm calling you from Go TV.' Then you call the customer's name, 'Mr Philip as a valued customer it's important we keep you entertained, please may we know why you have not subscribed on Go TV?' So, the customer tells me the reason, oh there has not been electricity or I do not have money right now.[10] Those are the most common excuses: money or light. Then you say to the customer 'we apologise and understand what is happening in the country. We know things are not easy. Please are you aware of our other affordable bouquets [products]'. Most of them are not aware of the cheaper subscription rates we have. And we try to enlighten them, educate them on all our bouquets. Then in the middle of the conversation you can try to solve the customer's issues. Then when you are through with her, we have the closing verbiage [statement]. 'Thank you very much for your time Mr Philip and thank you for choosing Go TV, have a nice day'.

Interviewer: Do they even tell you what responses to give to the customer?

> Rushd: They tell you what to say depending on the kind of problems because we have about 10 common problems customers face: financial, economic, kids in school, etc. We had our training for this. They [trainers] brief us on the ways to handle customers and the things we are supposed to say. Our quality assurance team is actually listening to our calls constantly. When you deviate in responses,

---

[9] When we spoke to the managers of the BPO firms, they did not disclose either the specifics of the software or the suppliers of those technologies. But through interviews with call centre agents, we found that some of the common CRM and WFM tools used in call centres in our case study countries were supplied by Ameyo, Aspect, or Oracle.

[10] Nigeria's electricity crisis is well known as it produces only about 4,000–5,000 MW per hour for over 195 million people (Olowosejeje, 2019). Power cuts are pervasive and diesel generators are used as back-up supply. By way of comparison, South Africa produces around 50,000 MW per hour.

> then they call you downstairs and tell you this is what you were supposed to say. There is always a particular response you should give to a customer.

We spoke to a number of quality assurance (QA) officers in our sample to understand the logic of listening to customer calls. One of them in South Africa who started her career as an agent told us that they have to listen to a certain number of calls per week to ensure agents are resolving customer issues properly and to check if the agents need further training. She told us that almost all worker interactions with customers (calls, chats, texts, messages) are controlled, stored, and analysed for quality purposes.

Overall, our argument here is that digital work's contribution to the freedom and flexibility of workers is not a given. Instead these are socio-political arrangements embedded in the social and cultural contexts and technological structures of digital economy activities, which are often dictated by the better positions of employers, management, and platforms vis-à-vis workers. Digital workers end up in harsh working conditions under the garb of individual freedom and flexibility. Workers in call centres often end up having to deal with high work intensity and the resulting negative impact on work–life balance (see Ananthram et al., 2018; Batt et al., 2009; Holman, 2004; Taylor et al., 2002). Gig workers spoke to us about unsocial working hours and a lack of stable work supply. Yet, African workers also framed various expectations around digital jobs. For some workers, like Karl in Nigeria, platforms like Upwork are a 'marketplace of benefits' (Group discussion, pers. comm., Abuja, March 2017), while for call centre agents, their job is seen as a potential stepping stone for their professional career. This can be described as a false consciousness developing among workers (Augoustinos, 1999), given the little hope for career progression in actual fact (see Anwar and Graham, 2019).

Precarity and Vulnerability

Contingent Employment Relations and Insecurities

Since gig work is based on short-term contracts, workers on platforms are often considered as self-employed or independent contractors rather than employees.[11] The flexible working typically associated with remote work

---

[11] One of the contentious issues in the gig economy is the misclassification of workers by platform companies (see Aloisi and De Stefano, 2020; Friedman, 2014; Stewart and Stanford, 2017;

can obscure the insecurities it brings because of the contingent nature of employment relations in the global gig economy. The UNDP (2015) has raised concerns that for gig workers who are already living in poverty, the distinction between work and personal life will be challenging since it is never clear to them when the next work opportunity will come their way. Almost every remote worker we interviewed noted that flexibility comes with significant insecurities associated with working in the gig economy, which affects them mentally and physically. We should note here that the majority of remote workers we interviewed told us that lack of a secure flow of work is a contributory factor to their high stress levels. As explained by Anu, an online writer in South Africa, 'freedom comes with a lot of uncertainty and stress because you need to make sure that you always have a job'. Even experienced workers like Ben, a virtual assistant in Nairobi, feel replaceable. Ben told us that he 'worries about his job every day' because 'it is risky and volatile. It is never constant. You may have had a good job before but it is not guaranteed'. There were various examples of clients cancelling workers' contracts. Pat, in South Africa, was hired on Upwork for customer service work for a French client. As soon as he started working, he was told that his accent was Belgian French and the client wanted French from France. His contract was cancelled overnight and he could not log into his account the next day.

The variable working hours on platforms further exacerbate these insecurities. For Amahle, a data entry worker in South Africa, variable working hours meant that she could not earn regular wages, which, according to her, contributed towards depression and stress. These insecurities may be further amplified for certain types of workers. For example, a female transcriber may experience a greater degree of economic freedom from her husband or father, but this work may also intensify her labour since she has to perform both productive and reproductive labour (McDowell, 2001). Timmy in South Africa had done various jobs, including call centre, before she started doing transcription and customer services work through Upwork. She described the challenges of working and raising children. She would wake up in the morning exhausted from her late-night work. She

---

Todolí-Signes, 2017). Prime examples include the ride-hailing companies such as Uber and Bolt, who misclassify workers as independent contractors and not as employees. Numerous court battles against these platforms have been waged in different parts of the world; prominent among them are in the US where a Californian court ruled in 2019 that Uber and Lyft must convert their drivers' status from independent contractors to employees with benefits (Bloomberg, 2020), Uber's case in the Supreme Court in the UK is well known, in which it lost against its drivers (Butler, 2021); similar court battles are going on in Nigeria (Kazeem, 2017) and South Africa (Moloi, 2018).

has to prepare breakfast, take the children to school and clean the house. By the time she is done with household chores, it will be around 1 pm. She would work from 2 pm until 10 pm (Interview, pers. comm., Johannesburg, August 2016). Her husband helps with child care while she is working. But for others this arrangement may not be available.

The contracts on platforms can be either 'fixed price' tasks or hourly paid. Fixed price gigs can last for as little as a few minutes to days, depending on the type of tasks (e.g. image tagging, transcription, video editing, translation, essay writing) (Figure 5.2). There are hourly wage contracts on platforms as well, which can be longer, sometimes lasting several months to a year (e.g. virtual assistant, web chat agents, search engine optimization). The contracts can be ended at the client's discretion, although platforms like Upwork provide some arbitration between the client and the worker to ensure contracts are respected. So, while in relative terms African gig workers might experience less insecurity on platforms compared to some local jobs, in absolute terms gig work is also insecure, and clients' actions on platforms contribute towards this precarity. In a different example, Shevchuk and Strebkov's (2018) study based on a sample of 5,756 Russian gig workers on a Russian language platform found that nearly 73 per cent

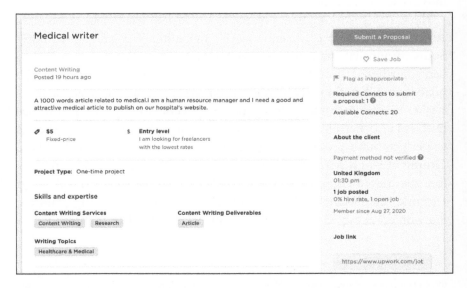

Fig. 5.2 A fixed price job for article writing advertised on Upwork by a UK-based client

Source: Reproduced with permission from Anwar and Graham, 2019: fig. 2.

of the workers faced agreement violation by clients, resulting in financial losses.

In many ways then, gig work has similar characteristics to other informal economy jobs (e.g. domestic workers, waste collectors, informal traders, and taxi drivers). The jobs on platforms are typically insecure, short-term, and carry no legal obligations on clients for employment benefits to workers. None of the remote workers we interviewed had benefits such as health care, pension funds, or other forms of social welfare contributions paid for by their clients/employers. There were some forms of state welfare provisions such as health care in countries like Ghana, public pension funds in Kenya, and social grants covering pensions, disability payments, and child support grants in South Africa. However, many African countries are financially constrained, which makes the provision of welfare benefits through jobs of utmost importance for workers' well-being. Most informal workers in Africa are not covered by such programmes such as pensions that are generally available to formal sector workers. Thus, the job and income insecurities found in various informal activities, such as waste collection, street vending, plumbing, shoe mending, etc. (see Chen and Carré, 2020) are also present in gig economy activities. For African workers gig work therefore presents a paradox, where opportunities to earn livelihoods go alongside the various economic and job insecurities they already face locally.

Regarding call and contact centres, the employment may be considered formal, but the sector operates with intense wage competition. As Peck (2017: 126) puts it, 'outsourcing is an activity with competition at its core, and often quite destructive competition at that'. Almost all the BPO executives we interviewed cited labour as their largest operational cost—as much as 60 per cent. As a result, service providers increasingly look to cut labour costs. At least in the African context, the lack of local work alternatives means that BPO firms have been able to suppress wages aggressively.

An agent in Kenya told us that he had started working for the inhouse customer service centre of Airtel, the world's second largest mobile network operator.[12] He was earning KSH35,000 (US$317) per month as an agent. Airtel outsourced their customer service centres to ISON around

---

[12] Bharti Airtel acquired Zain in 2010, for an estimated US$9 billion deal, to become the fifth largest mobile phone company by the number of subscribers. At that time this was the second biggest deal by an Indian firm to acquire a foreign firm after Tata's acquisition of Corus (Reuters, 2010a). The company is now the second largest mobile network operator in the world.

2013.[13] Workers were given new contracts by ISON and their starting salaries were brought down to KSH20,000 per month (US$183). When we asked one of the high-ranking executives of ISON why was this done, they replied bluntly, 'we are paying minimum wages according to the Kenyan law'. On condition of anonymity, the executive further explained the strategy deployed by them to lower wages for agents:

> When we took over the Airtel customer services centre, some agents were paid up to KSH50,000 per month. Now, straight away we could not bring them down to KSH20,000. But we have been hiring people at KSH20,000 which was giving other agents a clear indication that somehow the job is at risk because we would not like to continue with people at higher salary. . . We use a term called re-batch. Rebatch means suppose I am taking over a new business and a part of the department, for example the inbound customer services. So, the people who were in the call centre would be declared as redundant . . . So, to save their job they were rebatched, which can be of two forms. One, we take them on their existing terms and conditions, which is their salary, and benefits, everything as it is. It is just the employer changed from X to ISON. Another way of rebatching is on our terms and conditions, which is our wage policy and our employee benefits . . . There were people who were at KSH50,000 to a range of KSH70,000 as an agent; there were supervisors who were in the range of KSH120,000. But when we came and looked at outsourcing pay as per the minimum wage which is above KSH20,000 . . . That is the minimum wage policy in Kenya. So, we were hiring new people at the new wage policy. When we see a new process being taken over that can be a mixed experience for the employees, who were working there. It can be a good experience because in a way they can save their job, but the salary and benefits that they were getting from the previous employer might not be the same as the current employer.

This is a clear and deliberate assault by ISON on the wages of their workers. Under the Labour Institutions Act, Kenya's minimum wages are defined based on both occupations and geographical areas (Government of Kenya, 2018). While contact centre agents are not explicitly classified in the Kenyan regulation on minimum wages (see Government of Kenya, 2018), the minimum wage for telephone operators starts at KSH20,904 (US$183) per month in Nairobi and the minimum wage for cleaners and domestic

---

[13] ISON is one of the leading outsourcing services providers in Africa, and has been offering contact centre services to its clients in 16 African countries.

workers starts at KSH13,572 (US$123) per month. ISON workers in Nigeria also told us similar experiences of their wages being cut by the company. Call centre workers reported a lack of job alternatives locally and hence they accepted what was being paid. An agent in Kenya told us that:

> [T]he thing that we are crying for is the remuneration or salary. It is very little. In fact, you live from hand to mouth. But it is better than nothing because the unemployment rate in Kenya today is very high. So, as little as it is, we do appreciate it.

We asked call centre agents in our sample if they thought their income was fair. Most agents said their income was unfair. Ash, the agent in South Africa, who earns ZAR7,000 a month (US$477) said, 'for the work that we do and the amount of pressure or stress or abuse that we endure, I think we are grossly underpaid'. Workers had expectations to be earning higher salaries. An agent in Lagos told us that someone with his qualifications should be earning more than his N50,000 (US$131) per month. But the BPO employers rarely pays decent wages, and the issue of low income was particularly evident for the workers at outsourced centres. The agony of low pay was further highlighted for us by an agent in Kenya, who said:

> You find that you work a lot . . . If you compare with the remuneration we get for our work it is not much. I am working on a public holiday and the payment should be different but no. If I work at night the pay is supposed to be different. But with the BPO, it is not . . . We used to work five days, eight hours every day. But the company increased the working week to six days even though we still work seven and a half hours every day. We still earn minimum wages.

Agents repeatedly reported to us that they were struggling to meet their daily expenses and are getting into cycles of debt. An agent in Accra told us, 'before the month end my salary is finished. It's not enough'. When we asked them how they manage their expenses, they replied, 'I borrow money from my colleague. At the end of the month you pay them back and you are torn again'.

In a way, behind this façade of job creation lie constant efforts of BPO employers to underpay their employees. Along with the low wages, the management also employs bullying tactics as an effective strategy to discipline workers, which can contribute towards precariousness among workers (Einarsen et al., 2011). D'Cruz and Noronha (2014: 3) in their study on India's IT services sector highlighted lay-offs as a form of de-personalized workplace bullying, i.e. 'routine subjugation, both covert and overt, of employees by contextual, structural and processual elements of organizational design, implemented by managers'. This bullying in BPOs can also be done through the use of temporary contracts, which makes it easier for workers to be fired according to the whims of managers. The use of temporary contracts and agency workers who are hired on flexible employment terms have emerged as effective forms of managerial control over labour in the workplace (a review of this literature is given in Smith, 2015; also Crowley et al., 2010; Enright, 2013; Kalleberg, 2000; Kenny and Webster, 1998). In call centres, temporary contracts are common (Shire et al., 2009), and African workers are often powerless in the face of such managerial tactics. This is not to suggest that worker resistance does not take place in call centres; in fact, a large body of work already exists which has documented resistance in call centres (e.g. Bain and Taylor, 2002; Brophy, 2017; Mulholland, 2004; Taylor and Bain, 2003; Townsend, 2005; Woodcock, 2016). What we are saying is that workers' positionalities may make resistance less attractive for those who are already economically marginalized and poor, such as African workers. Take for example, a call centre agent Brian in Kenya, who explains how temporary contracts can subdue workers' actions in BPOs:

> Companies give us one year or six months contract. So, if you are not loyal and create problems like organising workers or joining a union, they will terminate your contract after six months. Previously, that was six months but the beginning of last year December [2015], contracts were reduced to three months and will be renewed if your performance and behaviour is good. If you are fighting for your rights, they will fire you at the end of the contract. This is what they did to one of the union organisers when I was working. They called him at 11 pm and told him your contract has expired, and we are not renewing your contract . . . I told them that they [employer] are violating the employees' rights. I am doing business management. I study labour laws related to that one. What I understand is that if you have made a mistake within the company you are supposed to be given first verbal warning. Then if you make another mistake you are given first written warning. Then, we have the second written warning and a third one. But at the company I worked for there was nothing like that. Once you have made a mistake you are gone. They have a term called 'zero tolerance'. If you do any mistake they will fire you. So, that makes the employee loyal to the company and in fact, most of the employees are pulling out of the union. You

have a family. You have children. Most of us were in colleges. You depend on this contract.

African digital workers' precariousness does not end there. Their work is defined by managerial control of the production process and workers themselves. This surveillance enabled by digital technologies allows management to ensure that the work gets done and quality is maintained. It also allows management to measure worker performance, which in turn affects the worker's experience, including high work intensity, long and irregular working hours, and lack of bargaining power.

Managerial Surveillance in the Gig Economy

Much has been written about managerial control and workplace regimes in the sociology and industrial relations literature (for an overview, see Thompson and van den Broek, 2010; also Meyers and Vallas, 2016). The strategies of control employed by management vary, and can be more complex than as typically understood by Taylorist forms of control (e.g. Burawoy, 1979, 1985; Edwards, 1979). As Burawoy (1985) has noted, there is a balance in the workplace between coercion and consent, which is in turn shaped by structural conditions, including social, cultural, and political institutions, and regulatory policies (see Degiuli and Kollmeyer, 2007).[14] There are convincing arguments developed for example by Callaghan and Thompson (2001), around integrated models of technological, bureaucratic, and normative controls, which highlight a shift towards the progressively hybridized nature of managerial systems (also see Fleming and Sturdy, 2011).

Technical and bureaucratic controls are often framed as being distinct from normative controls on the grounds that they can be 'direct' (see Thompson et al., 2004). Managerial attempts to impose a combination of 'unobtrusive' surveillance and team-based self-discipline have been studied (Sewell, 1998; Sewell and Wilkinson, 1992), including strategies of influencing workers' commitment and subjectivity (Casey, 1995; Willmott, 1993). Workers can be measured on their tacit, interpersonal, and affective skills (see Fuller and Smith, 1991), and there are also elements of encouraging self-discipline and attendance (Edwards and Scullion, 1982),

---

[14] We are aware of the studies that have highlighted the dynamics of control and consent, and also resistance at workplaces (e.g. Edwards and Scullion, 1982).

to make sure workers are more amenable and conducive to work and hence can be controlled easily. To give just one example, the Harambee Youth Employment Accelerator, a multi-stakeholder programme in South Africa with partnerships across public, private, and third-party organizations, trains work seekers in soft skills like punctuality and discipline among a variety of other skills in their work-readiness programme. After completion of training, workers are matched with prospective employers drawn from a variety of sectors (Interview, pers. comm. Harambee Official, Johannesburg, 2016).[15]

As we move towards the digital economy and work increasingly becomes digital in nature, new forms of labour process control and workplace surveillance have emerged.[16] The term 'electronic panopticon' has already been used to describe control in call centres (Fernie and Metcalfe, (1998); for a critique of this metaphor, see Bain and Taylor, 2000). Similar ones have been applied to new digital work activities, including 'algopticon' (Jamil, 2020), used to describe algorithmic management of the labour process and control over workers in the digital gig economy. An important aspect of the algorithmic control and surveillance found in various modern-day workplaces, including gig economy platforms, is the unobtrusive panoptic nature of control over both the labour process and workers.

For remote work, platforms like Upwork capture worker inputs and working hours to monitor their progress on a task. Workers are then rated by the platform and given a job success score, which reflects their clients' satisfaction as evidenced by relationships, feedback, and job outcomes over time. At the same time, the rating system is opaque and the platform rarely makes public how they generate ratings and score workers.[17] However, a number of empirical accounts from various gig economy activities have highlighted how platforms' use of algorithms and reputational scoring systems can affect job quality (e.g. for remote gig economy, see Anwar and

---

[15] Harambee's own assessment found that workers who had gone through their training have a lower attrition rate.

[16] Shoshana Zuboff's (2019) thesis of surveillance capitalism examines the wider trend in the world economy where surveillance is infused with the ideology of capital accumulation as the ultimate aim. Zuboff also makes it clear that surveillance capitalism should not be conflated with digital technologies such as algorithms, sensors, etc. alone even though it depends on these. She says (2019: 11), 'if technology is bone and muscle, surveillance capitalism is the soft tissue that binds the elements and directs them into action', i.e. to accumulate. The larger point Zuboff is making is that it is not the technology but the bigger assemblages of power and capital that institutionalize digital tools to shape accumulation.

[17] How Upwork generates job success score is available at https://support.upwork.com/hc/en-us/articles/211068358, accessed 19 July 2021. Also, see Veen et al. (2019) on how this obfuscation of performance management is designed to control workers.

Graham, 2020a; Milland, 2017; Rani and Furrer, 2020; Schörpf et al., 2017; Wood et al., 2019; and for place-based gig work, see Cant, 2019; Ravenelle, 2019; Rosenblat, 2018; Woodcock, 2020b). While these are important contributions to the research on the rise of algorithmic surveillance in the workplace, we also want to add that behind every use of technology to enhance productivity lies human decision making by the management (see Kellog et al., 2020). That is, placing emphasis on algorithms as a central cog in the control of labour processes should not mean ignoring the role of human management in digital work and also the possibilities of challenges to these production models.

In our sample, remote gig economy workers in Africa reported increased work intensity and unsocial working hours as a result of constant monitoring of their work by platforms and clients/employers.[18] Work intensity—understood as the pace of work and effort (Green, 2006), long and irregular working hours, and emotional and time demands (Boxall and Macky, 2014)—is a key indicator of job quality. Workers in our sample were increasingly looking to win excellent feedback from clients and a five-star rating, which enables them to gain a high job score on platforms. Workers also reported strict demands from clients in terms of work quality, with the concomitant risk of not receiving good feedback. This resulted in them working longer hours, which sometimes meant working through the night. Similar findings have been reported by Berg et al., (2018) and Rani and Furrer (2020).

For African gig workers, surveillance adds to their already existing vulnerable conditions by affecting their physiological and mental health. Workers are under constant pressure to sit in front of their screen for long hours, often late into the night, resulting in high physical and mental stress, weakening of eyesight, constant back pain, and a lack of sleep. This is particularly true for hourly rate work like virtual assistants, web chat agents, customer services, and sales. Even some of the most successful and experienced gig workers we met told us that they would be up way past midnight searching for jobs because this is when clients (mainly from the US and Canada) would normally post jobs. It was not uncommon for gig workers we met to work up to sixty hours a week. Dayo, an online sales agent in Nigeria, told us that during his busiest times he could end up working around eighty hours a week, and as a result he struggled to get enough sleep. Chris, a virtual assistant in Kenya, was working over seventy

---

[18] However, monitoring can vary based on types of contracts (e.g. fixed price or hourly wage contracts).

hours weekly in 2016 when we interviewed him. He explained his working routine and said:

> I work from home when my kid goes to school. My wife has her own salon business. So, she leaves early, comes late. So, I wake up at 3 am. I work till 5 am. From 5 am to 7 am I prepare my boy to go to school. Once he leaves for school, I take a shower and eat my breakfast. At 8 am, I start working. I work up till 4 pm. When my boy comes from school, I help him with his homework and then he goes to play. I work from around 5:30 pm till 7 pm. Then I take a break, I prepare supper. My boy comes back at 7.30 pm. He eats dinner and by 8:30–9 pm he goes to bed. I start working from 9:00 till midnight. Sometimes more depending on contracts.
>
> **Interview, pers. comm., Nairobi, 2016**

Another Kenyan worker, Dabiku, whose story we highlighted in the Prologue is an online video editor with a top-rated status on Upwork. He told us that he had to sacrifice his sleep to get to where he is now. When he joined Upwork in 2012, he was doing 16 hours per day every day from Monday to Sunday. He further added that he was going to sleep at around 3 or 4 am and developed migraines as a result (Interview, pers. comm., Nairobi, December 2016). The flexible working schedule which is very common among gig workers obscures the late-night work put in by these workers, which undermines their autonomy. This autonomy paradox is also highlighted by Shevchuk et al. (2019), who found in their study of Russian gig workers that night work has an adverse effect on workers' subjective well-being as measured by satisfaction with work–life balance, life satisfaction, and emotional exhaustion.

Surveillance and Monitoring in Call Centres

At the heart of call centre workplace monitoring is the calling system, which connects workers to end customers to create a cycle of continuous calls in order to maximize the length of time workers are on calls, resulting in what Taylor and Bain (1999) have referred to as 'an assembly line in the head'. Having said that, it is important to note here that despite the adoption of advanced technologies in call centres around the world, the organization of the work remains quite varied and depends on a number of variables, including the nature of the operations, the industrial sector, the type of technology integration, management styles, and human resource practices (Taylor et al., 2002).

In call centres almost all kinds of worker activities and interaction are monitored, stored, and analysed through the use of digital tools such as CRM and WFM software to enhance time management and employee productivity. Screens placed in the rooms where workers make and take calls display agents' daily performance and competence (see Figure 5.3) based on the number of calls answered, calls dropped, average call handling times, break times, login efficiency, attendance, meeting daily quotas, etc. These are often referred to as adherence levels. Workers are rated based on their adherence as well as work quality, whereby quality control managers rate workers based on their handling of customer calls and queries. A call centre worker, Akuwele, in Accra explained the daily schedule of an ordinary call centre worker. She said:

> Okay, so my daily schedule, I get out of my bed at about 4:00 am, latest 4:30 am. I would just do a few chores, hit the bathroom, get out, make sure I am done at about 5:30, get out of my house at 5:45 because my shift starts at 7:00 am. Latest for me at work is 6:40 and at 7:00 I should have spoken to a customer. I attend to customers till about 9:00, then I would have breakfast. I usually have breakfast for about 15–20 minutes . . . When I get back at 9:20 I would be at my desk until about 12:30. Then I would go for lunch and usually lunch is for 30 minutes. I am back and then I would sit through until about 3:30 am and take a break, walk around a little, come back and close my shift at 4:00 am. There are times when I do not log in too early, I would have to make up for the time because I would not be making up my KRAs (key responsibility areas). That is how a call centre agent is doing their average handling time (AHT), which is your time per call . . . Then we have quality control and assurance: where your calls are audited, what you are scored with. It is usually 86 per cent and above. Usually I get 90 per cent. Then we have our repeat percentage. Sometimes customers are just being customers: you have not satisfied the customer, that is one reason why they would call back. So, a lot of things count.

The average handling time is basically the time spent by agents on calls. Different call centre firms will have their own AHT. In the sample of workers we interviewed, this was typically in the range of 120 to 180 seconds. A call centre agent, Obiajulu, in Lagos explained what this AHT means for workers. He said:

> On an average I make about 150 calls a day but sometimes it can be 80–90 which affects my performance . . . We have an [AHT] of 180 seconds to solve customer queries . . . There are customers you talk for long and then there are calls that

last 50 seconds, and it affects your [AHT] meaning that you did not really talk much on that call. There are customers that instead of those three minutes you talk to them for like six minutes they are not done and you cannot cancel the call . . . You can tell the customer that you will call them back because you do not want to go over three minutes call time.

The pressure of performance on agents in call centres can lead to high work intensity among employees. Workers are under time pressure and they have to multitask while on call, while also maintaining high ratings. An agent, Eliza, in Accra told us:

We were given 120 seconds to handle one call and work up time. Work up time is after the call work. So, when the call ends you should have at least some seconds to work on what the customer requested before another call comes through . . . You have to lodge a complaint. Maybe the customer had a complaint. You have to either raise a ticket or transfer the complaint to the back office . . . But another customer would come on the line, so you could be doing this and still talking to the customer. A call centre job is you are working and talking and looking at the same time.

The high work intensity can affect the way workers perform their tasks. In terms of quality control and worker performance in call centres, a number of workers told us that if an agent makes a mistake it can have serious consequences. An agent in Nigeria, Obada, told us that 'If the quality is bad,

(a)   (b)

Fig. 5.3 Workers' performance boards, analog (left) and electronic (right)
Source: Reproduced with permission from Anwar and Graham, 2019: fig. 2.

the company will penalise you in the form of salary deduction'. In some extreme cases, workers can lose their jobs. Workers can be fired without any arbitration or settlement. Wan, an agent in South Africa said that it is common for workers to be fired at his company. In fact, he had his job terminated immediately over a complaint filed by a customer who was unhappy with a sales deal. Summing up her experience of working in call and contact centres, Ash, an agent in South Africa, said:

> I think the call centre industry is a bit stressful one, it is high paced and it is very demanding. You need to be able to work fast. Everything is based on statistics. So, whatever work comes, you need to be efficient enough to capture everything correctly and have it out by the time the next customer comes on the call. So, it is a very tense or complicated environment. You need to know your job. Sometimes you interact with clients over the phone, sometimes you interact with them via email. So, you need to have a good command of English. You need to be efficient because work piles up . . . If you take too long you have other calls that are building up and you need to be done by 5 pm. So, you need to have time management skills as well. You need to be able to get everything off your desk by 5 pm and have that job . . . In a call centre you are measured on keeping time, so that is schedule adherence. You are measured on how long you take your break, do you adhere to the amount of time given for your break. If you go over that time you are penalised. If you take long you will affect your team's performance as well. How long you actually spend on an interaction so that is either on a call or email, you get timed on that as well. How long you are actually spending with each line. You get an average of that on a monthly basis. How much work you do is also measured, i.e. your productivity . . . It affects you positively and negatively. It affects you positively because it helps your work ethic. It drives you to actually get your work done. It affects you negatively where maybe you have a difficult client and maybe this client needs 15 minutes of your time. So now that 15 minutes will bring you a whole day's average handling time down. Just that one call will affect your whole day's average handling time or just that email will affect your whole day.

Agents regularly complained that such workplace monitoring leads to demotivation and frustration, affecting both their personal and professional life. Ash told us that as a consequence of trying to finish her work tasks as quickly as possible, she has started treating her child and the household work professionally, and it is creating a distance between them. One worker, Jabulile in South Africa, likened the call centre's working space to 'packed sardines' due to the small size of the cubicles in which the agents sit. Multitasking with both voice and non-voice systems can also have damaging effects on workers both mentally and physically. Some of the words used by agents to describe the mental and psychological impacts of this work were 'stressful', 'strenuous', 'demotivating', and 'frustrating'. One call centre worker in South Africa told us that the job

> is really strenuous. We depend a lot on energy drinks because of the late-night shifts and the long working hours. You see a lot of Monsters [a brand of energy drink] there. Even in the cafeteria, you find the row for fresh water but no-one drinks water there. So, yes, it does give you that bit of financial freedom but then it comes with many sacrifices.

Woodcock (2016: 55) has argued that new labour practices in call centres reflect the exploitation of the 'minds' of workers, rather than a Fordist exploitation of their bodies. However, in every way entry-level call and contact centre activity is about the exploitation of both the minds and bodies of workers. The increasing use of digital technologies to monitor and control every aspect of the labour process is a contributing factor towards this.

Loneliness and Social Isolation

Workplace monitoring and strict control over labour processes can also be tough and isolating for workers. A key outcome of high work intensity coupled with working from home and irregular hours among remote workers was loneliness and social isolation, since their interpersonal contacts and communications are reduced. Social interactions between fellow workers, family, and friends have long been considered effective for the psychological and physiological health of workers (Jahoda, 1982).

Gig workers were often confined to their homes or cafes, which were the main places of work.[19] The fact that gig workers have to work late at night means they often do not get time to socialize. A Kenyan web researcher and virtual assistant on Upwork told us that she currently works between fifty-five and sixty hours a week to make sure the work gets completed and the client is satisfied. As a result, she did not have enough time for leisure

---

[19] Call centre workers do not face such issues as they work in an office space and interact with fellow workers regularly.

and social activities. Similar experiences were also reported to us during a group meeting of gig workers in Lagos, where participants told us that they often felt the need to talk to people, given how lonely home working could get.

This is not to suggest that all gig workers are atomized and individualized. To compensate for social isolation and loneliness, gig workers usually turn to digital communications with friends and fellow workers, whose importance is underscored in the survey of US and Indian gig workers by Gray and Suri (2019). Our own research has shown that gig workers form digital communities and that there is a great deal more interaction among them through social media than previously thought (Anwar and Graham, 2020c; more on this in Chapter 6).

The experiences of managerial surveillance that we described above are further amplified by the general lack of bargaining power and freedom of association among digital workers. Collective bargaining power among workers and their ability to unionize has been noted to have positive influence on job quality, resulting in higher wages, fewer redundancies, and class compromise with employers (Pahle, 2014; Silver, 2003; Wright, 2000). For workers in Africa, who often come from poor socio-economic backgrounds and have a precarious existence, freedom of association is even more important. African workers have often relied on trades union movements to win concessions in their workplaces (e.g. Alalade, 2004; Alexander, 2010; Dickinson, 2017; Von Holdt, 2002; Webster and Buhlungu, 2004) and for wider social activism (e.g. Ihonvbere, 1997; Karreth, 2018; Pillay, 2013; Webster, 2015). But as we discuss in the following subsections, the space for collective mobilization and freedom of association among African workers is narrowing, especially in the domain of digital economy.

Lack of Bargaining Power

Work in the remote gig economy and in call and contact centres affects workers' bargaining power in various ways. In the context of gig economy activities, where labour markets operate on a planetary scale (Graham and Anwar, 2019) and where the work gets done in the digital realm (Graham and Anwar, 2018a), workers rarely have the associational advantages that workers in manufacturing have, for example. Instead, remote workers have to rely on their structural power to influence their working conditions and gain concessions from managers.

Much remote work is characterized by an oversupply of labour (see Chapter 3; also Graham and Anwar, 2019). This has the potential to affect two key forms of bargaining power, i.e. associational and structural power (Silver, 2003; Wright, 2000). Because workers bid for jobs on Upwork, it is crucial to understand how their subjective perception of bargaining power affects their bidding behaviour, ability to demand higher wages, their understanding and awareness of online labour market competition, access to local alternatives, the potential cost of disrupting the production process, and also their ability to undertake collective action (Stillerman, 2017).

For African gig workers, both types of structural power—marketplace bargaining power and workplace bargaining power—are affected in multiple ways. Several workers told us that they struggled to find suitable jobs in their local labour markets despite having a university degree; a trend already noted by the ILO (2015b). Workers reported regulatory bottlenecks, favouritism, patronage, and discrimination to be some of the constraints to finding jobs locally. The handful of workers we interviewed who did indeed find a regular job in the local labour market were poorly paid and often endured long commutes due to bad traffic; an everyday reality in most large cities in Africa. Gig work therefore appears to be an attractive option, where workers can work from home and earn a livelihood.

However, the workers we interviewed noted that their workplace bargaining power is constrained in the gig economy. First, workers face intense competition on platforms. Almost every worker we met had the experience of being undercut by a lower bid, particularly from Indian, Bangladeshi, and Filipino workers who have a reputation for bidding extremely low. In fact, remote workers told us that they could not compete with Filipinos or Indians. In the words of Chris, a Kenyan transcriber on Upwork, 'the Filipinos will accept anything' (Interview, pers.comm. Nairobi, October 2017), while a Nigerian respondent told us that Indians can be very intimidating because they can accept as low as US$1 for any job and work like 'camels'. Second, platforms' rating systems can also influence the marketplace bargaining power of workers. On the one hand, the rating system allows workers to signal to clients about their reputation in order to attract more work and perhaps demand higher wages; but on the other hand, these reputational systems also affect their bargaining power if they receive low scores. Finally, very few gig workers would threaten to withdraw from contracts they find on platforms even if they are low paid.

We found that only experienced workers with good reviews and several hundred hours of work on platforms threatened their clients with cancellation of their contracts if their demands, such as increment in wages, were not met by clients. Workers were aware of their workplace bargaining power in extracting minor concessions and short-term gains to avoid the exploitation that comes with gig work (more on this in Chapter 6).

Additionally, global competition for remote work means a race to the bottom, rendering local minimum wages practically impossible in some circumstances (Graham et al., 2017b), further increasing income insecurity. An online virtual assistant or a data entry clerk may experience greater autonomy in terms of working hours and place of work but they may have to accept extremely low wages in order to secure work, which may be lower than the local minimum wage. Some data entry workers we met were earning a mere US$1–2 per hour, but felt that if they asked for higher wages, the client might replace them with other workers.[20] Noah, a data entry worker, worked for Hummingbird Connect, a mobile-based app for internet search and questions. He would answer fifty questions posted by mobile app users to earn US$1. It would take up to two hours for him to earn that dollar.

More surprisingly, gig workers are often threatened openly with the refusal of wages if their work is not satisfactory. Several platforms state on their websites that clients will only have to pay if they are satisfied with the completed work (Figure 5.4), a clear example of an attack on workers' wages and their bargaining power. This is particularly pronounced for fixed-price jobs like transcribing, proofreading, and article writing, i.e. tasks that are paid on a piecemeal basis. Ozigbodi, an online editor and proofreader in Ghana told us that a client had asked her to edit a book and she clocked well over forty hours for which she was supposed to receive US$400. However, Upwork suspended the client's account due to payment inaccuracies and cancelled her contract. Ozigbodi was still owed US$200 by the client when we last contacted her in 2019. Similarly, Kenyangi, from Uganda, was writing movie subtitles for a US-based client. She completed around three-quarters of the job, or roughly ten hours of work, but was unable to finish it within the time allotted by the client. Thus, the task was categorized as unfinished (though the client did receive the partially completed task from Kenyangi) and went unpaid. Piecemeal work has historical precedent and Marx (1954: 518) saw it as 'the most fruitful source of reduction of wages and capitalist cheating'. Under the ILO's

---

[20] Upwork introduced a minimum wage of US$3 per hour in 2014.

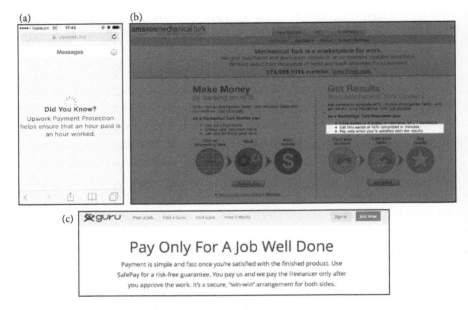

Fig. 5.4 Various platforms advertising pay protection for clients

Source: Reproduced with permission from Anwar and Graham, 2020a: fig. 1, published under the Creative Commons CC-BY 4.0 licence.

definition, withholding a worker's pay or refusing to pay constitutes forced labour (ILO, 2005), an important factor of vulnerability among workers (Waite et al., 2015).

Freedom of Association

Despite a few narratives of workers being able to exert their individual structural power over clients, there is little evidence of associational power of workers on platforms. Trades unions have long played a key role in establishing institutional protections against unfair practices of employers (Frege and Kelly, 2004). Therefore, a difficult question is how to convert workers' individual structural power into associational power in remote work. During a group discussion with Nigerian workers, the idea of having a labour union for remote workers in Africa was supported but workers were less clear on what such a labour union would look like and if it would help them overcome adverse working conditions. None of the gig workers we interviewed were members of any trades union, despite a particularly vibrant history of unions on the continent (Beckman et al., 2010).

Trades unions for remote work are actually rare globally, although there have been recent efforts around unionization and mobilization in the place-based gig economy. In various parts of the European Union, taxi drivers and delivery workers on various platforms such as Uber and Deliveroo have attempted to mobilize and organize (e.g. Jesnes et al., 2019; Tassinari and Maccarone, 2017). In Australia, negotiations between a trade union body in New South Wales and AirTasker, a place-based work platform, helped establish minimum standards for platform-based working (Minter, 2017). The efforts of Uber drivers to organize in the UK are also well known (Aslam and Woodcock, 2020).[21] Indeed, there is a growing social movement towards collective bargaining and mobilization among gig economy workers, especially during the COVID-19 pandemic. As gig economy platforms have largely shunned their responsibilities for protecting workers during the pandemic (Fairwork, 2020b), advocacy groups and gig workers have mobilized to form communities. A recent example is the recognition gained by the new App Drivers & Couriers Union, led by ride-hailing drivers in the UK. Similar movements have also emerged in Africa and other parts of the world, with the first conference convened at Oxford, UK on 29–30 January 2020 of app-based transport workers and their representatives from twenty-three countries (IWGB, 2020).

If there is one thing that unites the African digital workers we covered in our sample, it is non-unionization in their respective sectors. Remote workers rarely organize because their employer is often not based in the country of their residence, and home-based working means that networks in physical locations are rare. We found instances of Nairobi University students who worked for the same US-based employer on Upwork, but who had never met each other. However, we did also find some evidence of workers' digital interactions both locally and transnationally. During our interview with a Ugandan worker in Kampala, we found that he knew two of our respondents from Ghana, whom we had interviewed earlier. At the time of the interview, the Ugandan interviewee was chatting to the Ghanaian respondents on LinkedIn and he showed us their chat. They all worked for the same foreign-based agency on Upwork. These interactions also support the fact that despite the gig economy workforce being considered to be

---

[21] The court put the burden of proof on platforms to recognize gig workers as employees. But in 2020, backed by the funding and lobbying campaign of major platforms (Uber, Postmates, and Instacart), the state of California voted for the Prop 22 ballot, which effectively exempted platforms from AB5 and allowed them to continue to label gig workers as independent contractors. In 2021, a county superior in California ruled the ballot to be unconstitutional after the lawsuit filed by drivers (The Guardian, 2021).

atomized or individualized, worker networks exist, even though they may be spatially dispersed.

On the other side, i.e. BPOs the level of unionization in our sample countries is negligible, though unions do exist in these countries. We found some form of ground-level mobilization happening in Ghana and Kenya, but in South Africa—despite the extensive presence of trades unions, and the largest number of call centre workers—this was not the case. The Communications Workers Union of Kenya (COWU-K) was trying to organize call centre workers and had signed a collective bargaining agreement with two BPO firms when we interviewed their general secretary in 2016. In Ghana, in 2017 we spoke to the deputy secretary of the Communication Workers Union (CWU), who told us that they tried organizing the workers at Tech Mahindra two years ago but the workers were fearful of joining the union and management did not engage with the CWU.

Support for unions among workers is important for ground-level mobilization, but we found this to be missing among call centre workers. Although the workers we spoke to generally liked the prospect of a union, there were also some who thought 'the union is a bad idea' (Interview, pers. comm. call centre worker, South Africa, September, 2016). One such worker in South Africa explained:

> Because those guys they can put you into trouble . . . The unions will be the ones that will be talking to the employer, on behalf of the workers. Perhaps the employer will take time to solve the issue. The unions will be impatient. Then they will be informing the workers to say, 'we are going on a strike' . . . I think there should be a need for a union, at first. There should be a purpose to form a union, i.e. to solve a problem that I cannot solve by myself. I think it should start there first. If I have queries and problems that I cannot solve by myself or people that I think are supposed to assist me are not doing what they are supposed to be doing then that is when the union will come about . . . Anyway they will be deducting our money, I do not want that.

The transformation of trade unionism on the continent is well documented, with liberalization, revision of labour legislation, and changes to production processes often seen as reasons for declining union movements (see Chelghoum et al., 2016; Pitcher, 2007; Webster, 2007).[22] In new sectors of the economy, such as call and contact centres, union leaders told

---

[22] However, union mobilization among informal workers has gained traction lately, for example among domestic workers in Kenya and South Africa (Fischer, 2013; also Solidarity Centre, 2013).

us of a number of challenges to organizing workers in the sector. First, low income means union contributions are seen as a hefty expense workers cannot afford.[23] Second, call centre workers rarely work for an employer long enough to join a union, and because of the contractual nature of their jobs, workers may find themselves jobless after their contract ends. A team leader at a call centre in Nairobi, Ken, told us that he tried to recruit workers back in December 2015 and by April 2016 he had about 150 workers who agreed to join the union. But then seventy of them were fired from the company, and he had to start all over again. He told us that while he is working again with a union organizer, he is no longer giving it serious thought.

Joining a union is also risky for call centre workers. Ken told us that the management at his company had threatened to fire him if he tried to organize workers. He also said that call centre workers therefore do not speak out, because of the threat of losing their jobs. Where workers have joined a union and local unions have been active in mobilizing and entering into collective agreement with BPO firms (as has been the case in Kenya), the management punishes workers by firing those who join. A union organizer in Nairobi, Dave, who used to work for a BPO firm, told us that the company he worked for was going through collective bargaining discussion with COWU-K and he was one of the union representatives at the firm. The company waited until his contract was up and then decided not to renew it.

Some firms we spoke to told us that there is no need for workers to join a union if the management takes good care of them, and offers them a career path. A manager at a local firm in Accra said:

> We do not have any labour union in here and you ask how have we been able to do it? We do not stop anybody from joining a union, but we have a family thing going on in there, we work in teams. You do not even see the need to go and join a labour union where they are deducting your fees every month. At the end of the day, so long as you are working, you are earning money, you feel like there's a career path for you, you feel at home . . . We believe that we have issues, like any other company, but we are taking the problem one day at a time and trying to deal with it. You see, people want to work, they want job security, and they want a career path. I came in as a brand ambassador taking calls. I had

---

[23] Because BPO firms prefer hiring staff on temporary employment contracts wages can be very low (see Batt et al., 2009).

the opportunity to become a team leader, to become a supervisor, to become a manager. They can see a career path and we believe that is what we provide for these guys. We give them a future.

Interview, pers. comm., May 2017

However, the career trajectories of call and contact centre workers have long been the subject of scrutiny (e.g. Benner and Mane, 2011; Vira and James, 2012). On the one hand, call and contact centre jobs are understood to be suited to young people who are entering the labour market. On the other hand, there are genuine concerns that BPOs provide few career options.

Labour Mobility and Career Prospects

Occupational mobility—that is, the opportunity for future employment expressed as labour mobility both within and across the sectors of an economy—is seen as key for job quality. BPOs are considered to be flat organizations (Holman et al., 2007) with a high ratio of agents to team leaders and supervisors (Taylor and Bain, 1999). Therefore, there are few opportunities for internal progression of agents within a firm (Armistead et al., 2002; Benner and Mane, 2011; Del Bono et al., 2013; Gorjup et al., 2008). That said, Hunt and Rasmussen's (2010) study of women in call centres in New Zealand, found that call centre work may assist women in gaining promotion to management positions both internally and externally. But the small size of the industry and type of operations (government sector) may partially explain this outcome. In contrast, Belt (2002) holds that call centres can act as a 'female ghetto', in that they offer limited opportunities for women to progress to team leader roles, where they often reach a glass ceiling (also see Budhwar et al., 2009).

We asked industry experts and firm managers what they thought about the career trajectories of contact centre agents. An executive at an international BPO firm in South Africa said that these jobs are seen as a 'springboard for careers in other organisations, but not doing call and contact centre work'. Some experts were sceptical of the long-term sustainability of these jobs. Jon Browning, the President of Global BPO Solutions, told us that 'BPO companies do not like attrition after one year, [but] they do not mind it after 2–3 years' (Interview, pers. comm., Johannesburg,

2016). The attrition rates in this sector are certainly high, with BPESA suggesting it to be 30.9 per cent annually among contact centre workers in South Africa (BPESA, 2015b). A majority of our BPO workers did not see their jobs as 'agents' to be a long-term prospect, and instead wanted to move either to a different firm in search of higher income or to leave the sector entirely. However, this is not easy for the African workforce.

Job creation has slowed down since 2000 in most economies on the continent, and in countries like South Africa employment is becoming more skill intensive (World Bank, 2015). This has resulted in limited opportunities for the unskilled and semi-skilled workforce, both in the formal and informal sectors. In South Africa, youth, particularly young Blacks, struggle to secure meaningful jobs, making BPO jobs an attractive entry point into formal labour markets, albeit without much hope for career progression. The lack of career progression also has a particularly crucial racial element to it in South Africa. While there is no recent data on the racial composition of call and contact centre workers in South Africa, data from 2007 suggest that Blacks represent a significant proportion of contact centre agents, but make up only 7 per cent of managers, in comparison to whites who make up around 61 per cent of the management force (Benner et al., 2007).

We encountered a few respondents who had been call centre agents for more than five years, and asked them why they were still working in the sector. One of the common responses was that they do not have alternate employment opportunities in their local labour markets. One respondent in South Africa who had been a call centre agent for seven years replied that they had no choice but to continue to work and hope working conditions would eventually improve.

There are some indications that this could happen. The South African call centre industry has been growing for the last few years to emerge as one of the biggest on the continent. This certainly offers hope for workers, as a growing industry might allow new entrants and unemployed workers more options to seek jobs as call and contact centre agents. A growing industry might also offer workers opportunities for occupational mobility by switching companies and leveraging their experience to seek better incentives or higher salaries. This kind of tactic has been described by James and Vira (2012) in their study of BPO workers in India. They found that workers have been able to achieve career progression through what they call 'career staircases', where they undertake job hopping between firms to seek higher wages, improved working conditions, and more complex job roles. For workers in other countries in our sample, the career prospects of agents are curtailed by a smaller BPO sector, meaning that workers do not have such opportunities for job hopping. In Kenya, Nigeria, and Ghana, the agents we interviewed had often worked for various BPO firms, but this did not result in better pay or improved working conditions. Furthermore, workers can also leave the sector altogether to seek employment opportunities elsewhere, as has been the case with Indian call centre workers. Vira and James (2012), for example, in their survey showed how call centre workers develop transferable skills that can be exploited in India's burgeoning service-sector economy by moving on from the industry to seek education, or higher paying and complex jobs elsewhere, such as in banking, insurance, and real estate. Of course, we should be careful about comparing the BPO industry in our sample countries with India's.

India has a bigger national economy than most economies on the African continent and is the world's leading player in outsourced services (Kleibert, 2015). Its BPO industry is the biggest in the world with more than three million jobs. India's BPO firms are concentrated around a handful of large metropolitan cities, including New Delhi, Bangalore, and Mumbai. Similar developments are taking place in South Africa, with a BPO industry growing around Johannesburg, Cape Town, and Durban. Clustering of firms in a particular area is known to affect labour market outcomes. Freedman (2008), for example, noted that in IT clusters, workers can job hop within the sector or outside to achieve higher wages (also see Fallick et al., 2006; Tambe and Hitt, 2013). However, another study by D'Cruz and Noronha (2012) found that while opportunities for promotion were available to call and contact centre agents in India, these were limited in their number and scope, and where these are available it is very subjective. Therefore, any comparisons between African countries and other leading locations such as India and the Philippines should be drawn with care. This also applies to comparisons between South Africa's economy and that of other African economies.

While research on career progression in call centres is well established, in the gig economy this is a relatively new area of study (e.g. Idowu and Elbanna, 2020; Lehdonvirta et al., 2019; Yerby, 2020) with emerging discussions around boundary-less careers in the gig economy, i.e. concerning movement both within and between firms (Kost et al., 2020). The narratives around gig economy jobs portray them as a highly sought-after option to work and develop careers for a twenty-first-century workforce (see Kuek et al., 2015; Mckinsey and Company, 2016).[24] These narratives are further reinforced by the platform companies themselves. A 2015 survey conducted by Upwork in collaboration with the Freelancers Union in the US, found that 60 per cent of respondents started doing freelancing by choice. An earlier 2013 survey of freelancers conducted by oDesk found 72 per cent of those still in a regular job wanted to quit and work for themselves (Upwork, 2015). The policy rhetoric for development within international organizations like the World Bank is also to promote self-employment and entrepreneurship among the unemployed, and gig work platforms are seen as one of the means to foster this (Kuek et al., 2015). However, some of these self-employed might represent what Portes and Hoffman (2003: 55) have referred to as 'forced entrepreneurialism', arising from the limited choices available in the face of high unemployment, the loss of job opportunities in other sectors, dysfunctional local labour markets, and constrained opportunities in their workplaces (Burchell and Coutts, 2019). Workers joining gig work from Africa are often enticed by these narratives and discourses of gig work. But the reality of working in the gig economy is different, and numerous studies have begun to offer a rather bleak picture of tohe gig economy when it comes to workers' longer term career prospects (e.g. Anwar and Graham, 2020a; Kessler, 2018; Ravenelle, 2019).

In our interviews with gig workers, we explored how platform-based remote jobs can help workers develop skills and build careers in the long run. Indeed, gig workers can gain both tacit and explicit knowledge about their work and also acquire new technical skills (see Lehdonvirta et al., 2019). The workers we spoke to revealed that they have been able to acquire interpersonal skills, communication skills, confidence, and a positive outlook. Some workers developed technical skills (e.g. user interface design, and learning programming languages such as Java, mostly self-financed and self-directed), which theoretically opens up further avenues to seek complex and high paying jobs. Yet, where workers have been able to perform tasks successfully on platforms, that work experience and the skills gained have not necessarily been transferrable to other labour markets. For example, a worker with experience in transcription work would find it hard

---

[24] Deloitte in one of their studies describe changing attitudes among companies to use a variety of workers (incl. contractors, freelancers, and gig workers). This is suggested to lead to 'portfolio career' models, with careers involving multiple jobs, i.e. a mixture of part-time employment, contract work, and self-employment. However, full-time permanent is still the preferred employment contract among EU workers (Deloitte, 2018b).

to use that experience on their CV while applying for jobs locally. This was the key concern among workers in our sample, who told us that local employers do not recognize their work experience on platforms. They also told us that they cannot transfer their experience from one platform to another.

Our point is that gig work does not necessarily translate into a career path that helps workers achieve occupational and geographical mobility. Kost et al. (2020) raise this point that gig workers have limited chances for career management and development without adequate levels of support in the form of human resource management, and instead they depend on self-regulated learning strategies and self-development practices (see Margaryan, 2019b). While workers may have a greater degree of flexibility in terms of their work arrangements, only those with specialized skill sets can transition in and out of the gig economy (Kost et al., 2020) and better cope with the insecurities attached to non-standard work (Spreitzer et al., 2017). Unfortunately, in the context of the African continent, an estimated 58 per cent of the workforce is already employed in low-skilled occupations (ILO, 2020c). The ILO's study also highlights that skills mismatch remains a big issue in Africa, with 17.5 per cent of young workers reported to be over-skilled for their current jobs, and 28.9 per cent saying their skills were below the required levels. A young worker we interviewed in Uganda who had a degree in Ethics and Human Rights was working for a BPO doing entry-level data manipulation tasks. On the question of finding the right type of job for her education level, she explained the problem faced by most African youth who are entering the labour market:

> Yeah, I looked for the jobs. I looked and I am still looking for a job that fits my qualifications. But I know this is Uganda. The economy is bad. There is a high rate of youth unemployment. There are thousands of youths who graduate from different colleges and they are still loitering on the streets. They are doing nothing. So, it is either you get into something you say—it is called misplaced employment. You are not supposed to be where you belong. Either you do that or something else, like private business or try a start-up.
>
> **Interview, pers. comm., November 2017**

Thus, not only should policymaking on the continent look at addressing this skills mismatch, but it should also develop an educational system and training programmes that can not only equip the African workforce with the necessary skills to match contemporary labour market trends, but that are also integrated into wider national economic development plans. Having said that, we also want to point out that this does not mean digital workers cannot exercise their power over their employers, clients, and platforms to improve their working conditions and career prospects. In fact, in call centres workers' agency is well documented and analysed (e.g. Bain and Taylor, 2002; Mulholland, 2004; Taylor and Bain, 2003; Townsend, 2005; Woodcock, 2016). However, in gig economy activities this has so far been less studied (notable exceptions Anwar and Graham, 2020c; Barrat et al., 2020). Also, some of the implications of digital work that we discussed above are far more pronounced for the gig economy workers than call centre workers. Gig workers feel they are replaceable and the jobs on platforms can be given to anyone else if they demand concessions from employers. Additionally, because much of their work activities take place via platforms and their clients are often not based in the same country as workers, workers have less bargaining power in comparison to workers in activities that are based locally, i.e. call centre workers. As a result, it is not expected that gig economy workers have opportunities to exercise their agency. On the contrary, in Chapter 6, we discuss how African gig workers exert agency in the gig economy and the kinds of unique practices they deploy to counteract the adverse working conditions they face.

6

Resilience, Reworking, and Resistance

Hidden Transcripts of the Gig Economy

Introduction

In this chapter, we examine how African gig workers exercise agency to earn and sustain their livelihoods in the gig economy. As Chapter 5 has shown, in addition to the monetary and non-monetary rewards reaped by digital workers, they also face significant risks. Gig work platforms and clients/employers exert control over labour power and labour process through the mechanisms of ratings, feedback, payment methods, user profile registrations, and algorithmic workplace monitoring, thus constraining workers' autonomy and bargaining power. In fact, the opportunities for worker action in the gig economy are apparently fewer than in so-called 'Fordist' workplaces. This is even more apparent for remote gig work in comparison to place-based work—e.g. delivery couriers and taxi drivers who can form communities at or near restaurants and traffic junctions (see Tassinari and Maccarrone, 2019). Remote workers, as a result, are expected to have fewer opportunities to exert their agency—particularly so for workers in Africa, where a clear lack of well-paid work locally already constrains workers' ability to earn livelihoods. Further, in comparison to European workers, African workers have less state welfare support to fall back on, which can also limit their agency. In this chapter, we examine how remote gig workers in Africa manage these various constraints on one of the world's biggest gig economy platforms through their practices of everyday resilience, reworking, and resistance (after Katz, 2004).

Drawing from a rich labour geography tradition, which considers workers to 'actively produce economic spaces and scales' (Herod, 2001: 46), this chapter's main theoretical contribution is to offer a reformulation of Katz's (2004) notions of 'resistance', 'resilience', and 'reworking' as everyday practices of agency, best understood as 'hidden transcripts' of the gig economy (Scott, 1990). We documented these hidden transcripts—that is, acts and practices of workers that do not directly confront employers—among remote gig workers in Africa, both on and off the platform, to reveal how the socio-technical structures of platforms influence labour agency in the gig economy. In so doing, we contribute to the research on labour geography in the following ways.

First, the literature on the well-being of gig economy workers has grown tremendously in the last few years.[1] However, while gig workers' action and organizing have gained some traction in place-based work (see Cant, 2019; Tassinari and Maccarrone, 2019), discussion of labour agency in the remote gig economy has been generally limited to date. Some studies have noted how workers are developing a sense of online community through digital communication Wood et al. (2018). Similarly, Gray and Suri (2019) in their study of platform-based remote workers both in India and the US outlined the deeply intricate and interconnected nature of gig workers, often structured around current communication technologies. But beyond this there is a lack of discussion on what kinds of agency practices workers employ to overcome precariousness and vulnerability in the remote gig economy. This chapter, therefore, contributes to this emerging literature on labour agency and worker actions in the global gig economy by extending the scope of labour geography research from the context of African remote gig workers and its impact on their working conditions.

Second, whereas labour agency is generally understood to involve labour unions and collective bargaining, workers' individual actions are equally important (Rogaly, 2009). In this chapter, we discuss African gig workers' individual everyday practices of resilience, reworking, and resistance, and their consequences for working conditions. Cataloguing how these practices are performed at various scales and places helps us understand how the gig economy is negotiated and challenged by workers in low- and middle-income regions. In studying African gig workers, we advance the idea of 'hidden transcripts' (Scott, 1990) of the gig economy—that is, workers actions that do not confront clients or are in the public domain—which are attentive to the spatiality of work, socio-economic conditions of workers, and the labour processes guided by the technological structures of platforms.

---

[1] E.g. on the gig economy in high-income countries, see Berg (2016), Huws et al. (2017), Kessler (2018), Milland (2017), Ravenelle (2019), and Shibata (2019); and on low- and middle-income countries, see Anwar and Graham (2020a), Carmody and Fortuin (2019), D'Cruz and Noronha (2016), Graham et al. (2017), Rani and Furrer (2020), and Wood et al. (2019).

Third, while there is a long history of scholarship on labour studies in Africa (Beckman et al., 2010; Copper, 1987 Freund, 1984; Hilson, 2016), much of this literature is rooted in the mining-agricultural-industry complex. In this chapter, by contrast, we focus on African gig work, which until now has escaped the attention of scholars dealing with labour issues in Africa (for notable exceptions, see Carmody and Fortuin, 2019; Giddy, 2019). While there is already evidence to suggest that informal workers in Africa enjoy various sources of power (Lindell, 2013; Von Holdt and Webster, 2008), the spatially non-proximate nature of remote gig work means that coalitional and associational power are hardly available to these workers. In this chapter, we demonstrate how remote workers use their individual structural power to compensate for their weak associational power.

Conceptualizing Agency in Gig Work

Labour geography as a sub-discipline emerged in response to the Marxian-inspired economic geography literature of the 1970s, and other social science disciplines that neglected the agency of workers in their analyses of political–economic structures (see Herod, 1997, 2001). The basic premise in this 'labour geographies' turn is that workers can create and shape economic geographies through their own spatial fixes, just like capital can. But worker actions are enabled—and constrained—by the social, cultural, and political structures around them (Williams et al., 2017). In other words, agency and structures are intertwined and often influence each other (Coe and Jordhus-Lier, 2011).

Within the labour geography tradition, literature has emerged that asks how worker actions are determined both by their positions in production networks, and by the political systems (e.g. state, society, and labour markets) they find themselves in (Carswell and De Neve, 2013). The labour geography literature has also expanded to include non-standard employment relations in the new information economy (Benner, 2002), new modes of worker organization (see Lier and Stokke, 2006 on community unionism), and new geographical spaces (Lambert and Webster, 2001). Others have documented the influence of identity and intersectionality (gender, migrant status, and race) on agency (Batnitzky and McDowell, 2011). Further works exploring agency in the workplace and beyond it (Dutta, 2016; Hastings and MacKinnon, 2017), as well as individual agency

(Rogaly, 2009) have emerged, alongside the literature on the agency of unionized workers (Cumbers et al., 2010) and non-unionized workers (Benner and Dean, 2000). But the world of work is changing rapidly.

Work has always been connected to a place, e.g. a factory, farm, or home. However, the information-based economy is altering the meanings of employment, work, and workplaces, and how the labour process is organized, as a significant amount of work is now being done on digital labour platforms (Anwar and Graham, 2020a, 2020c; Graham and Anwar, 2018b, 2019 also see Chapter 3). Workers in the global gig economy are engaging in new forms of communication and organization. Thus, worker actions need to be examined in relation to changing work practices and unequal power relations in the gig economy, and how that influences platform structures and labour processes. Put differently, labour agency involves power—and also how effectively that power is wielded by gig workers in the context of their new digital workplaces, and the technological structures that both enable and constrain them.[2]

In studying gig workers in Africa, our point of departure is how labour agency is influenced by the relationship between labour and platforms as 'socio-technical systems' through which workers are brought under the control of capital for productive purposes.[3] Concretely, we show how worker actions are conditioned by platforms' technological controls such as ratings, feedback, monitoring systems, along with workers' socio-economic and cultural backgrounds. Finally, we will discuss how the gig economy is changing the spatial dynamics of labour agency by examining the social media interaction of gig workers as a useful space of agency, and considering the extent to which this impacts their working conditions.

Practices and Spaces of Labour Agency

We understand agency as a multifaceted concept that refers to both the intention and practice of taking action for one's self-interest or the

---

[2] Power here refers to the ability of workers to shape the social relations around them. In this context, the impact of agency will vary, depending on the types of power workers have and how that power is influenced and conditioned by the immediate contexts in which they live.

[3] Socio-technical systems refer to a combination of the technological artefacts, knowledge, capital, and human labour necessary for production and distribution of goods and services (Geels, 2004). Gig work platforms can be thought of as social-technical systems since they represent digital workplaces through which labour power performs various tasks.

interest of others (Rogaly, 2009: 1975; also Castree et al., 2004). A helpful way to understand labour agency in the gig economy is through Katz's (2004: 240–241) distinction between 'resilience', 'reworking', and 'resistance' strategies as three everyday practices of workers which emerge as a response to the changing world of work, and the political–economic transformations in their surroundings. In a way, Katz's conceptual distinction was informed by the early debates on resistance found in James Scott's work on Malay peasants (1985, 1990; also see Abu-Lughod, 1990).

Scott (1985) argues that oppression and resistance go hand in hand, and that by only focusing on visible actions and events, the subtle but powerful forms of everyday resistance get neglected. Scott characterized a wide variety of low-profile resistance practices that don't involve the collective defiance of powerful groups, but instead are often cryptic and opaque, and largely geared to the subordinated group's safety (Scott, 1990: 19). He distinguished two types of actions by such subordinated groups. One is the 'public transcript', i.e. open action in front of the other party in the power relationship (Scott, 1990: 2) and the other is the 'hidden transcript'—the discourse (both verbal and non-verbal actions) that takes place offstage so that power holders cannot see it (Scott, 1990: 4). Our concern in this chapter is with the hidden transcript, given that remote gig workers in Africa rarely come face to face with their employers, unlike with place-based work such as food delivery and taxi services. Scott's notion of the hidden transcript is a useful way to examine agency beyond observable actions, by looking into gig workers' daily lives to uncover practices that are not considered to be meaningful strategies for survival. For Katz (2004), not every autonomous act is an act of resistance, because there exists a variety of oppositional practices.[4] It is here that Katz's (2004) categorization of resistance, resilience, and reworking comes into play to understand labour agency in the gig economy.

Resistance, according to Katz (2004: 251), requires 'a critical consciousness to confront and redress historically and geographically specific conditions of oppression and exploitation'. For Ackroyd and Thompson (1999) resistance can also include misbehaviour and counterproductive practices towards work itself and the use of work material for non-work purposes.

---

[4] Hughes (2020) puts forward a similar argument that research, certainly within the discipline of human geography, has tended to conceptualize resistance by a 'predetermination of form', i.e. certain actions or actors constitute resistance. Instead, Hughes argues for framing resistance as emergent, whereby new actors and categories of resistance do not always cohere to an (expected) resistant form and yet condition the possibility for future claims to be made (pp. 1142–1143).

Thus, resistance can be seen as involving both the direct and indirect confrontation of workers, including challenging and subverting exploitative production regimes. Worker actions such as strikes and demonstrations are more direct forms of resistance, while indirect confrontations include wage negotiations. As employment relations become more contingent, and the workforce becomes unorganized, workers complement resistance with reworking and resilience to maximize their chances of survival (Katz, 2004).

Resilience refers to small acts of 'getting by' or coping with everyday realities without necessarily changing existing social relations (Katz, 2004: 244).[5] These acts include autonomous initiatives like education, training, and taking care of community members; and therefore may be neither progressive nor transformative. Workers also complement these with 'reworking' efforts in an attempt to redistribute resources and power by recalibrating oppressive and unequal power relations to improve their material conditions. Katz understood reworking as focused and pragmatic responses to problematic conditions faced by people. For example when facing eviction, residents of kampongs in North Jakarta use their local environmental knowledge and communal scavenging to rebuild their residences at an elevated site to avoid flooding (Betteridge and Webber, 2019).

Scott's and Katz's analyses both point to an important consideration of 'space'. Space is considered a key element in labour geography research—in particular, a key factor in the organization of production, collective mobilization of workers, institutional and regulatory practices at multiple scales, and labour mobility (Herod, 2001; Peck, 1996). But emerging spaces of digital work are both digitally distinct and digitally augmented (Graham and Anwar, 2018a).[6] The understanding of these digital spaces of production provides us with a way to think about how workers can produce their labour geographies. Since a large part of productive activities in the information economy take place in these digital spaces of work, digital channels have become central to production and reproduction, as well as to worker communication (Gray and Suri, 2019).

---

[5] For some, resilience can mean putting up with precarious life existence and inequality in society, and relocating the responsibility for well-being and change onto the individual (see Diprose, 2014).

[6] Gig work platforms are *digitally distinct* since they can be accessed from anywhere by anyone with access to a computer and internet connection. Digital technologies such as platforms also *augment* the positionalities of workers by transcending the temporal and spatial boundaries in which labour power is embedded. For example, African gig workers can perform certain tasks for employers in the US from a variety of spaces, which they were previously unable to do.

The proliferation of the internet has coincided with the rise of social media and new communication channels, such as WhatsApp and Skype.[7] These digital tools of communication have given rise to various social movements (Aouragh, 2012; Margetts et al., 2015) and have the potential to strengthen worker mobilization as well. In the age of platform capitalism (Srnicek, 2016), digital communication channels are fast becoming central to collective organization among workers (Wood et al., 2018), and are also a means to reduce overhead costs, perform work, and develop social bonds and support to make work manageable (Gray and Suri, 2019).

Following Scott (1990: 4) we have characterized remote gig workers' actions as hidden transcripts. We understand these as 'hidden' because workers and employers are rarely in the same location and hence do not confront each other. Also, worker actions will be hidden from employers when they use closed Facebook groups and WhatsApp messages,[8] rather than openly confronting them. For Silver (2003: 35), analysing 'anonymous or hidden forms of struggle . . . where strikes are illegal and open confrontation difficult or impossible', is just as important as analysing open resistance. We catalogue here a variety of socio-material practices of resilience and reworking, which are intended by workers to get by in their daily lives, as well as some resistance practices that are aimed at platform employers without the intention of their becoming full-fledged strikes, as used by factory or shop floor workers.

Katz's categorization further opens up the possibility to produce a revolutionary imagination in the minds of gig workers, who are often fragmented, individualized. and whose power is under continuous threat through the commodification of work (Graham and Anwar, 2018a, 2018b, 2019). While Africa has a long history of militant and progressive trades union movements opposing colonial and apartheid regimes, recent years have seen a decline in trades union movements across the continent (Andrae and Beckman, 1999; Beckman et al., 2010). Therefore, thinking about worker power in the gig economy that can complement labour unions is of utmost importance. The question here is: What types and sources of power do workers have in the gig economy?

---

[7] WhatsApp and Facebook are two of the most common messaging apps in Africa (Bobrov, 2018).
[8] Some of the Facebook groups used by gig workers are closed to the public; however, it is possible for employers to observe worker communications if they join these worker groups.

Types of Worker Power

Here it is important to think about different types of worker power, and workers' ability to exert agency vis-à-vis employers through a variety of acts (Schmalz et al., 2018). Structural power (Silver, 2003; Wright, 2000) can be used individually and collectively to improve labour's working conditions. Structural power is further divided into marketplace bargaining power (i.e. power derived by workers due to tight labour markets and shortage of skills) and workplace bargaining power (i.e. power derived through the position of workers in the production process), which can disrupt production through workers' collective action (Silver, 2003). Where workers' structural power has been weakened, symbolic power in combination with associational power has been a useful means for workers to articulate moral issues as social claims, and to build wider public pressure (Chun, 2009; Von Holdt and Webster, 2008). Similarly, associational power by workers is attained by being part of organizations—typically trades unions, which can serve as a front for collective action at multiple levels (Schmalz et al., 2018). A strategic combination of these worker powers is critical in order for workers' demands to be met (Mashayamombe, 2019; Webster et al., 2009).

In the near absence of institutionalized labour unions in the remote gig economy, it is crucial to explore how workers exert power in different spaces through individual practices that are informal, unorganized, and subtle, but which can nevertheless lead to positive outcomes. In this chapter we show how workers' everyday resilience, reworking, and resistance practices are built out of their structural power. We examine both productive and reproductive spaces, given that remote workers' daily practices also extend into the realm of social reproduction (Kelly, 2012).[9] Digital communication channels such as Facebook offer them a chance to forge community relations and build collective identity. Social media channels are also spaces where the interaction between markets, workers, civil society, and the state, have come to be made and remade daily, and hence are useful spaces to examine worker actions and labour market outcomes (Fuchs, 2014). Thus, gig workers' use of social media is an important

---

[9] Social reproduction includes a range of practices that maintain and reproduce production relations along with the material and social grounds on which they are produced (Katz, 2004). Social reproduction, therefore, has political–economic, cultural, and environmental aspects, all of which bear on the everyday lives of workers.

aspect to broaden the perspective of labour agency. The next section gives an account of agency practices undertaken by African remote workers.

The Variegated Landscape of Agency in the Gig Economy

On Upwork, bidding is determined by a worker's subjective perception of their marketplace bargaining power, which tends to be influenced by their awareness of the labour market competition. For example, newcomers tend to place more job bids compared to experienced workers, who prefer to filter jobs. New workers are also likely to bid at lower wages to win contracts. In contrast, experienced workers rely on their skills or reputation to command a higher price. Workers with positive reviews and top-rated status often do not even bid for jobs, since they get invited directly by clients through Upwork.

As part of our study, we examined the factors that enable African workers to succeed on platforms. Upwork categorizes successful workers in the form of 'Top Rated' workers, who maintain a job success score of at least 90 per cent, which is calculated based on both private and public feedback given to workers by clients. Workers with top-rated status often get more work from employers. Upwork also helps employers find top-rated workers based on the requirements of the job, a point made to us by several workers. As we show below, the already existing inequalities off-platform—including workers' education, economic status, and access to digital technologies—impact and influence who succeeds in finding work on Upwork and who does not. We further follow Carswell and De Neve's (2013) 'horizontal' approach to outline how workers' socio-economic status, identities, and livelihood strategies influence their agency.

Significantly different life goals among gig workers reflect the level of importance they assign to their work. In their multi-platform study in the US, Schor et al. (2020) found satisfaction to be higher and autonomy greater for workers with multiple sources of income, where the platform supplied just one portion of their total income. In contrast, those who were entirely dependent on platforms for their livelihoods expressed more dissatisfaction and experienced greater precarity. Similarly, in our sample, workers who were already in regular jobs were more likely to use gig work to earn extra income or simply to do something they are passionate about. Hence, they are also likely to filter jobs and select clients carefully, even if it took a few weeks to get their first contract. We found that those workers who were primarily dependent upon income from platforms (e.g. migrants) were more constrained in their actions, while educated workers tended to do complicated and highly skilled work such as article writing, and creative and multimedia activities. They were also more successful in setting up their profiles on multiple platforms, applying for jobs, and writing bids—compared with less-educated workers.

In the African context, workers' socio-economic backgrounds influence their ability to get work on digital platforms. We found that workers who were from poor backgrounds, had not completed higher education, and lacked necessary skills, often struggled to find jobs on Upwork. Their poor material conditions also prevented them from finding work on platforms, as they could not afford digital tools such as laptops. By contrast, workers who came from affluent socio-economic backgrounds and who had completed higher education, enjoyed success in winning bids on platforms. For example, Katy, a white migrant living in South Africa, explained that her privileged background, education, and material affordances had a direct bearing on her success as a gig worker. She explained:

> Yes, I have an advanced degree. I have the kind of life where I have always been able to go after something. I did not face racism and substandard education and I have had access to a computer. Whenever I have needed a computer and you know I have a network of friends who if my internet went down I could pick up and go to their houses and use it.
>
> **Interview, pers.comm., Johannesburg, 2016**

Similarly, Dean, a white remote worker in Johannesburg, has done thousands of hours of virtual assistant work on Upwork. He has a regular job as a sales agent in a local travel company. He also reiterated the importance of a worker's socio-economic status in finding work on platforms. He told us: 'I am able to exploit work opportunities on Upwork because I am privileged enough to enjoy all the necessities (internet, laptop, electricity) that are required to work on Upwork which many people in South Africa cannot afford' (Interview, pers.comm., September 2016). He further added that he gets 'paid a good salary from a regular job and has medical aid, pension, and other non-cash benefits. Online work definitely provides a cushion for extra money but if I lose my job on Upwork, which I think I can anytime, I am not concerned because I already have a job and enough money saved to survive'.

Gender and migrant status both shape and limit agency among workers. For migrant workers, gig work represents an alternative to the local labour markets, which can be exclusionary. For female workers, gig work offers freedom from certain forms of social relations, for example independence from male figures in the family. Crucially for migrant women workers, Rydzik and Anitha (2019) argue, agency acts can be differentiated as practices of resilience, reworking, and resistance, since gender, immigration status, and migration history (as well as low-status employment and educational level) shape both their understandings of particular experiences of exploitation and possible responses to these.

We examined a range of everyday individual practices and strategies of African gig workers through which they exert their agency both on and off the platform (Table 6.1). Workers often resorted to resilience and reworking strategies when they first joined Upwork. Those who found success on Upwork were then able to use more resistance strategies. Workers tended to exhibit similar agency 'off the platform', since the participation of workers on social media is less constrained by a platform's control mechanisms.

Remote gig workers' use of everyday reworking, resilience, and resistance strategies help them achieve autonomy at work and better bargaining power—where autonomy at work is understood as the ability of workers to control work intensity and working hours, and bargaining power includes a worker's capacity to negotiate their wages, withdraw from work at will, and control their employment conditions. We now discuss these everyday practices and their limits in the gig economy.

Everyday Resilience and Reworking

The most common everyday practices African gig workers have at their disposal are resilience and reworking, particularly among the new and less-educated workforce. The practices of these groups are often subtle and less confrontational than those of experienced workers or those already employed in their local labour markets. Less-educated workers often come from low-income backgrounds, and undertake insecure and low-paid work in informal local labour markets. Gig work is seen by them as an attractive substitute to the dysfunction of informal labour markets, and a significant livelihood opportunity. Hence, we found them to be less involved in acts of resistance, such as declining jobs or cancelling contracts. The importance of gig work for African labour's subsistence is underlined in both Research

Table 6.1 Heuristic framework for agency in the remote gig economy and its impacts

Spaces of labour agency	Types of agency practices			Agency impacts
	Resilience	*Reworking*	*Resistance*	
On the platform	Sharing computers and account. Buying reviews on platforms.	Negotiating working hours and wages. Creating multiple accounts Using two monitors.	Filtering of clients and jobs. Leaving negative feedback for client. Withholding the output from client.	Breaking barriers to entry. Improved Wages. Control over working hours. Discretion of work tasks. Scheduling of work.
Off the platform	Community formation (e.g. social media groups like Facebook). Advising fellow workers. Running training classes.	Using public Wi-Fi. Re-outsourcing jobs. Buying and selling accounts.	Exposing bad clients. Warning fellow workers.	Intensity of work. Collective identity formation.

Source: Reproduced with permission from Anwar and Graham, 2020c: 1278, tab 2.

ICT Africa's After Access survey (Insight2impact, 2019) and Wood et al.'s (2019) surveys, with a majority of the gig workers surveyed considering it crucial for their daily survival. The key target of gig workers is to break the barrier to entry on Upwork and find their first job, which is crucial for gig work: it helps workers get their first review score which, in turn, enables them to win further contracts. However, as we noted in Chapter 5, finding that first job is one of the biggest hurdles for workers.

In our sample, a majority of the workers (over 50 per cent) revealed that they spent anywhere from a month to a year of constant searching without winning any contracts on Upwork. That said, there are (dishonest) means to circumvent this problem. Newcomers who are starting out on the platform can buy feedback and reviews from clients on the platforms. The client posts a fake job, and workers pay the client in return for good feedback and a 5-star rating. Workers told us that this type of business transaction is undertaken primarily in local and personal networks. Additionally, workers might set up multiple accounts using the names of their family members and friends, thus giving them more 'connects' per month for job bidding.[10] One Kenyan worker, Isa, was using ten different Upwork accounts to increase the number of jobs he could bid for per month. Workers also resorted to sharing accounts with their friends and family members. We found examples of workers looking to buy highly rated pre-approved accounts with locations set for the European Union and the United States. These tend to be especially useful for African workers since it improves their chances of winning a bid, with a few workers reporting that clients seemed reluctant to outsource work to Africa.

Workers also told us how some clients will prey on newcomers with no feedback by demanding that they do free work in return for excellent reviews. Workers preferred jobs involving tasks that require less formal training and skills sets such as image tagging, which is easier than digital marketing, translation, and transcription work. A Nigerian worker, Ifeki, who is an online training instructor and has a university degree in public relations, spent one year bidding on Upwork. His first job was fixing the overheating problem on a laptop for an American client. A Ghanaian worker, Quinn, who primarily does editing and proofreading tasks, started on Upwork by finding the contact details of a South African businesswoman for a client. Both Ifeki and Quinn got paid and 5-star ratings

---

[10] Connects are like credits required by workers to apply for jobs. Number of 'connects' required to apply for jobs vary. Prior to May 2019, Upwork gave free connects to workers but that changed. Now, workers have to buy connects at US$0.15 per connect.

for their work, which led them to win further bids and ultimately several thousand dollars' worth of income through the platform.

Another issue among remote workers is that the gig economy is inherently dependent on internet access and computers, which is an added cost for them. Most workers reported using public internet hotspots such as coffee shops, libraries, and universities, to avoid paying internet access fees. Entry-level workers who could not afford a laptop worked at internet cafes, while others took out loans to buy a second-hand laptop and some even shared laptops in their non-work social networks, that is, with friends and family. An example of this was shared with us by Jess and Kenny, two friends from Ghana who both have undergraduate degrees. Upwork closed Kenny's account and told him that he was placing too many bids without actually winning any contracts. Kenny could not open a new account. Hence, he decided to use Jess's account, and now both share an account and a desktop to do data entry and article writing work (Interview, pers. comm., Takoradi, 2017). This practice has enabled them to overcome both the entry barrier and the technological barriers of platform work. These kinds of practices are also prevalent in place-based gig economy work such as ride-hailing. In a number of African countries, vehicle ownership is low and workers simply cannot join ride-hailing platforms such as Uber or Bolt, or other domestic platforms. However, the owner of a car with an approved account on a ride-hailing platform can add another driver as their 'driver partner' in order to share the car and any earnings (see Anwar, 2020; Graham and Anwar, 2018a; Otieno et al., 2020).[11]

Remote gig workers' problems are further compounded by the high levels of work monitoring on platforms. As discussed in Chapter 5, new digital technologies are enabling employers to exert authoritarian management practices remotely, through a form of 'Digital Taylorism' (The Economist, 2015a). This form of control is very much evident in the gig economy in both remote work and place-based work. Remote workers in our sample reported regular tracking of time and capturing of time-stamped screenshots of their laptops, leading to long working hours due to fear of non-payment of wages (Figure 6.1). Figure 6.1a shows a time-tracker on Upwork which records working hours regularly, and Figure 6.1b is the work diary of a remote worker showing screenshots of their computer captured by Upwork. If a worker's screenshot is captured while they are playing games or using

---

[11] That said, in practice, car owners have been able to extract rents as driver partners have to pay weekly rents for the car.

(a)

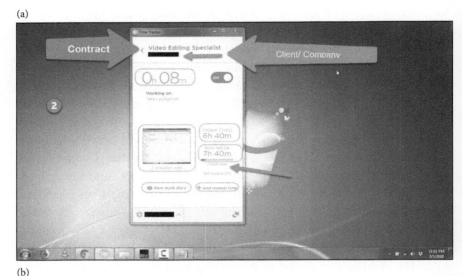

(b)

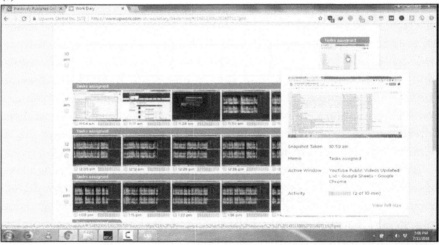

Fig. 6.1 Upwork's time tracker (a) and screenshot capture (b)
Source: Reproduced with permission from Anwar and Graham, 2020c: 1281, fig. 2.

social media, they may not get paid. The workers we spoke to subsequently felt that their client/employer and the platform are always watching them— a modern-day version of Jeremy Bentham's Panopticon (Semple, 1993). That said, some workers preferred screen-shot capturing, as this allowed regular payment of wages and protection against non-payment as reported by Wood et al. (2019).

To prevent such monitoring of non-work activities, some workers add a second display screen. This act can be thought of as both 'reworking' and 'resistance'. Reworking in a sense that workers tactically avoid monitoring of their work, and resistance because of the counterproductive work practices they do during working hours (Ackroyd and Thompson, 1999). It also provides workers with control over their pace of work and working hours, a key aspect of autonomy at work. While clients would often resort to regular monitoring of work early in the contract, experienced gig workers told us that once trust had been established, clients rarely tracked their time.

Another form of reworking strategy is to negotiate wages. While negotiation of wages is understood by Ackroyd and Thompson (1999) as an indirect form of resistance, Mann (2007) has argued that settlement of wage disputes is the working class's attempt to alter socio-economic relations from within the capitalist system, rather than by engaging in full-scale resistance. In the context of remote work, wage negotiations are often undertaken by workers to extract higher wages from the client, thus constituting an element of reworking.[12] This is largely possible due to the marketplace bargaining power of certain workers. Kelly, a transcriber from Uganda who has a '96 per cent job success' on Upwork, described how she uses a client's payment history to negotiate wages. She explained,

> If I go to a client's page and it says his average is $20 an hour, even if my profile states $15, I can confidently apply with a $20 an hour rate because that is what he pays . . . Sometimes you negotiate, he says your profile says $15, you are applying for $20. I tell him your page says you pay 20, so why do you want to pay me 15? And he says we compromise at 18, and I can work for 18.
>
> **Interview, pers. comm., October 2016.**

However, wage negotiation is not a viable option for many. The oversupply of labour power in the global gig economy creates a fear of replaceability, which means new workers work for low pay or unsocial working hours (Anwar and Graham, 2020a; see also Chapter 5). Thus, they resort to different types of strategies to cope with the everyday economic realities of low-paid and insecure work. Many of these tactics are built away from the workplace, and extend into the realm of their social and personal networks.

---

[12] Wage negotiation is not possible for place-based work such as ride-hailing at individual level. But collectively, Nigerian and Kenyan drivers have been able to do this via strikes (Alake, 2021). In call centres, there is a room for wage negotiations through trade unions. However, companies do very well in suppressing unions.

Workers' reliance on many non-work networks is critical to build the community and social relationships necessary for their own survival in the context of the precarious and informal work common in Africa (Lindell, 2013). For example, dockworkers in Durban, South Africa, combine wage labour with informal small-scale entrepreneurialism, pilferage, and petty trade in consumables for their livelihoods (Callebert, 2017). A similar account is given in Cooper (1987) of Mombasa dockers and their reliance on the nearby rural economy within the wider context of family, village, and regional life. The importance of non-work social networks in workers' lives has also become evident during the COVID-19 pandemic and subsequent lockdown. In Kenya and South Africa, after the lockdown, ride-hailing drivers experienced a significant drop in rides and as a result lost their income opportunities. Drivers resorted to various forms of alternative activities to generate livelihoods, for example, street vending and trading in consumables, or had to fall back on family support from partners, parents, and friends (Otieno et al., 2020). The social-economic networks on which informal workers have always depended are therefore extending into the digital sphere as well.

Digital communication technologies have also emerged as important spheres of social connection (Matassi et al., 2019; Miller and Venkatraman, 2018). Wong's (2020) study, on UK and Hong Kong youths who confine themselves to their rooms, reported deep interconnections and attachment to online communities in order to seek solace and solidarity. Social media networks and digital communication channels are also critical sites for political and social activity both globally (Gustafsson, 2012; Margetts et al., 2015; Milan and Barbosa, 2020) and in Africa (Aouragh, 2012; Bosch, 2017; Dwyer and Molony, 2019; Kadoda and Hale, 2015; Kharroub and Bas, 2016; Omanga, 2019). Digital communication tools are already used by civil society organizations and workers to support digital activism (Schradie, 2018; also, Chibita, 2016) and larger social movements (Aouragh, 2012; Margetts et al., 2015), as they enlarge new political space and accommodate new politics (Thigo, 2013). For example, social media networks are critical to the formation of collective identity, associational power, and ultimately in developing revolutionary consciousness (Aouragh, 2012). The significance of digital communications channels and social media networks in offsetting some of the adverse implications of gig work has already been underscored in recent studies (Anwar and Graham, 2020c; Gray and Suri, 2019; Johnston, 2020).

Selwyn (2012) has called for identification of sources of worker's structural power that might be turned into associational power (Selwyn, 2012), and African gig workers have indeed used their structural power to develop 'webs of care' (Katz, 2004: 246). African gig workers' community relations exist both in the digital sphere (i.e. through social media networks) and their immediate locality, i.e. personal networks. Much of the exercise of labour agency in these networks can be characterized as resilience, since these practices are intended to help workers cope with adverse outcomes of remote work such as low wages, exploitative clients, and the uncertainty of jobs. Social media networks among gig workers have become spaces where buying and selling of accounts, sharing strategies on bidding, re-outsourcing of jobs, running skills-training classes, and the discussion of a variety of interpersonal and work-related issues such as life, fair employment relationships, trust, and dealing with bad clients, are common. Our respondents stressed the importance of Facebook groups for worker interactions, where they can actually interact and communicate about their work and personal lives. Dabiku is a successful remote worker from Kenya and a member of a Facebook group in which he often offers tips for securing contracts, and also uses the group to re-outsource some of his work to locals, thus allowing him to manage a large number of contracts.

However, there are limitations to the use of social media by gig workers. Srauy (2015) makes the excellent point that while social media sites can enable community formation and social protest, at the same time these sites are designed to monetize users' labour. Users' activities and data can also be used for nefarious purposes by employers or management, such as monitoring workers and workplaces, and also by governments and the private sector for surveillance (e.g. Zuboff, 2019). Facebook, for example, has data sharing agreements with some of the largest technology companies in the world, including Amazon, which has come under fire for its intense monitoring of workers (Dance et al., 2018; also see Bloodworth, 2016).[13] There is evidence that employers can easily monitor and track workers' activities on social media platforms and take action against them. One case of this is Amazon's secret surveillance of its workers on private Facebook groups (Gurley and Cox, 2020). Similarly, Google has fired workers for engaging in labour activism (Lecher, 2019).

---

[13] Recently, Amazon had posted two job adverts for intelligence analysts to keep track of organized labour activities (Franceschi-Bicchierai, 2020). These job adverts were later removed from their website, but their archive is available at https://web.archive.org/web/20200901125940/ https://www.amazon.jobs/en/jobs/1026060/intelligence-analyst, accessed 20 July 2021.

Moving beyond social media networks, the non-digital personal networks and friendship circles of workers are also crucial for their survival. During our fieldwork, we met several workers who often helped each other in their local personal networks of friends and family. The case of two Kenyan gig workers, Jumapili and Seghen, from a small town about 100 km west of Nairobi, is a good illustration of such relationships. Jumapili used to be a teacher but after her husband passed away she started doing blog writing and social media marketing through gig work platforms. She later trained Seghen, who had an A-level certificate but could not go to university. She often re-outsources work to him and other workers in the town. In fact, in the north-eastern parts of Nairobi along the Thika Road, there is a small cluster of gig workers who often collaborate with one another and similar networks can be found in Ikeja area of Lagos, Nigeria and Legon in Accra, Ghana (also see Melia et al., 2019).

Everyday Resistance

Besides the important webs of care and support discussed above, targeted actions to disrupt the production process through acts of everyday resistance remain critical to altering the capitalist social relations found in the gig economy. Gig economy platforms exercise 'techno-normative control' driven by algorithms to control labour processes and workers (Gandini, 2019: 1041). Workers' use of resilience and reworking practices of survival go hand in hand with a variety of everyday resistance practices. For example, remote workers rely on personal networks to get by in their daily lives while also attempting to resist unscrupulous clients and platforms' system of control through unique resistance strategies. First, certain workers regularly use their new-found marketplace bargaining power on platforms to filter jobs and exclude clients and decline jobs; though this is mostly confined to workers who have gained some experience on platforms. An example of this is provided by Onochie, a top-rated virtual assistant and internet researcher in Nigeria with '100% Job Success'. He checks whether the prospective client has a verified payment method, reads reviews on Upwork to filter employers he wants to work with, and declines jobs that have unsociable working hours or pay very little. This enables him to eliminate exploitative clients.

The second strategy of resistance is remote workers' use of their marketplace power. In remote gig work, this relates to workers' threats of cancelling contracts and exiting work arrangements (Kiil and Knutsen,

2016). Ben, a virtual assistant in Nairobi, for example, considers himself as belonging to a middle-class family. He was educated in a private school and has an undergraduate degree in business studies. His first job was posting ads on Facebook for US$3 an hour. His first major contract was for a Canadian client as a virtual assistant. He gained the trust of his Canadian client over a year by handling his diary and appointments well. He was therefore able to cancel the contract with this client twice in order to demand an increase in his hourly wage—albeit only by an additional half-dollar. Similarly, a Lagos-based virtual assistant, Debare, informed his EU-based client about his intention to leave if his wages were not raised, and the client agreed to increase his salary from US$400 a month to US$550.[14]

Third, gig workers also withhold finished goods from clients due to non-payment of wages. While workers have some forms of protection against non-payment of wages by clients on Upwork, payment is only guaranteed if clients are satisfied with the work (Chapter 5). However, workers can push back against this practice, as demonstrated by Zain in Ghana. Zain only finished a Matric (equivalent to the UK's O-level) education and was doing odd jobs such as carpentry, selling clothes, and working in a salon. He sold some of his belongings to buy a second-hand laptop and learnt programming languages such as Java through donated books and YouTube. He began working on user interface designs for local clients (e.g. mobile apps for banks) before looking for work on platforms. One of his platform-based clients refused payment after Zain submitted the first batch of completed files through Dropbox. Zain therefore removed the remaining files from Dropbox, preventing the client from accessing them. The client then quickly moved to pay him to access the work files. Parallels can be drawn with the structural power of 'daladala' (minibus) drivers in Dar es Salaam, Tanzania, and their ability to bring the city's transport to a halt—eventually resulted in their gaining necessary labour rights (Rizzo, 2013).

There are also other forms of resistance among gig workers that affect employers' reputation on the platform. For example, gig workers can leave negative feedback and give low ratings if clients harass them. Workers regularly share information on social media networks about certain clients that offer extremely low-paying jobs or are harassing them—signalling

---

[14] Only a handful of workers in our sample transitioned to high-skilled complex work and were able to earn higher salaries.

others to avoid working for that client. That said, negative feedback given by clients hurts the workers more, since it affects their ability to win further contracts.

Identities and Agency in Gig Work

While some of the individual resistance acts discussed above are possible in the gig economy due to workers' structural power, worker agency is also influenced by their sociocultural identities. These identities can lead to the exclusion of certain segments from the local labour markets, such as women and migrants (Maume, 1999). We met eight international migrant remote workers in South Africa, most of whom were excluded by regulations from accessing jobs in the local labour market. Most migrants in the country face underpaid work, and hence gig work becomes an attractive option and even though unregulated, migrant identities are less relevant to source work on platforms. Platforms eliminate some of these identity barriers for workers, since their system of exchange depends primarily on ratings and feedback. For most migrants in our sample, income from remote work was critical for their household livelihoods. Thus, their agency acts were also limited to resilience and reworking strategies. They share computers and user accounts with family and friends and join online communities to find jobs and share best practices. Also, migrants' personal networks are critical for their work and livelihoods.[15] Tiffany, a migrant in Johannesburg who does customer services would seek regular help from her husband with her transcription work. Not only did this help ease the workload, but it also reduced the risk of losing contracts and income.

Similarly, gender also influences the actions of workers. As discussed by Carswell and De Neve (2013: 67), female workers' opportunities in the textile industry in Tiruppur, India, are structured by gendered norms, which constrain their spatial mobility. While spatial mobility is less relevant in the remote gig economy, income from gig work provides women with economic independence from patriarchal figures in the family. The importance of gig work income was highlighted by all the female workers in our sample, along with the development of new skills and future career

---

[15] To supplement their household income, migrants in South Africa are known for running corner shops or 'Spaza', which depend on dense networks of suppliers and buyers from the locality. Spazas are also the focus of xenophobic attacks in the country.

prospects. As Kenyangi in Uganda, who has ten siblings and economically supports her parents, explained:

This work has helped me see the world differently and gain new skills (e.g. subtitling videos, annotating data for machine learning). I feel like there are many possibilities. Now I feel like I do not have to sit home and mourn about not having a job. I know there are thousand and one places online where I can possibly look and get a job tomorrow. Skills, however small or big they may be, the ones you pick along the way gives you the confidence to apply for new jobs as they come.

Interview, pers. comm., November 2017

However, while female workers might exhibit similar agency potential to their male counterparts—such as filtering of jobs and clients, information sharing, training new workers, and re-outsourcing—they can still be constrained by their household positions and social status. Because remote work can involve unsocial hours, it can lead to an intensification of both productive and reproductive labour, thus limiting women's agency practices (McDowell, 2001). In our sample of remote workers, there were thirteen married women with children who preferred jobs with flexible working hours. Abi, a successful worker in Accra with three children, works from 8 a.m. until 2 p.m. on editing and social media management, which she says are easy to do and have negotiable working hours, even if that means less pay. Since her husband also does remote work, the family is now in a better economic position.

Nonetheless, a woman's agency potential is particularly impacted if she is a migrant and less educated (see Rydzik and Anitha, 2019). For example, Adele, a data entry worker who migrated with her husband to South Africa from Cameroon in 2007, could not find a job in Johannesburg. She therefore decided to work on digital platforms. However, given her lack of education, she resorted to doing menial tasks like document conversion to earn a living. Despite the simple nature of her digital jobs, Adele said it is challenging to care for her two children, do housework, and maintain the motivation and focus required to deliver quality work consistently.

So far, we have shown that despite the lack of opportunities for collective action, remote gig workers are able to exercise individual agency to influence their working conditions. But a fragmented workforce can also be easily stripped of its agency by capital. The high level of fragmentation of tasks in the gig economy is particularly worrying in this regard. Some gig jobs are one-time and short-term projects and often lack detailed description of the tasks involved, which makes them risky from the perspective of workers.

Commodification of Labour and Worker Power

The global gig economy has intensified the commodification of labour, presenting a challenge to labour agency. In fact, many observers would not expect workers in some of the world's economically marginalized regions to have much agency on platforms. However, gig workers can create their own labour geographies through everyday individual practices that are informal, subtle, and unorganized. This resonates with Rogaly's (2009) assertion that the 'everyday micro-struggles' of workers are critical for understanding labour agency. More importantly, many of the practices we have discussed in this chapter are performed offstage and hence could be understood as 'the hidden transcripts of the gig economy', because they rarely challenge or confront employers openly—unlike, for example, strikes, demonstrations, and protests. By contrast, in place-based work such as food delivery and taxi services, there is an element of 'public transcript' as workers have mobilized to stage strikes and demonstrations (e.g. Cant, 2019; Tassinari and Maccarrone, 2019).

By applying Katz's (2004) distinction between resilience, reworking, and resistance as forms of everyday practices, we have explored how gig workers use these strategies to influence their working conditions. Both resilience and reworking strategies were common among workers in our sample. Resistance acts seemed to be largely the domain of those workers who have already found success on platforms. Through these everyday practices, gig workers were able to avoid excessive workplace monitoring, representing a form of job autonomy. However, these resistance practices are largely confined to the domain of experienced remote workers who are able to exert their structural power over clients. As gig workers gain experience on Upwork, they also begin to choose their jobs and clients, are able to get flexible working hours, and even demand higher wages. This is not possible for most new workers who join platforms. In the absence of a collective bargaining mechanism like a union to help them overcome some of the poor practices found on platforms (e.g. inability to negotiate wages, and refusal of wages), workers have few options but to subsist on low wages. Also, digital work is footloose and can move from one location to the other, thus eroding workers' bargaining power. Therefore, it is important to think about how the structural power workers gain on platforms can be turned in associational power.

However, the agency of gig workers can be constrained by two key factors. One is the socio-economic and cultural contexts in which they are embedded. For the large proportion of the African workforce that lives in working poverty (ILO, 2020c), securing a job and maintaining that source of livelihood is all-important, even if that means working below a living wage. At the same time, workers' identities can also influence their actions. For example, a migrant worker can gain employment through gig economy platforms. But the kinds of platform jobs they can do are largely dependent on their education and family background. A migrant from a poor family and without higher education will generally only be able to do low-paid and low-skilled jobs such as data entry, image tagging, and transcription. Hence, they are likely to exert less agency than an educated worker who performs complex platform jobs such as article writing, web research, digital marketing, and software development.

The second important factor that constrains the agency of gig workers is the agency of capital, which encroaches on the class power of workers. Both clients and platforms have devised various mechanisms to develop the employment relations that suit them. Workplace control and monitoring through digital technologies, the short-term and fragmented nature of platform jobs, and the lack of job detail, are all attempts to curtail workers' autonomy and bargaining power (Figure 6.2). Thus, what opportunities do gig workers have to mobilize and organize themselves?

We are attentive to the fact that the untethered nature of remote work and a fragmented and geographically dispersed labour force makes collective action in the form of strikes or 'logging off' platforms nearly impossible.[16] However, we have also shown in this chapter how worker-led informal organizing can be achieved in digital spaces. There is therefore scope for developing more than just the ideological and materialist grounds for labour movements in the gig economy. African trades unions could engage in the politics of solidarity which speaks to the fragmented workers diverse

---

[16] Ride-hailing drivers have been able to log off the apps in order to push platforms to introduce surge pricing. This practice has been noted in Kessler (2018). Recently, in the aftermath of the COVID-19 pandemic a round of legislation passed by the Nigerian government to tax the driver and not the app companies led Nigerian ride-hailing drivers to log off and go on a week-long strike. The result of logging off and fewer drivers on the street has meant that platforms introduced surge pricing in various parts of Lagos.

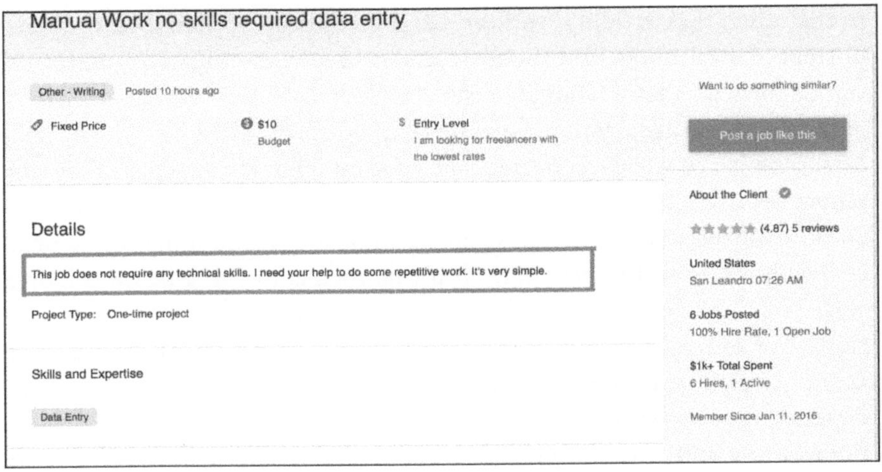

Fig. 6.2 The commoditized nature of jobs lacking details on Upwork
Source: Reproduced with permission from Anwar and Graham, 2020c: 1285, fig. 3.

experience of precarious life situations (Paret, 2016). Geographical diversity of such struggles may not necessarily contradict or be in conflict with each other, instead they can inspire movements beyond immediate and local contexts (Ibid). Unions could also take advantage of new spaces of recruitment for organizing and mobilizing gig workers around common interests. The networks of remote gig workers—both in their localities and on social media—are key to mobilizing workers and developing consciousness for collective action. Facebook and WhatsApp groups here offer a useful digital space for informal organizing, and as tools for new forms of labour movement in Africa. Social media not only have the advantage of enhancing member numbers but can also be used by local unions to tap into new occupational identities to organize workers, e.g. based on work types such as writers, data entry workers, Uber drivers, and delivery workers. Some of these tools are now widely used by African gig workers to engage in community building and to offer help to others, with some Facebook groups for remote gig workers each having thousands of members.

In the end, we want to stress the centrality of human labour to the global gig economy. The evidence of gig workers' everyday actions presented here is one component of a new class struggle of workers pitted against highly mobile capital. This class struggle must be fought in multiple spaces and at various scales—locally, regionally, and globally—for workers to be able to create their own labour geographies. We ultimately wish to emphasize that there is an urgent need to put the development of workers first. It is here that we want to renew Mario Tronti's call to bring back the role of workers into the mainstream analysis of capitalism:

> We too have worked with a concept that puts capitalist development first, and workers second. This is a mistake. And now we have to turn the problem on its head, reverse the polarity, and start again from the beginning: and the beginning is the class struggle of the working class.
>
> **Tronti, 1966: 1**

7

Futures of work

Making a Fairer World for Labour

Introduction

The book has made two key contributions. The first is that digital capitalism is bringing new jobs to Africa. The digitalization of production processes has generated new digital work activities (such as the digital gig economy and business process outsourcing), which mostly remain geographically untethered and can move around the world relatively easier than industrial goods like cars or garments. As a result, these activities can theoretically be performed from anywhere on the planet and the African continent is one of the newer locations for this type of work (Chapters 2 and 3).

Overall, we found that despite the proliferation of digital technologies and rapidly increasing internet connectivities, highly uneven economic geographies are emerging in the new world of digital work. These uneven geographies have a multi-scalar character. For example, there is a huge variation in terms of countries where digital work gets done globally and in Africa in particular. Countries like the US generate the bulk of the demand for digital work, and India and the Philippines are the major suppliers (Beerepoot et al., 2017; Graham and Anwar, 2019; Kässi and Lehdonvirta, 2018; Kleibert and Mann, 2020). However, many countries on the African continent have emerged as important suppliers of labour for digital work, with South Africa, Egypt, and Kenya being leading suppliers of remote labour in Africa. Other countries like Ghana, Nigeria, and Uganda have a smaller share, and countries like Libya, Sierra Leone, and South Sudan are virtually absent from the realm of digital work.

By examining the economic geographies of digital work, we are able to highlight that the remote gig economy and business process outsourcing are spatially organized and influenced by barriers to entry, competing interests, ideologies, trust, and power of various economic, political, and sociocultural actors. An underlying argument we have made in this book

The Digital Continent. Mohammad Amir Anwar and Mark Graham, Oxford University Press.
© Mohammad Amir Anwar and Mark Graham (2022). DOI: 10.1093/oso/9780198840800.003.0007

is that a global market for digital work now exists, which presents an economic opportunity for African workers. However, African workers face structural constraints (political, social, economic, cultural) which technology alone cannot transcend, despite the claims of many international development organisations.

The second key contribution of the book is that digital jobs are enabling 'digital Taylorism' (The Economist, 2015a). This is the same principle behind the 'Taylorism' of the early twentieth century, that is, a scientific management technique designed to increase managerial control of workplaces by breaking down work into simple tasks (i.e. commodification of work) to quantify worker performance on those tasks, and to link wages to performance. These techniques were widely adapted under Fordist-style industrial production (Frobel et al., 1981; Lipietz, 1987) and also for global services delivery through call centres which became synonymous with Taylorism in the late twentieth century (Taylor and Bain, 2005; Woodcock, 2016).

Recent technological innovations have given management the ability to control labour processes and workers remotely or from far beyond the place of production. This is nowhere better demonstrated than in the global gig economy, where managerial controls over workers through the use of algorithms are quite common. In call and contact centres, the integration of digital technologies has given the management increased powers over worker and labour process control. We argue that the digital Taylorism that sustains the contemporary digital economy activities is often stealthy, more intrusive and powerful than earlier versions, and affects the quality of jobs (Chapter 5).

These impacts of the new world of digital work on workers and their working conditions have already been noted in high-income countries (e.g. Ravenelle, 2019; Rosenblat, 2018; Schor, 2020), and there is an emerging literature concerning low- and middle-income countries (e.g. Anwar and Graham, 2020a, 2020c; Rani and Furrer, 2020). Our argument here is that in low- and middle-income regions the impact of digital Taylorism on job quality in digital work is greatly amplified due to workers' poor socio-economic backgrounds (e.g. lack of education, poor family backgrounds) and existing political environment, such as high rates of unemployment, inadequate social protection measures, weaker legal protection against misclassification of workers, and workplace harassment. Our analysis of new digital work activities shows that while these bring new employment opportunities for the African workforce, their job quality outcomes are quite varied.

On the one hand, these jobs can bring *freedom and flexibility* into the lives of workers. In the context of rampant poverty and inequality across the continent, remote gig work, for example offers a chance for African workers to earn livelihoods and allows some degree of control over work tasks and working hours. Similarly, call and contact centre work is also opening up new opportunities for the prospective workforce to join the labour markets. On the other hand, both these forms of work can also introduce *precarity and vulnerability* into the lives of workers. Remote work is gig-based and contractual, involves intense global competition, and workers face downward pressure on wages. While there are certain aspects of call and contact centre work which can be characterized as formal employment (e.g. health insurance and pensions), the sector is known for temporary contracts, suppression of wages, and high rates of attrition.

More importantly, the digital nature of both these jobs means that there is intense workplace monitoring and quality control which can lead to loss of wages and even termination of contracts. Another important aspect of these jobs is the lack of collective bargaining (both sectors remain largely non-unionized in the African context), which means workers are rarely able to negotiate wages. Additionally, national legal frameworks are rarely up to date with new digital economy activities, which means firms and employers exploit loopholes to their advantage, and avoid regulation and responsibilities towards worker welfare. This is particularly true for the gig economy, where platforms remain disembedded from national institutional and legal frameworks, even though the work activities take place in specific local contexts. Remote work platforms like Upwork have remained outside the purview of the state and its institutions, despite some recent attempts by governments, such as Kenya, to introduce taxation on remote workers who earn their income on platforms. Gig workers in Africa, as a result, experience poor working conditions; without adequate social protection measures they remain vulnerable.[1] Similarly, in call centre work, there is a trend towards the increasing use of contractual workforce (through employment agencies), which allows BPO companies to get access to labour at cheaper rates and avoid welfare responsibilities, such as pension contributions (Chapter 5).

Having said that, the digital jobs we discuss in this book don't suggest a complete absence of opportunities for worker power in these sectors. In fact, we have argued that due to the digital nature of work, there are new

---

[1] Gig workers' vulnerability is further exposed due to the COVID-19 pandemic as they experienced loss of livelihoods; governments emergency measures rarely cover them (see Fairwork, 2020a; Otieno et al., 2020).

spaces of digital activism opening up for worker actions and solidarity. In Chapter 6, we discussed labour agency in the gig economy context, including worker power vis-à-vis platforms and platform clients, and how workers exert their individual agency and use digital communication channels such as Facebook to develop solidarity and a sense of community. These digital spaces of communication have great implications for the new digital world of work both in Africa and elsewhere. Of course, we should note that while digital spaces remain useful for various forms of worker action, these need to be complemented with ground-level work including trades unions in different national settings.

Trades unions in Africa have a rich history of mobilization and resistance in the form of anti-colonial and anti-apartheid movements. Trades unions have won important battles in the form of negotiating wages, improved working conditions, and forcing employers to comply with national regulatory norms. However, the informalization of labour markets has eroded labour union density, and existing unions in Africa have not kept up with the changing structures of labour markets. The emergence of digital work also poses a challenge for unions to organize digital workers. This does not necessarily mean unions do not have opportunities to mobilize workers in these new digital sectors; in fact, digital communication tools have already been recognized as key to social movements (e.g. Margetts et al., 2015) and the future of unionism (e.g. Schradie, 2015). In the context of the COVID-19 pandemic, these digital spaces have become ever more important for activism and worker actions (e.g. Mendes, 2020; Otieno et al., 2020; Rosenblatt, 2020; Sanjay, 2020; Valls, 2020). Our research shows that unions worldwide can tap in to these digital spaces to develop solidarity among digital workers who now find and compete for work on a global scale.

Overall, this book has shown that the increasing digitization of work and recent advancements in automation and communication technologies don't just augment the labour process with digital data, digital processes, and machines; they also embed it in stretched-out networks of production, with tasks quickly passed in complex assemblages from person to person, person to machine, and machine to machine. Within these transformations, the future of digital work in Africa is still emerging and emergent. If that future is to contain decent jobs and fair outcomes for African workers, we need to ensure that we appropriately conceptualize the transnational networks in which those jobs are embedded. We need, in other words, to understand the current system if we hope to change it. To that end we find it productive to conceptualize a 'planetary labour market' in digital work. We end the chapter by outlining some principles for worker protection in a planetary market scenario, and examine the possibilities and future pathways for digital workers as they are drawn further into the networks of the digital economy.

A Planetary Labour Market?

To describe what is meant by a planetary labour market, it is first useful to describe what labour markets are. A nineteenth-century hiring fair, such as the one described by Thomas Hardy in *Far from the Madding Crowd*, is used by Fevre (1992) in his book about the sociology of labour markets, as a way of illustrating an abstract definition of labour markets through five key distinct processes. These are: informing employers (employers learning about availability and skills of workers), informing workers (workers learning about jobs), screening workers (employers obtaining enough information about workers to decide if they could be hired for a job), screening employers (workers learning about their employers), and offers to buy or sell labour (the actual negotiations and pitches made by workers and employers). Labour markets, in other words, are a way of describing a convergence of workers and employers in specific places and times. While scholars as far back as Karl Marx posited that this convergence in competitive labour markets is a fundamental characteristic of capitalist society, various planned economies in the late twentieth century likewise relied on the concept of a labour market to govern the management and distribution of the labour force (Brown, 1970).

In Hardy's hiring fair, the spatial and temporal co-presence of agricultural workers and employers allowed the five above-mentioned processes to converge. However, while co-presence has traditionally been a necessary condition for most of these conditions, it has not been a sufficient one. Kalleberg and Sørensen (1979: 351) understood labour markets as

> the arenas in which workers exchange their labour power in return for wages, status, and other job rewards. The concept, therefore, refers broadly to the institutions and practices that govern the purchase, sale, and pricing of labour services. These structures include the means by which workers are distributed among jobs and the rules that govern employment, mobility, the acquisition of skills and training, and the distribution of wages and other rewards obtained contingent upon participation in the economic system.

But, ultimately, those institutions and practices still require some level of space–time convergence between employers and workers.

It is important here to distinguish between the way that labour markets have been conceived in orthodox classical economics, and their actual characteristics. Orthodox conceptions put forward a perfectly competitive market that can provide both firms (buyers) and workers (sellers) with perfect information. Wages are set by the relationship between supply and demand, and 'workers can move freely in response to changes in supply and demand in different parts of the market' (Kalleberg and Sørensen, 1979: 354). Kalleberg and Sørensen (1979) give as examples of such markets the migrant labour market in California, and the 1970s labour market in Afghanistan. In both cases, wages were relatively uniform and institutional forces only had a small influence.

In practice, it is rare for labour markets to fit these sorts of properties perfectly; instead, labour markets function in imperfect and uneven ways. Workers comprise different classes, genders, races, nationalities, and other groups that can get segmented into different functions in labour markets. These markets are further built on, and performed through imperfect information, irrational social behaviours, politics, institutional arrangements and practices, customs, and prejudices. As Peck (1996: 5) has argued, labour markets are 'socially constructed and politically mediated' arenas, 'structured by institutional forces and power relations'. Thus, we get segmented labour markets functioning at multiple scales and spaces to produce variegated outcomes for workers (Craig et al., 1982). In these segmented markets, workers have little opportunity to cross into other groups and are thus constrained to a limited set of outcomes: with factors like gender or race influencing segmentation (with, for instance, women earning lower wages than men) (Bonacich, 1972; Reich et al., 1973).

The takeaway point here is that labour markets function in complex, imperfect, exclusionary ways. When speaking about a physical meeting place, like a hiring fair, the very concept serves as a multi-scalar abstraction. We use the idea of national or regional labour markets not to imply that everyone in those nations or regions have equal opportunities to read or access the market; but rather as a way of indicating that there are distinct economic, social, and political enablers and constraints that put rough, porous, but still real geographic boundaries around Fevre's five processes. This is not to say that workers are not enrolled into global-scale associations and production networks. Indeed, workers in many economic sectors have been for centuries (Hunt, 1994). But, as Fevre (1992: 14) notes, 'Labour markets need have neither a fixed time nor a fixed place, but they must have some sort of time and place otherwise how could people use them? If they do not know when and where, workers cannot find jobs and employers cannot hire workers'.

Much of this discussion assumes a located place of work—a farm, factory, or office in which a worker needs to be physically present, in order to perform their duties. But, as the nature of work changes, so too do our conceptions of the boundedness of labour markets. Here it is useful to draw on the concept borrowed from geography of a relational understanding of space (Massey, 2005). Rather than only thinking of space as a flat canvas, it is rather something that can also emerge from social relations (Hudson, 2001). This vision of space as relational and emergent, rather than fixed and pre-existing, is useful because it offers a productive way of understanding the impact of digital technologies on labour markets. Stephen Graham (1998: 174), in an influential piece on the intersections between technology and space, builds a relational understanding, noting that 'such a perspective reveals how new technologies become enrolled into complex, contingent and subtle blendings of human actors and technical artefacts, to form actor-networks'. He continues: '[N]ew information technologies, in short, actually resonate with, and are bound up in the active construction of space and place, rather than making it somehow redundant'.

If we apply these sorts of understandings to the contexts of work, the boundedness of earlier visions of labour markets evaporates. Building on an actor-network understanding of work as constituted through a broad range of associations with objects, Jones (2008: 12) argues that 'working practices, the experience of work, the nature of workplaces and the power relations in which people's working lives are entangled require a theoretical understanding of global-scale interrelationships if they are to be properly understood'. Describing how work is increasingly performed through global networks of human and non-human objects, he adds: 'Contemporary work is becoming less constituted through localized, physically-proximate relations and increasingly constituted through distanciated relations. These multiple spatial associations increasingly extend to the planetary scale' (Jones, 2008: 14). This starting point—moving beyond an understanding of work as inherently local—allows Jones (2008: 15) to then build his 'global work' thesis:

Rather than understanding work as a practice undertaken by social actors located in discrete material spaces and framed in a linear chronology, work is reconceptualised as a complex set of spatialised practices involving humans and non-humans . . . and which is constituted in relational space with a disjunctive, non-linear chronology . . . This is 'global' work because this reconfigured concept captures the qualitative degree to which all work practices are constituted through distanciated . . . socio-material relations.

As places of work move beyond single locations, this offers us a pathway for thinking through the impact of globalization on workers.

Towards a Planetary Labour Market

Although the 'global work' thesis is useful for providing a framework that allows us to carefully think through the impact of globalization on workers and the ways that the places of work move beyond single locations, in the rest of this chapter we will argue that it is important to think about the relationships between employers and workers as more than simply distanciated social relations. Using the idea of a 'planetary labour market' allows us to show that not just work can be highly (globally) connected, but rather temporary states of co-presence between workers and employers that can be brought into being.

Like Jones (2008), we build our understanding of a planetary labour market on a relational understanding of space. Specifically, we draw from Doreen Massey (1993: 61) who argued that:

Different social groups and different individuals are placed in very distinct ways in relation to . . . flows and interconnections. This point concerns not merely the issue of who moves and who doesn't, although that is an important element of it; it is also about power in relation to the flows and the movement. Different social groups have distinct relationships to this anyway—differentiated mobility: some are more in charge of it than others; some initiate flows and movement, others don't; some are more on the receiving end of it than others; some are effectively imprisoned by it.

As such, the moments of co-presence that will be described below rarely fit either the orthodox idea of labour markets or resemble Hardy's nineteenth-century hiring fair. While digital work platforms have enabled the potential coming together of employers and workers on a planetary scale, the labour market for digital work that is developing is characterized by both asymmetrical scalar relationships and uneven spatial ones: with workers and employers having very different possibilities to read and participate in the labour market. In other words, the argument put forward is that a planetary labour market is not simply a 'global' extension of Hardy's hiring fair. It facilitates a confluence that can transcend the spatial boundaries that constrained the convergence of employers and workers, but that is characterized by multi-scalar and asymmetrical technological, political, social, cultural, and institutional factors.

Planetary Labour Futures

Employers and workers, through the affordances of digital technologies, can seek each other out on a genuinely world-spanning scale, escaping some of the constraints that previously bound them exclusively to their local labour markets. Most importantly, many previously bounded labour markets were both transactionally and discursively insulated from the global reserve army of labour, and the downward pressure on wages and working conditions that it brings about (Huws, 2003).[2] A market that is planetary in scale will cease to have any of those brakes on the erosion of working conditions. Yet, while all of these interactions occur between economic actors in different parts of the world from one another, what we see is not just Hardy's hiring fair scaled-up to a global level or scaled-down onto the head of a pin. Instead of seeing the space of the labour market through a Euclidean lens in which geography is a pre-existing canvas on which economic relationships can be formed, the spaces of labour markets are instead relational and emergent.

It is this understanding of space that we seek to bring to discussions about digital work in Africa. We want to move away from thinking about labour markets as bounded spaces that you could draw on a map. In a planetary labour market, everything does not happen everywhere. However, key spatial constraints (such as the need for commuting, to leave the house, and to obtain visas and permits) can be circumvented. This forces us not to imagine away the already-existing economic geographies of work, but

---

[2] This is not to claim that local labour markets ever reach any sort of equilibrium. Indeed, much important scholarship has taken place refuting such ideas and instead arguing that labour markets are locally constituted (Craig et al., 1982; Hanson and Pratt, 1992; Harvey, 1989b; Peck, 1989). It is nonetheless clear than many bounded labour markets have been able to avoid an erosion of working conditions through the relative scarcity of labour power and better regulatory frameworks instituted by states.

to ask questions about how they will shape and be shaped by the potentials for planetary-scale interactions.

Thomas Friedman (2005: 110) famously pointed to a globalized world that would allow for 'the sharing of knowledge and work—in real time, without regard to geography, distance, or, in the near future, even language'. But, as much as some firms and clients might want it to, a planetary market doesn't do away with geography; it rather exists to take advantage of it. Companies use uneven geographies to facilitate labour arbitrage, cross-border competition, and are able to foster what Peck (2017: 42) refers to as an 'offshore consciousness'. To be clear, references to local labour markets, national labour markets, and planetary labour markets should never be made to ignore the myriad ways that those labour markets are brought into being by multi-scalar exogenous factors which, in turn, lead them to be socially and spatially segmented and fragmented. The spatial and scalar prefixes (urban-, local-, national-, etc.) that we add to labour markets are instead intended to signify enablers and constraints that serve to cluster a convergence of employers and workers within particular economic geographies. These enablers and constraints can be technological barriers (e.g. transportation costs and the availability of broadband), political (e.g. the availability of visas and work permits), social (e.g. availability of skills and language fluencies), economic (e.g. local reserve wages), and spatial (e.g. work and workers that inherently have to be in particular places).

Underlying material economic geographies of workers and clients are therefore never fully transcended, work is never fully commoditized, and there remain national and regional practices and institutions which govern the purchase, sale, and pricing of labour on platforms. But none of those national and regional practices determine the shape of the market as a whole. This is not to say that labour markets in non-digital contexts do not have similar ways of empowering and disempowering different groups. The material architectures, norms, laws, and relationships in traditional labour markets all bring particular power dynamics into being. However, what is different in the digital context is that co-presence and the transitory proximity that platforms bring into being is illusory. While workers can, in theory, connect from anywhere, they lose the ability to control a key part of their agency that they otherwise have in any other context: their control over space, and their ability to bring into being labour geographies that are at least in part on their own terms (see e.g. Herod, 2001). Because employers and workers have significantly different abilities to control space, the planetary labour market is a context that serves to further undermine the structural power of labour vis-à-vis that of capital.

This manifests in six key ways. First, mass global connectivity is bringing onstream a *massive oversupply of labour power, mainly from lower-income segments of the world population*. There are far fewer digital jobs than there are people able and willing to do them. The 'elemental rationale' of off-shoring has always been to cut and suppress costs (Peck, 2017); it should therefore come as no surprise that online outsourcing continues the trend.

Second, many workers seeking jobs in a planetary labour market are *replaceable and interchangeable*. This is not just due to the oversupply of labour power, but also to the fact that production networks can be footloose while workers are tethered to place.

Third, workers mostly interact as *competitors rather than collaborators*. For platform workers, this situation arises primarily because there are few physical sites at which to assemble with co-workers, and because the highly commodified nature of their jobs can lead to competition on price above all else. Digital platforms deliberately limit the amount of horizontal informa-tion that workers can glean about one another, and the distributed nature of work means that workers have few opportunities to engage in the collec-tive action afforded by spatial proximity. For contact centre workers, the highly commodified nature of their work makes it clear to all parties that workers around the world are in competition with one another, with wages being one of the most important dimensions on which they compete.

Fourth, there is a *lack of transparency*. Although workers can use digital tools to find jobs on the other side of the planet the networks and platforms used to mediate those jobs can also conceal much about the nature of those activities. In other words, workers often know little about the production networks that they are embedded into, and are offered few opportunities to economically upgrade skills or value chain positions.

Fifth, there is a relative *lack of agency* among workers to have their voice in, or to shape, their labour conditions. The affordances of most types of digital work tend to be closed to workers, in part because workers rarely have any stake or control in the physical or digital means of production in the digital economy. If we extend spatial metaphors to online labour plat-forms, they are not public markets; they are rather private spaces. That said, Chapter 6 has also demonstrated that even the most controlling and pan-topic systems will still always leave space for worker agency. The networks of work that bring jobs to Africa certainly do not facilitate or encourage agency among workers, but neither can they eradicate it.

Finally, *workers are unevenly protected by labour laws.* While call centre workers are considered employees and are covered by most national labour laws, BPO firms regularly use temporary staffing agencies to hire workers. For example, this trend is catching up in South Africa, with firms increasingly looking to hire workers to staffing agencies or on temporary contracts. This kind of employment relationship exposes workers to abuse both by employment contractors and BPO firms, such as through short-term contracts, low pay, and non-unionized workplaces. African outsourcing companies also regularly use 'low cost' as a way of attracting clients.[3] Most platform workers, by nature of their status as self-employed workers, meanwhile, do not benefit from protections under labour law at all. Because the labour market extends well beyond any individual jurisdiction's ability to regulate it, self-regulation tends to be carried out by platforms and clients.

These issues are all rooted in the specific designs of planetary labour markets that use space against workers. Once work becomes commodified, workers around the world are effectively largely competing on price and working conditions. The planetary nature of the market means that we have relatively mobile capital and relatively immobile workers. At the speed of light, capital can switch locations to find cheaper and less troublesome workers. It is a market in which labour power is traded globally and yet workers can only act locally.

Together, these issues all serve to undermine the structural power of workers, and especially workers at the world's economic margins. This is a grim vision of the future when thinking about the balance of power between workers and bosses, and the balance of power between economic actors in the world's cores and peripheries. But it is also a vision that is far from inevitable. An understanding of how today's planetary labour market works offers the foundations for imagining alternatives. We therefore end this book with reflections on how governments, researchers, and workers can resist some of the forces that seek to disempower workers.

---

[3] The private sector association of contact sector firms in South Africa, BPESA, regularly advertises the country as a low-labour cost destination. See https://www.bpesa.org.za/invest-in-south-africa.html, accessed 2 July 2021.

Beyond the Race to the Bottom

Research and Activism

Even though digital work is more globalized than the industries that have come before it, it is not without precedent. Other industries that have been built on commoditized skills or the production of tradable commodities have also done much to foster a race to the bottom in wages and working conditions.

The garment sector's value chains now span several countries and have been referred by Selwyn (2018) as 'global poverty chains'. The core of Selwyn's argument is that worker participation in these value chains generates new forms of worker poverty built around sub-par wages as firms search for locations where labour costs are low. In discussing the garment sector in Cambodia, Selwyn (2018: 84) points out that although workers are highly productive, they receive base wages (insufficient to meet their social reproduction requirements), are required by firms (often by force) and by economic necessity (as a consequence of insufficient base wages) to undertake large amounts of overtime, and consequently are physically and emotionally degraded. Similar results have been documented in other industries' value chains, including horticulture in Kenya (Dolan, 2004), fruit growing in South Africa (Barrientos and Kritzinger, 2004), and the footwear industry in Eastern Europe (Selwyn et al., 2020). Dolan (2004) notes that the fresh vegetable commodity chain linking Kenyan producers with consumers in the UK results in employment opportunities for Kenyan farm workers, but that the buyer-driven nature of the value chain and competitive pressure mean work is gendered and defined by insecure forms of employment, often low paid. Similarly, Barrientos and Kritzinger (2004) found that the South African fruit sector generates informality of work, which intensifies contractual and temporary work for low pay, lack of employment benefits, and as a result increases workers' risks and vulnerability to poverty (also see Barrientos, 2019).

However, some of these globalized industries have also been the centre of activism, primarily from consumers and also civil society to push back against the unethical business practices of big firms involved in global value chains. The Fair Trade movement is one such example, which promotes ethical production and consumption and also offers sustainable livelihood opportunities (see Lamb, 2008; Raynolds et al., 2004).[4] Activists have been able to successfully pressure lead firms in global value chains to change some of their business activities. For example, a 2015 report by the Human Rights Watch (HRW) on the Cambodian garment industry outlined labour rights abuses and substandard labour conditions which resulted in firms like H&M announcing that they will aim to put an end to short-term contractors and suppliers (HRW, 2015).

What we can learn from these industries is the important role that research and activism has played in attempting to prevent market forces pushing working conditions to inhumane levels. From foundations like Fair Trade, we can look to future research activism to be effective in three areas.

First, we can look to investigative research that seeks to make digital work more transparent. Such research is invaluable in exposing the structural dynamics of otherwise opaque production networks that operate within the planetary market. Lead firms—whether they engage in a direct or subcontracting relationship with distant workers—are rarely comfortable to be publicly seen to be implicated in ethically questionable practices. In uncovering the digital value networks used to coordinate the movement of informational products and services, investigative research is able not just to expose some of the worst and most concerning practices and experiences of exploitation, but also link those practices back to lead firms. Research that humanizes workers and amplifies their voices and concerns can go a long way to develop social and political responses to counteract the deeply harmful outcomes of such processes. In this book, we have taken one such step to expose the hidden and opaque practices that characterise digital capitalism.

Second, there are efforts to build on and systematize the kinds of research mentioned above into ratings, and certification schemes that seek to create a floor of standards that wages or working conditions cannot fall beneath. The practice of impact-sourcing is a forerunner to these efforts, that is, the hiring of people who are socio-economically disadvantaged, for example who are below national poverty lines or long-term unemployed. The Global Impact Sourcing Coalition (GISC) was launched in September 2016 in South Africa, supported by the Rockefeller Foundation in partnership with the Business for Social Responsibility (BSR), a global non-profit

---

[4] See https://www.fairtrade.org.uk/what-is-fairtrade/who-we-are/, accessed 22 July 2021. Also, to note that the Fair Trade movement which has its focus on ethical trade has its own problems (see Griffiths, 2012). There are concerns about reproduction of power asymmetries (Raynolds, 2017; Wilson and Jackson, 2016), elements of unfair and disempowering trading practices (Herman, 2019), and in some cases producers not receiving their fair share of wages (Cramer et al., 2017; Kilian et al., 2006; Valkila et al., 2010).

organization. The GISC have developed an Impact Sourcing Standard as 'minimum requirements and voluntary best practices for providers of business products and services to demonstrate their commitment to inclusive employment'.[5] In theory, impact sourcing can deliver some social goods in the form of economic opportunities through jobs to the disadvantaged and unemployed in Africa. It can also help establish minimum standards and avoid a race to the bottom for many workers. Several key players in Africa have adopted impact sourcing as a practice for hiring: DDD, and Samasource in Kenya, and BPESA and Harambee in South Africa are all active in their support of impact sourcing through training and outreach.

However, despite the genuine efforts of some in the impact sourcing space, the practice remains opaque, unmonitored, and under-regulated. There is a storied history of firms selling altruism on dubious foundations (Graham, 2013), and impact sourcing is no exception. In the context of African countries with high incidences of poverty and unemployment, most workers hired can be categorized as disadvantaged workers. So, there is a danger of impact sourcing becoming a mere public relations exercise for firms sourcing cheaper labour force. As we have shown in this book, the outsourcing space is driven by labour cost arbitrage meaning that firms still have little incentive to maintain labour standards, and disadvantaged workers could still experience adverse job quality impacts. For impact sourcing to be a trusted part of the digital work landscape, it will ultimately need to evolve into a practice that is regulated by state authorities and independent third-party observers.

The international Fairwork project has been trying to bring this sort of approach to the domain of platform work.[6] The project operates by co-developing a series of principles of fair platform work with workers, trades unions, and other key stakeholders. It then scores and ranks platforms against those principles through what is effectively an involuntary certification scheme—scoring all large platforms with or without their assent. The rankings are published on the Fair Work website. In doing so, it too encourages a move away from the race-to-the-bottom that characterizes so much digital work, and shows that there is nothing natural about indecent work.

Voluntary and involuntary certification or ranking schemes will always be limited in scope. They necessarily can't do the work that stronger

---

[5] Available at https://gisc.bsr.org/files/BSR_GISC_IS_Standard_Factsheet.pdf, accessed 22 July 2021.
[6] For disclosure, one of us (Graham) is the Founder and Director of this project.

regulation and stronger worker power can do (we will come to this later), but they can nonetheless have meaningful positive impacts on the lives of workers. Their impacts stretch well beyond the immediate features of work that they measure; they indirectly reframe how work is conceptualized, and how the power to regulate it is distributed in production networks.

That observation brings us to the third point—to move away from a world of commodified work and a race-to-the-bottom in tradable services that comes about because of a coming into being of a planetary-scale labour market; the ways that connections between users and workers are imagined need to be reconceptualized. We can do this through a focus on the 'power-geometry' of transnational connections. The geographer Doreen Massey (1993) coined the term to think about the ways that inter-place dependencies and connections have given rise to uneven relations of power that afford institutions, groups, and individuals in different places varying amounts of agency. These power-geometries take shape both because of the non-proximate connections that bind actors in uneven ways, but also because of the ways that they leave others out. To be either connected or disconnected is to be implicated in networks of power. A crucial project for an increasingly hyper-networked twenty-first century will be to find ever more ways of fostering shared understandings of power-geometries and how they impact upon the people and places who least benefit from their uneven configurations. Much can be accomplished from that starting point: more compassionate, kind, and empathetic ways of interacting with distant people are an essential ingredient to decommodify the labour power traded through impersonal networks. But shared understandings of winners and losers could also be the beginnings for targeted regulation and the building of powerful international solidarities. It is to those ideas that we now turn.

Government Action

At first glance, thinking about the roles government might play in supporting both the quantity and quality of jobs for footloose work that is traded in a planetary-scale market may seem pointless. If jobs can be easily moved from place to place, and if key actors in production networks are on the other side of the world, what role could local regulation ever play?

We deploy the aforementioned planetary lens as a way not of imagining that African digital workers are connected to powerful actors who operate out of a disembedded far-off undefinable place, but rather to highlight the transnational, but also always grounded nodes in every economic network. The market for digital work may be planetary in scale and scope, but—as we demonstrated in the book economic activity is characterized by distinct, grounded, geographies.

Chapter 3, for instance, showed that a majority of demand for platform work comes from the US, UK, Germany, Canada, and Australia. The demand for call- and contact-centre work is similarly geographically constrained. Here we can take inspiration from Germany's proposed Supply Chain Act. The Act would place legal obligations on German companies to ensure that social and ecological standards are upheld throughout their supply chains—irrespective of where any suppliers in their chain are based. A similar law passed in any of the countries that have a large demand for digital work could go a long way to upholding minimum standards of decent work around the world. A 'Cloudwork Act' could, at a basic level, stipulate that the rate of pay for all workers, irrespective of where they live and irrespective of employment status, must meet some sort of minimum legal threshold for wages (Wood et al., 2020). Wage differentials is a feature which sustains much of the global production networks, including digital outsourcing we described in this book. Workers in poor countries command lower wages in comparison to wages of workers in rich countries. In their recent paper, Hickel et al., (2021: 16) argue that wages in poor countries 'have been kept artificially low' (e.g. through colonialism, structural adjustment programmes, and free trade agreements), 'which enables patterns of imperial appropriation that remain a dominant feature of the contemporary world economy'. Such a system of unequal exchange they note drains trillions of dollars each year from poor countries to the rich countries (see Amin, 1976 who described this as a 'hidden transfer of value'). Digital labour platforms are one of the latest tools facilitating such unequal developments. One of the solutions discussed by several scholars and activists is to have a global minimum wage set at 50% of each country's median wage, though building political support can be difficult but not impossible (Hickel, 2017; also Palley, 2012; Gallant, 2019). A more ambitious Cloudwork Act could legislate that risks to workers are mitigated, that workers have due process, and that principles of equity and non-discrimination are baked into contracts and relationships through the value chain.

The history of offshoring also offers a warning to African governments who seek to attract jobs through the pull of low wages and a relative lack of regulation. In a region in which most of the world's poorest people have yet to connect to the internet, competing on low wages and under-regulated labour markets is a dangerous game. Highly commodified work that is traded in a planetary market could not be more footloose. Better then to make sure that minimum standards are upheld locally, and seek to attract jobs and businesses through other means.

Prioritizing education and skills development can be a way out of the race-to-the-bottom trap. We already see that a significant amount of digital work is offshored to both India and the Philippines, despite rising labour costs, because of highly-specialized services available in both countries. Within Africa, clusters are already emerging: notably copywriting in Kenya, customer service work in South Africa, and virtual assistance work in Nigeria. Those clusters of specialization are then likely to have a number of positive spillover effects in their respective regions. One reason why the Philippines is home to one of the world's largest number of platform workers is precisely because many of those workers learnt customer-facing digital work skills in the older BPO sector. The clusters that have already formed in Kenya, South Africa, and Nigeria can therefore not only contribute to local economic development through higher salaries for a more specialized workforce, but can also positively shape the future trajectory of economic development in those regions in unknown ways.

Building Worker Power and International Solidarities

Ultimately it is collective worker power and international solidarities that are needed to build a more sustainable industry. Historically, solidarities among workers were built in and around their places of work such as the factory or shop floor. Their pressure points were local and workers regularly used uniquely effective strategies to bring the production machinery to a halt. Workers also developed local solidarities in the communities, towns, or cities they lived and worked in. However, those strategies may not necessarily transfer neatly to an era of digital capitalism and planetary-scale transactions. Collective action becomes logistically and legally challenging for digital workers.

However, there have been numerous stories emerging around the world where workers have been able to develop international solidarities by engaging in innovative strategies and leveraging new digital communication tools to exercise their structural, associational, institutional, and symbolic power (Chun, 2009; Silver, 2003; Wright, 2000). There are multiple global campaigns that have demanded better protection and welfare rights for workers. The global union confederation, UNI Global, has for instance campaigned for the rights of essential workers such as cleaners, health care workers, and food delivery workers. The International Transport Workers Federation (ITF) is actively campaigning for delivery riders and taxi drivers for platforms such as Uber, Deliveroo, and Foodora (ITF, 2020b). Ride-hailing drivers around the world have also organized themselves from the ground up to form an International Alliance of App-Based Transport Workers (IAATW) (Varghese, 2020). The Independent Drivers Guild in the US, and the App Drivers and Couriers Union (ADCU) in the UK, emerged after a long campaign by drivers for Uber and other ride-hailing companies. Similar worker-led groups have emerged in Africa in the ride-hailing sector such as The Momentum (South Africa), the Digital Taxi Association (Kenya) and the National Union of Professional App-based Workers (NUPABW) (Nigeria).

These types of worker-led movements have taken concrete steps to push back against their employers. Drivers and couriers have used public spaces, misused the means of production to mobilize, and developed solidarity among themselves (Animento et al., 2017; Cant, 2019; Tassinari and Maccarrone, 2019). The Independent Workers Union of Great Britain (IWGB)'s campaign in London for courier workers resulted in delivery firm Citysprint dropping some of its lowest payment rates, while others have agreed to pay rises (Prassl, 2018). In New York City, the International Association of Machinists (IAM) associated Independent Drivers Guild managed to secure a minimum wage rate for app-based drivers (IAM, 2018). Ride-hailing driver groups in Africa have gone on strike in an effort to force ride-hailing platforms to change their behaviour. In Kenya, a nine-day strike in July 2018 resulted in drivers forcing Uber and Taxify to increase their fares, albeit marginally (Dahir, 2018). Strikes against ride-hailing platforms have expanded to include workers around the world simultaneously logging off the app (Campbell, 2019). More recently, the Transport Workers Union in Australia has entered an agreement with Doordash to provide workers with safety equipment and offer financial assistance for workers who tested positive for COVID-19 (ITF, 2020a).

There are important lessons to be learnt from such worker campaigns. Digital workers are fragmented and spatially dispersed, but the work is always performed in real spaces and always inherently falls under the jurisdiction of at least one place. This opens up possibilities for workers and their allies (e.g. civil society organizations) to take actions in specific jurisdictions that end up reshaping the economic geographies of digital work (Graham and Anwar, 2018a). Workers have the power to dismiss the idea that digital labour represents a final hegemonic spatio-temporal fix in which they have no agency due to atomization and the commodification of work. Workers do not necessarily need global campaigns but to build local strategies and find nodes at which the local can influence the non-local (Graham and Anwar, 2018a).

Therefore, rather than thinking of the end of organized labour, there are new opportunities for interventions to develop transnational solidarities across sectors, scales, and borders (Munck, 2019). The effectiveness of these alliances will depend not only on coordination across borders but also workers' ability to engage with institutions and stakeholders (local, national, and international) in ways that disrupt employers' core material interests (Brookes, 2019; also see Bieler and Lindberg, 2010).

The fact that an essential precondition for digital work is the international communications infrastructure over which it is transmitted also presents an important opportunity for digital workers. Worker groups have been able to overcome the structural constraints present in their work (e.g. a globally distributed workforce, contractual and agency workers) to find connections and develop networks beyond the physical realm. Those same networks can of course be used by workers to connect, collaborate, and strategize ways of exercising their collective, associational, power. The fact that a large part of digital production activities are transacted through digital technologies presents an opportunity for workers to use the same tools to disrupt such production (see Chapter 6).

The use of digital technologies opens up unique opportunities for both workers and trades unions to leverage them in uniting workers around the world. Said differently, if the coordination of global production networks of digital work occurs at a planetary scale, so too must the organization of workers. Trades unions would do well to develop transnational alliances with workers and tap into various sources of worker power (Dufour-Poirier and Hennebert, 2015; Sarkar and Kuruvilla, 2020; Webster, 2015). We can see the beginnings of such an idea in the Alphabet Workers Union (AWU), a trade union of a diverse range of workers who work either as direct employees of Alphabet (i.e. the parent company of Goggle) or who are temporary workers or contractors. While the union currently only counts US and Canadian workers as members, the organizing done by the AWU could potentially spread to the many African workers who are enrolled into the production networks of a variety of Alphabet products.[7] African workers who are tagging images to train machine learning systems and engineers in California, whether they know it yet or not, are ultimately working together and enrolled into the same chains of production.

These sorts of information asymmetries are, and have always been, used against workers. Multinational firms are able to enrol digital workers into networks in which they are pitted against one another as competitors. Those workers have fewer chances to connect vertically to downstream nodes on their production networks, or horizontally to other workers in other places doing similar work. A lack of those connections means the absence of a key structural condition needed for building associational collective power. However, it is also entirely possible that those asymmetries might begin to fade away precisely as more of the world is wired, and workers find ever more ways of developing international solidarities and engaging in cross-national organizing.

This book has shown that many African workers are embedded into chains of production that span the globe. Their work is integral to the development of products and services used the world over. However, they have been enrolled into these networks in relatively extractive and marginal ways, with the potential of any transformative upgrading hindered by long, opaque, and complex production networks. As such, while the digital moment has brought many jobs to Africa, we will continue to see relations premised upon extractivism if there is no meaningful change from either governments or collective associations of workers. It is in looking to new transnational solidarities that we see the most promise. As ever more is done to shed light on the structure of international production networks, and ever more pro-worker initiatives develop transnational campaigns, digital workers of the world may yet unite!

---

[7] There are examples of union alliances built globally. Uni Global Union represents 20 million workers from over 150 different countries in the skills and services sector. For alliances among unions in the low- and middle-income countries, the Southern Initiative on Globalisation and Trade Union Rights (SIGTUR) is another example. Though it has to be said Australia's inclusion in SIGTUR and the project itself has been criticized (on SIGTUR's history and genesis see Lambert and Webster, 2001 and Waterman, 2017 for a critique of the SIGTUR project).

Fieldwork Overview

A total of 207 participants were interviewed including digital workers (platform-based workers and call and contact centre workers), policymakers, labour union officials, businesses, small self-employed freelancers/entrepreneurs, private sector associations, industry experts, and development organizations. Some of the workers were interviewed twice. We kept in touch with workers and spoke to them on the phone and exchanged emails over the course of our research to do follow-up chats. Tables A1, A2, and A3 provide further details on the characteristics of interviewees. Names of all workers have been changed to protect their identities. Businesses, policymakers, labour union executives, and other participants who gave us permission to use their names appear by their name and designation, while all others have their identities protected.

All interviews were semi-structured and designed around certain central themes relevant to the scope of the study. All but three interviews were conducted face-to-face. Efforts were made to audio record the interviews. Just six participants declined our request to record them, in which case we took detailed notes during the interview and wrote detailed transcripts based on the notes immediately after the interview (see Rutakumwa et al., 2020). The interviews were transcribed by local transcribers based in South Africa, Kenya, and Ghana.

The transcripts were then transferred to NVivo for data analysis. For coding interviews of workers, a theoretical framework was derived from the initial literature review to sort the data into broad categories, based on the key job quality indicators we have outlined in Chapter 4. The transcripts were then systematically coded along those lines. For interviews with business executives, policymakers, labour unions, etc. open coding was done to sort data into broad categories, and revised during and after the data collection phase until condensed and comprehensive categories were achieved.

Remote Gig Economy Workers

We conducted in-depth interviews with sixty-five remote gig economy workers in our case study countries, on one of the world's biggest gig work platforms, Upwork. Upwork as a platform is very typical for global remote work, containing a standardized website structure and simple user interface, information on workers and clients, work and payment histories, and a reputation system. Workers bid for jobs posted by clients on Upwork. Upwork has a technological system of controlling the labour processes through a mix of algorithmic management and surveillance, which is also typical of other platforms such as Uber. Despite workers being able to register their profiles, fewer than 10 per cent of workers globally and just around 6 per cent of registered African workers on Upwork ever get to earn at least US$1 on the platform (see Chapter 4).

We selected participants with the aim of including a diversity of work experience, including types of work performed, education, number of hours worked, income earned, hourly rates, and gender (Table A1). We first sent invitations to workers via the platform. Since some workers were reluctant to speak to us, we used a number of other techniques

Table A1 Characteristics of remote gig economy workers interviewed

Characteristics	N=65
Gender	
Male	40
Female	25
Education	
Diploma or Matric (equivalent to UK's A Level)	11
Undergraduate degree and above	54
Age group	
18–24	15
25–29	29
30 and above	21
Total no. of hours worked*	
<100	17
100–500	20
Over 500	28
Total income earned (US$)*	
<500	17
500–1,000	8
Over 1,000	40
Types of gig work#	
Writing and Translation	14
Clerical and Data Entry (virtual assistant, transcription, proofreading, digitizing documents)	28
Professional Services (accounting, business consulting, legal advice)	3
Sales and Marketing Support	17
Creative and Multimedia (user interface and design, website development)	2
Software Development and Technology work	1

*at the time of the interview.
#Workers did multiple types of work, which makes categorizing difficult. So instead we chose their first listed work type on their profiles on Upwork.

to recruit them. We contacted them through their social media profiles (such as Facebook) and professional networking sites, e.g. LinkedIn and found that workers were more comfortable to speak if approached through these channels. We also undertook snowball sampling. In order to avoid sampling bias, we asked our initial respondents to encourage other workers in their networks to come forward and speak to us (see Heckathorn, 1997). This helped us examine the networks emerging in gig work, the levels of intermediation or re-outsourcing taking place—which are hard to discern when the workforce is dispersed and globally situated—and how these networks might influence job quality outcomes of workers. Thus, our results are indicative and not representative of the gig work taking place on the African continent.

Our semi-structured interviews lasted between 31 and 116 minutes, gathering in-depth information about the nature and types of work done by these workers, career prospects and challenges of livelihoods, worker perceptions and motivations for undertaking gig work, its impact on their lives and livelihoods, the meanings and expectations they attach to the work,

Table A2 Characteristics of call centre workers interviewed

Characteristics	N=67 (%)
Gender	
Male	40
Female	27
Education	
Diploma or Matric (equivalent to UK's A Level)	21
Undergraduate degree and above	46
Age group	
18–24	28
25–29	27
30 and above	12
Nature of work (key tasks)[*]	
Voice and Non-voice (sales, technical support, customer service)[**]	49
Data Manipulation (content generation, image annotation)	18

[*]Most workers did a combination of voice and non-voice work.
[**]Workers who did outbound calls tended to also have experience with inbound operations.

the challenges workers face, types of workers who find success in gig work, and the types who did not.

We also conducted two group discussions in Nigeria: one in Lagos and one in Abuja. We sent invitations to twenty-two gig workers in Lagos but only seven agreed to attend the meeting. In Abuja, we sent fifteen invitations and only five attended. We recruited workers from these two cities to gather feedback on some of the preliminary findings from our earlier fieldwork in South Africa and Kenya and to generate a range of opinions and ideas around topics such as the perceived flexibility in gig work (on group discussion see Stewart and Shamdasani, 1990). Another important reason was to examine the locally-specific social challenges workers face to do gig work; a case in point is the online scamming networks of Nigeria and their influence on workers' ability to win contracts on platforms. The characteristics of the gig economy workers are given in Table A1.

Call Centre Workers

We conducted in-depth interviews with a total of sixty-seven call and contact centre workers (Table A2) from eighteen different firms across five countries. We began our fieldwork by sourcing workers, asking firms directly to give us access to their employees. This proved to be difficult. In most cases, managers of the firms refused us permission to speak to workers since they have privacy/confidentiality agreements with their end clients. Some firms did give us access but only for a short time, because workers were on duty. In South Africa, one senior executive allowed us to speak to four workers in the firm's offices but for only 20 minutes at a time. We took the contact details of workers to speak to them at a later time after work or on a day when they are not working, but this effort proved futile as no one responded to our calls at a later time.

Table A3 Other participants and their breakdown

Location	BPO Firms' Managers	Government Officials	Industry Bodies	Industry Experts	Trades Unions/ Worker Bodies	Consulting Firm	Staffing Agency
South Africa	10	1	3	4		1	1
Kenya	11	4	1		8		
Uganda	4	2	1				
Nigeria	10	2	1				
Ghana	4	4			2		
Egypt		1					
Total	**39**	**14**	**6**	**4**	**10**	**1**	**1**

We then decided to meet workers in places they are known to congregate, such as near the street vendors outside their offices. We did that in South Africa (July–October 2016). We would wait outside call centre offices around lunch time when workers would be given a break and we would request an interview after their work or on their off day. Though not very successful, we were able to recruit two workers in South Africa.

We therefore decided to change our strategy of sourcing workers. We started sourcing respondents from LinkedIn. We would find profiles of the firm on LinkedIn and then browse their employees list and contact workers directly. While we were able to do some interviews, there were some issues in sourcing workers through social networking sites. Some workers, who agreed to meet, cancelled at the last moment. This was largely due to fear of management finding out about them and firing them (see Chapter 5 for more on hiring and firing in call centres). Second, workers often did not update their profiles even after they had left their jobs. We interviewed some of those ex-call centre workers anyway to hear about their experiences of work. We would exchange emails and phone numbers and have constant contact either through phone calls or text messages to build rapport. This proved useful for us to snowball for more respondents.

Workers recruited through this technique were comfortable and open to talk. In Kenya, our first interview with a call centre worker in October 2016 helped us connect with ten more workers from two of the major call centre firms operating in Nairobi. Apparently, the small size of the industry meant only a limited number of firms were operating in the city. Thus, workers knew people in other firms either in their locality, or because they had worked for the other firm. Similarly, in South Africa, our first three key respondents helped us connect with nine more workers. In Ghana, our first respondent connected us with two workers from their firm and the second participants connected us with three more workers.

There are several limitations with the snowball strategy. Sampling bias is a known in snowballing (Atkinson and Flint, 2001, 2004; Biernacki and Waldorf, 1981). Therefore, we would ask our key respondents to help us identify respondents based on certain criteria so that our sample would be as diverse as possible with workers from a range of experiences and backgrounds (see Heckathorn, 1997; Kirchherr and Charles, 2018). Some of the key traits for respondent characteristics we used were gender, type of work activities (e.g. inbound or outbound calling), and job category (call centre agent, team leader, supervisor). In most cases, they knew the socio-economic backgrounds of their co-workers (e.g. education, family background, previous employment history). Because workers knew their colleagues really well, we were able to get a diverse sample. This strategy proved helpful in recruiting workers as they were less concerned about managerial action and felt secure talking to us openly.

Most of our interviews with call centre workers lasted between 45 and 90 minutes, except four interviews in South Africa, which were only 20 minutes long BPO. Our interviews focused on the nature and types of their current and previous work, work-related impacts, and meanings derived from their work.

Other Participants

We interviewed thirty-nine executives from thirty firms in our case study countries. Most interviews were conducted in the major cities of our case countries (Johannesburg, Nairobi, Kampala, Lagos, Abuja, and Accra). Access to firms also presented a challenge. A senior figure in one of the largest international BPO firms in South Africa cancelled our meeting twice; some spoke to us on condition of anonymity; others never responded to our request for interview.

We also conducted interviews with members of industry bodies or private sector associations in the outsourcing sector. These included BPESA, KITOS, ATIS Uganda, AOPN, and NAITEOC.

In-depth interviews were also conducted with senior figures in government departments responsible for the ICT or digital economy sectors. These included Department of Trade and Industry (South Africa), National Information Technology (Uganda), ICT Authority (Kenya), NITDA Nigeria, and the National Information Technology Agency (Ghana). One telephonic interview was conducted with a government official in Egypt at ITIDA in 2019. This was primarily done to understand the nature and size of the outsourcing industry in Egypt and develop some comparative insights on the BPO sector in Africa. Finally, four industry experts, a member of the consulting firm in South Africa, and a member of a staffing agency in South Africa were interviewed. These interviews were geared to gain insights into the networks and scope of the wider outsourcing industry. Table A3 outlines the breakdown of other participants.

References

Abbott, P.Y. and Jones, M.R. 2012. Everywhere and nowhere: nearshore software development in the context of globalisation. *Eur. J. Inf. Syst.* 21, 529–551. https://doi.org/10.1057/ejis.2012.7

Abu-Lughod, L. 1990. The romance of resistance: tracing transformations of power through Bedouin women. *American Ethnologist* 17, 41–55.

Ackroyd, S. and Thompson, P. 1999. Organizational Misbehaviour. SAGE Publications, London.

Adera, E.O., Waema, T.M., May, J., et al. (eds) 2014. ICT Pathways to Poverty Reduction: Empirical Evidence from East and Southern Africa. Practical Action Publishing, Rugby, Warwickshire.

Adunbi, O. 2019. (Re)inventing development: China, infrastructure, sustainability and special economic zones in Nigeria. *Africa* 89, 662–679. https://doi.org/10.1017/S0001972019000846

AfDB 2012. African Economic Outlook: 2012. AfDB, Addis Ababa.

AfDB 2013. Connecting Africa: An Assessment of Progress Towards the Connect Africa Summit Goals. AfDB, Addis Ababa.

AfDB 2018a. African Development Bank Launches Coding for Employment Program: Unleashing Africa's Next Generation of Digital Innovators. AfDB, Addis Ababa.

AfDB 2018b. African Economic Outlook 2018. AfDB, Addis Ababa.

AfDB 2019. African Economic Outlook 2019. AfDB, Addis Ababa.

AfDB 2020. African Economic Outlook 2020: Developing Africa's Workforce for the Future. AfDB, Ethiopia.

AfDB, OECD, UNDP, UNECA 2012. African Economic Outlook: Promoting Youth Employment. AfDB, OECD, UNDP, UNECA, Addis Ababa.

Africa Partnership Forum 2008. ICT in Africa: Boosting Economic Growth and Poverty Reduction. Africa Partnership Forum, Addis Ababa.

Africa Renewal 2020. Innovative tech and connectivity key to fighting COVID-19 in Africa. UN. Available at https://www.un.org/africarenewal/news/coronavirus/innovative-tech-and-connectivity-key-fighting-covid-19-africa, accessed 2.6.20.

African Union 2018. Protocol to the Treaty Establishing the African Economic Community Relating to Free Movement of Persons, Right of Residence and Right of Establishment. African Union, Addis Ababa.

Aggad-Clerx, F. 2013. France: Out of Africa and back? Available at https://www.aljazeera.com/indepth/opinion/2013/12/france-out-africa-back-20131214112634946877.html, accessed 18.2.20.

Aglietta, M. 1979. A Theory of Capitalist Regulation: The US Experience. Verso, London.

Aker, J.C. 2010. Information from markets near and far: mobile phones and agricultural markets in Niger. *Am. Econ. J. Appl. Econ.* 2, 46–59. https://doi.org/10.1257/app.2.3.46

Aker, J.C. and Mbiti, I.M. 2010. Mobile phones and economic development in Africa. *J. Econ. Perspect.* 24, 207–232. https://doi.org/10.1257/jep.24.3.207

Akinyelure, D. 2018. Google launches free Wi-Fi hotspot network in Nigeria. Reuters.

Akpan-Obong, P.I. 2009. Information and Communication Technologies in Nigeria: Prospects and Challenges for Development. Peter Lang, New York.

Alake, T. 2021. Uber Raises Fares in Key African Markets After Driver Protests. Bloomberg. https://www.bloomberg.com/news/articles/2021-05-11/uber-raises-fares-in-key-african-markets-after-driver-protests. Accessed 5.8.2021.

Alalade, F.O. 2004. Trade unions and democratic option in Nigeria. *Journal of Social Sciences* 9, 201–206. https://doi.org/10.1080/09718923.2004.11892450

Alarcón-Medina, R. 2018. Informational returnees: deportation, digital media, and the making of a transnational cybertariat in the Mexican call center industry. *Dialect Anthropol.* 42, 293–308. https://doi.org/10.1007/s10624-018-9518-5

Alberti, G., Bessa, I., Hardy, K., et al. 2018. In, against and beyond precarity: work in insecure times. *Work, Employment and Society* 32, 447–457. https://doi.org/10.1177/0950017018762088

Alenda-Demoutiez, J. and Mügge, D. 2020. The lure of ill-fitting unemployment statistics: how South Africa's discouraged work seekers disappeared from the unemployment rate. *New Political Economy* 25(4), 590–606. https://doi.org/10.1080/13563467.2019.1613355

Alexander, A. 2010. Leadership and collective action in the Egyptian trade unions. *Work, Employment and Society* 24, 241–259. https://doi.org/10.1177/0950017010362144

Alliance for Affordable Internet 2019. New mobile broadband pricing data shows uneven progress on affordability. Available at https://a4ai.org/new-mobile-broadband-pricing-data-reveals-stalling-progress-on-affordability/, accessed 15.4.20.

Alliance for Affordable Internet. 2020. Mobile broadband pricing: data for 2020. Available at https://a4ai.org/extra/baskets/A4AI/2020/mobile_broadband_pricing_usd, accessed 9.8.21.

Aloisi, A. and De Stefano, V. 2020. Regulation, flexibility and the future of work: the case for the employment relationship as innovation facilitator. *International Labour Review* https://doi.org/10.1111/ilr.12160

Ambrose, M.L., Seabright, M.A., and Schminke, M. 2002. Sabotage in the workplace: the role of organizational injustice. *Organizational Behavior and Human Decision Processes* 89, 947–965. https://doi.org/10.1016/S0749-5978(02)00037-7

Amin, A. 1994. Post-Fordism: A Reader. Blackwell, Oxford.

Amin, S., 1976. *Unequal development: An essay on the social formations of peripheral capitalism.* Harvester Press, Sussex

Ananthram, S., Teo, S.T., Connell, J., et al. 2018. Control and involvement HR practices in Indian call centres: still searching for answers. *Asia Pacific Journal of Human Resources* 56, 196–215. https://doi.org/10.1111/1744-7941.12153

Andjelkovic, M. and Imaizumi, S. 2012. Mobile Entrepreneurship and Employment. *Innov. Technol. Gov. Glob.* 7, 87–100. https://doi.org/10.1162/INOV_a_00154

Andrae G. and Beckman B. 1999. Union Power in the Nigerian Textile Industry: Labour Regime and Adjustment. Transaction Publishers, New Brunswick, NJ.

Animento, S., Cesare, G.D., and Sica, C. 2017. Total eEclipse of wWork? Neue Protestformen in der gig economy am Beispiel des Foodora Streiks in Turin. *PROKLA* 47, 271–290. https://doi.org/10.32387/prokla.v47i187.145

Anwar, M.A. 2014. New modes of industrial manufacturing: India's experience with special economic zones. *Bull. Geogr. Socio-Econ. Ser.* 24, 7–25.

Anwar, M.A. 2019. Connecting South Africa: ICTs, uneven development and poverty debates, in Knight, J., and Rogerson, C.M. (eds), The Geography of South Africa: Contemporary Changes and New Directions, World Regional Geography Book Series.

Springer International Publishing, New York, pp. 261–267. https://doi.org/10.1007/978-3-319-94974-1_28

Anwar, M.A. 2020. 'We work for Uber': South Africa's gig drivers left alone at the wheel. *African Arguments*. Available at https://africanarguments.org/2020/04/28/we-work-for-uber-south-africa-covid-19-gig-drivers-alone-wheel/, accessed 29.9.20.

Anwar, M.A. and Carmody, P. 2016. Bringing globalization to the countryside: Special Economic Zones in India. *Singap. J. Trop. Geogr.* 37, 121–138. https://doi.org/10.1111/sjtg.12146

Anwar, M.A. and Graham, M. 2019. Does economic upgrading lead to social upgrading in contact centers? Evidence from South Africa. *Afr. Geogr. Rev.* 38, 209–226. https://doi.org/10.1080/19376812.2019.1589730

Anwar, M.A. and Graham, M. 2020a. Between a rock and a hard place: freedom, flexibility, precarity and vulnerability in the gig economy in Africa. *Compet. Change* 1024529420914473. https://doi.org/10.1177/1024529420914473

Anwar, M.A. and Graham, M. 2020b. Digital labour at economic margins: African workers and the global information economy. *Review of African Political Economy* 47, 95–105. https://doi.org/10.1080/03056244.2020.1728243

Anwar, M.A. and Graham, M. 2020c. Hidden transcripts of the gig economy: labour agency and the new art of resistance among African gig workers. *Environment and Planning A* 52(7):1269–1291. doi:10.1177/0308518X19894584

Anwar, M.A., Carmody, P., Surborg, B., et al. 2014. The diffusion and impacts of information and communication technology on tourism in the Western Cape, South Africa. *Urban Forum* 25, 531–545. https://doi.org/10.1007/s12132-013-9210-4

Aouragh, M. 2012. Social media, mediation and the Arab revolutions. *tripleC: Communication, Capitalism & Critique* 10(2): 518–536.

Appadurai, A. 1996. Modernity At Large: Cultural Dimensions of Globalization: 1, 1st edn. ed. University of Minnesota Press, Minneapolis, MN.

Appelbaum, R.P., Cao, C., Han, X., et al. 2018. Innovation in China: Challenging the Global Science and Technology System. Polity Press, Cambridge.

Archer, L. 2008. The new neoliberal subjects? Young/er academics' constructions of professional identity. *Journal of Education Policy* 23, 265–285. https://doi.org/10.1080/02680930701754047

Armistead, C., Kiely, J., Hole, L., et al. 2002. An exploration of managerial issues in call centres. *Managing Service Quality* 12, 246–256. https://doi.org/10.1108/09604520210434857

Arnold, D. and Bongiovi, J.R. 2013. Precarious, informalizing, and flexible work. *American Behavioral Scientist* 57, 289–308. https://doi.org/10.1177/0002764212466239

Aroles, J., Mitev, N., and de Vaujany, F.-X. 2019. Mapping themes in the study of new work practices. *New Technol. Work Employ.* 34, 285–299. https://doi.org/10.1111/ntwe.12146

Asamoah, D., Takieddine, S., and Amedofu, M. 2020. Examining the effect of mobile money transfer (MMT) capabilities on business growth and development impact. *Information Technology for Development* 26, 146–161. https://doi.org/10.1080/02681102.2019.1599798

Aslam, Y. and Woodcock, J. 2020. A history of Uber organizing in the UK. *South Atlantic Quarterly* 119, 412–421. https://doi.org/10.1215/00382876-8177983

Asongu, S.A. 2013. The 'Knowledge Economy' – finance nexus: how do IPRs matter in SSA and MENA countries? *Econ. Bull.* 33, 78–94.

Asongu, S.A. and Nwachukwu, J.C. (2019) The role of openness in the effect of ICT on governance. *Information Technology for Development* 25(3), 503–531. https://doi.org/10.1080/02681102.2017.1412292

Atkinson, R. and Flint, J. 2001. Accessing hidden and hard-to-reach populations: snowball research strategies. *Social Research Update* 33, 1–4.

Atkinson, R. and Flint, J. (2004) Snowball sampling, in Lewis-Beck, M.S., Bryman, A., and Liao, T.F. (eds) The Encyclopaedia of Social Science Research Methods. Sage, London, 1043–1044.

Attwood, H., Diga, K., Braathen, E., et al. 2013. Telecentre functionality in South Africa: re-enabling the community ICT access environment. *Journal of Community Informatics* 9. https://doi.org/10.15353/joci.v9i4.3137

Augoustinos, M. 1999. Ideology, false consciousness and psychology. *Theory & Psychology* 9, 295–312. https://doi.org/10.1177/0959354399093002

AU/OECD, 2018. Africa's Development Dynamics 2018: Growth, Jobs and Inequalities. OECD. AU/OECD, Addis Ababa/Paris.

Avgerou, C. 2010. Discourses on ICT and development. *Inf. Technol. Int. Dev.* 6, 1–18.

Azmeh, S. 2014. Labour in global production networks: workers in the qualifying industrial zones (QIZs) of Egypt and Jordan. *Glob. Netw.* 14, 495–513. https://doi.org/10.1111/glob.12047

Bailard, C.S. 2009. Mobile phone diffusion and corruption in Africa. *Polit. Commun.* 26, 333–353. https://doi.org/10.1080/10584600903053684

Bain, P. and Taylor, P. 2000. Entrapped by the 'electronic panopticon'? Worker resistance in the call centre. *New Technol. Work Employ.* 15, 2–18. https://doi.org/10.1111/1468-005X.00061

Bain, P. and Taylor, P. 2002. Ringing the changes? Union recognition and organisation in call centres in the UK finance sector. *Industrial Relations Journal* 33, 246–261. https://doi.org/10.1111/1468-2338.00233

Bain, P., Watson, A., Mulvey, G., et al. (2002), Taylorism, targets and the pursuit of quantity and quality by call centre management. *New Techn. Work Employ.* 17: 170–185. https://doi.org/10.1111/1468-005X.00103

Ball, K.S. and Margulis, S.T. 2011. Electronic monitoring and surveillance in call centres: a framework for investigation. *New Techn. Work Employ.* 26, 113–126. https://doi.org/10.1111/j.1468-005X.2011.00263.x

Bangasser, P. 2000. The ILO and the Informal Sector: An Institutional History. ILO, Geneva.

Bardhan, A., Jaffee, D.M., and Kroll, C.A. 2013. The Oxford Handbook of Offshoring and Global Employment. Oxford University Press, Oxford.

Barker, K. and Christensen, K. 1998. Contingent Work: American Employment Relations in Transition. ILR Press, Ithaca, NY.

Barley, S. 1990. The alignment of technology and structure through roles and networks. *Adm. Sci. Q.* 35, 61–103.

Barley, S.R. and Kunda, G. 2006. Contracting: a new form of professional practice. *Acad. Manage. Perspect* 20, 45–66. https://doi.org/10.5465/AMP.2006.19873409

Barnes, T.J. 1989. Place, space, and theories of economic value: contextualism and essentialism in economic geography. *Trans. Inst. Br. Geogr.* 14, 299–316. https://doi.org/10.2307/622690

Barnes, T.J. and Sheppard, E. 2010. 'Nothing includes everything': towards engaged pluralism in Anglophone economic geography. *Prog. Hum. Geogr.* 34, 193–214. https://doi.org/10.1177/0309132509343728

Barnet, R. and Muller, R. 1974. Global Reach: The Power of the Multinational Corporations. Simon & Schuster, New York.

Barrett, C.B., Christiaensen, L., Sheahan, M., et al. 2017. On the structural transformation of rural Africa. *J Afr. Econ.* 26, i11–i35. https://doi.org/10.1093/jae/ejx009

Barrientos, S. 2013. Corporate Purchasing Practices in Global Production Networks: A Socially Contested Terrain. *Geoforum* 44, 44–51.

Barrientos, S. 2019. Gender and Work in Global Value Chains: Capturing the Gains? Cambridge University Press, Cambridge.

Barrientos, S. and Kritzinger, A. 2004. Squaring the circle: global production and the informalization of work in South African fruit exports. *Journal of International Development* 16, 81–92. https://doi.org/10.1002/jid.1064

Barrientos, S., Knorringa, P., Evers, B. et al. 2016. Shifting regional dynamics of global value chains: implications for economic and social upgrading in African horticulture. *Environ. Plan. Econ. Space* 48, 1266–1283. https://doi.org/10.1177/0308518X15614416

Bassier, I. and Woolard, I. 2018. The top 1% of incomes are increasing rapidly even with low economic growth. *Econ 3x3*. Available at http://www.econ3x3.org/sites/default/files/articles/Bassier%20&%20Woolard%202018%20Top%20incomes_0.pdf, accessed 9.8.21.

Bateman, M., Duvendack, M., and Loubere, N. 2019. Is fin-tech the new panacea for poverty alleviation and local development? Contesting Suri and Jack's M-Pesa findings published in science. *Rev. Afr. Polit. Econ.* 46, 480–495. https://doi.org/10.1080/03056244.2019.1614552

Batnitzky A. and McDowell, L. 2011. Migration, nursing, institutional discrimination and emotional/affective labour: ethnicity and labour stratification in the UK National Health Service. *Social & Cultural Geography* 12(2): 181–201.

Batt, R., Holman, D., and Holtgrewe, U. 2009. The globalization of service work: comparative institutional perspectives on call centers. *Introduction to a Special Issue of the Industrial & Labor Relations Review* 62, 453–488. https://doi.org/10.1177/001979390906200401

Bauman, Z. 2003. Wasted Lives: Modernity and Its Outcasts. Wiley-Blackwell, London.

Bayart, J.F. 2000. Africa in the world: a history of extraversion, trans. Stephen Ellis. *Afr. Aff.* 99, 217–267. https://doi.org/10.1093/afraf/99.395.217

Beckman, B., Buhlungu, S., and Sachikonye, L. 2010. Trade Unions & Party Politics: Labour Movements in Africa. HSRC Press, Cape Town.

Beerepoot, N. and Hendriks, M. 2013. Employability of offshore service sector workers in the Philippines: opportunities for upward labour mobility or dead-end jobs? *Work, Employment & Society*. https://doi.org/0950017012469065.

Beerepoot, N. and Keijser, C. 2015. The service outsourcing sector as driver of development: the expectations of Ghana's ICT for Accelerated Development Programme. *Tijdschr. Voor Econ. En Soc. Geogr.* 106, 556–569.

Beerepoot, N. and Lambregts, B. 2015. Competition in online job marketplaces: towards a global labour market for outsourcing services? *Global Networks* 15, 236–255.

Beerepoot, N., Lambregts, B., and Kleibert, J. (eds) 2017. Globalisation and Services-Driven Economic Growth: Perspectives from the Global North and South, 1st edn. Routledge, Abingdon.

Beers, T.M. 2000. Flexible schedules and shift work: replacing the 9-to-5 workday. *Monthly Lab. Rev.* 123, 33.

Beinin, J. 2015. Workers and Thieves: Labor Movements and Popular Uprisings in Tunisia and Egypt, 1st edn. Stanford Briefs, Stanford, CA.

Belt, V. 2002. A female ghetto? Women's careers in call centres. *Hum. Resour. Manag. J.* 12, 51–66. https://doi.org/10.1111/j.1748-8583.2002.tb00077.x

Benanav, A. 2019. The origins of informality: the ILO at the limit of the concept of unemployment. *Journal of Global History* 14, 107–125. https://doi.org/10.1017/S1740022 818000372

Benner, C. 2002. Work in the New Economy: Flexible Labor Markets in Silicon Valley. Oxford: Wiley-Blackwell.

Benner, C. 2006. 'South Africa On-call': information technology and labour market restructuring in South African call centres. *Reg. Stud.* 40, 1025–1040. https://doi.org/10.1080/00343400600928293

Benner, C. and Dean, A. 2000. Labour in the new economy: lessons from labour organising in Silicon Valley, in Carre, F.J., Ferber, M.A., Golden, L., et al. (Eds) Nonstandard Work: The Nature and Challenges of Changing Employment Arrangements. Cornell University Press, Ithaca, NY, pp. 361–376.

Benner, C. and Mane, F. 2011. From internal to network labor markets? Insights on new promotion processes from the call center industry. *Industrial Relations: A Journal of Economy and Society* 50, 323–353. https://doi.org/10.1111/j.1468-232X.2011.00638.x

Benner, C. and Rossi, J. 2016. An island off the West Coast of Australia: multiplex geography and the growth of transnational telemediated service work in Mauritius, in Mirchandani, K. and Poster, W. (eds), Borders in Service: Enactments of Nationhood in Transnational Call Centers. University of Toronto Press, Toronto, ON, pp. 86–120.

Benner, C., Lewis, C. and Omar, R. 2007. The South African call centre industry: a study of strategy, human resource practices and performance. *The Global Contact Centre Study Report*. URL: https://tinyurl.com/c7jwn99r Retrieved Novemb. 22.

Berg, J. 2016. Income Security in the On-Demand Economy: Findings and Policy Lessons from a Survey of Crowdworkers, Conditions of Work and Employment Series No. 74. ILO, Geneva.

Berg, J., Furrer, M., Harmon, E., et al. 2018. Digital Labour Platforms and the Future of Work: Towards Decent Work in the Online World. ILO, Geneva.

Berg, L.D., Huijbens, E.H., and Larsen, H.G. 2016. Producing anxiety in the neoliberal university. *Canadian Geographer/Le Géographe canadien* 60, 168–180. https://doi.org/10.1111/cag.12261

Bernards, N., 2018. The Global Governance of Precarity: Primitive Accumulation and the Politics of Irregular Work. Routledge, London.

Bessa, I., Charlwood, A., and Valizade, D. 2020. Do unions cause job dissatisfaction? Evidence from a quasi-experiment in the United Kingdom. *British Journal of Industrial Relations*. https://doi.org/10.1111/bjir.12543

Betteridge, B. and Webber, S. 2019. Everyday resilience, reworking, and resistance in North Jakarta's kampungs. *Environment and Planning E: Nature and Space* 2(4): 944–966.

Bhattacharyya, G. and Murji, K. 2013. Introduction: race critical public scholarship. *Ethnic and Racial Studies* 36, 1359–1373. https://doi.org/10.1080/01419870.2013.791399

Bhorat, H. and Khan, S. 2018. Structural change and patterns of inequality: in the South African labour market. DPRU Working Paper 201801, University of Cape Town.

Bieler, A. and Lindberg, I. 2010. Global Restructuring, Labour and the Challenges for Transnational Solidarity. Taylor & Francis Group, London.

Biernacki, P. and Waldorf, D. 1981. Snowball sampling—problems and techniques of chain referral sampling. *Social Methods Res.* 10(2), 141–63.

Bishara, D. 2018. Contesting Authoritarianism: Labor Challenges to the State in Egypt. Cambridge University Press, Cambridge.

Blaya, J.A., Fraser, H.S.F., and Holt, B. 2010. E-health technologies show promise in developing countries. *Health Aff. Proj. Hope* 29, 244–251. https://doi.org/10.1377/hlthaff. 2009.0894

Bloodworth, J. 2016. Hired: Six Months Undercover in Low-Wage Britain. Atlantic Books, London.

Bloomberg 2020. California Wins Preliminary Injunction against Uber, Lyft. Bloomberg.

Bobrov, L.H. 2018. Mobile Messaging App Map – February 2018. Available at https://www. similarweb.com/blog/mobile-messaging-app-map-2018, accessed 3.7.19.

Bohle, P. 2016. Work-life conflict in 'flexible work': precariousness, variable hours and related forms of work organization, in Iskra-Golec, I., Barnes-Farrell, J., and Bohle, P. (eds), Social and Family Issues in Shift Work and Non Standard Working Hours. Springer International Publishing, New York, pp. 91–105. https://doi.org/10.1007/978-3-319-42286-2_5

Boisen, C. 2013. The changing moral justification of empire: from the right to colonise to the obligation to civilise. *Hist. Eur. Ideas* 39, 335–353. https://doi.org/10.1080/01916599. 2012.716603

Bonacich, E. 1972. A theory of ethnic antagonism: the split labor market. *American Sociological Review* 37(5), 547–559. doi: https://doi.org/10.2307/2093450

Bond, P. 2006. Looting Africa: The Economics of Exploitation. University of KwaZulu-Natal Press; London; Scottsville, South Africa.

Bond, P. 2014. Elite Transition: From Apartheid to Neoliberalism in South Africa. Revised and Expanded edn. Pluto Press, London.

Bond, P. and Garcia, A. (eds) 2015. BRICS: An Anti-Capitalist Critique. Pluto Press, London.

Bonekamp, L. and Sure, M. 2015. Consequences of industry 4.0 on human labour and work organisation. *J. Bus. Media Psychol.* 6, 33–40.

Booth, R. 2020. Uber drivers' fight for workers' rights reaches UK supreme court. The Guardian. https://www.theguardian.com/technology/2020/jul/21/uber-drivers-fight-for-workers-rights-reaches-supreme-court, accessed 21.6.21

Bornman, E. 2016. Information society and digital divide in South Africa: results of longitudinal surveys. *Inf. Commun. Soc.* 19, 264–278. https://doi.org/10.1080/1369118X.2015. 1065285

Bosch, T. 2017. Twitter activism and youth in South Africa: the case of #RhodesMustFall. *Information, Communication & Society* 20, 221–232. https://doi.org/10.1080/1369118X. 2016.1162829

Boxall, P. and Macky, K. 2014. High-involvement work processes, work intensification and employee well-being. *Work, Employment and Society* 28, 963–984. https://doi.org/10. 1177/0950017013512714

Boyer, R. and Saillard, Y. (eds) 2002. Regulation Theory: The State of the Art. Routledge, London.

BPESA (Business Process Enabling SA) 2015a. South Africa's BPO Proposition. BPESA, Johannesburg.

BPESA (Business Process Enabling SA) 2015b. South Africa Business Process Management: Key Indicator Report 2015. BPESA, Johannesburg.

BPESA (Business Process Enabling SA) 2018. South Africa Business Process Management: Key Indicator Report 2018. BPESA, Johannesburg.

Bratton, M. 2013. Briefing: citizens and cell phones in Africa. *Afr. Aff.* 112, 304–319. https:// doi.org/10.1093/afraf/adt004

Bräutigam, D. and Xiaoyang, T. 2011. African Shenzhen: China's special economic zones in Africa. *Journal of Modern African Studies* 49(1), 27–54. doi:10.1017/S0022278X10000649

Braverman, H. 1974. Labor and Monopoly Capital: The Degradation of Work in the Twentieth Century. Monthly Review Press, New York, NY.

Britz, J.J., Lor, P.J., Coetzee, I.E.M., et al. 2006. Africa as a knowledge society. *Int. Inf. Libr. Rev.* 38, 25–40. https://doi.org/10.1080/10572317.2006.10762700

Brookes, M. 2019. The New Politics of Transnational Labor. Cornell University Press, Ithaca, NY.

The Brookings Institution. 2020. Foresight Africa: Top priorities for the continent 2020-2030. New York. Available at https://www.brookings.edu/wp-content/uploads/2020/01/ForesightAfrica2020_20200110.pdf. accessed 10.5.21

Brophy, E. 2017. Language Put to Work: The Making of the Global Call Centre Workforce. Springer, New York.

Brown, A., Charlwood, A., and Spencer, D.A. 2012. Not all that it might seem: why job satisfaction is worth studying despite it being a poor summary measure of job quality. *Work, Employment and Society*. https://doi.org/10.1177/0950017012461837

Brown, E.C. 1970. Continuity and change in the Soviet labor market. *ILR Review* 23(2), 171–190.

Brown, P. 2003. The opportunity trap: education and employment in a global economy. *European Educational Research Journal* 2, 141–179. https://doi.org/10.2304/eerj.2003.2.1.4

Brynjolfsson, E. and Kahin, B. (eds) 2000. Understanding the Digital Economy: Data, Tools, and Research. MIT Press, Cambridge, MA.

Brynjolfsson, E. and Mcafee, A. 2014. The Second Machine Age: Work, Progress, and Prosperity in a Time of Brilliant Technologies. W. W. Norton, New York.

Bryson, J.R. 2007. The 'second' global shift: the offshoring or global sourcing of corporate services and the rise of distanciated emotional labour. *Geogr. Ann. Ser. B Hum. Geogr.* 89, 31–43. https://doi.org/10.1111/j.1468-0467.2007.00258.x

Buehler, E.M., Crowley, J.L., Peterson, A.M., et al. 2019. Broadcasting for help: a typology of support-seeking strategies on Facebook. *New Media & Society* 21(11–12), 2566–2588. doi:10.1177/1461444819853821

Bukht, R. and Heeks, R. 2017. Defining, conceptualising and measuring the digital economy. *Centre for Development Informatics, Manchester*. https://doi.org/10.2139/ssrn.3431732.

Bulut, E. 2015. Glamor above, precarity below: immaterial labor in the video game industry. *Critical Studies in Media Communication* 32, 193–207. https://doi.org/10.1080/15295036.2015.1047880

Burawoy, M. 1979. Manufacturing Consent: Changes in the Labor Process under Monopoly Capitalism. University of Chicago Press, Chicago, IL.

Burawoy, M. 1985. The Politics of Production. Verso, London.

Burchell, B., Sehnbruch, K., Piasna, A., et al. 2014. The quality of employment and decent work: definitions, methodologies, and ongoing debates. *Camb J Econ* 38, 459–477. https://doi.org/10.1093/cje/bet067

Burchell, B.J. and Coutts, A.P. 2019. The experience of self-employment among young people: an exploratory analysis of 28 low- to middle-income countries. *American Behavioral Scientist* 63, 147–165. https://doi.org/10.1177/0002764218794240

Burrell, J. 2012. Invisible Users: Youth in the Internet Cafes of Urban Ghana. MIT Press, Cambridge, MA.

Burrell, J. 2016. How the machine 'thinks': understanding opacity in machine learning algorithms. *Big Data & Society* 3. https://doi.org/10.1177/2053951715622512

Buskens, I. and Webb, A. (eds) 2009. African Women and ICTs: Investigating Technology, Gender, and Empowerment. Zed Books, London.

Butare, A., Adam, L., Okello, D., et al. 2013. Connecting Africa: An Assessment of Progress towards the Connect Africa Summit Goals. African Development Bank, Tunis.

Butler, S. (2021). Uber drivers entitled to workers' rights, UK supreme court rules. Guardian. Available at https://www.theguardian.com/technology/2021/feb/19/uber-drivers-workers-uk-supreme-court-rules-rights, accessed 10.8.21.

Calderon, C., Kambou, G., Korman, V., et al. 2019. Africa's Pulse: An Analysis of Issues Shaping Africa's Economic Future (No. 19). World Bank, Washington, DC.

Callaghan, G. and Thompson, P. 2001. Edwards revisited: technical control and call centres. Economic and Industrial Democracy 22, 13–37. https://doi.org/10.1177/0143831X01221002

Callaghan, G. and Thompson, P. 2002. 'We Recruit Attitude': the selection and shaping of routine call centre labour. J. Manag. Stud. 39, 233–254. https://doi.org/10.1111/1467-6486.00290

Callebert, R. 2017. On Durban's Docks: Zulu Workers, Rural Households, Global Labor. University of Rochester Press, Rochester, NY.

Campbell, A.F. 2019. The worldwide Uber strike is a key test for the gig economy Vox. Available at https://www.vox.com/2019/5/8/18535367/uber-drivers-strike-2019-cities, accessed 8.1.21.

Campbell, I., Fincher, R., and Webber, M. 1991. Occupational mobility in segmented labour markets: the experience of immigrant workers in Melbourne. Australian and New Zealand Journal of Sociology 27, 172–194. https://doi.org/10.1177/144078339102700202

Cant, C. 2019. Riding for Deliveroo: Resistance in the Gig Economy. Polity Press, London.

Carmody, P. 1998. Constructing alternatives to structural adjustment in Africa. Rev. Afr. Polit. Econ. 25, 25–46. https://doi.org/10.1080/03056249808704291

Carmody, P. 2010. Globalization in Africa: Recolonization or Renaissance? Lynne Rienner, Boulder, CO.

Carmody, P. 2012. The informationalization of poverty in Africa? Mobile phones and economic structure. Information Technologies & International Development 8, 1–17.

Carmody, P. 2013a. A knowledge economy or an information society in Africa? Thintegration and the mobile phone revolution. Inf. Technol. Dev. 19, 24–39. https://doi.org/10.1080/02681102.2012.719859

Carmody, P. 2013b. The Rise of the BRICS in Africa: The Geopolitics of South-South Relations. Zed Books, London.

Carmody, P. 2016. The New Scramble for Africa, 2nd edn. Polity, Cambridge.

Carmody, P. and Fortuin, A. 2019. 'Ride-sharing', virtual capital and impacts on labor in Cape Town, South Africa. African Geographical Review 38(3), 196–208.

Carmody, P. and Taylor, D. 2016. Globalization, land grabbing, and the present-day colonial state in Uganda: ecolonization and its impacts. Journal of Environment & Development 25(1), 100–126. https://doi.org/10.1177/1070496515622017

Carswell, G. and De Neve, G. 2013. Labouring for global markets: Conceptualising labour agency in global production networks. Geoforum 44: 62–70.

Casey, C. 1995. Work, Self and Society: After Industrialism. London: Routledge.

Casilli, A. and Posada, J. 2019. The platformization of labor and society, in Mark Graham, Mark and Durron, William H. (eds), Society and the Internet. How Networks of Information and Communication are Changing Our Lives, 2nd edn. Oxford University Press, Oxford, 293–306.

Castree N., Coe, N.M., Ward, K., et al. 2004. Spaces of Work: Global Capitalism and Geographies of Labour. Sage, London.

Chapela, J.G. 2015. Split or straight? Evidence of the effects of work schedules on workers' well-being, time use, and productivity. *SERIEs* 6, 153–177. https://doi.org/10.1007/s13209-015-0125-2

Charbonneau, B. 2016. France and the New Imperialism: Security Policy in sub-Saharan Africa. Routledge, Oxford. https://doi.org/10.4324/9781315582948

Chatterjee, A., Czajka, L., and Gethin, A. 2020. Estimating the distribution of household wealth in South Africa. Working Paper no. 2020/06 UNU-WIDER, Helsinki.

Chaudhuri, A. 2012. ICT for development: solutions seeking problems? *J. Inf. Technol.* 27, 326–338. http://dx.doi.org/10.1057/jit.2012.19

Chelghoum, A., Takeda, S., Wilczek, B., et al. 2016. The challenges and future of trade unionism in Algeria: a lost cause? *Employee Relations* 38, 351–372. https://doi.org/10.1108/ER-11-2014-0135

Chen, M. and Carré, F. 2020. The Informal Economy Revisited: Examining the Past, Envisioning the Future. Routledge, London. https://doi.org/10.4324/9780429200724

Cheru, F. 2017. Africa's development trajectory: past, present, and future directions, in Lopes, C., Hamdok, A., and Elhiraika, A. (eds), Macroeconomic Policy Framework for Africa's Structural Transformation. Springer International Publishing, New York, pp. 37–62. https://doi.org/10.1007/978-3-319-51947-0_2

Cheru, F. and Modi, R. 2013. Agricultural Development and Food Security in Africa: The Impact of Chinese, Indian and Brazilian Investments. Zed Books, London.

Chibita, M.B. 2016. Digital Activism in Uganda, in Mutsvairo, B. (ed.), Digital Activism in the Social Media Era: Critical Reflections on Emerging Trends in Sub-Saharan Africa. Springer International Publishing, New York, pp. 69–93. https://doi.org/10.1007/978-3-319-40949-8_4

Chowdhury, S.K. 2006. Investments in ICT-capital and economic performance of small and medium scale enterprises in East Africa. *J. Int. Dev.* 18, 533–552. https://doi.org/10.1002/jid.1250

Chun, J.J. 2009. Organizing at the Margins: The Symbolic Politics of Labor in South Korea and the United States. Cornell University Press, Ithaca, NY.

Churchill, B. and Craig, L. 2019. Gender in the gig economy: men and women using digital platforms to secure work in Australia. *Journal of Sociology* 55, 741–761. https://doi.org/10.1177/1440783319894060

CIPD (Chartered Institute of Personnel and Development) 2015. Zero-Hours and Short-Hours Contracts in the UK: Employer and Employee Perspectives. CIPD, London.

CIPD (Chartered Institute of Personnel and Development) 2017. To Gig or Not to Gig? Stories from the Modern Economy. CIPD, London.

Clark, A.E. 2005. Your money or your life: changing job quality in OECD countries. *British Journal of Industrial Relations* 43, 377–400. https://doi.org/10.1111/j.1467-8543.2005.00361.x

Clark, G.L., Feldman, M.P., Gertler, M.S., et al. 2018. The New Oxford Handbook of Economic Geography. Oxford University Press, Oxford.

CNBC (Consumer News and Business Channel) 2020. Coronavirus pandemic highlights productivity, environmental benefits of remote work. Available at https://www.youtube.com/watch?v=DCaxXiHKOhY, accessed 9.8.21.

CNN, 2011. Mobile phone: Weapon against global poverty. CNN. Available at http://www.cnn.com/2011/10/09/tech/mobile/mobile-phone-poverty/index.html, accessed 9.8.21.

Coates, T.N. 2013. What we mean when we say 'race is a social construct'. *The Atlantic.* Available at https://www.theatlantic.com/national/archive/2013/05/what-we-mean-when-we-say-race-is-a-social-construct/275872/, accessed 9.8.21.

Coe, N., Hess, M., Yeung, H., et al. 2004. Globalizing regional development: a global production networks perspective. *Trans. Inst. Br. Geogr.* 29, 468–484.

Coe, N.M. and Jordhus-Lier, D.C. 2011. Constrained agency? Re-evaluating the geographies of labour. *Progress in Human Geography* 35, 211–233. https://doi.org/10.1177/0309132510366746

Coe, N.M. and Yeung, H.W.-C. 2015. Global Production Networks: Theorizing Economic Development in an Interconnected World. Oxford University Press, Oxford.

Coe, N.M., Johns, J., and Ward, K. 2009. Agents of casualization? The temporary staffing industry and labour market restructuring in Australia. *J Econ Geogr* 9, 55–84. https://doi.org/10.1093/jeg/lbn029

Coe, N.M., Jones, K., and Ward, K. 2010. The business of temporary staffing: a developing research agenda. Geography Compass 4(8), 1055–1068.

Coenen, M. and Kok, R.A.W. 2014. Workplace flexibility and new product development performance: the role of telework and flexible work schedules. *European Management Journal* 32, 564–576. https://doi.org/10.1016/j.emj.2013.12.003

Cooper, F. 1987. On the African Waterfront: Urban Disorder and the Transformation of Work in Colonial Mombasa. Yale University Press, New Haven, CT.

Cooper, F. 1996. Decolonization and African Society: The Labor Question in French and British Africa. Cambridge University Press, Cambridge.

Cooper, F. (2017). 'From enslavement to precarity? The labour question in African history'. In W. Adebanwi (ed.), *The Political Economy of Everyday Life in Africa: Beyond the Margins.* Woodbridge: James Currey.

Corporaal, G. and Lehdonvirta, V. 2017. Platform Sourcing How Fortune 500 Firms Are Adopting Online Freelancing Platforms. Oxford Internet Institute, University of Oxford, Oxford.

Costello, S. 2020. Where Is the iPhone Made? (Hint: Not Just China). *Lifewire.* Available at https://www.lifewire.com/where-is-the-iphone-made-1999503, accessed 21.4.20.

Cotula, L., Vermeulen, S., Leonard, R., et al. 2009. Land Grab or Development Opportunity? Agricultural Investment and International Land Deals in Africa. IIED/FAO/IFAD, London; Rome.

Couldry, N. and Mejias, U.A. 2019. The Costs of Connection: How Data Is Colonizing Human Life and Appropriating It for Capitalism. Stanford University Press, Stanford, CA.

Craig, C., Rubery, J., Tarling, R., et al. 1982. Labour market structure, industrial organisation, and low pay. University of Cambridge, Department of Applied Economics, Occasional paper, number 54. Cambridge: Cambridge University Press.

Cramer, C., Johnston, D., Mueller, B., et al. 2017. Fairtrade and labour markets in Ethiopia and Uganda. *Journal of Development Studies* 53, 841–856. https://doi.org/10.1080/00220388.2016.1208175

Crane, D., Stachura, J., Dalmat, S., et al. 2007. International sourcing of services: the 'Homeshoring' alternative. *Serv. Bus.* 1, 79–91. https://doi.org/10.1007/s11628-006-0008-5

Crowley, M., Tope, D., Chamberlain, L.J., et al. 2010. Neo-Taylorism at work: occupational change in the post-Fordist era. *Social Problems* 57, 421–447. https://doi.org/10.1525/sp.2010.57.3.421

Cruz, M.D. 2018. Offshore migrant workers: return migrants in Mexico's English-speaking call centers. *RSF: Russell Sage Foundation Journal of the Social Sciences* 4, 39–57. https://doi.org/10.7758/RSF.2018.4.1.03

Cumbers, A., Nativel, C., and Routledge, P. 2008. Labour agency and union positionalities in global production networks. *J Econ Geogr* 8, 369–387. https://doi.org/10.1093/jeg/lbn008

Cumbers A., Helms, G., and Swanson, K. (2010) Class, agency and resistance in the old industrial city. *Antipode* 42(1), 46–73.

Dahir, A.L. 2018. Uber and other ride-hailing apps are facing a major test in Kenya—from drivers themselves Quartz Africa. Available at https://qz.com/africa/1327568/uber-taxify-little-cab-kenya-drivers-end-strike/, accessed 1.8.21.

Dance, G., LaForgia, M., and Confessore, N. 2018. As Facebook Raised a Privacy Wall, It Carved an Opening for Tech Giants. *New York Times*. Available at https://www.nytimes.com/2018/12/18/technology/facebook-privacy.html, accessed 10.8.21.

Dannenberg, P., Yejoo, K., and Schiller, D. 2013. Chinese special economic zones in Africa: a new species of globalisation? *Afr. East-Asian Aff.* 0. https://doi.org/10.7552/0-2-103

Daramola, J.O. 2020. Africa's health systems should use AI technology in their fight against COVID-19. *The Conversation*. Available at http://theconversation.com/africas-health-systems-should-use-ai-technology-in-their-fight-against-covid-19-135862, accessed 2.6.20.

Davies, R.B. and Vadlamannati, K.C. 2013. A race to the bottom in labor standards? An empirical investigation. *J. Dev. Econ.* 103, 1–14. https://doi.org/10.1016/j.jdeveco.2013.01.003

De Bustillo, R.M., Fernández-Macías, E., Esteve, F., et al. 2011. E pluribus unum? A critical survey of job quality indicators. *Socioecon Rev* 9, 447–475. https://doi.org/10.1093/ser/mwr005

Dehghan, A., Ortiz, E., Shu, G., Masood, S.Z. 2017. Deep Age, Gender and Emotion Recognition Using Convolutional Neural Networks. URL. https://arxiv.org/pdf/1702.04280.pdf

Desta, Z. F., Bitga, A., & Boyson, J. (2018). *USAID/Ethiopia Cross-Sectoral Youth Assessment Situational Analysis*. USAID and Youth Power. Available at : https://www.youthpower.org/resources/usaidethiopia-cross-sectoral-youth-assessment-situational-analysis-report

De Stefano, V. 2016. The Rise of the 'Just-In-Time Workforce': On-Demand Work, Crowdwork and Labour Protection in the 'Gig-Economy'. ILO, Geneva.

De´, R., Pal, A., Sethi, R., et al. 2018. ICT4D research: a call for a strong critical approach. *Inf. Technol. Dev.* 24, 63–94.

D'Cruz, P. and Noronha, E. 2012. High commitment management practices re-examined: the case of Indian call centres. *Economic and Industrial Democracy* 33(2), 185–205.

D'Cruz, P. and Noronha, E. 2013. Hope to despair: the experience of organizing Indian call centre employees. *Indian Journal of Industrial Relations* 48, 471–486.

D'Cruz, P. and Noronha, E. 2014. Workplace bullying and pluralism. Industrial Relations Journal 45, 2–21. https://doi.org/10.1111/irj.12039

D'Cruz, P. and Noronha, E. 2016. Positives outweighing negatives: the experiences of Indian crowdsourced workers. *Work Organisation, Labour & Globalisation* 10, 44–63. https://doi.org/10.13169/workorgalaboglob.10.1.0044

Dedrick, J., Linden, G., and Kraemer, K.L. 2018. We estimate China only makes $8.46 from an iPhone – and that's why Trump's trade war is futile. *The Conversation*.

Available at http://theconversation.com/we-estimate-china-only-makes-8-46-from-an-iphone-and-thats-why-trumps-trade-war-is-futile-99258, accessed 21.4.20.

Degiuli, F. and Kollmeyer, C. 2007. Bringing Gramsci back in: labor control in Italy's new temporary help industry. *Work, Employment and Society* 21, 497–515. https://doi.org/10.1177/0950017007080011

Del Bono, A., Gorjup, M.T., Henry, L., et al. 2013. Call centres' employment practices in global value networks: a view from Argentina as a receiving economy. *Economic and Industrial Democracy* 34, 693–717. https://doi.org/10.1177/0143831X12462488

Deloitte 2015. Outsourcing is Good for Job Creation in South Africa. Deloitte, Johannesburg.

Deloitte 2016. Kenya: Grounding Africa's Economic Growth. Deloitte, Johannesburg.

Deloitte 2017. Leveraging Digital to Unlock the Base of the Pyramid Market in Africa. Deloitte, Johannesburg.

Deloitte 2018a. Business Services Outlook 2018. Available at https://www2.deloitte.com/uk/en/pages/business-and-professional-services/articles/business-services-outlook.html, accessed 2.6.20.

Deloitte 2018b. Voice of the Workforce in Europe: Understanding the Expectations of the Labour Force to Keep Abreast of Demographic and Technological Change. Deloitte, Brussels.

Department for Business, Energy & Industrial Strategy 2017. Race in the Workplace: The Mcgregor-Smith Review. Department for Business, Energy & Industrial Strategy, London.

Desjardins, J. 2019a. How much data is generated each day? *World Econ. Forum.* Available at https://www.weforum.org/agenda/2019/04/how-much-data-is-generated-each-day-cf4bddf29f/, accessed 20.2.20.

Desjardins, J. 2019b. Infographic: what happens in an internet minute in 2019? Visual-Capitalist. Available at https://www.visualcapitalist.com/what-happens-in-an-internet-minute-in-2019/, accessed 19.12.19.

Desrosières, A. 2002. The Politics of Large Numbers: A History of Statistical Reasoning. Harvard University Press, Cambridge, MA.

Díaz Andrade, A. and Urquhart, C. 2012. Unveiling the modernity bias: a critical examination of the politics of ICT4D. *Inf. Technol. Dev.* 18, 281–292. https://doi.org/10.1080/02681102.2011.643204

Dicken, P. 2011. Global Shift: Mapping the Changing Contours of the World Economy, 6th Edition. SAGE, London.

Dicken, P. 2015. Global Shift: Mapping the Changing Contours of the World Economy, 7th Edition. SAGE, London.

Dickinson, D. 2017. Institutionalised conflict, subaltern worker rebellions and insurgent unionism: casual workers' organisation and power resources in the South African Post Office. *Review of African Political Economy* 44, 415–431. https://doi.org/10.1080/03056244.2017.1322947

Diga, K. and May, J. 2012. Africa: Tweeting Out of Poverty – A Comparison of Access to Information and Communication Technology (ICT) as a Pathway from Poverty in South and East Africa. Carnegie3, Cape Town.

Diprose, K. 2014. Resilience is futile. *Soundings* 58, 44–56.

Doellgast, V. Holtgrewe, U. and Deery, S. 2009. the effects of national institutions and collective bargaining arrangements on job quality in front-line service workplaces. *ILR Review.* https://doi.org/10.1177/001979390906200402

Dolan, C.S. 2004. On farm and packhouse: employment at the bottom of a global value chain. *Rural Sociology* 69, 99–126. https://doi.org/10.1526/003601104322919928

Dolan, P. Peasgood, T. and White, M. 2008. Do we really know what makes us happy? A review of the economic literature on the factors associated with subjective well-being. *Journal of Economic Psychology* 29, 94–122. https://doi.org/10.1016/j.joep.2007.09.001

Donner, J. 2006. The use of mobile phones by microentrepreneurs in Kigali, Rwanda: changes to social and business networks. *Inf. Technol. Int. Dev.* 3, 3–19.

Donner, J. 2015. After Access: Inclusion, Development, and a More Mobile Internet. MIT Press, Cambridge, MA.

Donovan, K. and Martin, A. 2014. The rise of African SIM registration: the emerging dynamics of regulatory change. *First Monday* 19(2–3). https://firstmonday.org/ojs/index.php/fm/article/view/4351/3820

Dorling, D., Simpson, S. (eds) 1998. Statistics in Society: The Arithmetic of Politics. Hodder Education, London; New York.

Dossani, R. and Kenney, M. 2007. The next wave of globalization: relocating service provision to India. *World Dev.* 35, 772–791. https://doi.org/10.1016/j.worlddev.2006.09.014

Dossani, R. and Kenney, M. 2009. Service provision for the global economy: the evolving Indian experience. *Rev. Policy Res.* 26, 77–104. https://doi.org/10.1111/j.1541-1338.2008.00370.x

DTI (Department of Trade and Industry) 2018. Minister Davies launches the global business process services (BPS) incentive to prospective investors in London, United Kingdom. Available at http://www.thedti.gov.za/editmedia.jsp?id=5728, accessed 10.7.19.

Du Preez, J. 2019. The 4th industrial revolution in Africa: the next great frontier. IOA. Available at https://www.inonafrica.com/2019/06/24/the-4th-industrial-revolution-in-africa-the-next-great-frontier/, accessed 19.2.20.

Dufour-Poirier, M. and Hennebert, M.A. 2015. The transnationalization of trade union action within multinational corporations: a comparative perspective. *Economic and Industrial Democracy* 36, 73–98. https://doi.org/10.1177/0143831X13495743

Duhigg, C. and Bradsher, K. 2012. How the U.S. lost out on iPhone work. NY Times.

Dunning, J.H. 2002. Regions, Globalization, and the Knowledge-Based Economy. Oxford University Press, Oxford.

Dutta, M. 2016. Place of life stories in labour geography: Why does it matter? *Geoforum* 77, 1–4.

Dwyer, M. and Molony, D.T. (eds) 2019. Social Media and Politics in Africa: Democracy, Censorship and Security. Zed Books, London.

The Economist 2005. The rise of nearshoring. Special Report 3rd December. Available at https://www.economist.com/special-report/2005/12/01/the-rise-of-nearshoring, accessed 21.3.19.

The Economist 2011. Africa rising. Available at https://www.economist.com/leaders/2011/12/03/africa-rising, 11.7.17.

The Economist 2015a. Digital Taylorism – Schumpeter. Available at https://www.economist.com/business/2015/09/10/digital-taylorism, accessed 26.7.19.

The Economist 2015b. Why trade unions are declining. Available at https://www.economist.com/the-economist-explains/2015/09/29/why-trade-unions-are-declining, accessed 16.01.19.

Edelman, B., Luca, M., and Svirsky, D. 2017. Racial discrimination in the sharing economy: evidence from a field experiment. *American Economic Journal: Applied Economics* 9, 1–22. https://doi.org/10.1257/app.20160213

Edwards, P.K., Scullion, H. 1982. The Social Organisation of Industrial Conflict. Blackwell, Oxford.

Edwards, R. 1979. Contested Terrain: The Transformation of the Workplace in the Twentieth Century. Heinemann, London.

Einarsen, S., Hoel, H., Zapf, D., et al. (eds) 2011. Bullying and Harassment in the Workplace. Taylor & Francis, London.

Elcioglu, E.F. 2010. Producing precarity: the temporary staffing agency in the labor market. *Qual Sociol* 33, 117–136. https://doi.org/10.1007/s11133-010-9149-x

Elding, C. and Morris, R. 2018. Digitalisation and its impact on the economy: insights from a survey of large companies (ECB Economic Bulletin). ECB, Brussels.

Eliasson, K., Lindgren, U. and Westerlund, O. 2003. Geographical labour mobility: migration or commuting? *Regional Studies* 37, 827–837. https://doi.org/10.1080/0034340032000128749

Elms, D.K. and Low, P. (eds) 2013. Global Value Chains in a Changing World. World Trade Organisation, Geneva.

Engardio, P., Bernstein, A., Kriplani, M., et al.. 2003. Is your job next? *Bus. Week* 3, 50–60.

Engels, B. 2017. Not all glitter is gold: mining conflicts in Burkina Faso, in Engels, B. and Dietz, K. (eds), Contested Extractivism, Society and the State: Struggles over Mining and Land, Development, Justice and Citizenship. Palgrave Macmillan, London, pp. 149–169.

Enright, B. 2013. (Re)considering new agents: a review of labour market intermediaries within labour geography. *Geography Compass* 7, 287–299. https://doi.org/10.1111/gec3.12035

Etzo, S. and Collender, G. 2010. The mobile phone 'revolution' in Africa: rhetoric or reality? *Afr. Aff.* 109, 659–668. https://doi.org/10.1093/afraf/adq045

European Commission 2001. Employment and social policies: a framework for investing in quality. Available at http://eur-lex.europa.eu/legal-content/EN/TXT/HTML/?uri=CELEX:52001DC0313&from=EN, accessed 16.3.16.

European Commission 2007. Towards Common Principles of Flexicurity: More and Better Jobs through Flexibility and Security. Commission of the European Communities. European Commission, Directorate-General for Employment, Social Affairs and Equal Opportunities. Unit D2, Luxembourg.

European Commission 2012. New Skills and Jobs in Europe: Pathways towards Full Employment. European Commission, Brussels.

European Commission 2017. Digital4Development: Mainstreaming Digital Technologies and Services into EU Development Policy. European Commission, Brussels.

European Commission 2019. The Changing Nature of Work and Skills in the Digital Age. European Commission, Brussels.

Eurostat 2020. Temporary employment: 14.1% of employees. Available at https://ec.europa.eu/eurostat/en/web/products-eurostat-news/-/DDN-20190524-1, accessed 10.1.20.

Everest Group 2012. South Africa's BPO proposition. Discussion document. Everest Group, London.

Fairwork 2020a. If platforms do not protect gig workers, who will? Available at https://blog.geographydirections.com/2020/05/22/if-platforms-do-not-protect-gig-workers-who-will/, accessed 1.7.21.

Fairwork 2020b. The Gig Economy and Covid-19: Fairwork Report on Platform Policies. Fairwork, Oxford.

Fallick, B., Fleischman, C.A., and Rebitzer, J.B. 2006. Job-hopping in silicon valley: some evidence concerning the microfoundations of a high-technology cluster. *Review of Economics and Statistics* 88, 472–481. https://doi.org/10.1162/rest.88.3.472

Farole, T. and Moberg, L. 2017. Special Economic Zones in Africa: Political Economy Challenges and Solutions. Oxford University Press, Oxford.

Farrell, D., Grieg, F., and Hamoudi, A. 2018. The Online Platform Economy in 2018: Drivers, Workers, Sellers and Lessors. JP Morgan Chase Institute, New York.

Featherstone, D. and Griffin, P. 2016. Spatial relations, histories from below and the makings of agency. *Progress in Human Geography* 40, 375–393. https://doi.org/10.1177/0309132515578774

Felstead A., Gallie, D., Green, F., et al. 2019. The determinants of skills use and work pressure: a longitudinal analysis. *Economic and Industrial Democracy* 40(3),730–754. https://doi.org/10.1177/0143831X16656412

Feltrin, L. 2019. Labour and democracy in the Maghreb: the Moroccan and Tunisian trade unions in the 2011 Arab Uprisings. *Economic and Industrial Democracy* 40, 42–64. https://doi.org/10.1177/0143831X18780316

Fernández-Macías, E. and Hurley, J. 2017. Routine-biased technical change and job polarization in Europe. *Socioecon Rev* 15, 563–585. https://doi.org/10.1093/ser/mww016

Fernandez-Stark, K., Bamber, P., and Gereffi, G. 2011. The Offshore Services Global Value Chain Economic Upgrading and Workforce Development. Duke Centre on Globalization, Governance and Competitiveness, Durham, NC

Fernie, S. and Metcalf, D. 1998. (Not) Hanging on the Telephone: Payment Systems in the New Sweatshops. Centre's Industrial Relations Programme, LSE, London.

Fevre, F. 1992. The Sociology of Labour Markets. Harvester Wheatsheaf, Hemel Hempstead.

Financial Times 2015. Zero-hours workers as happy in their jobs as full-time employees. Available at https://www.ft.com/content/ac067b7c-99b1-11e5-987b-d6cdef1b205c, accessed 16.6.20.

Financial Times 2016. Kenyans start to roam Silicon Savannah. Financial Times.

Findlay, P., Kalleberg, A.L., and Warhurst, C. 2013. The challenge of job quality. *Human Relations* 66(4). https://doi.org/10.1177/0018726713481070

Finnemore, I., Kim, G., and Pande, A. 2010. IT Services: The New Allure of Onshore Locales. McKinsey & Company, New York.

Fischer, G. 2013. Revisiting abandoned ground: Tanzanian trade unions' engagement with informal workers. *Labor Studies Journal* 38, 139–160. https://doi.org/10.1177/0160449X13494846

Fleming, P. and Sturdy, A. 2011. Being yourself' in the electronic sweatshop: new forms of normative control. *Human Relations* 64, 177–200.

Forbes 2019. Top 100 Digital Companies List. Available at https://www.forbes.com/top-digital-companies/list/#tab:rank, accessed 31.10.19.

Foroohar, R. 2019. Don't Be Evil. Penguin Books, New York.

Foster, C., Graham, M., Mann, L., et al. 2018. Digital control in value chains: challenges of connectivity for East African Firms. *Economic Geography* 94, 68–86. https://doi.org/10.1080/00130095.2017.1350104

Franceschi-Bicchierai, L. 2020. Amazon is hiring an intelligence analyst to track 'labour organising threats'. *Vice*. Available at https://www.vice.com/en_uk/article/qj4aqw/amazon-is-hiring-an-intelligence-analyst-to-track-labour-organising-threats, accessed 10.8.21.

Franssen, L. 2019. Capturing value in South–South and South–North value chains: evidence from East Africa. *Eur J Dev Res*. https://doi.org/10.1057/s41287-019-00248-w

Freedman, M.L. 2008. Job hopping, earnings dynamics, and industrial agglomeration in the software publishing industry. *Journal of Urban Economics* 64, 590–600. https://doi.org/10.1016/j.jue.2008.07.002

Frege, C. and Kelly, J. 2004. Varieties of Unionism: Strategies for Union Revitalization in a Globalizing Economy. Oxford University Press, Oxford.

Freund, B. 1984. Labor and labor history in Africa: a review of the literature. *African Studies Review* 27(2): 1–58.

Freund, B. 1988. The African Worker, 1st edn. Cambridge University Press, Cambridge; Cambridge, MA.

Friederici, N., Ojanperä, S., and Graham, M. 2017. The impact of connectivity in Africa: grand visions and the mirage of inclusive digital development. Electronic *Journal of Information Systems in Developing Countries* 79, 1–20. https://doi.org/10.1002/j.1681-4835. 2017.tb00578.x

Friederici, N., Wahome, M., and Graham, M. 2020. Digital Entrepreneurship in Africa. MIT Press, Boston, MA.

Friedman, G. 2014. Workers without employers: shadow corporations and the rise of the gig economy. *Review of Keynesian Economics* 2, 171–188. https://doi.org/10.4337/roke. 2014.02.03

Friedman, T. 2005 The World Is Flat: A Brief History of the Twenty-First Century. Farrar, Straus and Giroux, New York.

Frischmann, B. and Selinger, E. 2017. Robots have already taken over our work, but they're made of flesh and bone. *The Guardian.*

Fröbel, F., Heinrichs, J., and Kreye, O. 1981. The New International Division of Labour. Structural Unemployment in Industrialised Countries and Industrialization in Developing Countries. Cambridge University Press; Maison des sciences de l'homme, Cambridge; Paris.

Frost and Sullivan, 2018. Digital Market Overview: Kenya (White Paper Commissioned by the UK Government). Frost and Sullivan, London.

Fuchs, C. 2014. Digital prosumption labour on social media in the context of the capitalist regime of time. *Time Soc.* 23, 97–123. https://doi.org/10.1177/0961463X13502117

Fuchs, C. and Horak, E. 2008. Africa and the digital divide. *Telematics and Informatics* 25, 99–116. https://doi.org/10.1016/j.tele.2006.06.004

Fuchs, C. and Sevignani, S. 2013. What is digital labour? What is digital work? What's their difference? And why do these questions matter for understanding social media? TripleC Communication, Capitalism & Critique. *Open Access J. Glob. Sustain. Inf. Soc.* 11, 237–293.

Fuller, L. and Smith, V. (1991) 'Consumers' reports: management by customers in a changing economy. *Work, Employment and Society* 5(1), 1–16.

Galant, M. 2019. The Time Has Come for a Global Minimum Wage. Inequality.Org. Available at https://inequality.org/research/ilo-global-minimum-wage/

Gallie, D. 2009. Employment Regimes and the Quality of Work. Oxford University Press, Oxford.

Gandini, A. 2019. Labour process theory and the gig economy. *Hum. Relat.* 72, 1039–1056. https://doi.org/10.1177/0018726718790002

Gareis, K., Lilischkis, S., and Menturp, A. 2006. Mapping the mobile eWorkforce in Europe, in Andriessen, J.H. and Vartiainen, M. (eds), Mobile Virtual Work: A New Paradigm? Springer, Berlin, pp. 45–69.

Garson, B. 1988. The Electronic Sweatshop: How Com- puters are Transforming the Office of the Future into the Factory of the Past. Simon & Schuste, NewYork.

Gautié, J. and Schmitt, J. (eds) 2010. Low-Wage Work in the Wealthy World, Illustrated Edition. Russell Sage Foundation, New York.

Geels F.W. 2004. From sectoral systems of innovation to socio-technical systems: insights about dynamics and change from sociology and institutional theory. *Research Policy* 33(6), 897–920.

Gerber, C. and Krzywdzinski, M. 2019. Brave new digital work? New forms of performance control in crowdwork, in Vallas, S.P. and Kovalainen, A. (eds), Work and Labor in the Digital Age, Research in the Sociology of Work. Emerald, Bingley, pp. 121–144. https://doi.org/10.1108/S0277-2833201933

Gereffi, G. 1999. International trade and industrial upgrading in the apparel commodity chain. *Journal of International Relations* 48, 37–70.

Gereffi, G. 2014. Global value chains in a post-Washington Consensus world. *Rev. Int. Polit. Econ.* 21, 9–37. https://doi.org/10.1080/09692290.2012.756414

Gereffi, G. and Lee, J. 2016. Economic and social upgrading in global value chains and industrial clusters: why governance matters. *J. Bus. Ethics* 133, 25–38. https://doi.org/10.1007/s10551-014-2373-7

Gereffi, G., Humphrey, J., and Sturgeon, T. 2005. The governance of global value chains. *Rev. Int. Polit. Econ.* 12, 78–104.

Ghai, D. 2003. Decent work: concept and indicators. *International Labour Review* 142, 113–145. https://doi.org/10.1111/j.1564-913X.2003.tb00256.x

Ghani, E., Kerr, W.R., and Stanton, C. (2014) Diasporas and outsourcing: evidence from oDesk and India. Management Science 60(7), 1677–1697.

Ghemawat, P. 2009. Why the world isn't flat. *Foreign Policy*. Available at https://foreignpolicy.com/2009/10/14/why-the-world-isnt-flat/, accessed 20.12.19.

Giannecchini, P. and Taylor, I. 2018. The eastern industrial zone in Ethiopia: catalyst for development? *Geoforum* 88, 28–35. https://doi.org/10.1016/j.geoforum.2017.11.003

Gibbon, P. 1993. The World Bank and the new politics of aid. *Eur. J. Dev. Res.* 5, 35–62.

Gibbon, P. and Mkandawire, T. 1995. Towards a Political Economy of the World Bank 1970–90. CODESRIA, Dakar.

Giddy, J.K. 2019. The influence of e-hailing apps on urban mobilities in South Africa. *African Geographical Review* 38(3), 227–239.

Gillwald, A. 2019. South Africa is caught in the global hype of the fourth industrial revolution. *The Conversation*. Available at http://theconversation.com/south-africa-is-caught-in-the-global-hype-of-the-fourth-industrial-revolution-121189, accessed 19.2.20.

Ginzberg, E. 1979. Good Jobs, Bad Jobs, No Jobs. Harvard University Press, Cambridge, MA.

Giordano, L. 2016. Beyond Taylorism: Computerization and the New Industrial Relations. Springer, New York.

Glucksmann, M.A. 2004. Call configurations: varieties of call centre and divisions of labour. *Work Employ. Soc.* 18, 795–811. https://doi.org/10.1177/0950017004047965

Golash-Boza, T. 2016. 'Negative credentials,' 'foreign-earned' capital, and call centers: Guatemalan deportees' precarious reintegration. *Citizenship Studies* 20, 326–341. https://doi.org/10.1080/13621025.2016.1158357

Goodfellow, T. 2014. Rwanda's political settlement and the urban transition: expropriation, construction and taxation in Kigali. *Journal of Eastern African Studies* 8(2), 311–329 https://doi.org/10.1080/17531055.2014.891714

Gorjup, M.T., Valverde, M., and Ryan, G. 2008. Promotion in call centres: opportunities and determinants. *Journal of European Industrial Training* 32, 45–62. https://doi.org/10.1108/03090590810846566

Gorwa, R., Binns, R., and Katzenbach, C. 2020. Algorithmic content moderation: technical and political challenges in the automation of platform governance. *Big Data & Society*. https://doi.org/10.1177/2053951719897945

Government of Kenya 2018. The Regulation of Wages (General) (Amendment) Order, 2018. Department of Labour and Social Protection, Nairobi.

Gradín, C. 2019. Occupational segregation by race in South Africa after apartheid. *Review of Development Economics* 23, 553–576. https://doi.org/10.1111/rode.12551

Graham, L. and Lannoy, A. 2016. Youth unemployment: what can we do in the short run? | *Econ 3x3*. Available at http://www.econ3x3.org/sites/default/files/articles/Graham%20%26%20De%20Lannoy%202016%20Youth%20unemployment%20FINAL.pdf, accessed 13.11.18.

Graham, L., Williams, L., and Chisoro, C. 2019. Barriers to the labour market for unemployed graduates in South Africa. *Journal of Education and Work* 32, 360–376. https://doi.org/10.1080/13639080.2019.1620924

Graham, M. 2013. Thai silk dot com: authenticity, altruism, modernity and markets in the Thai silk industry. *Globalisations* 10(2), 211–230.

Graham, M. and Anwar, M.A. 2018a. Two models for a fairer sharing economy, in Davidson, N., Finck, M., and Infranca, J. (eds), Cambridge Handbook on Law and Regulation of the Sharing Economy. Cambridge University Press, Cambridge, pp. 328–340. https://doi.org/10.1017/9781108255882.025

Graham, M. and Anwar, M.A. 2018b. Labour, in Ash, J. Kitchin, R., and Leszczynski, A. (eds), Digital Geographies. SAGE Publications, London, pp. 177–187.

Graham, M. and Anwar, M.A. 2019. The global gig economy: towards a planetary labour market? *First Monday* 24. https://doi.org/10.5210/fm.v24i4.9913

Graham, M. and Mann, L. 2013. Imagining a silicon savannah? Technological and conceptual connectivity in Kenya's BPO and software development sectors. *Electron. J. Inf. Syst. Dev. Ctries* 56, 1–19.

Graham, M., Andersen, C., and Mann, L. 2015. Geographical imagination and technological connectivity in East Africa. *Trans Inst Br Geogr* 40, 334–349. https://doi.org/10.1111/tran.12076

Graham, M., Mann, L. Friederici, N., et al. 2016. Growing the Kenyan business process outsourcing sector. *The African Technopolitan* 5, 93–95.

Graham, M., Ojanperä, S., Anwar, M.A., et al. 2017a. Digital connectivity and African knowledge economies. *questions de communication* 32, 345–360.

Graham, M., Hjorth, I., and Lehdonvirta, V. 2017b. Digital labour and development: impacts of global digital labour platforms and the gig economy on worker livelihoods. *Transfer* 23, 135–162. https://doi.org/10.1177/1024258916687250

Graham, S. 1998. The end of geography or the explosion of place? Conceptualizing space, place and information technology. *Prog. Hum. Geogr.* 22, 165–185. https://doi.org/10.1191/030913298671334137

Granovetter, M. 2005. The impact of social structure on economic outcomes. *Journal of Economic Perspectives* 19(1), 33–50.

Gray, H. and Khan, M. 2010. Good governance and growth in Africa: What can we learn from Tanzania?, in Padayachee, V. (ed.), The Political Economy of Africa. Routledge, London, pp. 339–356.

Gray, M. and Suri, S. 2019. Ghost Work: How to Stop Silicon Valley from Building a New Global Underclass? Houghton Mifflin, New York.

Gray, M. and Suri, S. 2019. Ghost Work: How to Stop Silicon Valley from Building a New Global Underclass? Houghton Mifflin, New York.

Green, F. 2006. Demanding Work: The Paradox of Job Quality in the Affluent Economy. Princeton University Press, Princeton, NJ.

Green, F., Felstead, A., Mayhew, K., et al. 2002. The impact of training on labour mobility: individual and firm-level evidence from Britain. *British Journal of Industrial Relations* 38, 261–275. https://doi.org/10.1111/1467-8543.00162

Greenberg, J. 1990. Employee theft as a reaction to underpayment inequity: the hidden cost of pay cuts. *Journal of Applied Psychology* 75, 561–568. https://doi.org/10.1037/0021-9010.75.5.561

Gregory, K. 2017. Digital labor in the Blackwell Encyclopedia of Sociology. *American Cancer Society*, pp. 1–4. https://doi.org/10.1002/9781405165518.wbeos0992

Griffiths, P. 2012. Ethical objections to Fairtrade. *J Bus Ethics* 105, 357–373. https://doi.org/10.1007/s10551-011-0972-0

GSMA (Global System for Mobile Communications Association) 2018. State of the Mobile Money Industry in Sub-Saharan Africa 2018. GSMA, London.

GSMA (Global System for Mobile Communications Association) 2019a. The Mobile Economy: Sub-Saharan Africa 2019. GSMA, London.

GSMA (Global System for Mobile Communications Association) 2019b. GSMA 618 active tech hubs: The backbone of Africa's tech ecosystem | Mobile for Development. Available at https://www.gsma.com/mobilefordevelopment/blog/618-active-tech-hubs-the-backbone-of-africas-tech-ecosystem/, accessed 31.7.19.

Gurley, L.K. and Cox. J. 2020. Inside Amazon's secret program to spy on workers' Private Facebook Groups. Available at https://www.vice.com/en/article/3azegw/amazon-is-spying-on-its-workers-in-closed-facebook-groups-internal-reports-show, accessed 10.8.21.

Gustafsson, N. 2012. The subtle nature of Facebook politics: Swedish social network site users and political participation. *New Media & Society* 14, 1111–1127. https://doi.org/10.1177/1461444812439551

Hackl, A. 2018. Mobility equity in a globalized world: reducing inequalities in the sustainable development agenda. *World Development* 112, 150–162. https://doi.org/10.1016/j.worlddev.2018.08.005

Hannák, A., Wagner, C., Garcia, D., et al. 2017. Bias in Online Freelance Marketplaces: Evidence from TaskRabbit and Fiverr. CSCW '17: Proceedings of the 2017 ACM Conference on Computer Supported Cooperative Work and Social Computing. Presented at the Association for Computing Machinery, New York, pp. 1914–1933.

Hannif, Z. and Lamm, F. 2005. When non-standard work becomes precarious: insights from the New Zealand call centre industry. *Management Revue* 16, 324–350.

Hanrahan, O. 2015. We Must Protect the On-Demand Economy to Protect the Future of Work. Wired. Avialble at: https://www.wired.com/2015/11/we-must-protect-the-on-demand-economy-to-protect-the-future-of-work/, accessed 13.10.18

Hanson S. and, Pratt, G. 1992. Dynamic dependencies: a geographic investigation of local labor markets. *Economic Geography* 68, 373–405. https://doi.org/10.2307/144025, accessed 20.3.19.

Harris, K. and Scully, B. 2015. A hidden counter-movement? Precarity, politics, and social protection before and beyond the neoliberal era. *Theor Soc* 44, 415–444. https://doi.org/10.1007/s11186-015-9256-5

Hart, K. 1973. Informal income opportunities and urban employment in Ghana. *Journal of Modern African Studies* 11, 61–89.

Hart, K. 1985. The informal economy. *Cambridge Anthropology* 10, 54–58.

Hart, K. 2006. Bureaucratic form and the informal economy, in Guha-Khasnobis, B., Kanbur, R., and Olstrom, E. (eds), Linking the Formal and Informal Economy: Concepts and Policies. Oxford University Press, Oxford, pp. 21–35.

Hart, K. 2009. On the informal economy: the political history of an ethnographic concept. (No. 09–042.RS), Working Papers CEB. ULB—Université Libre de Bruxelles, Brussels.

Hartshorn, I. 2019. Labor Politics in North Africa: After the Uprisings in Egypt and Tunisia. Cambridge University Press, Cambridge.

Harvey, D. 1978. The urban process under capitalism: a framework for analysis. *Int. J. Urban Reg. Res.* 2, 101–131. https://doi.org/10.1111/j.1468-2427.1978.tb00738.x

Harvey, D. 1982. The Limits to Capital. Blackwell, Oxford.

Harvey, D. 1989a. The Condition of Postmodernity: An Enquiry into the Origins of Cultural Change. Wiley-Blackwell, Oxford; Cambridge, MA.

Harvey, D. 1989b. The Urban Experience. Johns Hopkins University Press, Baltimore, MD.

Harvey, D. 2001. Globalization and the 'spatial fix'. *Geographische Revue* 2, 23–30. http://geographische-revue.de/gr2-01.htm, accessed 20.03.19.

Harvey, D. 2003. The New Imperialism, Clarendon Lectures in Geography and Environmental Studies. Oxford University Press, Oxford; New York.

Harvey, D. 2005. A Brief History of Neoliberalism. Oxford University Press, Oxford.

Harvey, D. 2009. Reshaping Economic Geography: The World Development Report 2009. *Dev. Change* 40, 1269–1277. https://doi.org/10.1111/j.1467-7660.2009.01602.x

Harvey, D. 2011. The Enigma of Capital and the Crises of Capitalism. Profile Books, London.

Harvey, D. 2014. Seventeen Contradictions and the End of Capitalism. Profile Books, London.

Hastings, T. and MacKinnon, D. 2017. Re-embedding agency at the workplace scale: workers and labour control in Glasgow call centres. *Environment and Planning A* 49(1), 104–120.

Heeks, R. 2006. Theorizing ICT4D Research. *Inf. Technol. Int. Dev.* 3, 1–4.

Heckathorn, D. 1997. Respondent-driven sampling: a new approach to the study of hidden populations. Social Problems, 44(2), 174–199,

Heeks, R. 2009. Worldwide Expenditure on ICT4D. *ICTs Dev.* Available at https://ict4dblog.wordpress.com/2009/04/06/worldwide-expenditure-on-ict4d/, accessed 10.1.16.

Heeks, R. 2017. Digital Economy and Digital Labour Terminology: Making Sense of the 'Gig Economy', 'Online Labour', 'Crowd Work', 'Microwork', 'Platform Labour', etc. Centre for Development Informatics, University of Manchester, Manchester.

Heeks, R. and Krishna, S. 2016. ICTs and hope for development: a theoretical framework. *Electron. J. Inf. Syst. Dev. Ctries* 77, 1–19. https://doi.org/10.1002/j.1681-4835.2016.tb00563.x

Henderson, J., Dicken, P., Hess, M., et al. 2002. Global production networks and the analysis of economic development. *Rev. Int. Polit. Econ.* 9, 436–464.

Herman, A. 2019. Asymmetries and opportunities: power and inequality in Fairtrade wine global production networks. *Area* 51, 332–339. https://doi.org/10.1111/area.12467

Herod, A. 1997. From a geography of labor to a labor geography: labor's spatial fix and the geography of capitalism. *Antipode* 29, 1–31.

Herod, A. 2001. Labor Geographies: Workers and the Landscapes of Capitalism. Guilford Press, New York.

Herrington, M., Kew, J., and Kew, P. 2010. Tracking Entrepreneurship in South Africa: A GEM Perspective. Graduate School of Business, University of Cape Town, Cape Town.

Hilbert, M. 2016. Big data for development: a review of promises and challenges. *Dev. Policy Rev.* 34, 135–174. https://doi.org/10.1111/dpr.12142

Hickel, J. 2017. *The Divide: A Brief Guide to Global Inequality and its Solutions.* Windmill Books, London.

Hickel, J., Sullivan, D. & Zoomkawala, H. 2021. Plunder in the Post-Colonial Era: Quantifying Drain from the Global South Through Unequal Exchange, 1960–2018, *New Political Economy*, DOI: 10.1080/13563467.2021.1899153

Hilson, G. 2016. Farming, small-scale mining and rural livelihoods in sub-Saharan Africa: a critical overview. *Extractive Industries and Society* 3(2), 547–563.

Hirst, P. and Thompson, G. 2019. 'The future of globalisation', in Michie, J. (Ed.), The Handbook of Globalisation, 3rd edn, chap. 1, pp. 16–31, Edward Elgar Publishing, Cheltenham.

Holborow, M. 2015. Language and Neoliberalism. Routledge, London; New York.

Holland, P. and Brewster, C. 2020. Contemporary Work and the Future of Employment in Developed Countries. Routledge, London.

Holman, D. 2004. Employee well-being in call centres, in Deery, S. and Kinnie, N. (eds), Call Centres and Human Resource Management: A Cross-National Perspective. Palgrave Macmillan, London, pp. 223–244. https://doi.org/10.1057/9780230288805_10

Holman, D. 2013. An explanation of cross-national variation in call centre job quality using institutional theory. *Work, Employment and Society* 27, 21–38. https://doi.org/10.1177/0950017012460309

Holman, D., Batt, R., and Holtgrewe, U. 2007. The Global Call Center Report: International Perspectives on Management and Employment. Cornell University Press, New York.

Honest Accounts 2017. Honest Accounts 2017 – How the world profits from Africa's wealth. Available at https://www.globaljustice.org.uk/resource/honest-accounts-2017-how-world-profits-africas-wealth/, accessed 1.8.21.

Honneth, A. 1996. The Struggle for Recognition. MIT Press, Cambridge, MA.

Hoogvelt, A. 2001. Globalisation and the Postcolonial World: The New Political Economy of Development, 2nd edn. Macmillan Education, London.

Horner, R. 2014. Strategic decoupling, recoupling and global production networks: India's pharmaceutical industry. *J Econ Geogr* 14, 1117–1140. https://doi.org/10.1093/jeg/lbt022

Horton, J. 2010. Online labor markets, in Saberi, A. (ed.), Internet and Network Economics. Springer, Berlin, pp. 515–522.

Hoskyns, C. and Rai, S.M. 2007. Recasting the global political economy: counting women's unpaid work. *New Political Economy* 12, 297–317. https://doi.org/10.1080/13563460701485268

Howe, J. 2009. Crowdsourcing: Why the Power of the Crowd Is Driving the Future of Business. Crown Business, New York.

Hudson, R. 2001. Producing Places. Guilford Press, New York.

Hughes S.M. 2020. On resistance in human geography. Progress in Human Geography 44(6), 1141–1160. https://doi:10.1177/0309132519879490

Human Right Watch 2015. 'Work Faster or Get Out' – Labor Rights Abuses in Cambodia's Garment Industry. HRW, New York.

Hunt, E. 1994. The Medieval Super-Companies: A Study of the Peruzzi Company of Florence. Cambridge University Press, Cambridge.

Hunt, V. and Rasmussen, E. 2010. Patterns and motivations of successful women pursuing their careers in New Zealand call centres. *Asia-Pacific Journal of Business Administration* 2, 167–184. https://doi.org/10.1108/17574321011078201

Hunter, M. and Hachimi, A. 2012. Talking class, talking race: language, class, and race in the call center industry in South Africa. *Soc. Cult. Geogr.* 13, 551–566. https://doi.org/10.1080/14649365.2012.704642

Huws, U. 2003. The Making of a Cybertariat: Virtual Work in a Real World. Monthly Review Press, New York.

Huws, U. 2013. Working online, living offline: labour in the internet age. *Work Organisation, Labour & Globalisation* 7, 1–11. https://doi.org/10.13169/workorgalaboglob.7.1.0001

Huws, U. 2014. Labor in the Global Digital Economy: The Cybertariat Comes of Age. Monthly Review Press, New York.

Huws, U., Spencer, N.H., Syrdal, D., et al. 2017. Work in the European Gig Economy: Research Results from the UK, Sweden, Germany, Austria, the Netherlands, Switzerland and Italy. FEPS/Uni Global/University of Hertfordshire, Hatfield.

IAM (International Association of Machinists) 2018. IAM's independent drivers guild wins historic victory for New York drivers. IAMAW. Available at https://www.goiam.org/news/iams-independent-drivers-guild-wins-historic-victory-for-new-york-drivers/, accessed 1.8.21.

IBM 2017. IBM Launches 'Digital – Nation Africa': invests $70 million to bring digital skills to Africa with free, Watson-powered skills platform for 25 million people. IBM News Room. Available at https://newsroom.ibm.com/2017-02-08-IBM-Launches-Digital-Nation-Africa-Invests-70-Million-to-Bring-Digital-Skills-to-Africa-with-Free-Watson-Powered-Skills-Platform-for-25-Million-People, accessed 9.5.19.

IBM n.d. IBM brings Watson to Africa for Project Lucy. Available at http://www.research.ibm.com/labs/africa/project-lucy.shtml, accessed 6.12.20).

IDC (International Data Corporation) 2018. The Digitization of the World from Edge to Core. IDC, Needham, MA. Available at https://resources.moredirect.com/white-papers/idc-report-the-digitization-of-the-world-from-edge-to-core, accessed 3.2.20.

Idowu, A. and Elbanna, A. 2020. Digital platforms of work and the crafting of career path: the crowdworkers' perspective. *Inf Syst Front*. https://doi.org/10.1007/s10796-020-10036-1

Ihonvbere, J.O. 1997. Organized labor and the struggle for democracy in Nigeria*. *African Studies Review* 40, 77–110. https://doi.org/10.2307/524967

ILO 1972. Employment, Incomes and Equality: A Strategy for Increasing Productive Employment in Kenya. ILO, Geneva.

ILO 1993a. Resolution Concerning Statistics of Employment in the Informal Sector. Adopted by the 15th International Conference of Labour Statisticians (January 1993). ILO, Geneva.

ILO 1993b. Resolutions Concerning International Classification of Status in Employment Adopted by the 15th International Conference of Labour Statisticians, para. 10. ILO, Geneva.

ILO 1999. Decent Work. Geneva. (Report of the Director-General to the 89th Session of the International Labour Conference.) ILO, Geneva.

ILO 2005. Human Trafficking and Forced Labour Exploitation: Guidance For Legislation and Law Enforcement (Report). ILO, Geneva.

ILO 2010 A Skilled Workforce for Strong, Sustainable and Balanced Growth. ILO, Geneva.

ILO 2013. Measuring Informality: A Statistical Manual on the Informal Sector and Informal Employment. ILO, Geneva.

ILO 2014. World of Work Report 2014: Developing with Jobs. ILO, Geneva.

ILO, 2015. Recommendation Concerning the Transition from the Informal to the Formal Economy: Recommendation 204. ILO, Geneva.

ILO 2016. Non-Standard Employment around the World: Understanding Challenges, Shaping Prospects. ILO, Geneva.

ILO 2017a. ILO calls for global action to boost youth employment in North Africa. ILO. Available at http://www.ilo.org/global/about-the-ilo/newsroom/news/WCMS_577397/lang—en/index.htm, accessed 17.2.20.

ILO 2017b. World Social Protection Report 2017/19: Universal Social Protection to Achieve the Sustainable Development Goals. ILO, Geneva.

ILO 2018. Women and Men in the Informal Economy: A Statistical Picture. ILO, Geneva.

ILO 2019. Work for a Brighter Future: Global Commission on the Future of Work. ILO, Geneva.

ILO 2020a. ILO: As job losses escalate, nearly half of global workforce at risk of losing livelihoods. Available at http://www.ilo.org/global/about-the-ilo/newsroom/news/WCMS_743036/lang—en/index.htm, accessed 18.5.20.

ILO 2020b. Global Employment Trends for Youth 2020: Technology and the Future of Jobs. ILO, Geneva.

ILO 2020c. World Employment and Social Outlook: Trends 2020. ILO, Geneva.

ILOSTAT n.d. Trade union density rate (%) – annual. Available at https://www.ilo.org/shinyapps/bulkexplorer29/?lang=en&segment=indicator&id=ILR_TUMT_NOC_RT_A, accessed 10.8.21.

Insight2impact 2019. Africa's Digital Platforms and Financial Services: An Eight-Country Overview. CENFRI, Cape Town.

Internet World Stats 2020. Internet users statistics for Africa. Available at https://www.internetworldstats.com/stats1.htm, accessed 13.07.21.

ITC (International Trade Centre) 2015. NTF III: Access to finance programme devised for ITES and BPO SMEs in Uganda and Kenya to boost export. Available at http://www.intracen.org/news/NTF-III-Access-to-Finance-Programme-Devised-for-ITES-and-BPO-SMEs-in-Uganda-and-Kenya-to-Boost-Export/, accessed 28.8.19.

ITF (International Transport Worker Federation) 2020a. Australian gig workers secure important Covid-19 protections. ITF. Available at https://www.itfglobal.org/en/news/australian-gig-workers-secure-important-covid-19-protections, accessed 1.6.21.

ITF (International Transport Worker Federation) 2020b. Delivery riders forum plans on cleaning up the gig economy. Available at https://www.itfglobal.org/en/news/delivery-riders-forum-plans-cleaning-gig-economy, accessed 1.6.21.

ITIDA (Information Technology Industry Development Agency) 2018. Export-IT rebate program 2018. Available at http://beta.itida.gov.eg/En/OurPrograms/IndustrySupport/ExportIT2013/Pages/default.aspx, accessed 4.6.20.

ITIDA (Information Technology Industry Development Agency) 2020. Future work is digital. ITIDA. Available at https://itida.gov.eg/English/Programs/future-work-is-digital/Pages/default.aspx, accessed 10.8.21.

ITU (International Telecommunications Union) 2017**a**. ICT Development Index 2017. ITU, Geneva.

ITU (International Telecommunication Union) 2017b. ICT Prices, 2017. International Telecommunication Union, Geneva.

ITU (International Telecommunication Union) 2017c. Global E-waste Monitor 2017. Available at https://www.itu.int/en/ITU-D/Environment/Pages/Toolbox/Global-E-waste-Monitor-2017.aspx, accessed 28.8.18.

ITU (International Telecommunication Union) 2019. Measuring Digital Development: Facts and Figures 2019, ITU. Geneva.

IWGB (Independent Workers' Union of Great Britain) 2020. First-ever international meeting of app-based transport workers to develop global strategy to challenge platform companies. Available at https://iwgb.org.uk/post/first-ever-international-meeting-of-app-based-transport-workers-to-develop-global-strategy-to-challenge-platform-companies, accessed 26.10.20.

Jack, W. and Suri, T. 2011. Mobile money: The economics of M-PESA (Working Paper No. 16721), Working Paper Series. National Bureau of Economic Research, Cambridge, MA. https://doi.org/10.3386/w16721

Jack, W. and Suri, T. 2014. Risk sharing and transactions costs: evidence from Kenya's mobile money revolution. *Am. Econ. Rev.* 104, 183–223.

Jacques, V. 2006. International Outsourcing Strategy and Competitiveness: Study on Current Outsourcing Trends: IT, Business Processes, Contact Centers. Editions Publibook, Paris.

Jahoda, M. 1982. Employment and Unemployment: A Social-Psychological Analysis. Cambridge University Press, Cambridge.

Jalakasi, W. 2019. After years of rapid growth in Africa we're about to enter the age of Mobile Money 2.0. *Quartz*. Available at https://qz.com/africa/1721818/africa-mobile-money-industry-is-entering-its-next-stage-of-growth/, accessed 4.10.19

James, A. and Vira, B. 2012. Labour geographies of India's new service economy. *Journal of Economic Geography* 12, 841–875. https://doi.org/10.1093/jeg/lbs008

Jamil, R. 2020. Uber and the making of an Algopticon – insights from the daily life of Montreal drivers. *Capital & Class.* https://doi.org/10.1177/0309816820904031

Jesnes, K., Ilsøe, A., and Hotvedt, M. 2019. Collective Agreements for Platform Workers? Examples from the Nordic Countries (Nordic Future of Work Brief 3). Fafo, Oslo.

Jessop, B. 2001. Regulationist Perspectives on Fordism and Post-Fordism, Regulation Theory and the Crisis of Capitalism; 3. Edward Elgar, Cheltenham.

Jessop, B. 2006. Spatial fixes, temporal fixes, and spatio-temporal fixes, in David Harvey (ed.), A Critical Reader. Blackwell, Malden; Oxford, pp. 142–166.

Johnston, H. 2020. Labour geographies of the platform economy: understanding collective organizing strategies in the context of digitally mediated work. *International Labour Review* 159, 25–45. https://doi.org/10.1111/ilr.12154

Jones, A. 2008. The rise of global work. *Transactions of the Institute of British Geographers* 33, 12–26. doi: https://doi.org/10.1111/j.1475-5661.2007.00284.x

Jubilee Debt Campaign 2020. The Growing Global South Debt Crisis and Cuts in Public Spending. Jubilee Debt Campaign, London.

Juma, C. and Agwara, H. 2006. Africa in the global knowledge economy: strategic options. *International Journal of Technology and Globalisation* 2, 218–231. https://doi.org/10.1504/IJTG.2006.011911

Kadoda, G. and Hale, S. 2015. Contemporary youth movements and the role of social media in Sudan. *Canadian Journal of African Studies/Revue canadienne des études africaines* 49, 215–236. https://doi.org/10.1080/00083968.2014.953556

Kalleberg, A. 2013. Good Jobs, Bad Jobs: The Rise of Polarized and Precarious Employment Systems in the United States, 1970s to 2000s, 1st pbk. edn. Rose Series in Sociology. Russell Sage Foundation, New York.

Kalleberg A. and Sørensen, A. (1979) The sociology of labor markets. *Annual Review of Sociology* 5, 351–379. doi: https://doi.org/10.1146/annurev.so.05.080179.002031

Kalleberg, A.L. 2000. Nonstandard employment relations: part-time, temporary and contract work. *Annual Review of Sociology* 26, 341–365.

Kalleberg, A.L. 2003. Flexible firms and labor market segmentation – effects of workplace restructuring on jobs and workers. *Work and Occupations* 30, 154–175. https://doi.org/10.1177/0730888403251683

Kamau, M. 2016. Business outsourcing: Hype versus reality. *The Standard.* Available at https://www.standardmedia.co.ke/article/2000227370/n-a, accessed 25.9.19.

Kamel, L. 2018. Torpedoing Africa, and then complaining about 'migration'. Available at https://www.aljazeera.com/indepth/opinion/torpedoing-africa-complaining-migration-180817133759141.html, accessed 18.2.20.

Kane, P.S. 2017. Macron's Francafrique. Available at https://www.aljazeera.com/indepth/opinion/2017/07/macron-francafrique-170721190500965.html, accessed 18.2.20.

Kariuki, E. (2010). Progress Report Implementation of the Mckinsey Report BPO/ITES Study Recommendations. Kenya ICT Board. Available at http://www.horizoncontact centers.com/ke/userfiles/Mckinsey_Report.pdf, accessed 10.8.21.

Karreth, A.K. 2018. Schools of democracy: how trade union membership impacts political participation in Africa's emerging democracies. *Democratization* 25, 158–177. https://doi.org/10.1080/13510347.2017.1339273

Kässi, O. and Lehdonvirta, V. 2018. Online labour index: measuring the online gig economy for policy and research. *Technological Forecasting and Social Change* 137, 241–248. https://doi.org/10.1016/j.techfore.2018.07.056

Kässi, O, Lehdonvirta, V, and Stephany, F. (2021). How many online workers are there in the world? A data-driven assessment. Open Research Europe. 1:53. https://doi.org/10.12688/openreseurope.13639.3

Katz, C. 2004. Growing up Global: Economic Restructuring and Children's Everyday Lives. University of Minnesota Press, Minneapolis, MN.

Kawar, M. 2011. Skills development for job creation, economic growth and poverty reduction (Background Paper), Doha Forum on Decent Work and Poverty Reduction. International Labour Organisation, Geneva.

Kazeem, Y. 2017. Uber drivers inLagos are suing it for employee status. Quartz Africa. Available at https://qz.com/africa/1125087/uber-drivers-in-lagos-nigeria-sue-for-employee-status/, accessed 27.8.20.

Kazeem, Y. 2018. Africa's smaller economies are leading business reforms on the continent. *Quartz Africa*. Available at https://qz.com/africa/1445788/mauritus-rwanda-rank-high-on-world-bank-doing-business-report/, accessed 7.10.19.

Kearney, 2019. The 2019 Kearney Global Services Location Index. Available at https://www.kearney.com/digital/gsli/2019-full-report, accessed 10.8.21.

Kellogg, K.C., Valentine, M.A., and Christin, A. 2020. Algorithms at work: the new contested terrain of control. *Acad. Manag. Ann.* 14, 366–410. https://doi.org/10.5465/annals.2018.0174

Kelly, M. 2018. Facebook details data sharing agreements with Amazon, Qualcomm, and AT&T among others. The Verge. Available at https://www.theverge.com/2018/7/2/17526716/facebook-cambridge-analytica-apple-microsoft-data-sharing, accessed 10.8.21.

Kelly, P. 2012. Labor movement: migration, mobility and geographies of work in Barnes, T.J., Peck. J., and Sheppard, E. (eds) The Wiley-Blackwell Companion to Economic Geography. Oxford: Blackwell, 431–443.

Kennedy, R.E., Sheth, S., London, T., et al. 2013. Impact Sourcing: Assessing the Opportunity for Building a Thriving Industry. The Rockefeller Foundation & The William Davidson Institute, University of Michigan, Ann Arbor, MI.

Kenny, B. and Webster, E. 1998. Eroding the core: flexibility and the re-segmentation of the South African labour market. *Crit Sociol* 24, 216–243. https://doi.org/10.1177/089692059802400304

Kenya ICT Authority 2019. THE Draft FY 2019–2023 Strategic Plan: Promoting Digital Inclusion for Sustained Economic Growth. Ministry of ICT, Nairobi.

Kenya National Bureau of Statistics 2019. Economic Survey 2019. Nairobi.

Kessler, S. 2018. Gigged: The End of the Job and the Future of Work. Macmillan USA, New York.

Keune, M. and Serrano, A. 2014. Deconstructing Flexicurity and Developing Alternative Perspectives: Towards New Concepts and Approaches for Employment and Social Policy. Routledge Advances in Sociology. Routledge, New York.

Khan, F. and Ghadially, R. 2010. Empowerment through ICT education, access and use: a gender analysis of Muslim youth in India. *J. Int. Dev.* 22, 659–673. https://doi.org/10.1002/jid.1718

Kharroub, T. and Bas, O. 2016. Social media and protests: an examination of Twitter images of the 2011 Egyptian revolution. *New Media & Society* 18, 1973–1992. https://doi.org/10.1177/1461444815571914

Kiil, M.B. and Knutsen, H.M. 2016. Agency by exit: Swedish nurses and the 'not below 24,000' movement. *Geoforum* 70, 105–114.

Kilian, B., Jones, C., Pratt, L., et al. 2006. Is sustainable agriculture a viable strategy to improve farm income in Central America? A case study on coffee. *Journal of Business Research, Strategic Management in Latin America* 59, 322–330. https://doi.org/10.1016/j.jbusres.2005.09.015

Kincses, A. and Tóth, G. 2020. The geographical network of international migration. *Environ Plan A.* https://doi.org/10.1177/0308518X20904737

Kinyanjui, M.N. 2014. Women and the Informal Economy in Urban Africa: From the Margins to the Centre. Zed Books, London.

Kinyanjui, M.N. 2019. African Markets and the Utu-Ubuntu Business Model A Perspective on Economic Informality in Nairobi. African Minds. Cape Town.

Kirchherr, J. and Charle, K. 2018. Enhancing the sample diversity of snowball samples: recommendations from a research project on anti-dam movements in Southeast Asia. PLOS ONE 13(8). https://doi.org/10.1371/journal.pone.0201710

Kleibert, J.M. 2014. Strategic coupling in 'next wave cities': local institutional actors and the offshore service sector in the Philippines. *Singap. J. Trop. Geogr.* 35, 245–260. https://doi.org/10.1111/sjtg.12044

Kleibert, J.M. 2015. Islands of globalisation: offshore services and the changing spatial divisions of labour. *Environ. Plan. Econ. Space* 47, 884–902. https://doi.org/10.1068/a140119p

Kleibert, J.M. 2016. Global production networks, offshore services and the branch-plant syndrome. *Reg. Stud.* 50, 1995–2009. https://doi.org/10.1080/00343404.2015.1034671

Kleibert, J.M. and Mann, L. 2020. Capturing value amidst constant global restructuring? Information-technology-enabled services in India, the Philippines and Kenya. *Eur. J. Dev. Res.* https://doi.org/10.1057/s41287-020-00256-1

Kleine, D. and Unwin, T. 2009. Technological revolution, evolution and new dependencies: what's new about ict4d? *Third World Q.* 30, 1045–1067. https://doi.org/10.1080/01436590902959339

Komlosy, A. 2018. Work: The Last 1,000 Years. Verso, London; New York.

Kopf, D. 2019. Union membership in the US keeps on falling, like almost everywhere else. Quartz.

Kost, D., Fieseler, C., and Wong, S.I. 2020. Boundaryless careers in the gig economy: an oxymoron? *Human Resource Management Journal* 30, 100–113. https://doi.org/10.1111/1748-8583.12265

Krishna, V. 2019. On the job: the state of the blue-collar gig economy in India. YourStory.com. Available at https://yourstory.com/2019/03/job-blue-collar-gig-econom-w132hse8o8, accessed 3.7.19.

Kuek, S.C., Paradi-Guilford, C., Fayomi, T., et al. 2015. The Global Opportunity in Online Outsourcing. World Bank, Washington, DC

Lamb, H. 2008. Fighting the Banana Wars and Other Fairtrade Battles. Random House, New York.

Lambert, L. 2020. Over 42.6 million Americans have filed for unemployment during the coronavirus pandemic. *Fortune.* Available at https://fortune.com/2020/06/04/us-unemployment-rate-numbers-claims-this-week-total-job-losses-june-4-2020-benefits-claims/, accessed 19.6.20.

Lambert, R. and Herod, A. 2016. Neoliberal Capitalism and Precarious Work: Ethnographies of Accommodation and Resistance. Edward Elgar, Northampton, MA.

Lambert, R. and Webster, E. 2001. Southern unionism and the new labour internationalism. *Antipode* 33(3), 337–362.

Lambert, S.J. 2008. Passing the buck: Labor flexibility practices that transfer risk onto hourly workers. *Human Relations* 61, 1203–1227. https://doi.org/10.1177/0018726708094910

Lambert, S.J., Haley-Lock, A., and Henly, J.R. 2012. Schedule flexibility in hourly jobs: unanticipated consequences and promising directions. *Community, Work & Family* 15, 293–315. https://doi.org/10.1080/13668803.2012.662803

Lane, N. 1999. Advancing the digital economy into the 21st century. *Inf. Syst. Front.* 1, 317–320. https://doi.org/10.1023/A:1010010630396

Langley, P. and Leyshon, A. 2017. Platform capitalism: the intermediation and capitalisation of digital economic circulation. *Finance Soc.* 3, 11–31. https://doi.org/10.2218/finsoc.v3i1.1936

Lavers, T. and Boamah, F. 2016. The impact of agricultural investments on state capacity: a comparative analysis of Ethiopia and Ghana. *Geoforum* 72, 94–103. https://doi.org/10.1016/j.geoforum.2016.02.004

Lawlor, C. 2013. Review: the precariat. *Global Discourse* 3, 536–538. https://doi.org/10.1080/23269995.2014.880253

Lawrence, P.R. and Lorsch, J.W. 1967. Organization and Environment. Harvard Business School, Division of Research, Boston, MA.

Lawrence, T.B. and Robinson, S.L. 2007. Ain't misbehavin: workplace deviance as organizational resistance. *Journal of Management* 33, 378–394. https://doi.org/10.1177/0149206307300816

Lecher, C. 2019. Google employee says she was fired for sending internal pop-ups about labor rights. *The Verge.* Available at https://www.theverge.com/2019/12/17/21024472/google-employee-fired-labor-rights-notification-tool, accessed 10.8.21.

Lefebvre, H. 1991. The Production of Space, trans. Donald Nicholson Smith. Blackwell, Oxford.

Lehdonvirta, V. 2016. Algorithms that divide and unite: delocalization, identity, and collective action in 'microwork', in Flecker, J. (ed.), Spatial Dynamics of Digital Work: Dynamics of Virtual Work. Palgrave Macmillan, London, pp. 53–80.

Lehdonvirta, V. 2018. Flexibility in the gig economy: managing time on three online piecework platforms. *New Technology, Work & Employment* 33(1), 13–29.

Lehdonvirta, V., Barnard, H., Graham, M., et al. 2014. Online Labour Markets – Levelling the Playing Field for International Service Markets? University of Oxford, Oxford.

Lehdonvirta, V., Kässi, O., Hjorth, I., et al. 2019. The global platform economy: a new offshoring institution enabling emerging-economy microproviders. *J. Manag.* 45, 567–599. https://doi.org/10.1177/0149206318786781

Leonardi, P. 2013. When does technology use enable network change in organizations? A comparative study of feature use and shared affordances. *MIS Q.* 37, 749–775.

Leonardi, P.M. and Barley, S.R. 2010. What's under construction here? Social action, materiality, and power in constructivist studies of technology and organizing. *Acad. Manag. Ann.* 4, 1–51. https://doi.org/10.5465/19416521003654160

Levien, M. 2018. Dispossession without Development: Land Grabs in Neoliberal India. Oxford University Press, Oxford.

Lewis, C. 2005. Unions and cyber-activism in South Africa. *Critical Perspectives on International Business* 1, 194–208. https://doi.org/10.1108/17422040510595672

Lewis, H., Dwyer, P., Hodkinson, S., et al. 2015. Hyper-precarious lives: migrants, work and forced labour in the Global North. *Prog Hum Geogr* 39, 580–600. https://doi.org/10.1177/0309132514548303

Lier, D.C. and Stokke, K. 2006. Maximum working class unity? Challenges to local social movement unionism in Cape Town. *Antipode* 38(4), 802–824.

Lin, B.Y.-J., Lin, Y.-K., Lin, C.-C., et al. 2013. Job autonomy, its predispositions and its relation to work outcomes in community health centers in Taiwan. *Health Promot Int* 28, 166–177. https://doi.org/10.1093/heapro/dar091

Lindell, I. 2013. Africa's Informal Workers: Collective Agency, Alliances and Transnational Organizing in Urban Africa. Zed Books, London.

Linsi, L. and Mügge, D.K. 2019. Globalization and the growing defects of international economic statistics. *Review of International Political Economy* 26, 361–383. https://doi.org/10.1080/09692290.2018.1560353

Lipietz, A. 1982. Towards global Fordism? *New Left Rev.* 132. Available at https://newleftreview.org/issues/i132/articles/alain-lipietz-towards-global-fordism, accessed 21.04.16.

Lipietz, A. 1987. Mirages and Miracles: The Crises of Global Fordism. Verso, London.

Lipietz, A. 1997. The post-Fordist world: labour relations, international hierarchy and global ecology. *Rev. Int. Polit. Econ.* 4, 1–41. https://doi.org/10.1080/096922997347841

Liu, A. 2019. Africa's future is innovation rather than industrialization. *World Econ. Forum.* Available at https://www.weforum.org/agenda/2019/09/africa-innovation-rather-than-industrialization/, accessed 20.2.20).

Long, J. and Ferrie, J. 2003. Labour mobility, in Wokyr, J. (ed.), Oxford Encyclopedia of Economic History. Oxford University Press, Oxford, Available at https://www.oxfordreference.com/view/10.1093/acref/9780195105070.001.0001/acref-9780195105070-e-0415?rskey=K6M0QO&result=415, accessed 6.9.17.

Lopes, C. and Kararach, G. 2020. Structural Change in Africa: Misperceptions, New Narratives and Development in the 21st Century, Routledge, London.

Low, P. 2013. The role of services in global value chains. in Elms, D. and Low, P. (eds), Global Value Chains in a Changing World. WTO, Geneva, pp. 61–81.

McDowell, L. 2001. Father and Ford revisited: gender, class and employment change in the new millennium. *Transactions-IBG* 26(4), 448–464.

McDuie-Ra, D. 2012. Cosmopolitan tribals: frontier migrants in Delhi. *South Asia Research* 32, 39–55. https://doi.org/10.1177/026272801203200103

McGrath, S. 2013. Fuelling global production networks with slave labour? Migrant sugar cane workers in the Brazilian ethanol GPN. *Geoforum, Global Production Networks, Labour and Development* 44, 32–43. https://doi.org/10.1016/j.geoforum.2012.06.011

McGregor-Smith, R. (2017). *Race in the Workplace*. Department of Business, Energy and Industrial Strategy. London.

MacKenzie, D.A. and Wajcman, J. 1999. The Social Shaping of Technology. Open University Press, Maidenhead.

MacKinnon, D. 2012. Beyond strategic coupling: reassessing the firm-region nexus in global production networks. *J Econ Geogr* 12, 227–245. https://doi.org/10.1093/jeg/lbr009

MacKinnon, D. 2013. Strategic coupling and regional development in resource economies: the case of the Pilbara. *Australian Geographer* 44, 305–321. https://doi.org/10.1080/00049182.2013.817039

McKinsey & Company, 2016. How technology is creating a new world of work?. Available at https://www.mckinsey.com/business-functions/mckinsey-digital/our-insights/how-technology-is-creating-a-new-world-of-work, accessed 15.4.20.

MacLachlan, I. and Aguilar, A.G. 1998. Maquiladora myths: locational and structural change in Mexico's export manufacturing industry. *Prof. Geogr.* 50, 315–331. https://doi.org/10.1111/0033-0124.00123

McMenamin, T.M. 2007. A time to work: recent trends in shift work and flexible schedules. *Monthly Lab. Rev.* 130, 3.

Mail and Guardian 2017. Ramaphosa signs minimum wage agreement of R20/h. Available at http://mg.co.za/article/2017-02-08-ramaphosa-signs-national-minimum-wage-agreement-of-r20h/, accesssed 23.02.17.

Mains, D. 2007. Neoliberal times: progress, boredom, and shame among young men in urban Ethiopia. *American Ethnologist* 34, 659–673.

Malecki, E.J. and Moriset, B. 2007. The Digital Economy: Business Organization, Production Processes and Regional Developments. Routledge, Abingdon.

Mallonee, L. 2018. The techies turning Kenya into a Silicon Savannah. Wired. Available at https://www.wired.com/story/kenya-silicon-savannah-photo-gallery/, accessed 10.8.21.

Mamba, M.S.N. and Isabirye, N. 2015. A framework to guide development through icts in rural areas in South Africa. *Inf. Technol. Dev.* 21, 135–150. https://doi.org/10.1080/02681102.2013.874321

Manek, S. 2018. Egypt's IT/ITeS exports on track to achieve ambitious growth targets as offshoring industry embraces 3rd platform technologies. *IDC*. Available at https://www.idc.com/getdoc.jsp?containerId=prCEMA43545618, accessed 8.8.19.

Mann, L. 2018. Left to other peoples' devices? A political economy perspective on the big data revolution in development. *Dev. Change* 49, 3–36. https://doi.org/10.1111/dech.12347

Mann, L. and Berry, M. 2016. Understanding the political motivations that shape Rwanda's emergent developmental state. *New Political Economy* 21(1), 119–144. https://doi.org/10.1080/13563467.2015.1041484

Mann, L. and Graham, M. 2016. The domestic turn: business process outsourcing and the growing automation of Kenyan organisations. *Journal of Development Studies* 52(4), 530–548. https://doi.org/10.1080/00220388.2015.1126251.

Mann M. 2007. Our Daily Bread: Wages, Workers, and the Political Economy of the American West. University of North Carolina Press, Chapel Hill, NC.

Manning, S., Larsen, M.M., and Kannothra, C. 2017. Global sourcing of business processes: history, effects, and future trends, in Clark, G., Feldman, M., Gertler, M., et al. (eds), The New Oxford Handbook of Economic Geography. Oxford University Press, Oxford, pp. 407–426.

Mantz, J. 2008. Blood diamonds of the digital age: Coltan and eastern Congo. *Glob. Stud. Rev.* 4, 12–14.

Manwaring, T. 1984. The extended internal labour market. *Camb. J. Econ.* 8, 161–187. https://doi.org/10.1093/oxfordjournals.cje.a035543

Manyika, J. 2015. How technology is transforming the world of work. World Econ. Forum. Available at https://www.weforum.org/agenda/2015/10/how-technology-is-transforming-the-world-of-work/, accessed 15.4.20.

Margaryan, A. 2019a. Comparing crowdworkers' and conventional knowledge workers' self-regulated learning strategies in the workplace. *Human Computation* 6, 83–97. https://doi.org/10.15346/hc.v6i1.5

Margaryan, A. 2019b. Workplace learning in crowdwork: comparing microworkers' and online freelancers' practices. *Journal of Workplace Learning* 31, 250–273. https://doi.org/10.1108/jwl-10-2018-0126

Margetts, H., John, P., Hale, S., et al. 2015. Political Turbulence: How Social Media Shape Collective Action. Princeton University Press, Princeton, NJ; Oxford.

Maru, M.T. 2019. Barriers to free movement in Africa: How to remove them? Migration Policy Centre Blog.

Marx, K. 1954. Capital: A Critique of Political Economy. Progress Publishers, Moscow.

Mashayamombe, J. 2019. Evaluation of labor agency strategy: the case of a strike at a South African opencast mine in 2012. *Labor Studies Journal* 45(4), 351–369

Massey, D. 1993. Power geometry and a progressive sense of place, in Bird, John, Curtis, Barry, Putnam, T., et al. (Eds). Mapping the Futures: Local Cultures, Global Change. London: Routledge, pp. 59–69.

Massey, D. 1995. Spatial Divisions of Labor: Social Structures and the Geography of Production, 2nd Edition. Routledge, New York.

Massey, D. 2005. For Space. SAGE Publications, London.

Massey, D. 2013. Neoliberalism has hijacked our vocabulary. Available at https://www.theguardian.com/commentisfree/2013/jun/11/neoliberalism-hijacked-vocabulary, accessed 9.12.17.

Mastercard Foundation, 2019. Mastercard Foundation to enable three million young people to access employment opportunities in Ghana. Mastercard Foundation. Available at https://mastercardfdn.org/mastercard-foundation-to-enable-three-million-young-people-to-access-employment-opportunities-in-ghana/, accessed 17.6.20.

Matassi, M., Boczkowski, P.J., and Mitchelstein, E. 2019. Domesticating WhatsApp: family, friends, work, and study in everyday communication. *New Media & Society* 21, 2183–2200. https://doi.org/10.1177/1461444819841890

Matfess, H. 2015. Rwanda and Ethiopia: developmental authoritarianism and the new politics of African strong men. *African Studies Review* 58(2), 181–204. https://doi.org/10.1017/asr.2015.43

Matondi, P.B., Havnevik, K., and Beyene, A. (eds.) 2011. Biofuels, Land Grabbing and Food Security in Africa. Zed Books, London.

Mattingly, D.J., Leitch, V., Duckworth, C.N., et al. (eds) 2017. Trade in the Ancient Sahara and beyond. Cambridge University Press, Cambridge.

Maume, D. 1999. Glass ceilings and glass escalators: occupational segregation and race and sex differences in managerial promotions. *Work and Occupations* 26(4), 483–509.

Mboya, T. 1956. Kenyan trade unions fight for freedom. *Africa Today* 3, 2–5.

Meagher, K. 2016. The scramble for Africans: demography, globalisation and Africa's informal labour markets. *Journal of Development Studies* 52(4), 483–497.

Meer, N. 2014. Key Concepts in Race and Ethnicity, 3rd edn. Sage, London. https://doi.org/10.4135/9781473906051

Mehmet, O. 2006. Race to the bottom: the impact of globalization on labor markets – a review of empirical and theoretical evidence, in Ghosh, B.N. and Guven, H.M. (eds), Globalization and the Third World: A Study of Negative Consequences. Palgrave Macmillan, London, pp. 148–161. https://doi.org/10.1057/9780230502567_9

Melachrinoudis, E. and Olafsson, M. 1995. A microcomputer cashier scheduling system for supermarket stores. *Int Jnl Phys Dist & Log Manage* 25, 34–50. https://doi.org/10.1108/09600039510080180

Melia, E., Kässi, O., Karanja, P., et al. 2019. The Constraints of Online Work in Kenya, Conference on Digital Economy Africa. University of Johannesburg, Johannesburg; University of Oxford, Oxford.

Mendes, L. (2020) How can we quarantine without a home? Responses of activism and urban social movements in times of COVID-19 pandemic crisis in Lisbon. *Tijdschrift voor economische en sociale geografie* 111, 318–332.

Meyers, J.S.M. and Vallas, S.P. 2016. Diversity regimes in worker cooperatives: workplace inequality under conditions of worker control. *Sociological Quarterly* 57, 98–128. https://doi.org/10.1111/tsq.12114

Milan, S. and Barbosa, S. 2020. Enter the WhatsApper: reinventing digital activism at the time of chat apps. *First Monday*. https://doi.org/10.5210/fm.v25i12.10414

Milland, K. 2017. Slave to the keyboard: the broken promises of the gig economy. *Transfer: European Review of Labour and Research* 23, 229–231. https://doi.org/10.1177/1024258917696233

Miller, D. and Venkatraman, S. 2018. Facebook interactions: an ethnographic perspective. *Social Media + Society* 4. https://doi.org/10.1177/2056305118784776

Minter, K. 2017. Negotiating labour standards in the gig economy: Airtasker and unions New South Wales. *Economic and Labour Relations Review* 28, 438–454. https://doi.org/10.1177/1035304617724305

Mkandawire, T. 2014. Can Africa turn from recovery to development? *Curr. Hist.* 113, 171–177.

Möhlmann, M. and Zalmanson, L. 2017. Hands on the Wheel: Navigating Algorithmic Management and Uber Drivers' Autonomy, in ICIS. Presented at the International Conference on Information Systems, Seoul.

Molla, A. and Heeks, R. 2007. Exploring e-commerce benefits for businesses in a developing country. *Information Society* 23, 95–108. https://doi.org/10.1080/01972240701224028

Moloi, S. 2018. South Africa's labour court overturns Uber drivers ruling. *iAfrikan.com*. Available at https://www.iafrikan.com/2018/01/23/uber-south-africa-labour-court/, accessed 27.8.20.

Molony, T. 2006. 'I don't trust the phone; it always lies': trust and information and communication technologies in Tanzanian micro- and small enterprises. *Inf. Technol. Int. Dev.* 3, 67–83.

Monteith, W. and Giesbert, L. 2017. 'When the stomach is full we look for respect': perceptions of 'good work' in the urban informal sectors of three developing countries. *Work, Employment and Society* 31, 816–833. https://doi.org/10.1177/0950017016650606

Moore, P.V. 2018. The Quantified Self in Precarity: Work, Technology and What Counts. Routledge, Abingdon.

Moore, P.V., Upchurch, M., and Whittaker, X. 2017. Humans and Machines at Work: Monitoring, Surveillance and Automation in Contemporary Capitalism. Springer, New York.

Moorhead, P. 2019. Who Are Apple's iPhone Contract Manufacturers?. Forbes. Available at https://www.forbes.com/sites/patrickmoorhead/2019/04/13/who-are-apples-iphone-contract-manufacturers/, accessed 21.4.20.

Morgan, G. and Nelligan, P. 2018. The Creativity Hoax: Precarious Work in the Gig Economy. Anthem Press, London; New York.

Morris, M., Plank, L., and Staritz, C. 2016. Regionalism, end markets and ownership matter: shifting dynamics in the apparel export industry in sub-Saharan Africa. *Environ Plan A* 48, 1244–1265. https://doi.org/10.1177/0308518X15614745

Morsy, H. 2020. How can Africa succeed in the Fourth Industrial Revolution? Project Syndicate. Available at https://www.project-syndicate.org/commentary/how-africa-can-close-education-skills-gap-by-hanan-morsy-2020-08, accessed 15.03.21.

Mosese, M. and Mearns, M. 2016. Leveraging management information in improving call centre productivity: original research. *South African Journal of Information Management* 18, 1–9. https://doi.org/10.4102/sajim.v18i1.690

Moyo, D. 2009. Dead Aid: Why Aid Is Not Working and How There Is a Better Way for Africa. Penguin Books, London.

Mulholland, K. 2004. Workplace resistance in an Irish call centre: slammin', scammin' smokin' an' leavin'. *Work, Employment and Society* 18, 709–724. https://doi.org/10.1177/0950017004048691

Munck, R. 2013. The precariat: a view from the South. *Third World Quarterly* 34, 747–762. https://doi.org/10.1080/01436597.2013.800751

Munck, R. 2019. Workers of the world unite (at last). *Great Transition Initiative.* Available at https://greattransition.org/publication/workers-of-the-world-unite, accessed 8.1.21.

Murphy, J.T. 2019. Global production network dis/articulations in Zanzibar: practices and conjunctures of exclusionary development in the tourism industry. *J. Econ. Geogr.* 19, 943–971. https://doi.org/10.1093/jeg/lbz009

Murphy, J.T. and Carmody, P. 2015. Africa's Information Revolution: Technical Regimes and Production Networks in South Africa and Tanzania. John Wiley & Sons, Hoboken, NJ.

Murphy, J.T., Carmody, P., and Surborg, B. 2014. Industrial transformation or business as usual? Information and communication technologies and Africa's place in the global information economy. *Rev. Afr. Polit. Econ.* 41, 264–283. https://doi.org/10.1080/03056244.2013.873024

Muto, M. and Yamano, T. 2009. The impact of mobile phone coverage expansion on market participation: panel data evidence from Uganda. *World Dev.* 37, 1887–1896. https://doi.org/10.1016/j.worlddev.2009.05.004

Nadler, D.A. and Lawler, E.E. 1983. Quality of work life: perspectives and directions. *Organizational Dynamics* 11, 20–30. https://doi.org/10.1016/0090-2616(83)90003-7

Nair, R. das, Chisoro, S., and Ziba, F. 2018. The implications for suppliers of the spread of supermarkets in southern Africa. *Development Southern Africa* 35, 334–350. https://doi.org/10.1080/0376835X.2018.1452715

NASSCOM (National Association of Software and Services Companies) 2018. Annual Report 2018-19: Catalysing IT-BPM Industry in India. NASSCOM, Noida.

NCEUS (National Commission for Enterprises in the Unorganised Sector) 2008. Report on Definitional and Statistical Issues Relating to Informal Economy. NASSCOM, New Delhi.

Ncube, M. and Ondiege, P. 2013. Silicon Kenya: Harnessing ICT Innovations for Economic Development. African Development Bank, Addis Ababa.

Ndemo, P.B. n.d. Using policy to develop a BPO industry in Africa. APR. Available at http://africapolicyreview.com/using-policy-to-develop-a-bpo-industry-in-africa/, accessed 7.10.19.

Neff, G. 2012. Venture Labor: Work and the Burden of Risk in Innovative Industries, Acting with Technology. MIT Press, Cambridge, MA.

Nest, M. 2013. Coltan. John Wiley & Sons, Hoboken, NJ.

Ngai, P. 2007. Gendering the dormitory labor system: production, reproduction, and migrant labor in south China. *Feminist Economics* 13, 239–258. https://doi.org/10.1080/13545700701439465

NITDA (National Information Technology Development Agency) 2007. National Outsourcing Policy and Institutional Framework for Nigeria 2007. NITDA, Abuja.

NITDA (National Information Technology Development Agency) 2020. National Outsourcing Strategy 2020. NITDA, Abuja.

Nkrumah, K. 1965. Neo-colonialism, the last stage of imperialism. Available at https://www.marxists.org/subject/africa/nkrumah/neo-colonialism/introduction.htm, accessed 10.8.21.

Noble, S.U. 2018. Algorithms of Oppression: How Search Engines Reinforce Racism. New York University Press, New York.

Noman, A., Botchwey, K., Stein, H., et al. (eds) 2012. Good Growth and Governance in Africa: Rethinking Development Strategies. Oxford University Press, Oxford.

Noronha, E. and D'Cruz, P. 2009. Engaging the professional: organising call centre agents in India. *Ind. Relat. J.* 40, 215–234. https://doi.org/10.1111/j.1468-2338.2009.00522.x

Norris, P. 2001. Digital Divide: Civic Engagement, Information Poverty, and the Internet Worldwide. Cambridge University Press, Cambridge. https://doi.org/10.1017/CBO9781139164887

Nothias, T. 2020. Access granted: Facebook's free basics in Africa. *Media Cult. Soc.* https://doi.org/10.1177/0163443719890530

Nsengimana, J.P. 2018. How Africa Wins The 4th Industrial Revolution. *Forbes*. Available at https://www.forbes.com/sites/startupnationcentral/2018/10/10/how-africa-wins-the-4th-industrial-revolution/, accessed 9.5.19.

Nyang'oro, J.E. and Shaw, T.M. (eds) 1992. Beyond Structural Adjustment in Africa: The Political Economy of Sustainable and Democratic Development. Praeger, New York.

OECD 2017. Key Issues for Digital Transformation in the G20. OECD, Paris.

OECD 2020. Going Digital – Organisation for Economic Co-operation and Development. OECD, Paris.

OECD Stats n.d. Overseas development assistance. Available at https://stats.oecd.org/Index.aspx?DataSetCode=Table2A, accessed 10.8.21.

OECD/ILO, 2019. Definitions of Informal Economy, Informal Sector and Informal Employment, in Tackling Vulnerability in the Informal Economy. OECD Publishing, Paris.

Ohmae, K. 1990. The Borderless World: Power and Strategy in the Interlinked Economy. Harper Collins, New York.

Okpaku, J.O. 2006. Leapfrogging into information economy: harnessing information and communications technologies in Botswana, Mauritania and Tanzania, in Fox, L. and Leibenthal, R. (eds), Attacking Africa's Poverty: Experiencing from the Ground. World Bank, Washington DC, pp. 149–175.

Olowosejeje, S.A. 2019. Nigeria's unreliable electricity costs its economy $29 bln a year—solar power would save billions. *Quartz Africa*. Available at https://qz.com/africa/1632978/nigeria-solar-power-could-fix-costly-electricity-problems/, accessed 27.7.20.

Olssen, M. 2016. Neoliberal competition in higher education today: research, accountability and impact. *British Journal of Sociology of Education* 37, 129–148. https://doi.org/10.1080/01425692.2015.1100530

Omanga, D. 2019. WhatsApp as 'digital publics': the Nakuru analysts and the evolution of participation in county governance in Kenya. *Journal of Eastern African Studies* 13, 175–191. https://doi.org/10.1080/17531055.2018.1548211

Omi, M. 2001. The changing meaning of race, in Smelser, N., Wilson, W., and Mitchell, F. (eds), America Becoming: Racial Trends and Their Consequences: Volume I. National Academy Press, Washington DC, pp. 243–263. https://doi.org/10.17226/9599

O'Neill, J. 2011. Varieties of Unfreedom. University of Manchester Press, Manchester.

Oonk, G. 2013. Settled Strangers: Asian Business Elites in East Africa, 1st Edition. SAGE, Los Angeles, CA.

Orlikowski, W.J. and Scott, S.V. 2008. 10 Sociomateriality: challenging the separation of technology, work and organization. *Acad. Manag. Ann.* 2, 433–474. https://doi.org/10.1080/19416520802211644

Orr, C.A. 1966. Trade unionism in colonial Africa. *Journal of Modern African Studies* 4, 65–81. https://doi.org/10.1017/S0022278X00012970

Oseland, S.E., Haarstad, H., and Floysand, A. 2012. Labour agency and the importance of national scale: emergent acquaculture unonis in Chile. *Political Geography* 31, 94–103.

Oshri, I., Kotlarsky, J., and Willcocks, L.P. 2015. The Handbook of Global Outsourcing and Offshoring, 3rd edn. Springer, New York.

Osterman, P. 2013. Introduction to the Special Issue on job quality: what does it mean and how might we think about it? *ILR Review* 66, 739–752. https://doi.org/10.1177/001979391306600401

Otieno, E. Stein, M. and Anwar, M.A. (2020) Ride hailing drivers left alone at the wheel: experiences from South Africa and Kenya. In Carmody, P. McCann, G., Colleran, C., et al. COVID-19 in the Global South: Impacts and Responses, Bristol, Bristol University Press, pp. 95–104. Available at https://library.oapen.org/bitstream/handle/20.500.12657/42662/9781529217278_web_revised.pdf?sequence=7#page=118, accessed 9.8.21.

Ovadia, J. 2016. The Petro-Developmental State in Africa: Making Oil Work in Angola, Nigeria and the Gulf of Guinea, 1st edn. Hurst, London.

Oxfam, 2020. Time to Care: Unpaid and Underpaid Care Work and the Global Inequality Crisis. Oxfam, Oxford.

Oya, C. 2013. The Land rush and classic agrarian questions of capital and labour: a systematic scoping review of the socioeconomic impact of land grabs in Africa. *Third World Quarterly* 34(9), 1532–1557.

Oyelaran-Oyeyinka, B. and Lal, K. 2006. Learning new technologies by small and medium enterprises in developing countries. *Technovation* 26, 220–231. https://doi.org/10.1016/j.technovation.2004.07.015

Pahle, S. 2014. What difference does the International Labour Organisation make? Freedom of association norms, supervision and promotion vis-à-vis Brazil. *Labor History* 55, 465–485. https://doi.org/10.1080/0023656X.2014.932525

Pai, H-H. 2013. Scattered Sand: The Story of China's Rural Migrants, Verso, London.

Palley, T. 2012. *From Financial Crisis to Stagnation: The Destruction of Shared Prosperity and the Role of Economics*. Cambridge University Press, New York.

Panteli, N., Rapti, A., and Scholarios, D. 2020. 'If He Just Knew Who We Were': microworkers' emerging bonds of attachment in a fragmented employment relationship. *Work, Employment and Society*. https://doi.org/10.1177/0950017019897872

Paret M. 2016. Towards a precarity agenda. *Global Labour Journal* 7(2), 111.

Parker, G.G., Alstyne, M.W.V., and Choudary, S.P. 2016. Platform Revolution: How Networked Markets Are Transforming the Economy and How to Make Them Work for You. W. W. Norton, New York.

Parthasarathy, B. 2004. India's silicon valley or silicon valley's India? Socially embedding the computer software industry in Bangalore. *Int. J. Urban Reg. Res.* 28, 664–685. https://doi.org/10.1111/j.0309-1317.2004.00542.x

Parthasarathy, B. and Aoyama, Y. 2006. From software services to R&D services: local entrepreneurship in the software industry in Bangalore, India. *Environ Plan A* 38, 1269–1285. https://doi.org/10.1068/a38102

Paul, K. 2020. Twitter announces employees will be allowed to work from home 'forever'. Available at https://www.theguardian.com/technology/2020/may/12/twitter-coronavirus-covid19-work-from-home, accessed 6.7.20.

Peck J. 1989. Reconceptualizing the local labour market: space, segmentation and the state, *Progress in Human Geography* 13, 42–61. https://doi.org/10.1177/030913258901300102

Peck, J. 1996. Work-Place: The Social Regulation of Labor Markets. Guilford Press, New York.

Peck, J. 2017. Offshore: Exploring the Worlds of Global Outsourcing. Oxford University Press, Oxford; New York.

Peck, J. and Theodore, N. 2016. The business of contingent work: growth and restructuring in Chicago's temporary employment industry. *Work, Employment and Society*. https://doi.org/10.1177/0950017098124004

Peck, J. and Tickell, A. 2002. Neoliberalizing space. *Antipode* 34, 380–404. https://doi.org/10.1111/1467-8330.00247

Peet, R. 1983. Introduction: the global geography of contemporary capitalism. *Econ. Geogr.* 59, 105–111. https://doi.org/10.2307/143608

Perrow, C. 1967. A framework for the comparative analysis of organizations. *Am. Sociol. Rev.* 32, 194–208. https://doi.org/10.2307/2091811

Perry, A. 2012. Africa Rising. *Time.* Available at http://content.time.com/time/subscriber/article/0,33009,2129831,00.html, accessed 23.12.16

Pfeffermann, G. 1967. Trade unions and politics in French West Africa during the Fourth Republic. *African Affairs* 66, 213–230. https://doi.org/10.1080/0034340022000033385

Phillips, J., Hailwood, E., and Brooks, A. 2016. Sovereignty, the 'resource curse' and the limits of good governance: a political economy of oil in Ghana. *Rev. Afr. Polit. Econ.* 43, 26–42. https://doi.org/10.1080/03056244.2015.1049520

Pillay, D. 2013. Between social movement and political unionism: COSATU and democratic politics in South Africa. *Rethinking Development and Inequality* 2, 10–27.

Pitcher, M.A. 2007. What has happened to organized labor in Southern Africa? *International Labor and Working-Class History* 72, 134–160.

Polanyi, K. 2001. The Great Transformation: The Political and Economic Origins of Our Time, 2nd Beacon pbk. edn. Beacon Press, Boston, MA.

Portes, A. and Hoffman, K. 2003. Latin American class structures: their composition and change during the neoliberal era. *Latin American Research Review* 38, 41–82.

Posada, J. 2019. From the computer to the streets. Notes from Below. Available at https://notesfrombelow.org/article/computer-streets, accessed 19.6.19.

Posel, D., Casale, D., andVermaak, C. 2014. Job search and the measurement of unemployment in South Africa. *South African Journal of Economics* 82, 66–80. https://doi.org/10.1111/saje.12035

Poster, W.R. and Yolmo, N.L. 2016. Globalisation and outsourcing, in Edgell, S., Granter, E., and Gottfried, H. (eds), Sage Handbook of the Sociology of Work and Employment. Ond: Sage, London, pp. 576–596.

Poveda, S. and Roberts, T. 2018. Critical agency and development: applying Freire and Sen to ICT4D in Zambia and Brazil. *Inf. Technol. Dev.* 24, 119–137. https://doi.org/10.1080/02681102.2017.1328656

Prassl, J. 2018. Humans as a Service: The Promise and Perils of Work in the Gig Economy. Oxford University Press, Oxford; New York.

Pratten, S. 1993. Structure, agency and Marx's analysis of the labour process. *Review of Political Economy* 5, 403–426. https://doi.org/10.1080/09538259300000029

Qiang, C. and Rossotto, C. 2009. Economic Impacts of Broadband (http://siteresources.worldbank.org/EXTIC4D/Resources/IC4D_Broadband_35_50.pdf No. 48791). Information and Communications for Development: Extending Reach and Increasing Impact. World Bank, Washington, DC.

Qureshi, S. 2015. Are we making a better world with information and communication technology for development (ICT4D) research? Findings from the field and theory building. *Inf. Technol. Dev.* 21, 511–522. https://doi.org/10.1080/02681102.2015.1080428

Radelet, S. 2010. Emerging Africa: How 17 Countries Are Leading the Way. Centre for Global Development, Washington, DC

Radelet, S. 2015. The Great Surge: The Ascent of the Developing World. Simon & Schuster, New York.

Rakowski, C.A. 1994. Convergence and divergence in the informal sector debate: a focus on Latin America, 1984–92. *World Development* 22, 501–516. https://doi.org/10.1016/0305-750X(94)90107-4

Rani, U. and Furrer, M. 2020. Digital labour platforms and new forms of flexible work in developing countries: algorithmic management of work and workers. *Competition & Change.* https://doi.org/10.1177/1024529420905187

Ravenelle, A.J. 2019. Hustle and Gig: Struggling and Surviving in the Sharing Economy. University of California Press, Berkeley, CA.

Raynolds, L.T. 2017. Fairtrade labour certification: the contested incorporation of plantations and workers. *Third World Quarterly* 38, 1473–1492. https://doi.org/10.1080/01436597.2016.1272408

Raynolds, L.T., Murray, D., and Leigh Taylor, P. 2004. Fair trade coffee: building producer capacity via global networks. *J. Int. Dev.* 16, 1109–1121. https://doi.org/10.1002/jid.1136

Reich, M., Gordon, D., and Edwards, R. (1973) A theory of labor market segmentation. *American Economic Review* 63, 359–365.

Reinardy, S. 2014. Autonomy and perceptions of work quality. *Journalism Practice* 8, 855–870. https://doi.org/10.1080/17512786.2014.882481

Research ICT Africa 2017. What is the State of Micro-Work in Africa? A View from Seven Countries. Research ICT Africa, Cape Town.

Research ICT Africa 2018. Lagging ICT Adoption in SA Reflects Social and Economic Inequalities. Research ICT Africa, Cape Town.

Reuters 2010a. Bharti closes $9 billion Zain Africa deal. Available at https://www.reuters.com/article/us-zain-bharti-idUSTRE6570VJ20100608, accessed 9.7.2015.

Reuters 2010b. Egypt targets incentives for outsourcing industry. Available at https://www.reuters.com/article/egypt-callcentres/egypt-targets-incentives-for-outsourcing-industry-idUSLDE62L2AU20100323, accessed 21.10.18.

Reuters, 2018. Nigeria's internet fraudsters zero in on corporate email accounts. Available at https://www.reuters.com/article/us-nigeria-cyber-crime-idUSKBN1I42BG, accessed 10.5.18.

Rizzo, M. 2013. Informalisation and the end of trade unionism as we knew it? Dissenting remarks from a Tanzanian case study. *Review of African Political Economy* 40, 290–308. https://doi.org/10.1080/03056244.2013.794729

Rockefeller Foundation 2013a. Digital Jobs: Building Skills for the Future. Rockefeller Foundation, New York.

Rockefeller Foundation 2013b. Digital Jobs in Africa: Catalyzing Inclusive Opportunities for Youth. Rockefeller Foundation, New York.

Rockefeller Foundation 2014. Online Work: A New Frontier for Digital Jobs Africa. Rockefeller Foundation, New York. Available at https://www.rockefellerfoundation.org/blog/online-work-new-frontier-digital-jobs/, accessed 26.2.16.

Rodney, W. 2012. How Europe Underdeveloped Africa. Pambazuka Press, Cape Town.

Rodrik, D. 1997. Has Globalization Gone Too Far? Institute for International Economics, Washington, DC.

Rogaly, B. 2009. Spaces of work and everyday life: labour geographies and the agency of unorganised temporary migrant workers. *Geography Compass* 3, 1975–1987.

Rosenblat, A. 2018. Uberland: How Algorithms Are Rewriting the Rules of Work. University of California Press, Oakland, CA.

Rosenblatt, K. 2020. How 2020 became the summer of activism both online and offline. NBC News. Available at https://www.nbcnews.com/news/us-news/summer-digital-protest-how-2020-became-summer-activism-both-online-n1241001, accessed 19.11.20.

Rosenthal, N.H. 1989. More than wages at issue in job quality debate (cover story). *Monthly Labor Review* 112, 4.

Roser, M. and Ortiz-Ospina, E. 2016. Literacy. OurWorldInData.org. Available at https://ourworldindata.org/literacy, accessed 10.8.21.

Roser, M. and Ortiz-Ospina, E. 2019. Global extreme poverty. OurWorldInData.org. Available at https://ourworldindata.org/extreme-poverty, accessed 10.8.21.

Roser, M., Ritchie, H., and Ortiz-Ospina E. 2015. 'Internet'. OurWorldInData.org. Available at https://ourworldindata.org/internet, accessed 19.11.20.

Rossiter, A. 2014. Axel Honneth's theory of recognition and its potential for aligning social work with social justice. *Critical and Radical Social Work* 2, 93–108. https://doi.org/10.1332/204986014X13912564145762

Royal Geographical Society n.d. ICTs: a technological fix? Available at https://www.rgs.org/NR/rdonlyres/27A6CB1E-5AAE-4B8C-A42C-FBFD6569A20C/0/ICTsAtechnologicalfix.pdf, accessed 11.4.16.

Roztocki, N., Soja, P., and Weistroffer, H.R. 2019. The role of information and communication technologies in socioeconomic development: towards a multi-dimensional framework. *Inf. Technol. Dev.* 25, 171–183. https://doi.org/10.1080/02681102.2019.1596654

Rubery, J. and Grimshaw, D. 2001. ICTs and employment: the problem of job quality. *International Labour Review* 140, 165–192. https://doi.org/10.1111/j.1564-913X.2001.tb00219.x

Rutakumwa, R., Mugisha, J., Bernays, S., et al. 2020. Conducting in-depth interviews with and without voice recorders: a comparative analysis. *Qualitative Research* 20(5), 565–581.

Rydzik, A. and Anitha, S. 2019 Conceptualising the agency of migrant women workers: resilience, reworking and resistance. *Work, Employment and Society*. https://doi.org/10.1177/0950017019881939.

S&P Global 2020. Top 30 banks by assets in Africa and Middle East, 2020. Available at https://www.spglobal.com/marketintelligence/en/news-insights/latest-news-headlines/top-30-banks-by-assets-in-africa-and-middle-east-2020-58040885, accessed 14.1.21.

Sachs, J. 2005. The End of Poverty: How We Can Make it Happen in Our Lifetime. Penguin, London.

Sadowski, J. 2019. When data is capital: datafication, accumulation, and extraction. *Big Data Soc.* 6. https://doi.org/10.1177/2053951718820549

Sadowski, J. 2020. The internet of landlords: digital platforms and new mechanisms of rentier capitalism. *Antipode* 52, 562–580. https://doi.org/10.1111/anti.12595

Sainato, M. 2020. Amazon is cracking down on protesters and organizing, workers say. *The Guardian*. Available at https://www.theguardian.com/technology/2020/may/05/amazon-protests-union-organizing-cracking-down-workers, accessed 5.5.20.

Sanjay, S. 2020. Online Activism in the Time of Coronavirus. *Vice*. Available at https://www.vice.com/en/article/qj4akq/online-activism-in-coronavirus-drives-change, accessed 19.11.20.

Saraswati, J. 2014. Konza City and the Kenyan software services strategy: the great leap backward? *Review of African Political Economy* 41, S128–S137. https://doi.org/10.1080/03056244.2014.976189

Sarkar, S. and Kuruvilla, S. 2020. Constructing transnational solidarity: the role of campaign governance. *British Journal of Industrial Relations* 58, 27–49. https://doi.org/10.1111/bjir.12465

Sassen, S. 2001. The Global City: New York, London, Tokyo. 2nd edn. Princeton University Press, Princeton, NJ.

Schawbel, D. 2013. Millennials and the future of work study. Available at http://millennialbranding.com/2013/millennials-future-work-study/, accessed 6.10.17.

Schmalz, S., Ludwig, C., and Webster, E. 2018. The power resources approach: developments and challenges. *Global Labour Journal* 9, 113–134. http://dx.doi.org/10.15173/glj.v9i2.3569

Scholz, T. (ed.) 2012. Digital Labor: The Internet as Playground and Factory, 1st edn. Routledge, New York.

Scholz, T. 2016. Uberworked and Underpaid: How Workers Are Disrupting the Digital Economy, 1st edn. Polity, Cambridge; Malden, MA.

Schor, J. 2020. After the Gig: How the Sharing Economy Got Hijacked and How to Win It Back. University of California, Berkeley, CA.

Schor, J.B. Attwood-Charles, W. Cansoy, M., et al. 2020. Dependence and precarity in the platform economy. *Theory and Society* 49, 833–861. https://doi.org/10.1007/s11186-020-09408-y

Schörpf, P., Flecker, J., Schönauer, A., et al. 2017. Triangular love–hate: management and control in creative crowdworking. *New Technology, Work and Employment* 32, 43–58. https://doi.org/10.1111/ntwe.12080

Schradie, J. 2015. Political ideology, social media, and labor unions: using the internet to reach the powerful not mobilize the powerless? *International Journal of Communication* 9: 1987–2006.

Schradie, J. 2018. Digital activism gap: how class and costs shape online collective action? *Social Problems* 65, 51–74.

Schwab, K. 2016. The Fourth Industrial Revolution. World Economic Forum, Geneva.

Scott, A.J. 1988. Flexible production systems and regional development: the rise of new industrial spaces in North America and Western Europe. *Int. J. Urban Reg. Res.* 12, 171–186. https://doi.org/10.1111/j.1468-2427.1988.tb00448.x

Scott, A.J. 2001. Capitalism, cities, and the production of symbolic forms. *Trans. Inst. Br. Geogr.* 26, 11–23. https://doi.org/10.1111/1475-5661.00003

Scott, J. 1985. Weapons of the Weak: Everyday Forms of Peasant Resistance. Yale University Press, New Haven, CT.

Scott, J.C., 1990. Domination and the Arts of Resistance: Hidden Transcripts. Yale University Press, New Haven, CT.

Scully, B. 2016. From the shop floor to the kitchen table: the shifting centre of precarious workers' politics in South Africa. *Review of African Political Economy* 43, 295–311. https://doi.org/10.1080/03056244.2015.1085378

Seacom Live 2009. Connecting Africa to the world. Available at https://www.dailymotion.com/video/x2zg5l6, accessed 12.10.21.

Selwyn, B. 2012. Beyond firm-centrism: re-integrating labour and capitalism into global commodity chain analysis. *Journal of Economic Geography* 12(1), 205–226.

Selwyn, B. 2013. Social upgrading and labour in global production networks: a critique and an alternative conception. *Competition & Change* 17, 75–90. https://doi.org/10.1179/1024529412Z.00000000026

Selwyn, B. 2018. Poverty chains and global capitalism. *Competition & Change*. https://doi.org/10.1177/1024529418809067

Selwyn, B., Musiolek, B., and Ijarja, A. 2020. Making a global poverty chain: export footwear production and gendered labor exploitation in Eastern and Central Europe. *Review of International Political Economy* 27, 377–403. https://doi.org/10.1080/09692290.2019.1640124

Semple, J. 1993. Bentham's Prison: A Study of the Panopticon Penitentiary. Oxford University Press, Oxford.

Sen, A. 2001. Development as Freedom. Oxford University Press, Oxford.

Sengenberger, W. 2011. Beyond the Measurement of Unemployment and Underemployment: The Case for Extending and Amending Labour Market Statistics. ILO, Geneva.

Sewell, G. 1998. The discipline of teams: the control of team-based industrial work through electronic and peer surveillance, *Administrative Science Quarterly* 43(2), 406–469.

Sewell, G. and Wilkinson, B. 1992. Someone to watch over me: surveillance, discipline and the just-in-time labour process. *Sociology* 26(2), 271–289.

Shah, A. and Lerche, J. 2020. Migration and the invisible economies of care: production, social reproduction and seasonal migrant labour in India. *Transactions of the Institute of British Geographers*. https://doi.org/10.1111/tran.12401

Shellenbarger, S. 2008. Work at home? Your employer may be watching. WSJ. Available at https://www.wsj.com/articles/SB121737022605394845, accessed 8.12.20.

Sheppard, E. 2002. The spaces and times of globalization: place, scale, networks, and positionality. *Econ. Geogr.* 78, 307–330. https://doi.org/10.1111/j.1944-8287.2002.tb00189.x

Shevchuk, A. and Strebkov, D. 2018. Safeguards against Opportunism in Freelance Contracting on the Internet. *British Journal of Industrial Relations* 56, 342–369. https://doi.org/10.1111/bjir.12283

Shevchuk, A., Strebkov, D., and Davis, S.N. 2019. The autonomy paradox: how night work undermines subjective well-being of internet-based freelancers. *ILR Review* 72, 75–100.

Shibata, S. 2019. Gig work and the discourse of autonomy: fictitious freedom in Japan's digital economy. *New Political Economy* 0, 1–17. https://doi.org/10.1080/13563467.2019.1613351

Shire, K.A., Schönauer, A., Valverde, M., et al. 2009. Collective bargaining and temporary contracts in call centre employment in Austria, Germany and Spain. *European Journal of Industrial Relations* 15, 437–456. https://doi.org/10.1177/0959680109344370

Silver, B.J. 2003. Forces of Labor: Workers' Movements and Globalization since 1870. Cambridge University Press, Cambridge.

Smaje, C. 1997. Not just a social construct: theorising race and ethnicity. Sociology 31(2), 307–327. https://doi.org/10.1177/0038038597031002007

Smith, C. 2006. The double indeterminacy of labour power: labour effort and labour mobility. *Work, Employment and Society* 20, 389–402. https://doi.org/10.1177/0950017006065109

Smith, C. 2015. Continuity and change in labor process analysis forty years after labor and monopoly capital. *Labor Studies Journal* 40, 222–242. https://doi.org/10.1177/0160449X15607154

Smith, N. 1983. Uneven Development: Nature, Capital and Production of Space. Blackwell, Oxford.

Smith, R.E. 2019. Rage Inside the Machine: The Prejudice of Algorithms, and How to Stop the Internet Making Bigots of Us All. Bloomsbury Business, New York.

Solidarity Centre 2013. Trade Unions Organizing Workers 'informalized from above': Case Studies from Cambodia, Colombia, South Africa, and Tunisia. USAID, Washington, DC.

Solon, O. 2018. Amazon patents wristband that tracks warehouse workers' movements. The Guardian. Available at https://www.theguardian.com/technology/2018/jan/31/amazon-warehouse-wristband-tracking, accessed 20.03.18.

Solutions for Youth Employment 2018. Digital Jobs for Youth: Young Women in the Digital Economy. World Bank, Washington, DC.

Song, M. 2018. Why we still need to talk about race. *Ethnic and Racial Studies* 41, 1131–1145. https://doi.org/10.1080/01419870.2018.1410200

Sonn, J.W. and Lee, D. 2012. Revisiting the branch plant syndrome: review of literature on foreign direct investment and regional development in Western advanced economies. *International Journal of Urban Sciences* 16(3), 243–259.

Southall, R. 1988. Labour and Unions in Asia and Africa: Contemporary Issues. Macmillan Press, London.

Southall, R. and Melber, H. (eds) 2009. A New Scramble for Africa? Imperialism, Investment and Development. University Kwazulu Natal Press, Scottsville, South Africa.

Spicer, A. 2018. Amazon's 'worker cage' has been dropped, but its staff are not free. *The Guardian*. Avilable at https://www.theguardian.com/commentisfree/2018/sep/14/amazon-worker-cage-staff, accessed 14.9.18.

Spreitzer, G.M., Cameron, L., and Garrett, L. 2017. Alternative work arrangements: two images of the new world of work. *Annu. Rev. Organ. Psychol. Organ. Behav.* 4, 473–499. https://doi.org/10.1146/annurev-orgpsych-032516-113332

Squawk Box Today 2016. CNBC exclusive: Uber co-founder & CEO Travis Kalanick on CNBC's. CNBC. Available at https://www.cnbc.com/2016/04/27/cnbc-exclusive-cnbc-excerpts-uber-co-founder-ceo-travis-kalanick-on-cnbcs-squawk-box-today.html, accessed 20.7.20.

Srauy S. 2015. The limits of social media: what social media can be, and what we should hope they never become. *Social Media + Society* 1(1), 1–3. https://doi.org/10.1177/2056305115578676

Srnicek, N. 2016. Platform Capitalism. Polity Press, Cambridge; Malden, MA.

Standing, G. 2014. The Precariat: The New Dangerous Class, Trade pbk edn. Bloomsbury Academic, London; New York.

Standing, G. 2018. The precariat: today's transformative class? Great Transition Initiative. Available at https://greattransition.org/publication/precariat-transformative-class, accessed 3.8.21.

Statistics South Africa 2014. Employment, Unemployment, Skills and Economic Growth: An Exploration of Household Survey Evidence on Skills Development and Unemployment between 1994 and 2014. Statistics South Africa, Government of South Africa, Pretoria.

Statistics South Africa 2017. Three Facts about the ICT Sector. Government of South Africa, Pretoria.

Statistics South Africa 2019a. Unemployment Rises Slightly in Third Quarter of 2019. Government of South Africa, Pretoria.

Statistics South Africa. 2021. Quarterly Labour Force Survey Quarter 1: 2021. Available at http://www.statssa.gov.za/publications/P0211/P02111stQuarter2021.pdf, accessed 10.8.21.

Stephany, F., Kässi, O., Rani, U., & Lehdonvirta, V. (2021). Online Labour Index 2020: New ways to measure the world's remote freelancing market. Big Data & Society. doi:10.1177/20539517211043240

Stewart, A. and Stanford, J. 2017. Regulating work in the gig economy: what are the options? *Economic and Labour Relations Review* 28, 420–437. https://doi.org/10.1177/1035304617722461

Stewart, D.W. and Shamdasani, P.N. 1990. Focus Groups: Theory and Practice. Sage Publications, Thousand Oaks, CA; London.

Steyn, L. 2014. The downward spiral of SA unions. *The M&G Online.* Available at https://mg.co.za/article/2014-11-13-the-downward-spiral-of-sa-unions/, accessed 20.9.19.

Stillerman, J. 2017. Explaining strike outcomes in Chile: associational power, structural power, and spatial strategies. *Latin American Politics and Society* 59, 96–118. https://doi.org/10.1111/laps.12012

Stockman, F. and Mureithi, C. 2019. Cheating, Inc.: How writing papers for American college students has become a lucrative profession overseas, *New York Times.* Available at https://www.nytimes.com/2019/09/07/us/college-cheating-papers.html, accessed 12.9.19.

Storper, M. 1997. The Regional World: Territorial Development in a Global Economy. Guilford Press, New York; London.

Storper, M. and Christopherson, S. 1987. Flexible specialization and regional industrial agglomerations: the case of the U.S. motion picture industry. *Ann. Assoc. Am. Geogr.* 77, 104–117. https://doi.org/10.1111/j.1467-8306.1987.tb00148.x

Stuart, E., Samman, E., and Hunt, A. 2018. Informal is the New Normal Improving the Lives of Workers at Risk of being Left Behind. ODI, London.

Sundararajan, A. 2016. The Sharing Economy: The End of Employment and the Rise of Crowd-Based Capitalism. MIT Press, Cambridge, MA.

Suri, T. and Jack, W. 2016. The long-run poverty and gender impacts of mobile money. *Science* 354, 1288–1292. https://doi.org/10.1126/science.aah5309

Swart, G. 2013. The future of work in the digital age. *The European.* Available at https://www.theeuropean.de/en/gary-swart-2/7117-the-future-of-work-in-the-digital-age-4, accessed 26.2.16.

Tambe, P. and Hitt, L.M. 2013. Job hopping, information technology spillovers, and productivity growth. *Management Science.* https://doi.org/10.1287/mnsc.2013.1764

Tapscott, D. 1996. The Digital Economy: Promise and Peril in the Age of Networked Intelligence, 1st edn. McGraw-Hill, New York, NY.

Tassinari, A. and Maccarrone, V. 2017. The mobilisation of gig economy couriers in Italy: some lessons for the trade union movement. *Transfer: European Review of Labour and Research* 23, 353–357. https://doi.org/10.1177/1024258917713846

Tassinari, A. and Maccarrone, V. 2019. Riders on the storm: workplace solidarity among gig economy couriers in Italy and the UK. *Work, Employment and Society.* https://doi.org/10.1177/0950017019862954

Taylor, F.W. 1911. The Principles of Scientific Management. Harper & Brothers, New York.

Taylor, I. 2016. Dependency redux: why Africa is not rising. *Rev. Afr. Polit. Econ.* 43, 8–25. https://doi.org/10.1080/03056244.2015.1084911

Taylor, P. and Bain, P. 1999. 'An assembly line in the head': work and employee relations in the call centre. *Ind. Relat. J.* 30, 101–117. https://doi.org/10.1111/1468-2338.00113

Taylor, P. and Bain, P. 2003. 'Subterranean Worksick Blues': humour as subversion in two call centres. *Organization Studies* 24, 1487–1509. https://doi.org/10.1177/0170840603249008

Taylor, P. and Bain, P. 2005. 'India calling to the far away towns': the call centre labour process and globalization. *Work Employ. Soc.* 19, 261–282. https://doi.org/10.1177/0950017005053170

Taylor, P., Mulvey, G., Hyman, J., et al. 2002. Work organization, control and the experience of work in call centres. *Work, Employ. Soc.* 16, 133–150. https://doi.org/10.1177/09500170222119281

Taylor, P., D'Cruz, P., Noronha, E., et al. 2013. The experience of work in India's domestic call centre industry. *Int. J. Hum. Resour. Manag.* 24, 436–452. https://doi.org/10.1080/09585192.2011.561216

Theodore, N. 2016. Worlds of work: changing landscapes of production and the new geographies of opportunity. *Geography Compass* 10, 179–189. https://doi.org/10.1111/gec3.12261

Theodore, N. and Peck, J. 2002. The temporary staffing industry: growth imperatives and limits to contingency. *Economic Geography* 78, 463–493. https://doi.org/10.1111/j.1944-8287.2002.tb00196.x

Thigo, P. 2013. People, technology and spaces: towards a new generation of social movements. *J. Contemp. Afr. Stud.* 31, 255–264.

Thompson, C. 2020. AI, the transcription economy, and the future of work. Wired.

Thompson, J.D. 1967. Organizations in Action: Social Science Bases of Administrative Theory. Routledge, Abingdon.

Thompson, M. 2004. Discourse, 'development' & the 'digital divide': ICT & the World Bank. *Rev. Afr. Polit. Econ.* 31, 103–123.

Thompson, P., Callaghan, G., and van den Broek, D. 2004. Keeping up appearances: recruitment, skills and normative control in call centres, in Deery, S. and Kinnie, N. (eds), Call Centres and Human Resource Management: A Cross-National Perspective. Palgrave Macmillan, London, pp. 129–152.

Thompson, P. and van den Broek, D. 2010. Managerial control and workplace regimes: an introduction. *Work, Employment and Society* 24, 1–12. https://doi.org/10.1177/0950017010384546

Tilly, C. 1997. Arresting the decline of good jobs in the USA? *Industrial Relations Journal* 28, 269–274. https://doi.org/10.1111/1468-2338.00062

Times Live 2015. Fewer people joining trade unions. Available at https://www.timeslive.co.za/news/south-africa/2015-02-09-fewer-people-joining-trade-unions/, accessed 20.9.19.

Times of India 2013. It's BPM now, but many still see it as BPO. *Times of India.* Available at http://timesofindia.indiatimes.com/business/india-business/Its-BPM-now-but-many-still-see-it-as-BPO/articleshow/22734976.cms, accessed 10.11.17.

Todolí-Signes, A. 2017. The 'gig economy': employee, self-employed or the need for a special employment regulation? *Transfer: European Review of Labour and Research* 23, 193–205. https://doi.org/10.1177/1024258917701381

Topping, A. 2017. Union membership has plunged to an all-time low, says DBEIS. The Guardian. Available at https://www.theguardian.com/politics/2017/jun/01/union-membership-has-plunged-to-an-all-time-low-says-ons, accessed 26.03.18.

The Guardian, 2021. Blow for Uber as judge finds California's gig-worker law unconstitutional. Available at https://www.theguardian.com/technology/2021/aug/20/california-gig-worker-law-proposition-22-unconstitutional, accessed 21.8.21

Torquati, L., Mielke, G., Brown, W., et al. 2019. Shift work and poor mental health: a meta-analysis of longitudinal studies. *American Journal of Public Health*. https://doi.org/10.2105/AJPH.2019.305278

Touré, H. 2013. Speech by ITU Secretary-General, Dr Hamadoun I. Touré, ITU.

Townsend, K. 2005. Electronic surveillance and cohesive teams: room for resistance in an Australian call centre? *New Technology, Work and Employment* 20, 47–59. https://doi.org/10.1111/j.1468-005X.2005.00143.x

Troaca, V. and Bodislav, D. 2012. Outsourcing. *The Concept. Theor. Appl. Econ.* 19, 51–58.

Tronti, M. 1966. Operai e capitale [Workers and Capital]. Einaudi, Turin.

Tubaro, P., Casilli, A.A., and Coville, M. 2020. The trainer, the verifier, the imitator: three ways in which human platform workers support artificial intelligence. *Big Data Soc.* https://doi.org/10.1177/2053951720919776

TUC (Trades Union Congress) Commission on Vulnerable Employment 2008. Hard Work, Hidden Lives: The Full Report of the Commission on Vulnerable Employment. TUC Commission on Vulnerable Employment. TUC, London.

TUC, 2017. *Insecure work and Ethnicity*. London.

Tuma, A. 1998. Configuration and coordination of virtual production networks. *Int. J. Prod. Econ. Spec. issue Production Economics: The Link between Technology and Management* 56–57, 641–648. https://doi.org/10.1016/S0925-5273(97)00146-1

Turnbull, A. 2020. How coronavirus set the stage for a techno-future with robots and AI. *The Conversation*. Available at http://theconversation.com/how-coronavirus-set-the-stage-for-a-techno-future-with-robots-and-ai-136475, accessed 6.2.20.

UN 2013. A New Global Parternship: Eradicate Poverty and Transform Economies through Sustainable Development. Report of the High Level Panel of Eminent Persons on the Post-2015 Development Agenda. United Nations, New York.

UN Global Pulse 2012. Big Data for Development: Opportunities and Challenges (White Paper). United Nations, New York.

UN News 2017. Electronic waste poses 'growing risk' to environment, human health, UN report warns. *UN News*. Available at https://news.un.org/en/story/2017/12/639312-electronic-waste-poses-growing-risk-environment-human-health-un-report-warns, accessed 28.8.18.

UN News 2020. 'Business as unusual': How COVID-19 could change the future of work. *UN News*. Available at https://news.un.org/en/story/2020/05/1064802, accessed 6.12.20.

UNCTAD 2004. World Investment Report 2004: The Shift towards Services. UNCTAD, Geneva.

UNCTAD 2017. Information Economy Report 2017: Digitalization, Trade and Development. UNCTAD, Geneva.

UNCTAD 2019a. Digital Economy Report 2019: Value Creation and Capture: Implications For Developing Countries. UNCTAD, New York.

UNCTAD 2019b. Made in Africa: Rules of Origin for Enhanced Intra-African Trade. UNCTAD, Geneva.

UNCTAD 2019c. State of Commodity Dependence. UNCTAD, Geneva.

UNCTAD 2019d. World Investment Report 2019: Special Economic Zones. UNCTAD, Geneva.

UNCTAD 2020. World Investment Report 2020. International Production beyond the Pandemic. UNCTAD, Geneva. Available at https://unctad.org/system/files/official-document/wir2020_en.pdf, accessed 10.8.21.

UNDP 2015. Human Development Report 2015: Work for Human Development. UNDP, Geneva.

UNDP 2016. Human Development Report 2016: Human Development for Everyone. UNDP, New York.

UNDP 2017. Income Inequality Trends in sub-Saharan Africa: Divergence, Determinants, and Consequences. UNDP, New York.

UNDP 2019. Human Development Report 2020. UNDP, Geneva.

UNDP 2020. Global Multidimensional Poverty Index (MPI) 2020: Charting Pathways out of Multidimensional Poverty: Achieving the SDGs. UNDP, Geneva.

UNECA 2020. COVID-19 in Africa: Protecting Lives and Economies. Available at https://www.uneca.org/publications/covid-19-africa-protecting-lives-and-economies, accessed 6.1.20.

Unwin, P.T.H. 2009. ICT4D: Information and Communication Technology for Development. Cambridge University Press, Cambridge.

Unwin, T. 2017. A Critical Reflection on ICTs and 'Development.' Oxford University Press, Oxford.

Upwork 2015. Freelancers Union and Upwork release new study revealing insights into the almost 54 million people freelancing in America. Press, News & Media Coverage. Available at https://www.upwork.com/press/2015/10/01/freelancers-union-and-upwork-release-new-study-revealing-insights-into-the-almost-54-million-people-freelancing-in-america/, accessed 20.7.20.

Upwork 2018. Fortune 500 enterprises shift their contingent workforce to Upwork platform saving both time and money. Available at https://www.upwork.com/press/releases/fortune-500-enterprises, accessed 10.8.21.

Valkila, J., Haaparanta, P., and Niemi, N. 2010. Empowering coffee traders? the coffee value chain from Nicaraguan fair trade farmers to Finnish consumers. *J Bus Ethics* 97, 257–270. https://doi.org/10.1007/s10551-010-0508-z

Vallas, S. and Prener, C. 2012. Dualism, job polarization, and the social construction of precarious work. *Work and Occupations* 39, 331–353. https://doi.org/10.1177/0730888412456027

Vallas, S. and Schor, J.B. 2020. What do platforms do? Understanding the gig economy. *Annu. Rev. Sociol.* https://doi.org/10.1146/annurev-soc-121919-054857

Valls, D. 2020. Activism in times of COVID-19. *Amnesty International.* Available at https://www.amnesty.org/en/latest/campaigns/2020/05/activism-in-times-of-covid-19/, accessed 19.11.20.

Van Doorn, N. 2017. Platform labor: on the gendered and racialized exploitation of low-income service work in the 'on-demand' economy. *Inf. Commun. Soc.* 1–17. https://doi.org/10.1080/1369118X.2017.1294194

Varghese, S. 2020. Gig economy workers have a new weapon in the fight against Uber. *Wired UK.* Available at https://www.wired.co.uk/article/gig-economy-uber-unions, accessed 17.2.20.

Veen, A., Kaine, S., Goods, C., et al. 2019. The gigigfication of work in the 21st century, in Holland, P. and Brewster, C. (eds), Contemporary Work and the Future of Employment in Developed Countries. Routledge, Abingdon, pp. 15–32.

Venugopal, R. 2015. Neoliberalism as concept. *Economy and Society* 44, 165–187.

Vira, B. and James, A. 2011. Researching hybrid 'economic'/'development' geographies in practice. Methodological reflections from a collaborative project on India's new service economy. *Prog. Hum. Geogr.* 35, 627–651. https://doi.org/10.1177/0309132510394012

Vira, B. and James, A. 2012. Building cross-sector careers in India's new service economy? Tracking former call centre agents in the national capital region. *Development and Change* 43, 449–479. https://doi.org/10.1111/j.1467-7660.2012.01768.x

Visser, M.A. 2019. Restructuring opportunity: employment change and job quality in the United States during the Great Recession. *Socioecon Rev* 17, 545–572. https://doi.org/10.1093/ser/mwy002

Von Holdt, K. 2002. Social movement unionism: the case of South Africa. *Work, Employment and Society* 16, 283–304. https://doi.org/10.1177/095001702400426848

Von Holdt, K. and Webster, E. 2008. Organising on the periphery: new sources of power in the South African workplace. *Employee Relations* 30(4): 333–354.

Wachter-Boettcher, S. 2017. Technically Wrong: Sexist Apps, Biased Algorithms, and Other Threats of Toxic Tech. W. W. Norton, New York, NY.

Waite, L., Craig, G.P., Lewis, H., et al.. 2015. Vulnerability, Exploitation and Migrants: Insecure Work in a Globalised Economy [electronic resource], Migration, Diasporas and Citizenship. Palgrave Macmillan, Basingstoke.

Walsham, G. 2017. ICT4D research: reflections on history and future agenda. *Information Technology for Development* 23(1), 18–41. https://doi.org/10.1080/02681102.2016.1246406

Warschauer, M. 2003. Technology and Social Inclusion: Rethinking the Digital Divide. MIT Press, Cambridge MA.

Waterman, P. 2017. The Southern initiative on globalisation and trade union rights 'Futures Report': springboard or tombstone? South Asia Citizens Web. Available at http://www.sacw.net/article13292.html, accessed 10.8.21.

Waverman, L., Meschi, M. and Fuss, M. 2005. The impact of telecoms on economic growth in developing countries (No. 2), Moving the Debate: Africa: The impact of mobile phones. Vodafone Policy Paper Series. Vodafone, London.

Webster, E. 2007. Trade Unions and Political Parties in Africa: New Alliances, Strategies and Partnerships. Friedrich-Ebert-Stiftung, Bonn.

Webster, E. 2015. The shifting boundaries of industrial relations: insights from South Africa. *International Labour Review* 154, 27–36. https://doi.org/10.1111/j.1564-913X.2015.00223.x

Webster, E. and Buhlungu, S. 2004. Between marginalisation & revitalisation? The state of trade unionism in South Africa. *Review of African Political Economy* 31, 229–245.

Webster, E., Lambert, R., and Bezuidenhout, A. 2009. Grounding Globalization: Labour in the Age of Insecurity. Blackwell, Oxford.

Webster, E., Joynt, K., and Sefalafala, T. 2016. Informalization and decent work: labour's challenge. *Progress in Development Studies* 16, 203–218. https://doi.org/10.1177/1464993415623152

WEF (World Economic Forum) 2018. Digital Transformation Initiative: Unlocking $100 Trillion for Business and Society from Digital Transformation. WEF, Davos.

Wen, L. and Maani, S. 2018. Job Mismatches and Career Mobility (No. IZA DP No. 11844). IZA Institute of Labour Economics, Bonn.

Whitney, R. 2017. US provides military assistance to 73 percent of world's dictatorships. *Truthout.* Available at https://truthout.org/articles/us-provides-military-assistance-to-73-percent-of-world-s-dictatorships/, accessed 17.2.20.

Williams, P., James, A., McConnell, F., et al. (2017) Working at the margins? Muslim middle class professionals in India and the limits of 'labour agency'. *Environment and Planning A* 49(6), 1266–1285.

Willmott, H. 1993. Strength is ignorance, slavery is freedom: managing culture in modern organisations. *Journal of Management Studies* 30(4), 515–552.

Wilson, M. and Jackson, P. 2016. Fairtrade bananas in the Caribbean: towards a moral economy of recognition. *Geoforum* 70, 11–21. https://doi.org/10.1016/j.geoforum.2016.01.003

Winant, H. 2001. The World Is A Ghetto Race and Democracy Since World War II. Basic Books, New York.

Wong, M. 2020. Hidden youth? A new perspective on the sociality of young people 'withdrawn' in the bedroom in a digital age. *New Media & Society* 22, 1227–1244. https://doi.org/10.1177/1461444820912530

Wonolo, 2019. America's Thriving Blue-Collar Gig Economy. Wonolo. Available at https://www.wonolo.com/whitepapers/blue-collar-gig-economy/, accessed 7.3.19.

Wood, A.J. 2020. Despotism on Demand: How Power Operates in the Flexible Workplace. Cornell University Press, Ithaca, NY.

Wood A.J, Graham M and Anwar A, 2020. Minimum Wages for Online Labor Platforms? Regulating the Global Gig Economy. 'In Larsson A and Teigland R (Eds)' *The Digital Transformation of Labor (Open Access): Automation, the Gig Economy and Welfare*. Routledge, London.

Wood, A.J, Lehdonvirta, V. and Graham M. 2018. Workers of the internet unite? Online freelancer organisation among remote gig economy workers in six Asian and African countries. *New Technology, Work and Employment* 33(2): 95–112.

Wood, A.J., Graham, M., Lehdonvirta, V., et al. 2019. Good gig, bad gig: autonomy and algorithmic control in the global gig economy. *Work, Employment and Society* 33, 56–75. https://doi.org/10.1177/0950017018785616

Wood, G. and Brewster, C. 2007. Industrial Relations in Africa. Palgrave MacMillan, Basingstoke.

Woodcock, J. 2016. Working the phone: Control and Resistance in Call Centres. Pluto Press, London.

Woodcock, J. 2020a. How to beat the boss: game workers unite in Britain. *Capital & Class*. https://doi.org/10.1177/0309816820906349

Woodcock, J. 2020b. The algorithmic panopticon at Deliveroo: measurement, precarity, and the illusion of control. *Ephemera: Theory & Politics in Organization* 20(3), 67–95.

Woodcock, J. and Graham, M. 2019. The Gig Economy: A Critical Introduction. Cambridge: Polity.

Woodward, J. 1958. Management and Technology, Problems of Progress in Industry. HMSO, London.

World Bank 2000. Improving Governance, Managing Conflict, and Rebuilding States', in Can Africa Claim the 21st Century? World Bank, Washington, DC, pp. 48–82.

World Bank 2009. World Development Report 2009: Reshaping Economic Geography. World Bank, Washington, DC.

World Bank 2012. E-Transform Africa: The Transformational Use of Information and Communication Technologies in Africa. World Bank, Washington, DC.

World Bank 2013a. World Development Report 2013: Jobs. World Bank, Washington, DC.

World Bank 2013b. Connecting to Work: How ICTs Are Expanding Job Opportunities Worldwide. World Bank, Washington, DC.

World Bank 2015. South Africa economic update: jobs and South Africa's changing demographics (Working Paper Issue No. 7). World Bank Group, Washington, DC.

World Bank 2016. World Development Report 2016: Digital Dividends. World Bank, Washington, DC.

World Bank 2019a. Achieving Africa's Digital Transformation is an Ambition that Requires Game-Changing Cooperation. World Bank, Washington, DC. Available at http://www.worldbank.org/en/news/feature/2019/05/06/achieving-africas-digital-transformation-is-an-ambition-that-requires-game-changing-cooperation, accessed 5.9.19.

World Bank 2019b. Supporting Africa's Transformation World Bank Africa Strategy for 2019–2023. World Bank. Washington, DC. Available at http://pubdocs.worldbank.org/en/485321579731572916/AFREC-Strategy-Trifold-Brochure.pdf, accessed 10.8.21.

World Bank 2019c. World Development Report 2019: The Changing Nature of Work. World Bank, Washington DC.

World Bank 2020. Phase II: COVID-19 Crisis through a Migration Lens. Migration and Development Brief 33. World Bank. Washington, DC. Available at https://www.knomad.org/sites/default/files/2020-11/Migration%20%26%20Development_Brief%2033.pdf, accessed 15.1.21.

World Bank n.d. Poverty and Equity Data. Available at https://povertydata.worldbank.org/poverty/region/SSF, accessed 5.10.20.

Wright, E.O. 2016. Is the Precariat a Class? *Global Labour Journal* 7(2), 189.

Wright, E.O. 2000. Working-class power, capitalist-class interests, and class compromise. *American Journal of Sociology* 105, 957–1002. https://doi.org/10.1086/210397

Xing, Y. 2019. How the iPhone widens the US trade deficit with China: The case of the iPhone X. VoxEU.org. Available at https://voxeu.org/article/how-iphone-widens-us-trade-deficit-china-0, accessed 21.4.20.

Yerby, E. 2020. Frayed careers in the gig economy: rhythms of career privilege and dis-advantage, in Page-Tickell, R. and Yerby, E. (eds), Conflict and Shifting Boundaries in the Gig Economy: An Interdisciplinary Analysis, The Changing Context of Managing People. Emerald Publishing, Bingley, pp. 161–181. https://doi.org/10.1108/978-1-83867-603-220201013

Yeung, H.W. 2016. Strategic Coupling: East Asian Industrial Transformation in the New Global Economy. Cornell Studies in Political Economy. Cornell University Press, Ithaca, NY.

Yonazi, E., Kelly, T., Halewood, N., et al. 2012. The Transformational Use of information and Communication Technologies in Africa (No. 74550), E-Transform Africa. World Bank, Washington, DC.

Young, T. 1999. The state and politics in Africa. *J. South. Afr. Stud.* 25, 149–154.

Zaller, A. 2012. What is a Split Shift? (California Employment Law Report). California IWC Wage Orders. Available at https://www.californiaemploymentlawreport.com/2012/05/what-is-a-split-shift/, accessed 3.8.21.

Zhang, K.H. (ed.) 2006. China as the World Factory. Routledge, London.

Zuboff, P.S. 2019. The Age of Surveillance Capitalism: The Fight for a Human Future at the New Frontier of Power: Barack Obama's Books of 2019, 1st edn. Profile Books, London.

Index